The Lake District

written and researched by

Jules Brown

with additional contributions from

Kate Stephenson, Mark Murray and Jean Brown

NEW YORK • LONDON • DELHI

www.roughguides.com

Contents

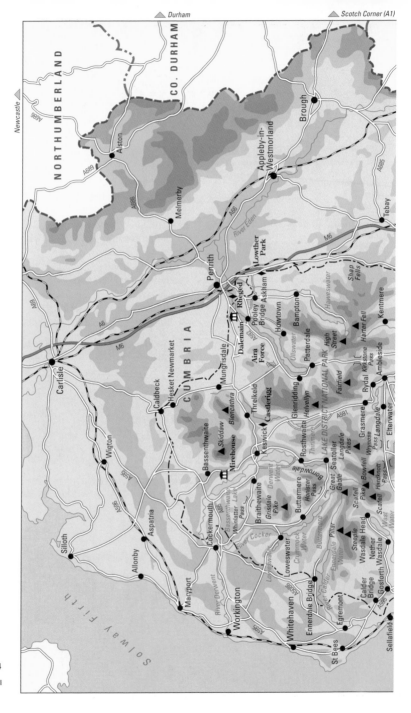

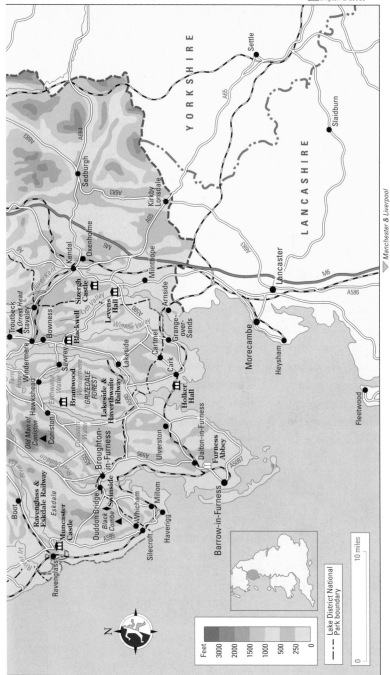

Skipton & Leeds

YORKSHIRE

LANCASHIRE

Settle

Slaidburn

A65

A684

Sedbergh

Oxenholme

A683

Kirkby Lonsdale

Kendal

A65

Milnthorpe

Arnside

Lancaster

M6

A586

Morecambe

Heysham

Fleetwood

Manchester & Liverpool

River Kent

A6

Troutbeck

Orrest Head

Staveley

Windermere

Bowness

Blackwell

Sizergh Castle

Levens Hall

Lyth Valley

Winster Valley

Grange-over-Sands

Cartmel

Sawrey

Esthwaite Water

Brantwood

GRIZEDALE FOREST

Lakeside

Cark

Holker Hall

Hawkshead

Windermere

Lakeside & Haverthwaite Railway

Coniston Water

Old Man of Coniston

Coniston

Broughton-in-Furness

Ulverston

Dalton-in-Furness

Furness Abbey

A595

A590

Boot

Ravenglass & Eskdale Railway

Eskdale

River Esk

Muncaster Castle

Duddon Bridge

Swinside

Black Combe

Whicham

Millom

Silecroft

Haverigg

Barrow-in-Furness

River Irt

Ravenglass

Tarn Hows

River Duddon

A595

A5087

N

Lake District National Park boundary

Feet
3000
2000
1500
1000
500
250
0

10 miles

0

5

© Crown copyright

Introduction to the

Lake District

The Lake District is England's most celebrated, most visited and most hyped scenic area. Tucked into a bulge between the industrial cities of northwest England and the Scottish borders, the small region – just thirty miles across – is literally irresistible to the twelve million visitors a year who pour in to experience its famous lakes, picturesque villages and alpine landscape. To many, the lure is of a misty-eyed English past – quiet country lanes, ivy-clad inns, agricultural shows and sheep-dog trials – while others seek to tick off English superlatives, including the country's highest mountain (Scafell Pike), and its largest and deepest lakes (Windermere and Wast Water respectively). The sundry pastoral images could hardly be better known, whether bolstered by the siren words of the Lake Poets or embedded in the minds of the nation's children who grow up with the lakeland tales of Beatrix Potter, Arthur Ransome and John Cunliffe's _Postman Pat_.

It's hard to think of a region in Britain with a similar breadth of scenery – wild fells to walled grazing land, glacial lakes to forested valleys, steeply pitched mountains to tumbling waterfalls – in such a small area. Tourist numbers are concentrated in fairly specific areas and, even on the busiest of summer days, it's relatively easy to escape the crowds by climbing to the higher fells or exploring more remote valleys. There are parts of the region, particularly in the north and west, where tourism is still decidedly low-key. Choose to come in the early spring, late autumn or winter – when magical crisp, clear days often enhance the natural backdrop – and even the most beaten paths and over-visited sights can be refreshingly uncluttered.

Fact file

• The Lake District National Park was established in 1951 and covers 880 square miles (half a million acres).

• Most of the land within the park (59 percent) is privately owned. The rest is owned by the National Trust (24.8 percent) and water and forestry concerns (12.4 percent), with 3.8 percent owned by the National Park Authority itself.

• There are 42,000 people living within the National Park. Up to fifty percent of all jobs are attributable in some way to tourism.

• Farming accounts for just ten percent of the Park's working population – and the National Trust alone owns 91 farms.

• The highest mountains are Scafell Pike (3210ft), Scafell (3162ft), Helvellyn (3118ft) and Skiddaw (3053ft); the deepest lakes are Wast Water (243ft), Windermere (204ft) and Ullswater (200ft).

The scenery is, of course, the major attraction and if **hiking and the great outdoors** isn't your bag, it's tempting to say that you're on the wrong holiday. The central lakeland crags – the birthplace of British rock-climbing – still lure climbers from far and wide, while the lakes, paths and valleys support an entire industry of adventure activities, from kayaking and windsurfing to pony-trekking and off-road biking.

However, the Lake District has more than enough to satisfy less boisterous interests. The region's **literary connections** are justly famous, though you may be surprised to find that it's not all Wordsworth, Coleridge, Southey and De Quincey: writers and poets as diverse as Sir Hugh Walpole, Norman Nicholson and John Ruskin have left their mark, and their houses, haunts and places of inspiration form the backbone of many a lakeland literary trail. There's a long **industrial history**, too, which manifests itself in scattered mining works, scarred quarry sites, surviving mills (one still working at Stott Park) and a couple of old railway lines – Ravenglass to Eskdale, and Lakeside to Haverthwaite – now converted to tourist use.

▼ Rural postbox, St John's in the Vale

Lakeland names and terms

Many lakeland place-names, geographical features and dialect words have origins which go back to Norse, Saxon or even Celtic times. The most common are appended to features you'll see every time you stride out into the countryside – like "fell" (hill, mountain, or high common land), "mere" (lake), "holme" (island), "beck" (stream), "force" (waterfall) and "tarn" (small mountain lake). With other names, it helps to know the derivation in order to figure out exactly what you're looking at, thus place-names ending in "-thwaite" (signifying a clearing), or those incorporating the words "ghyll" or "gill" (narrow ravine or mountain stream), "hause" (summit of a pass), "how" or "howe" (rounded hill), "pike" (peak), "raise" (summit of a ridge), "rake" (natural rock passage) or "wyke" (bay). Farming language is deeply rooted in the past – words like "heaf" (grazing area), "garth" (enclosed land or field) or "lath" (barn) have ancient roots – and there was once an entire counting system for keeping tabs on sheep (yan, tyan, tethera, or one, two, three . . .). That's not to mention scores of dialect words, many still in use, for describing traditional skills and pastimes, from basket-weaving to wrestling.

The Lake District has one of the country's highest concentrations of classic rural **pubs and inns**, many of them former coaching inns dating back several hundred years. Locally brewed beer is widely available, and a circular walk and a pint in front of a roaring fire at the end of it takes some beating for an afternoon out. Stay overnight and you can experience another Lake District speciality, the **country-house hotel**: some of the grandest specimens in England occupy exclusive lakeview positions. Finally, in summer the region hosts many of its annual **sports**, **festivals**, **shows** and **events**, providing a fascinating snapshot of traditional rural life.

Where to go

It's easy to see a great deal of the Lake District in just a few days, even if you are travelling by public transport or getting around on foot. If you're pushed for time, you could tour around most of what's detailed below in a week, but you'd be doing precious little hiking or relaxing. It's far better to pick a base and see what you can from there, walking rather than driving between villages, and building in time for doing nothing more strenuous on occasion than taking out a rowboat or picnicking in a meadow.

Windermere is the longest and largest lake, featuring a cruise service which calls at all points north and south. Two late-Victorian mansions on its shores provide must-see attractions: the National Park's Lake District Visitor Centre at **Brockhole**, and **Blackwell**, whose restored Arts and Crafts interior is one of England's architectural gems. The lake's towns – Windermere, Bowness and, especially, **Ambleside** – have populations of just a few thousand but are among the region's busiest settlements and, given their choice of accommodation, cafés, restaurants and pubs, they make obvious bases. Even if they don't plan to stay there, most people at least pass by Windermere on the way to **Grasmere** and the famous Wordsworth houses of **Rydal Mount** and **Dove Cottage**, or to pretty Hawkshead and Beatrix Potter's house at **Hill Top**.

Nearby **Coniston** sits at the head of Coniston Water which boasts the big draw of **Brantwood**, comfortably endowed home of the critic and essayist John Ruskin. Nearby natural attractions include **Grizedale Forest**, where you can cycle or hike the shaded trails, and **Tarn Hows**, many visitors' favourite splash of water in the entire Lakes. Away from the literary trail, there are renowned hikes, peaks and tarns in central **Langdale** – and, arguably, the finest hikers' inn in the region (the *Old Dungeon Ghyll*) from which to explore them. Less dramatic rural pockets in the hills and dales south of Windermere and Coniston offer easy rambles, village visits and pub lunches in the **Duddon** or **Winster** valleys.

On the whole, the scenery is more dramatic in the north, where four peaks – **Scafell Pike**, **Scafell**, **Helvellyn** and **Skiddaw** – top out at over 3000 feet, and several other equally famous mountains (including **Great Gable** and **Blencathra**) don't lag far behind. The quite different lakes of **Derwent Water** and **Ullswater** provide superb backdrops for a day's cruising and walking. **Keswick**, the main town in the north (with a population of around 5000), is the one major lakeland settlement with real year-round character, and it makes a handy base for exploring: south through the precipitous delights of **Borrowdale**, a valley for which the word pictur-esque might have been invented; west over the forested **Whinlatter Pass**; or north around the little-visited region known as **Back o' Skiddaw**.

The summer crowds thin out in the western side of the Park. Although **Buttermere** and **Crummock Water** see a fair amount of traffic, **Wast Water**, **Ennerdale Water** and **Loweswater** lie further off the beaten track. All these lakes provide supreme walking opportunities, from simple lake-circuits to fell-top clambers, and anyone looking for typical rural accommodation – whether a room above a pub, a farmhouse B&B or lake-side hotel – will find the western lakes and fells irresistible. Keep heading west and you find the only part of the Cumbrian **coastline** that lies within the National Park. This stretches twenty miles south from **Ravenglass**, an undistinguished village with a Roman past, but which provides a bucolic route into the heart of dramatic **Eskdale** by either following the snaking road or the Ravenglass and Eskdale Railway.

This book concentrates on the natural attractions, towns and villages within the National Park, but people's itineraries and interests don't always follow the somewhat arbitrary Park boundaries. Outside the National Park, most visitors make time for Kendal and its excellent museums, the revitalized Georgian port of Whitehaven, and the peripheral historic market towns of Ulverston, Penrith and Cockermouth, the last also famous as the birthplace of Wordsworth. These are bigger settlements than anywhere in the National Park, so they make useful bases; and they're also rainy-day boltholes of sorts, offering a varied set of attractions, including the startling **Rheged** visitor centre near Penrith, fashioned to blend in with the local fells. More reflective destinations lie on the southern flanks of the National Park where **Furness Abbey** and the priory church in the highly attractive village of **Cartmel** provide a glimpse of the erstwhile religious influence on the Lakes.

Kendal Mintcake

You'll see blocks of **Kendal Mintcake** on sale throughout the Lake District, though "cake" is perhaps a misleading term for such a solid confection of molar-shattering properties. It does come from Kendal, though – first produced in the town in 1869 – and it is undeniably minty. As is the way with many great inventions, its initial production came about as a mistake made during the process of combining sugar and peppermint oil for clear mint sweets. It was quickly apparent that the grainy, energy-giving "mintcake" would go far in a region where you often needed a quick boost if you were to scale the local fells and crags. **Romney's of Kendal**, established 1919, is still the biggest producer, famous since Sir Edmund Hillary carried their mintcake up to the top of Everest in 1953. Stick some in your backpack and there's not a Lake District peak you can't knock off before breakfast.

When to go

High **summer** may be the warmest season – usually – but it isn't the ideal time to visit the Lakes. July and August can see accommodation (and the roads) stretched to capacity as the bulk of the annual visitors descend. If you're thinking of swimming in the lakes, it's worth knowing that late August and September see the waters at their warmest, as they've had time to soak up the summer sun. To be honest, though, you'll barely notice the difference: the inland waters are pretty cold, at best, year-round. Other busy periods include **Easter week**, the few days around **New Year**, and school **half-term holidays** (usually Feb & late Oct).

▲ Burthwaite, Wast Water

Fewer people visit the Lakes in the **late autumn**, **winter** and **early spring**, so if you're looking for relative peace and quiet, these are the seasons to choose. Many of the indoor sights and attractions remain open year-round, so you shouldn't be unduly inconvenienced, and while some hotels, guesthouses and campsites are closed, those that do stay open tend to offer reduced rates. Spring usually arrives a little later than in the south of England, though in mild seasons you sometimes get the famous **daffodils** flowering as early as February. Mostly, though, before May you might get bright, blue days, but you can also expect chilly mornings, overnight frosts and cold conditions (snow can linger on north-facing slopes as late as June). December has the shortest and rainiest days; November and January aren't much better.

Average daily temperatures and rainfall in the Lake District

	Jan	Feb	Mar	Apr	May	June	July	Aug	Sept	Oct	Nov	Dec
°F	38	42	45	50	58	62	65	63	60	52	44	42
°C	4	5	7	10	14	17	19	18	15	11	7	6
inches	2	1.75	1.75	1.75	1.9	1.8	2.2	2.2	2	2.1	2.3	1.9
mm	50	44	44	44	48	45	55	55	50	53	58	48

18

things not to miss

It's not possible to see everything that the Lake District has to offer in one trip – and we don't suggest you try. What follows is a selective taste of the highlights of the region. They're arranged in five colour-coded categories, which you can browse through to find the very best things to see and experience. All entries have a page reference to take you straight into the guide, where you can find out more.

01 **Tarn Hows** Page **128** • The most beautiful spot in the Lake District? Many people think so, but you decide as you stroll the undulating paths around this most serene of tarns.

03 **Helvellyn** Page **200** • Climb Helvellyn (3114ft) via the infamous Striding Edge route – one of the most challenging of Lake District walks.

02 **Honister Slate Mine** Page **159** • Don a hard hat and explore the caverns and tunnels of the historic slate mine on Honister Pass.

05 **Aira Force** Page **201** • The sparkling waterfall with a seventy-foot drop is a cherished location – Wordsworth "wandered lonely as a cloud" among the neighbouring daffodils.

04 **Dove Cottage, Grasmere** Page **98** • The most famous literary house in the Lake District – the early home of William and Dorothy Wordsworth, containing a wealth of memories.

06 Castlerigg Stone Circle Page **144**
• The dramatically sited standing stones at Castlerigg, above Keswick, are the most prominent reminder of Lakeland's ancient inhabitants.

08 A cruise on Windermere Page **62** • Cruises and boat trips depart all year round from Bowness piers on Windermere, England's largest lake.

07 Stylish lodgings Page **79** • Contemporary style meets traditional England in the *Waterhead*, one of the Lake District's most fashionable lodgings.

09 Farm life Page **32** • Staying in a farmhouse B&B is the best way to learn something about rural life in the Lake District.

10 Hardknott Roman Fort Page **180** • The finest Roman remains in the Lakes stretch across a blustery hillside.

12 Grizedale Forest Page 130 •
The remarkable sculptures lurking in Grizedale Forest are the backdrop to an adventurous day's walking or cycling.

11 The #79 bus ride in Borrowdale Page 154 •
The Lakes' most scenic bus ride flanks Derwent Water and runs through the stunning valley of Borrowdale, with rustic stops at packhorse bridges, waterfalls, crags, woods and hamlets.

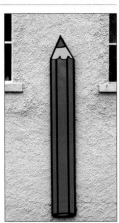

13 Ravenglass & Eskdale Railway Page 175 •
A ride on "La'al Ratty", as the train is known, makes a great family outing, with easy walks possible straight off the platforms of the tiny Eskdale stations.

14 Cumberland Pencil Museum Page 141 •
Trace the history of one of the region's oldest industries at the quirky Pencil Museum in Keswick.

ACTIVITIES | CONSUME | EVENTS | NATURE | SIGHTS

15

15 Langdale Page **106** • For the best rugged walking in the central fells, head for the dramatic Langdale valley.

17 Furness Abbey Page **225** • The beautiful Cistercian abbey ruins provide a contemplative corner in an unsung region.

16 Townend Page **81** • Get close to the life of a yeoman farmer in one of the Lake District's best-preserved domestic houses.

18 Pubs Page **36** • The Lake District has some of the best old inns and pubs in the country, many dating back hundreds of years and still offering a hearty welcome, rooms for the night, local beer and filling bar meals.

Basics

Basics

Getting there

The Lake District is in the county of Cumbria, in the northwest of England, 80 miles north of Manchester and 270 miles from London. The M6 motorway gets you within a few miles' drive of the eastern side of the region, while public transport links are good, with trains or buses providing reasonably direct access from most major British cities (and from Manchester Airport). The major points of access are Lancaster, Kendal and Windermere to the south, and Penrith and Carlisle to the north.

This section tells you how to reach the Lake District by bus, train or car, and gives all the contact details you'll need for planning routes and booking tickets. Touring around the Lakes by either public transport or car is covered in the next section, "Getting around".

A number of operators offer **organized holidays** in the Lakes for those who'd rather someone else made the day-to-day arrangements. Large-scale package-tour operators tend to concentrate on whirlwind trips through the region, bussing passengers in en masse to see the famous lakes and literary sites. Generally speaking, you can do much better than that on your own – either using public transport or booking local minibus tours (covered in "Getting around"). But if you're interested in a residential outdoor activity or pastime-based holiday – from cycle-touring to art appreciation in the Lakes

– you may prefer to let the specialists take charge. We've picked out some of the more interesting options in the "Walking and climbing" (p.40) and "Organized holidays, courses and outdoor activities" (p.44) sections.

For more guidance on holidaying in the Lake District, contact the **Cumbria Tourist Board**: ☎015394/44444, brochure line ☎0870/513 3059, ⓦwww.golakes.co.uk, ⓦwww.gocumbria.co.uk.

By bus

National Express buses from London's Victoria Coach Station run twice daily to Windermere, a seven-hour ride (£35 return; £27 if booked seven days in advance). This service continues from Windermere on to Ambleside (15min), Grasmere (30min) and Keswick (45min). From Manchester's Chorlton Street Coach Station there's one National Express service bus a day

Getting there for overseas visitors

Overseas visitors heading straight for the Lake District should consider taking a connecting **flight** from London, or flying directly to Manchester Airport, northern England's major airport, from where there are direct train services to Kendal and Windermere. Other services from or via Manchester sometimes require a change of trains at Oxenholme, the station for the Lakes on the west-coast main line.

Travelling from Ireland by **ferry**, the most logical port to use is Liverpool (sailings from Belfast and Dublin), from where it's an easy train ride to Manchester and on to the Lakes. Using the Belfast service to Stranraer in Scotland, you'll need to travel first by train to Glasgow and on from there; arriving in Holyhead from Dublin, take the train via Crewe to Oxenholme. From the rest of Europe, using the North Sea crossings makes most sense. Docking at Hull (from Rotterdam and Zeebrugge), take the train to York and Manchester, changing for the onward service to the Lakes; from Newcastle (Hamburg, Amsterdam, Norway and Sweden), take the train to Carlisle, changing for the service south to Penrith and Oxenholme.

to Windermere, which takes three hours (£20 return; £17 if booked seven days in advance) and which also stops in Ambleside, Grasmere and Keswick. This service starts its route at Manchester Airport, providing a useful connection for recent arrivals. From Birmingham, there are two daily services to Windermere, taking under five hours (£32 return; £28 if booked seven days in advance). National Express services from York, Newcastle and Scotland all route via Manchester to the Lakes; from the south, east and west you'll have to change in London or Birmingham. A £3–5 supplement is charged on all National Express routes for travelling on a Friday. Make bookings with your local travel agent, or with National Express, either by phone or online (see below).

Regional bus operators provide other services to the Lake District, though these are often limited to weekend departures in summer from towns and cities in northern England. Stagecoach has the most useful year-round, direct regional service (#555/556), from Carlisle (three daily) to Keswick and points beyond, or from Lancaster (hourly) to Kendal, Windermere, Ambleside, Grasmere and Keswick. For these journeys it's cheapest to buy an Explorer Ticket (see p.22).

Bus information

National Express ☎08705/808080,
ⓦwww.nationalexpress.com.
Stagecoach ☎0870/608 2608,
ⓦwww.stagecoachbus.co.uk/cumbria.

By train

Virgin Trains operates the west-coast mainline service between London and Glasgow. For the Lake District, you must change at **Oxenholme** for the First North Western branch line service to Kendal (3min) and Windermere (20min). The only other places in the region directly accessible by train are Penrith (also on the west-coast main line) and Carlisle (west-coast main line, plus connections from Newcastle upon Tyne). First North Western also has direct services from Manchester to Kendal and Windermere; and from Manchester, Preston and Lancaster to

the towns along the Furness and Cumbrian coast. This latter service runs via Ulverston, Barrow-in-Furness, Ravenglass and the Cumbrian coastal towns to Carlisle, providing a leisurely approach to the south and western Lakes (though there's no service on Sunday).

From London (Euston Station) there are up to ten departures a day, changing at Oxenholme for Kendal and Windermere, a four- to five-hour trip. Prices vary wildly, depending on when you book your ticket, but booking fourteen days in advance can bring the return fare down to £32, and booking seven or three days in advance to £44 or £54. If you buy your ticket on the day, expect to pay more like £67 return, and a lot more if you intend to travel on a Friday or during peak commuter hours. To reach Keswick and the northern Lakes, either take the train from Oxenholme to Windermere and continue from there by bus or stay on the main-line service to Penrith or Carlisle, from where buses also run to Keswick.

From Manchester (Airport, and both Piccadilly and Oxford Road train stations), there are five direct trains daily to Windermere, the quickest of which takes 1hr 45min (seven-day advance £14, three-day £20, standard return £24). Coming **from Yorkshire**, a longer, more scenic approach is provided by the famous **Settle to Carlisle Railway** (connections from Leeds and Bradford), which runs through stunning Yorkshire Dales countryside. At Carlisle, you'll have to switch to local buses to get you to Keswick, Penrith or Cockermouth. The best deal on this route is the Settle to Carlisle Freedom Ticket (£35 for three days), which gives unlimited travel between Leeds and Carlisle. Anyone seeing the Lakes as part of a wider northern England trip might consider buying a **North West Rover** ticket (seven days £52.50; any three days in seven £42.50), valid for unlimited rail travel in a region which stretches between Carlisle, the Cumbrian coast and Lancaster east into Yorkshire.

Services from **Glasgow Central** (9 daily; 2hr 30min–3hr 30min) and **Edinburgh** (8 daily; 3hr–3hr 30min) run to Oxenholme for connections to Windermere, with stops en route at Carlisle and Penrith. Return fares to Windermere from either city start at around

£31, though you'll need to book at least two weeks in advance to get this fare. If buying your ticket on the day, expect to pay £41 return, or up to £63 if you travel on a Friday or at peak times.

Train information and tickets

First North Western ☎ 0845/600 1159, Ⓦ www.firstnorthwestern.co.uk. Timetables and ticket sales.
National Rail Enquiries ☎ 08457/484950, Ⓦ www.nationalrail.co.uk. Timetable, route and service information, with links to ticket-sale sites.
The Train Line Ⓦ www.thetrainline.com. Online timetables, ticket sales and seat reservations.
Virgin Trains ☎ 08457/222333, Ⓦ www.virgintrains.co.uk. Timetables and ticket sales.

By car

The Lake District lies to the west of the M6 motorway, which – as it approaches the hills and troughs of the Lakes and the Eden Valley – displays one of the best feats of road engineering in the country: the section between Kendal and Penrith is as impressive as major highways get in England. Where you come off the motorway depends on your ultimate destination – for Keswick and Penrith, take junction 40; for Kendal and Windermere, take junction 38 (north) or 36 (south); for Cartmel and Ulverston, take junction 36.

Count on a driving time of five hours from London and the southeast, an hour and a half from Manchester or Newcastle, two and half hours from York or Birmingham,

Distances in miles from major cities

Distances in miles from major cities

	Windermere	Keswick
London	270	305
Birmingham	150	190
Manchester	80	115
York	100	115
Newcastle-upon-Tyne	90	80
Edinburgh	145	135
Glasgow	140	135

and three hours from Glasgow or Edinburgh. Once you leave the motorway, the nature of the roads and the summer traffic can slow you right down, so allow plenty of time if you're aiming for the central fells, Borrowdale or the western Lakes. Local radio stations (see p.27) carry regular traffic and weather reports. Both the AA (Ⓦ www.theaa.co.uk) and RAC (Ⓦ www.rac.co.uk) have useful **route-planning services**.

For information, brochures, maps and leaflets en route, there are three useful tourist information offices on the M6: **Cumbria Gateway** (☎ 01524/792181) at Lancaster Services (formerly Forton Services), between junctions 32 and 33, six miles south of Lancaster; **Killington Lake Services** (☎ 015396/20138), one mile south of junction 37 (southbound side only) and seven miles east of Kendal; and **Southwaite Services** (☎ 016974/73445), between junctions 41 and 42, twelve miles north of Penrith.

Getting around

Too many people bring cars to the Lake District and, as a consequence, once-quiet valleys and villages can be adversely affected by the amount of traffic. However, over the last few years – recognizing the damage that's being done to the environment – the local authorities have made great improvements to the public transport network within the National Park to encourage people to leave their cars at home. As well as providing public transport information, this section also recommends local minibus tours, which are a good way of seeing the region quickly. There are also full details about the ups and downs of getting around by car, and a section on cycling in the Lake District (though for cycling holiday operators, see p.44).

The southern, central and northern band – from Windermere and Coniston through Ambleside and Grasmere to Keswick – is the easiest section of the Lakes to tour by public transport. In summer especially, when services are at their peak, there's no longer any real excuse not to use public transport for at least some journeys. In the western Lakes and valleys, and in the far north beyond Keswick, getting around by bus becomes trickier, though nearly everywhere is connected by some sort of service, however limited.

Timetables and information

Major bus routes and frequencies of the services on them are listed at the end of each chapter in "Travel details". For extensive coverage of all public transport services – bus, rail and ferry – get hold of a copy of the free *Getting Around Cumbria and the Lake District Timetable*, available twice a year from Traveline (see below), tourist information centres and National Park offices. It's complemented by a county public transport map, called *To and Through Cumbria and the Lake District*, available from the same offices.

For all public transport enquiries in Cumbria – bus, coach, rail and ferry services – call **Traveline**. If you're calling from outside Cumbria, ask to be transferred to "Traveline Cumbria". The website gives access to a searchable database of all public transport services in the area; the office can send out timetables on request.

Public transport information

Traveline ☎0870/608 2608, ⊛www.traveline .org.uk. Telephone enquiries service available daily 7am–8pm.

By bus

Stagecoach (☎0870/608 2608, ⊛www .stagecoachbus.co.uk/cumbria) is the biggest bus operator in the Lakes, though many of its routes are subsidized by Cumbria County Council, the Countryside Agency or the National Parks Authority to ensure coverage of areas that wouldn't otherwise be economically viable. Dozens of routes connect every major town and village, and although travel frequencies vary you can usually count on being able to reach most places at least once a day throughout the year. The most frequent services on all routes are between Easter and the end of the school holidays in August, though some peak-period timetables continue into September and October (often at weekends only). Local services connect with express routes at Windermere, Ambleside and Keswick to places outside the National Park, such as Cockermouth, the Cumbrian coast, Carlisle, Penrith, Kendal, Ulverston and Barrow.

You can buy tickets on the bus as you go, though the best deal is the Stagecoach **Explorer Ticket** (one-day £8.50; four-day £19; seven-day £26.50), which is valid on the entire network and available on any bus from the driver. With a passport-sized photograph, you can get a week's unlimited travel within Cumbria on a **Cumbria Goldrider** card (£21), while other special Stagecoach **discount tickets** offer hop-on-hop-off transport between Bowness and Grasmere, and bus-and-boat combinations for Windermere, Coniston and Ullswater – specific details are included in the Guide.

Current Stagecoach routes and ticket details are spelt out exhaustively in the invaluable, free, **Lakeland Explorer** timetable, published annually before Easter and available from tourist offices and on board buses in Cumbria. Most tourist offices also have individual route timetables available.

Other services in the Lakes are run by a partnership of agencies and operators, most notably the useful **Cross-Lakes Shuttle** (Easter–Oct), which combines launch and minibus to connect Bowness-on-Windermere with the Beatrix Potter house at Hill Top and Hawkshead. In the past, this service has also continued to Tarn Hows and Coniston, though the future of this section of the route is unclear. In addition, the post office's **postbus** service covers a few outlying areas and takes fee-paying passengers, though departures are often very early in the morning, while some local taxi and minibus operators fill in other gaps on an ad hoc basis. Finally, the **YHA** operates a shuttle-bus service from Ambleside hostel to the Hawkshead, Coniston, Elterwater, Langdale and Grasmere hostels (Easter–Oct; £2.50 a journey; ☎0870/770 5672).

If you're short on time, or just want to let someone else do the driving, then a **minibus tour** through the Lakes can show you an awful lot quickly. Most day tours are in small vehicles, which means that, compared to the big tour buses, you get much more time at the sights and share them with fewer people. The specialist operators listed below have some interesting itineraries and can arrange pick-ups from most of the major lakeland towns. Prices usually start at around £20 for a half-day to £30–35 for a full day out on the road. As well as calling the contact numbers given, you can book most bus tours at local tourist information offices.

Specialist bus tour operators

Fellrunner ☎01768/890063, and at the Penrith tourist office ☎01768/867466. Community-run minibus service offering bargain-priced summer-holiday day tours (mid-July to mid-Sept selected Sun & Mon) of Cumbria, concentrating on the Eden Valley and Ullswater.

Furness Adventure Tours ☎01229/474547. Eight-seater tours concentrating on the southern Lakes and Furness peninsula (Furness Abbey, Cartmel etc), though other Lake District tours too.

Lakeland Safari Tours ☎015394/33904, ⓦwww.lakesafari.co.uk. Small (maximum six-seater) safaris with an environmental emphasis, featuring out-of-the-way circuits and themed historic tours. There's scope for requesting your own day's itinerary or special stops. Departures from Windermere, Bowness, Ambleside and Grasmere.

Lakes Supertours ☎015394/42751 or 88133, ⓦwww.lakes-supertours.com. Eleven- and sixteen-seater, all-day minibus tours – lakes and mountains or literary themes – with some cruises and house entries included.

Mountain Goat ☎015394/45161, ⓦwww.mountain-goat.com. Minibus tours that get off the beaten track: Duddon Valley and Back o'Skiddaw as well as the usual lakes and passes. Daily departures from Windermere, Bowness, Grasmere, Ambleside and Keswick. Also offers themed four- to seven-night touring holidays (such as the five-night "Summer gardens of the Lake District", £395).

Touchstone Tours ☎017687/79599, ⓦwww.touchstonetours.co.uk. Small (maximum eight people) Keswick-based historical tours – lakeland legends, Romans in Cumbria, prehistoric stone circles – that involve some walking and are a bit pricier than the rest but include a country pub lunch and admission fees. Also tailor-made tours, and walking and weekend trips.

By train

After years of service cuts and the whole-hearted embrace of the car, the only place in the Lake District National Park you can now reach on a regular train service is Windermere, on the branch line from Oxenholme (on the London–Manchester–Glasgow west-coast main-line route) via Kendal and Staveley. Outside the park, but still a handy approach to the northern Lakes, Penrith is also a stop on the west-coast main-line route; while the Furness and Cumbrian Coast branch line from Lancaster runs via Ulverston, Ravenglass and the Cumbrian coastal towns to Carlisle. All timetable and ticket details are available from National Rail Enquiries (℡08457/484950).

A **Lakes and Furness Day Ranger** ticket (adult £10.30, child £5.15, family £20) is valid after 8.30am Monday to Friday, and all day at weekends and on public holidays, on services from Lancaster to the Cumbrian coast, and between Oxenholme and Windermere. There's also a **Lakes Day Tripper** ticket (various prices), valid for return rail-and-bus travel to Grange-over-Sands and Windermere from Manchester, Liverpool and other northwestern towns and cities. The three-/seven-day North West Rover ticket (£42.50/£52.50) covers a much wider geographical area and is little use for a tour of the Lakes.

What the Lakes lack in a regular train network is made up for in a couple of scenic steam-train lines. Both **Lakeside and Haverthwaite** (southern end of Windermere) and **Ravenglass and Eskdale** (western fells and valleys) lines are covered in the Guide. The former is the more popular (and easiest to access); the latter provides the more enjoyable ride and operates a year-round service.

By ferry

Of the lakes themselves, Windermere, Coniston Water, Derwent Water and Ullswater have ferry or cruise services of varying degrees of usefulness, all covered in detail in the Guide. Windermere and Ullswater are the most popular choices for a round-trip cruise; the service on Derwent Water is extremely useful for hopping around the lake and accessing Borrowdale walks; while the Coniston launches are used mainly as a means of reaching Ruskin's house, Brantwood.

For steering yourself around lakeland waters, see p.43.

By car

While driving around the Lakes might seem convenient, it soon loses its attraction on July and August weekends when the roads are busy, it takes ages to get from village to village and you can't find anywhere to park once you arrive. Leave the car at home, or at your hotel or B&B, whenever

you can and you'll get more enjoyment out of the region.

Parking is difficult throughout the Lakes, especially in the towns and villages. There is free on-street parking in places such as Ambleside, Windermere, Bowness, Coniston, Grasmere and Keswick, but there's not very much of it and it's usually limited to thirty minutes. The best advice, every time, is to follow the signs to the car parks and pay up. All car parks mentioned in the Guide – and marked on our maps – are **pay-and-display** unless otherwise stated, so a supply of change is a necessity. Expect to pay £1.50–2 for up to four hours' parking, and up to £5 for a full day, even in car parks on National Trust land in out-of-the-way places. Most hotels and some B&Bs have private parking, mentioned in the reviews where available.

Most A and B **roads** in the area are in good condition, though single-track driving is common – don't park in passing places. Surfaces on high ground and off the beaten track tend to deteriorate rapidly, being little more than unmetalled tracks in places: many routes can be adventurous at the best of times and downright treacherous in winter or bad weather. The steepest road gradients and most difficult driving are on the following **lakeland passes**: Blea Tarn Road (between Great and Little Langdale), Hardknott Pass (Eskdale and Duddon Valley), Honister Pass (Buttermere and Borrowdale), Kirkstone Pass (Ullswater and Windermere), The Struggle (Ambleside and Kirkstone Pass), Whinlatter Pass (Braithewaite and Lorton Vale) and Wrynose Pass (Duddon Valley and Little Langdale).

Car rental companies

National

Avis ℡0870/010 0287, www.avis.co.uk.
Budget ℡0870/153 9170, www.budget.co.uk.
Hertz ℡0870/844 8844, www.hertz.co.uk.
Holiday Autos ℡0870/400 0099, www.holidayautos.co.uk.
Thrifty ℡01494/751600, www.thrifty.co.uk.

In Cumbria

Barrow-in-Furness Avis ℡01229/811211; Hertz ℡01229/836666.

Carlisle Avis ℡01228/590580; Hertz ℡01228/524273.
Kendal Westmorland Vehicle Hire ℡01539/728532.
Keswick Keswick Motor Company ℡01687/72064.
Penrith Can be arranged through Westmorland Vehicle Hire, Kendal (see above).
Ulverston Alan Myerscough (Ford) ℡01229/581058.
Windermere Lakes Car Hire ℡015394/44408.

Local taxi firms

Ambleside Billy's Taxis ℡015394/31287; Brown's Taxis ℡015394/33263; John's Taxis ℡015394/32857; Kevin's Taxis ℡015394/32371; Sarah's Taxis ℡015394/41171; Steve's Taxis ℡015934/33544.
Bowness/Windermere Bowness Taxis ℡015394/46664; Lakes Village Taxis ℡015394/46777 or 015394/44055; Windermere Taxis ℡015934/42355.
Cockermouth Cockermouth Taxis ℡01900/826649; G. & J. Taxis ℡01900/826307; Karl's Taxis ℡01900/827393.
Coniston Coniston Taxis ℡015394/41683.
Grasmere Grasmere Taxis ℡015394/35506.
Kendal Blue Star Taxis ℡01539/723670; Crown Taxis ℡01539/732181; Cumbria Cars ℡01539/720620; K. & C. Taxis ℡01539/724117.
Keswick Davies Taxis ℡017687/72676; Derwent Taxis ℡017687/75585; Skiddaw Taxis ℡017687/75600 or 0800/654321.
Penrith A Taxis ℡01768/863354; Cumbria Taxis ℡01768/892886; Express ℡01768/890890; Lakeland ℡01768/865722; Moorside Taxis ℡01768/899066.

By bicycle

Off-road cycling is becoming increasingly popular in the Lakes, though walkers and environmental organizations are concerned by the detrimental effect that mountain biking can have on ancient bridleways. Local cycle businesses do much to promote responsible cycling within the National Park and by following agreed routes, exercising caution and respecting walkers' rights of way you'll help to ensure continued co-operation. If you're not bringing your own bike, then local **bike-rental outfits** (see the list below) can kit you out with all the gear. The going rate

is around £18 for a full-day's rental of a mountain bike, with helmets, locks and often route maps usually included in the price. Children's bikes, trailer bikes and tandems are also often available. A limited number of local buses will carry bikes: call Traveline Cumbria (℡0870/608 2608) for details.

Cycle touring in the Lakes per se isn't much fun, given the traffic, the narrow roads and the severe hills (some of the passes are the steepest roads in England), but it's still a popular pastime. Many youth hostels have bike sheds, though you should call ahead to check facilities at B&Bs and hotels.

Long-distance tourers have the choice of shadowing walkers on the **Sea-to-Sea (C2C)** cycle route, a 140-mile trip between Whitehaven/Workington and Sunderland/Newcastle (information from Sustrans: ℡0845/113 0065, ⓦwww.sustrans.org .uk), or using the **Cumbria Cycle Way**, which circles the region. For more information, and touring information route sheets (free to members) for Cumbria and the Lakes, contact the Cyclists' Touring Club (CTC: ℡0870/873 0061, ⓦwww.ctc.org .uk). If you'd like someone else to make all the arrangements, then contact one of the specialist **cycling tour operators** (listed on p.44), who can arrange fully inclusive cycling holidays in the Lakes.

Bike rental

Ambleside

Biketreks ℡015394/31505, ⓦwww.biketreks.co.uk.
Ghyllside Cycles ℡015394/33592, ⓦwww.ghyllside.co.uk. Nov–Easter closed Wed.

Bowness-on-Windermere

Windermere Canoe & Cycle Hire ℡015394/44451, ⓦwww.windermerecanoecycle.co.uk.

Coniston

Summitreks ℡015394/41212, ⓦwww.summitreks.co.uk.

Grizedale Forest

Grizedale Mountain Bikes ℡01229/860369, ⓦwww.grizedalemountainbikes.co.uk.

Hawkshead

Croft Mountain Bike Hire ☎015394/36374,
ⓦwww.hawkshead-croft.com. Closed Dec & Jan.

Keswick

Keswick Mountain Bikes ☎017687/75202,
ⓦwww.keswickmountainbikes.co.uk.

Staveley

Millennium Cycles ☎01539/821167. Closed Mon.

Ullswater

St Patrick's Landing ☎017684/82393. Closed
Nov–Feb.

Ulverston

Gill Cycles ☎01229/581116. Closed Sun.

Windermere

Country Lanes ☎015394/44544,
ⓦwww.countrylanes.co.uk.

Information, websites and maps

There's plenty of free information available about the Lakes before you go
– either from the official information authorities or from a plethora of useful websites. There's also a visitor information office in virtually every town and village,
which is the best first stop for any kind of information once you're there, while
local newspapers, magazines and radio stations offer useful insights into Lake
District life. Almost everyone in the region has a favourite walk and will be eager
to share it with you, but keen hikers and hill walkers – in fact, anyone intending
to do more than just stroll by the lakeside – will need to buy proper maps; the
best are reviewed below.

Visitor information

For information before you go, contact
the **Cumbria Tourist Board** or the **Lake
District National Park Authority** (NPA),
both of which maintain useful websites
and can send you a variety of brochures.
In the Lake District itself, a series of visitor
information offices provide help on
the ground – all are listed in the guide.
The offices are funded and run by the
tourist board, the NPA and by local councils: opening hours vary, though in the
summer most of the main offices are open
daily from 10am to 6pm, sometimes an
hour earlier in the morning and an hour
later in the evening. Opening hours are
reduced in winter and, in some offices,
may be restricted to weekends only (usually Fri to Sun) from 10am to 4pm. At each
office you'll be able to book accommodation, check on local weather conditions,
and buy guides and maps.

Visitor information

Cumbria Tourist Board Ashleigh, Holly Rd,
Windermere, Cumbria LA23 2AQ ☎015394/44444,
brochure line ☎0870/513 3059, from abroad
☎44-(0)1271/336039, ⓦwww.golakes.co.uk,
ⓦwww.gocumbria.co.uk.
Lake District National Park Authority
Brockhole, Windermere, Cumbria LA23 1LJ
☎015394/46601, ⓦwww.lake-district.gov.uk.

Local publications

Local **newspapers** (published weekly) are
a good source of information about lakeland events, politics and personalities. Look
for the *Westmorland Gazette* (which covers
eastern Cumbria and the southern and central Lakes); the *Lake District Herald* (Penrith,
Keswick and the northern Lakes); the *Keswick Reminder* (covering just Keswick); and
the *Cumberland News* (Carlisle, Keswick
and Penrith). Two daily evening papers carve
up the region between them: the *North West*

Evening Mail (southern Cumbria) and the *Evening News and Star* (northern Cumbria).

Cumbria, the small-format monthly **magazine**, and the bigger, glossier, bi-monthly *Cumbria Life* concentrate on the history, culture and social and natural fabric of the Lakes. The quarterly *Lakeland Walker* is a chatty periodical aimed at hikers and lakeland lovers, featuring walks, news, reviews and equipment-testing. *Park Life* is the free newspaper published twice a year by the National Park Authority, containing news and events from around the region. You should also pick up the NPA's annual *Events* guide, listing all the region's festivals, activities and events.

Local radio

BBC Radio Cumbria North Cumbria 95.6 FM/756 AM; West Cumbria 104.1 FM/1458 AM; South Cumbria 96.1 FM/837 AM; Windermere 95.2 FM/104.2 FM.
The Bay North 96.9 FM; Lakes/South 102.3 FM; Cumbria 103.2 FM.

Maps and walking guides

The best general map of the National Park area is the Ordnance Survey (OS) inch-to-the-mile (1:63,360) Touring Map and Guide no. 3, with hill shading and principal footpaths illustrated. For more detail of Cumbria as a whole (including Carlisle and the coast), you'll need the pink (1:50,000) OS Landranger series of maps (nos. 85, 89, 90, 91, 96 and 97).

Essential for **hikers** are the yellow (1:25,000) OS Outdoor Leisure series – four maps (nos. 4, 5, 6 and 7) which cover the whole Lake District National Park. Map no. 33 (same scale) shows the western half of the Coast-to-Coast walk, the part which cuts through the Lakes. Some prefer the Harvey's Superwalker series of waterproof maps (also 1:25,000) covering north, east, northwest, west, south and central Lakeland.

Most bookshops, outdoors stores and information offices sell the full range of maps, as well as various **local walk map-leaflets**. Recommended series include the packs of *Lakeland Leisure Walks* (five assorted walks in each of the major areas), local fell expert Paul Buttle's various walking

booklets, and the National Park Authority's *Walks in the Countryside* leaflets. For **hiking guides** for the Lake District, see p.251.

Useful websites

Websites devoted to Cumbria and the Lake District have multiplied rapidly in recent years. Those maintained by official, regional organizations – including the tourist board, the National Park Authority and local newspapers – are kept fully up to date and are still the best first stop for general information about the area. Others are sponsored by local businesses and, provided you accept that the listings and reviews aren't necessarily comprehensive, they offer plenty of help if you want to find a B&B or a local taxi firm. The best of all these sites are covered below, along with some of the more interesting, noteworthy or downright quirky sites devoted to Lake District life.

Many local towns and villages also have their own **community websites**, all offering the same breadth of information – from potted village histories and weather reports to hotel lists and forthcoming events. We've included these in the relevant "Practicalities" sections in the Guide.

Travel and tourism

ⓦ **www.cumbria.com** Cumbria on the Internet: a useful searchable database of Cumbrian tourist resources (from information offices to accommodation lists) and businesses (from fish suppliers to quarry companies).
ⓦ **www.thecumbriadirectory.com** Guide to Cumbria and the Lakes, with useful round-ups of towns, villages, people, attractions, books, news and traditions.
ⓦ **www.golakes.co.uk,** ⓦ **www.gocumbria .co.uk** Official website of the Cumbria Tourist Board, with an interactive map, accommodation databases and webcams showing views of Windermere, Coniston and Keswick.
ⓦ **www.lake-district.gov.uk** Official website of the National Park Authority – all you need to know about National Park work, services and events.
ⓦ **www.lake-district-peninsulas.co.uk** Official website for the Lake District peninsulas region – information, accommodation and events for Broughton-in-Furness, Lakeside and Newby Bridge, Ulverston and Cartmel.
ⓦ **www.lakesnet.co.uk** Leisure, travel and business resource, with plenty of useful links and searchable databases.

ⓦ **www.western-lakedistrict.co.uk** Website of the Western Lake District Tourism Partnership, covering events, accommodation and attractions in the lakes and towns west of Keswick to the coast.

Regional news, features and services

ⓦ **www.cumbria.gov.uk** Cumbria County Council site – the place to come for local community, social, government and business information, with useful links to other sites.

ⓦ **www.cumbria-online.co.uk** The online presence of a local newspaper group, with daily news and features from the *Evening Mail, Cumberland News* and *Cumbria Life* among others. This is the best one-stop site for Cumbrian news, sport, entertainment, property, classified ads, message boards, photographs, webcams and so on.

ⓦ **www.thisisthelakedistrict.co.uk** Official site of the *Westmorland Gazette* – daily updated news and features, plus full coverage of everything to do with eastern Cumbria and the southern and central Lakes.

Walking and the mountains

ⓦ **www.bassplace.freeserve.co.uk/wildcamp** Backpacking, camping and walking in Britain, with particular emphasis on the Lake District – click on any of the 214 Wainwright fells for a full description, or check out the pictures, routes, trip reports, camping tips and more.

ⓦ **www.bonington.com** Official site for the grand old man of British climbing, Chris Bonington, born in London but based for many years in Caldbeck in the northern Lakes. There's more in his biography, plus expedition details, Lake District views and signed copies of his books.

ⓦ **http://homepages.enterprise.net/ldsamra** Cumbria's Search and Mountain Rescue Association site, packed full of useful advice for walkers and mountaineers, and a forbidding tally of accident stats.

ⓦ **www.lakedistrictoutdoors.co.uk** Cumbria Tourist Board site featuring walks and cycle rides, water-sports and hang-gliding, together with safety advice, weather information and other useful bits and pieces.

ⓦ **www.lakedistrictwalks.com** John Dawson's incredibly detailed Lake District hiking site features over forty classic walks, complete with route descriptions, photos and a distance calculator.

ⓦ **www.ukclimbing.com** Mountaineers should go straight to this site, the definitive online climbing resource – walls, climbs and crag summaries, photos, features, news and events, online shop and message forums.

Lakeland scenery

ⓦ **www.keswick.u-net.com** Ann Bowker's site claims she's "Mad About Mountains" – and she certainly is. Digital pix, routes and ascents of Skiddaw, her local mountain, plus an incredibly comprehensive photo-gallery of ascents and views of each of the 214 Wainwright peaks.

ⓦ **www.lakelandcam.co.uk** Beautiful shots of lakeland scenery and the weather in all seasons and conditions from the roving digital camera of Tony Richards.

Regional crafts, food and language

ⓦ **www.kendal.mintcake.co.uk** All you ever wanted to know about Kendal's famous energy-boosting sweetie, made by Romney's of Kendal, complete with a list of stockists.

ⓦ **www.lakelanddialectsociety.org** Browse the dialect poems and stories, learn to count sheep the Cumbrian way, or study the online dictionary in an attempt to avoid looking like a *garrack* (awkward stupid person).

ⓦ **www.madeincumbria.co.uk** Dedicated to Cumbrian crafts, gifts and food, with over four hundred craftspeople and local suppliers offering everything from handmade baskets to furniture. The food section includes a list of Cumbrian farmers' markets.

Phone, mail and email

There are telephone boxes all over the Lake District, even in isolated rural areas, which is just as well because you'll sometimes find that coverage from your mobile phone network is patchy to say the least. Each town and major village in the Lakes also has a single post office, listed below for reference. As for email, there's an increasing number of cafés, Internet points, guest houses and hotels where you can log on and check your mail.

Telephones and email

It doesn't pay to rely on being able to use your **mobile phone** in the Lakes. The nature of the terrain means you sometimes can't get a signal (though you're usually all right in the main towns and villages), which is one reason why it's not recommended that hikers rely solely on their phones – rather than their navigational skills – to get them out of trouble on the fells. **Telephone boxes**, on the other hand, are ubiquitous in the towns and villages, and most take phone- and credit cards. Local telephone codes are included for all numbers listed in the Guide.

There are **Internet points** in all the major towns and villages and we've listed the most useful places in the Guide. It's rarely cheap (around £2 for 30min is standard), though local libraries now all have Internet access, too, which can be free or inexpensive. Most youth hostels, B&Bs, guest houses and hotels are also online these days, and you might be able to persuade them to let you check for mail.

Post offices

Apart from the usual postal services, you can exchange travellers' cheques and foreign currency at most lakeland post offices. Normal **opening hours** are Monday to Friday from 9am to 5.30pm and Saturday from 9am to 12.30pm, though smaller offices may have restricted hours. It's worth noting that not all post offices are stand-alone businesses – the smaller ones, especially, are often housed in village stores.

The **list of post offices** below covers all the main tourist areas of the Lake District, though for any further information about postal services in Cumbria and the Lakes you can contact the post office enquiry line on ☏ 0845/722 3344.

Ambleside Market Place ☏ 015394/32267.
Bowness 2 St Martin's Parade ☏ 015394/46964.
Broughton-in-Furness Princes St ☏ 01229/716220.
Cockermouth Main St ☏ 01900/822277.
Coniston Yewdale Rd ☏ 015394/41259.
Elterwater Maple Tree Cnr ☏ 015394/37221.
Grasmere Red Lion Sq ☏ 015394/35261.
Hawkshead Main St ☏ 015394/36911.
Kendal 75 Stricklandgate ☏ 01539/725592.
Keswick 48 Main St ☏ 017687/72269.
Patterdale Ullswater ☏ 017684/82220.
Penrith Crown Sq ☏ 01768/863942.
Ravenglass Main St ☏ 01229/717821.
Rosthwaite Borrowdale ☏ 017687/77304.
Troutbeck Troutbeck village ☏ 015394/33302.
Windermere 21 Crescent Rd ☏ 015394/43245.

Costs, money and banks

Banks are fairly plentiful, in the towns at least, and the reciprocal use of cash dispensers (ATMs) means you are unlikely to be stuck for money, whoever you bank with. How far the cash will go is another matter. As with anywhere in England, travelling around the Lakes isn't particularly cheap, though the glorious countryside is of course free to enjoy. In addition, a vast network of B&Bs and youth hostels keep prices down for anyone on a budget, and it doesn't cost a penny if you walk from place to place – the best way to enjoy the scenery in any case.

Costs and discounts

As always, accommodation will be your major expense, and there's a full rundown of the costs in the next section. Generally speaking, though, even if staying in a B&B, buying a picnic or café lunch, hiking or taking the bus, and eating and drinking in a pub, you're unlikely to spend less than £35 a day. Camping, hostelling and self-catering shaves a few pounds off this figure. Upgrade to a better room, or eat in a restaurant, and you can double it easily. Meanwhile, dinner, bed and breakfast alone in one of the region's celebrated country-house hotels can run to well over £100 per person.

If you're counting the cost, however, there are plenty of ways to keep to a more moderate budget. Nearly all accommodation options – from simple B&Bs to luxury hotels – offer special **off-season deals** or discounts or even free nights for longer stays. It always pays to ask when booking. Youth hostels and **self-catering** cottages – the Lakes has the most extensive network of either in the country – mean you can save money by cooking for yourself. **Children** and **senior citizens** get discounts on most forms of transport in the Lakes, and on entrance to the sights, museums and historic houses. If you're a **YHA member**, you qualify for discounts and special deals on all sorts of activities and at attractions and retail outlets. And **National Trust** and **English Heritage** members (see p.46 for contact details) have free entry to all relevant sights and attractions. As far as **events and activities** go, many of the traditional festivals or local attractions are free, while the National Park Authority organizes free or low-cost activities, courses, walks and events throughout the year.

Banks, exchange and credit cards

Normal **banking hours** are Monday to Friday from 9.30am to 3.30pm, with some branches in the major towns open on Saturday morning too. Conversely, in smaller lakeland villages, bank branches sometimes only open a couple of days a week. At least one of the major banks (Abbey, Barclays, Halifax, HSBC, Lloyds-TSB or NatWest) has a cash dispenser (ATM) in each of the main settlements (Ambleside, Bowness, Cockermouth, Kendal, Keswick, Penrith, Ulverston and Windermere) and addresses for each are listed at the end of town accounts in the Guide. In addition, stand-alone ATMs are increasingly found in village shops and petrol stations, though note that these nearly all charge a fee for withdrawing cash with your card. Apart from at the banks, you'll be able to exchange travellers' cheques and foreign currency at major post offices.

Credit cards are widely accepted in shops, hotels, restaurants and service stations, but don't count on being able to use plastic in B&Bs, guest houses, pubs and cafés: we indicate all those that don't accept credit cards in the Guide. Be aware, however – even those that do accept credit cards often don't accept American Express.

Accommodation

The Lake District has no shortage of accommodation, though it sometimes seems like it at peak periods. At New Year, Easter, public holidays and school holidays (particularly the six-week summer break from late July to the end of August) it's always wise to book ahead – though tourist information centres will always be able to find a room for anyone arriving without a reservation. Accommodation listed in the Guide is open year-round unless otherwise stated, though note that, even so, many places close for a few days over Christmas and New Year.

The Cumbria Tourist Board has a Booking Hotline, ☎0808/100 8848, for short breaks, special offers and late bookings; check its website, too, ⓦwww.lastminutelakedistrict .co.uk, for up-to-the-minute special offers. Otherwise, local information offices can provide assistance: all offer a free **room-booking service** where you'll be charged a deposit (usually ten percent) that's then deducted from your accommodation bill. For full lists of Lake District accommodation you'll need the following four annual publications: *Where To Stay in Central and Southern Lakeland*, *Keswick and the Northern Lakes Visitor Guide*, *Western Lake District Visitor Guide* and *Discover Cumbria's Eden* (covers Ullswater, Penrith and the Eden Valley). All are available from information offices in the Lakes, or by mail if you call local tourist offices.

Hotels, guest houses and B&Bs

Bed-and-breakfast (B&B) rates in the Lake District start at around £16 per person per night. Even in the most basic of places, you should get a sink, a TV and a kettle in the room, and the use of a guest lounge. These days, most B&Bs and guest houses have added en-suite shower and toilet cubicles to their rooms, for which you'll pay from £20–25 per person – don't expect a great deal of space (or indeed a bath) in these "bathrooms". Once above these prices – say from £30–35 per person – you can expect a range of services and facilities that you won't get in a standard B&B, from fresh flowers and gourmet breakfasts to king-sized beds and quality bathrooms. Many B&Bs and small guest houses have raised their game in recent years – some are truly excellent – and we've highlighted the best choices in every area.

Hotels in the Lakes tend to charge what they can get away with and, as location is everything, lakeside or isolated fellside retreats can get away with an awful lot – you can easily spend £150–200 for a room in one of the famous country-house hotels, like *Miller Howe*, *Sharrow Bay* or *Gilpin Lodge*. However, there's a lot of choice in

---

Accommodation price codes

All **hotel** and **B&B** accommodation in the Guide is priced on a scale of ❶ to ❾, indicating the **average price** you could expect to pay per night for a **double/twin room** in high season. **Breakfast** is usually included, and rooms are **en suite**, unless otherwise stated.

❶ under £40	❹ £61–70	❼ £111–150
❷ £41–50	❺ £71–90	❽ £151–200
❸ £51–60	❻ £91–110	❾ £201 and over

the £70–110 range, though it pays to pick and choose – a classy, personally run B&B often has the edge over a traditional hotel. Again, though, overall standards are slowly improving, as contemporary style, designer fabrics and new technology make inroads into the Lakes. Several places have had makeovers, adding fancy linen, marble and slate detailing, and flatscreen TVs and DVD players to rooms – Ambleside's townhouse-style *Waterhead* hotel is the most dramatic example, though other hotels and guest houses are following suit.

Rooms are also available in many town-centre and country **pubs and inns**. Often this is traditional B&B in old-fashioned or modernized rooms, starting at around £25 per person, rising to around £40–45 in the best-known traditional hikers' inns (like Langdale's *Britannia Inn* and the *Old Dungeon Ghyll,* and Wasdale's *Wasdale Head Inn*). However, several country inns in particular have gone contemporary, with sharp styling, snappy service and good food now the norm at places like the *Drunken Duck Inn*, outside Hawkshead, and Loweswater's *Kirkstile Inn*.

Prices in all establishments are often higher at weekends, during summer and over public holidays: conversely, it's always worth asking about off-season **discounts**, which might shave a couple of quid off a B&B room, or up to forty off a hotel.

At weekends, many places insist upon two- or (over public holidays) even three-night **minimum stays**. There again, staying more than a couple of nights in many places brings the standard price down a pound or two a night. There aren't a great many **single rooms** available, and solitary hikers or holidaymakers won't often get much knocked off the price of a double room if that's the only option. Finally, many guest houses, and inns hotels offer a discounted **dinner, bed and breakfast** (D, B&B) rate which – provided you want to eat there in the first place – is often a better deal than the standard B&B rate: the Guide picks out those D, B&B places where the cooking is particularly good. Note, though, that some hotels *only* offer stays on a D, B&B basis while others are so remote that there's nowhere else to eat anyway.

At all the establishments listed in this book, **payment by credit card** is accepted unless otherwise stated. However, even where credit cards are accepted, American Express cards often aren't – pack another card, just in case.

Farm stays

Not surprisingly, one of England's most rural regions offers plenty of opportunity to see country life at close quarters by staying on a farm. At its most basic this might be simple farmhouse B&B, offered on many farms as a way of boosting income. Accommodation might be in the farmhouse itself or in cottages on the farm, and you can expect to pay standard bed-and-breakfast rates. Sometimes accommodation is on a self-catering basis and then the price depends on the property and length of stay. You'll see signs advertising rooms on farms all over the Lake District and while it helps to have your own transport (because of the isolated nature of many farms), some farms sited on the edge of villages are easy to reach on foot. Although there's no obligation, many farms provide a more in-depth experience and, where it's appropriate, you'll have a lot more opportunity to muck in, either feeding the animals or finding out more about farming life.

Farm stay contact

Farm stay UK ☎ 0247/669 6909, free brochure on ☎ 01271/336141, ⊕ www.farmstayuk.co.uk.

Youth hostels and backpackers' accommodation

There are 23 Youth Hostel Association (YHA) **youth hostels** in the Lake District, plus one in Carlisle and one in Arnside on Morecambe Bay. Several, including those in Ambleside and Grasmere, are amongst the most popular in the country, so advance booking is a good idea at any time of the year. Gone are the days of curfews, tasks and sackcloth comforts: many Lake District hostels have rooms with just two, three, four or six beds, all bed linen is provided, and nearly all are well-equipped with kitchen, laundry and drying-room facilities; some have licensed cafés, bike rental and Internet access. A YHA shuttle bus runs between the major Lake District hostels (see p.23); alternatively, buy a copy of *The Lake District Youth Hosteller's Walking Guide* by Martin Hanks (Landmark Publishing), which describes walks between every hostel.

You need to be a hostel member to stay at a YHA hostel: either join your home country's hostelling association before you go (which gives you access to YHA hostels), or simply join on your first night at the hostels themselves. **Prices** start at £11 per night for a bed at simple, remote establishments such as those at Black Sail and Honister Hause, rising to £18 (including breakfast) for the flagship Ambleside hostel. Breakfast costs an extra £3.80 and a three-course dinner (where available) £5.50; packed lunches (£4.30) are usually provided too. Many hostels also have **family rooms** available, giving you exclusive use of a small dorm, and some will let couples stay in rooms or have specific **twin rooms** (usually with bunk-beds) available. Prices are usually around £25–30 for couples and between £35 and £60 for families, depending on the room. A **YHA reservation service** (Easter–Oct daily 9.30am–5.30pm; ☎015394/31117) lets you book any hostel in the Lake District up to seven days in advance, free of charge. Only Ambleside and Keswick YHAs are open daily, year-round. Most other hostels have restricted opening periods in the winter, which are detailed in the Guide, though you should call the hostels themselves for specific details. At many hostels you can't check in until 5pm; reception opening hours are noted in the Guide.

The few **independent backpackers'** hostels in the Lakes (in Ambleside, Windermere, Grasmere and Keswick) have very similar facilities and are pitched at roughly the same prices as the higher-grade YHA hostels. On the whole, they have a more laid-back feel than the YHA hostels and tend to attract a more international crowd. There are no membership requirements for backpackers' hostels and they are usually open year-round, with someone generally on hand throughout the day.

Youth hostel associations

Australia Australian Youth Hostels Association ☎02/9565 1699, ⊛www.yha.com.au.
Canada Canadian Hostelling Association ☎1-800/663 5777 or 613/237 7884, ⊛www.hostellingintl.ca.
England & Wales Youth Hostel Association ☎0870/770 8868, ⊛www.yha.org.uk.
New Zealand New Zealand Youth Hostels Association ☎03/379 9970, ⊛www.yha.co.nz.
Northen Ireland Hostelling International Northern Ireland ☎028/9032 4733, ⊛www.hini.org.uk.
Republic of Ireland An Óige ☎01/8430 4555, ⊛www.irelandyha.org.
Scotland Scottish Youth Hostel Association ☎01786/891400, ⊛www.syha.org.uk.
USA American Youth Hostels ☎202/783-6161, ⊛www.hiayh.org.

Holiday property rental

The dream of renting a pretty rural holiday cottage in the Lakes is easily accomplished. The hardest thing is deciding what you want, with choices ranging from simple stone cottages to large country houses, by way of barn conversions, former mills, town houses and shooting lodges. There are lots of companies out there vying for your custom but all offer the same kind of basic deal. The minimum rental period is usually a week, though outside the summer season and especially in the winter you may be able to negotiate a three-day/long-weekend rate – except, that is, at Christmas, New Year and Easter when prices are at their highest and demand at its most intense. All properties come with a fully equipped kitchen and many (but not all) provide bed linen and towels. Prices vary dramatically – from £160 to £200 a week for the smallest properties to as much as £1000 for a week in a large, luxury property with admission to the local pool and health club thrown in.

The list of **agencies** below should help in finding the property you want, but it's worth scanning accommodation brochures and notices in local shop windows for other choices. Throughout the Guide we've also picked out recommended individual self-catering properties, while an advance-booking service, based at Windermere tourist information centre (℡015394/46499), can provide up-to-date information about lots of other self-catering properties, mainly but not exclusively in the southern and central Lakes.

Holiday property agencies

Coppermines and Coniston Cottages ℡015394/41765, ⓦwww.coppermines.co.uk. Specialist in the Coniston area, with unique properties in Coppermines Valley as well as around Coniston Water.

CottageNet.co.uk ⓦwww.cottagenet.co.uk. Internet-based reservations company for holiday cottages, with a large selection in the Lakes.

Country Holidays ℡0870/078 1200, ⓦwww.country-holidays.co.uk. National firm with over a hundred properties in the Lakes.

Cumbrian Cottages ℡01228/599960, ⓦwww.cumbrian-cottages.co.uk. A wide range of over 300 cottages and apartments in the Lake District and Cumbria.

Goosemire Cottages ℡015395/68102, ⓦwww.goosemirecottages.co.uk. Thirty conversions and traditional cottages in the Ullswater and Haweswater region.

Heart of the Lakes ℡015394/32321, ⓦwww.heartofthelakes.co.uk. Excellent choice of over 300 quality properties all over the Lakes.

Hideaway Cottages ℡015394/42435, ⓦwww.lakeland-hideaways.co.uk. Cottages, barn and farm conversions in Hawkshead and around Esthwaite Water.

Holidays in Lakeland ℡0870/078 0162, ⓦwww.holidays-in-lakeland.co.uk. Anything from modern studios to traditional cottages in the southeastern area of the Lakes.

Keswick Cottages ℡017687/73895, ⓦwww.keswickcottages.co.uk. A good selection of cottages in and around Keswick, Braithewaite and Threlkeld in the northern Lakes.

Lakeland Cottage Co. ℡015395/30024, ⓦwww.lakeland-cottage-company.co.uk. Southern Lakes specialist – from simple cottages to large country houses – with outdoor activities, baby-sitting and catering services offered too.

Lakeland Cottages ℡017687/76065, ⓦwww.lakelandcottages.co.uk. Period cottages and farmhouses in the Keswick area, and also in Borrowdale and Lorton Vale.

Lakelovers ℡015394/88855, ⓦwww.lakelovers.co.uk. A large range of properties mainly in the western and southern Lakes.

National Trust ℡0870/458 4422, ⓦwww.nationaltrustcottages.co.uk. Eighteen lakeland properties – mainly around Ambleside, Little Langdale, Eskdale, Loweswater and Penrith.

Wheelwright's ℡015394/37635, ⓦwww.wheelwrights.com. Best starting-place for cottages in and around Elterwater, Chapel Stile and Langdale.

Campsites, bunkhouses and camping barns

The Lake District has scores of **campsites**, though in the Guide we've tended to recommend those that favour tents over the large family-style caravan-RV parks. Many sites close between November and March, while in July and August it's always worth booking a pitch in advance.

Prices vary considerably, from a couple of quid to stick your tent in a farmer's field (and possibly the use of a toilet and cold tap) to £10 a night for the use of all the facilities in one of the super-sites, complete with shop, bar and hot showers. The National Trust also maintains three popular campsites – Great Langdale, Low Wray and Wasdale Head (all featured in the Guide) – in fantastic locations and moderately priced at around £4 a head per night.

The number of **bunkhouses** in the Lakes is slowly increasing, as farms, pubs and individuals make good use of old barns and other buildings to provide simple accommodation for hikers and backpackers. At its most basic, a bunkhouse might provide a mattress on the floor and a shower room, though others provide bunk beds, kitchens, lounges and other comforts. You'll have to provide your own sleeping bag and prices usually run to between £6 and £10 per person per night. In a similar vein, the YHA co-ordinates a series of thirteen **camping barns** within the National Park: self-catering converted farm buildings with basic, communal facilities. The cost is £5 per person per night and you'll need your own sleeping bag, foam mat and other camping equipment (not all have cooking utensils available). To check availability and make reservations, call the Lakeland Barns Booking Office on ℡017687/72645, and consult ⓦwww.lakelandcampingbarns.co.uk for details.

Food and drink

Few people come to the Lakes purely for the gastronomic experience, but many are pleasantly surprised by the range and quality of food on offer. Pub and café meals have improved immeasurably over the last few years, while in restaurants right across the region there's good lakeland cooking in abundance, using local ingredients – fish, lamb, locally grown veg, homemade bread – and a dash of flair. Those with more cosmopolitan tastes will be relieved that cappuccino machines have continued their steady march north, and though there aren't any sushi bars in the Lakes there are decent pizzerias, Modern-British and Thai restaurants, gastro-pubs and gourmet vegetarian places. There just aren't very many of them.

Traditionally, fine dining in the Lakes – as in the rest of England – was very much a silver-service roast-and-veg affair, or heavily Anglo-French in character, a state of affairs that still survives in many old-fashioned lakeland hotels. But some regional chefs have married contemporary flavours and trends with well-sourced local ingredients to produce something slightly different: if not a specific lakeland style of cuisine then at least a welcome change to old-school menus. At the more adventurous places expect to see plenty of pan-searing and char-grilling of local meat and fish, together with seasonal veg, soups and fruit given ethnic and fusion twists. The Lake District also offers a dozen of the finest **country-house dining** experiences in England, notably the Michelin-starred *Holbeck Ghyll*, as well as renowned foodie locations like *Sharrow Bay*, *Miller Howe* and *Gilpin Lodge*. However, for sheer style and panache,

nothing beats Cartmel's *L'Enclume* restaurant-with-rooms, also Michelin-starred, which has few peers in Britain, never mind the Lakes.

You're as likely to come across good food in a tearoom or café as in a restaurant or hotel. As a rule, meals in **pubs and inns** are a bit more hit and miss, though many in the Lakes are carving out a reputation for their food as much as for their beer. In the Guide we've picked out our favourite choices for pub meals, whether it's a good sandwich in a town-centre hostelry or gourmet food in a rural gastro-pub, of which there are increasing numbers.

All cafés, restaurants and pubs listed in the Guide serve **lunch and dinner** daily unless otherwise stated. Winter opening hours are notoriously fickle, so a phone call before you set out never does any harm. Listed places all take **credit cards** unless otherwise stated (though this often doesn't include American Express, except in the more expensive hotels and restaurants).

Local specialities

It's pretty much as you would expect in farming and fishing country. Beef and pork tends to be overshadowed by the local **lamb**, particularly by Herdwick lamb, the traditional lakeland breed which finds its way onto menus across the county. It also forms the basis of filling dishes such as "tattie pot", a traditional lamb stew topped with potato. This is supplemented on menus by local **trout** (farmed on Ullswater and elsewhere, as well as found wild), Morecambe Bay

Restaurant price codes

Restaurants listed in this Guide have been assigned one of four price categories:
Inexpensive under £12.50
Moderate £12.50–20
Expensive £20–35
Very expensive over £35
This is the price you can expect to pay per person for a three-course meal or equivalent, excluding drinks and service.

shrimps and, on occasion, the lake-caught **char** (see p.62), a trout-like fish peculiar to the Lake District. **Bread** is at its best from the Village Bakery, Melmerby (near Penrith) – on sale in shops and supermarkets across the region – while **cheese** from the Thornby Moor Dairy, in Thursby (near Carlisle) is well-regarded too, either plain (a smooth, creamy variety), smoked, or flavoured with garlic and herbs. The Old Smokehouse at Brougham Hall (near Penrith) **smokes** everything from garlic to goose, and supplies Fortnum & Mason as well as local outlets – try its award-winning smoked Penrith Pepperpot sausage.

As you go, keep an eye out at roadside stalls, craft outlets and village shops for locally made honey and preserves – the Lyth Valley's **damson** harvest, for example, ends up in jams and even beer. The Hawkshead Relish Company and others supply locally made **chutneys and pickles**, often served as part of a ploughman's lunch, and Alston in northern Cumbria provides many outlets with speciality mustards.

In many places, **breakfast** is the best meal of the day – no surprise in England. Even the humble B&B makes an occasional outstanding effort (the best are noted in the Guide), with homemade bread and muesli, yoghurt, muffins, pancakes, rissoles and other delights appearing alongside the ubiquitous fry-up. And on that subject, the Lake District is the best place to try **Cumberland sausage**, a thick, spicy, herby pork sausage (traditionally made in a spiral shape); the supreme example is that made by Woodall's of Waberthwaite (near Millom), suppliers by Royal Warrant to the Queen, and purveyors, too, of fine dry-cured hams and bacon.

No rundown of local treats would be complete without **Kendal Mintcake**, a brutal peppermint confection favoured by strongtoothed hikers. There are plaudits too for Cartmel Village Shop's **sticky toffee pudding** and **Penrith fudge and toffee**, while creamy lakeland **ice cream** is increasingly available in local shops and cafés.

Vegetarians

Vegetarians are increasingly well catered for in the Lakes. Most B&Bs these days at least make a stab at a non-meat breakfast, while if you want a true **vegetarian guest house** you can choose between (among others) the *Beech Tree* in Coniston, *Yewfield* at Hawkshead, *Lakeland Natural* in Kendal and Ulverston's *Walkers' Hostel*. There is also a fair number of vegetarian/wholefood **cafés and restaurants** in the Lakes, notably in Keswick, Kendal, Grasmere, Ambleside and Cockermouth, while Grasmere's *Lancrigg Vegetarian Country House Hotel* combines gourmet veggie dining with country-house living.

Pubs and beer

There's a fine selection of country pubs and former coaching inns throughout the region, many dating back several hundred years. Those tied to the major breweries feature the same range of drinks you'll find all over England, but it's worth seeking out those owned by the main regional breweries and other independent (ie free house) pubs for the best selection of local beer.

Jennings (ⓦwww.jenningsbrewery.co.uk) has the main lakeland stranglehold and offers brewery tours (see p.230) at its base in Cockermouth. You'll come across its beers everywhere – both a Bitter and Cumberland Ale, and the stronger Cocker Hoop and Sneck Lifter ales. Meanwhile, the **Bitter End Brewery** (ⓦwww.bitterend.co.uk), based at the *Bitter End* pub in Cockermouth, bravely brews a small range of beers on Jennings' home soil.

Several other small brewers also have just single-pub outlets, or are confined to the pubs in one village or local area. Ones to keep an eye out for include: the **Coniston Brewing Company** (ⓦwww.conistonbrewery.com), which sells its award-winning Bluebird bitter, Old Man, Opium and winter Blacksmith's ales at the village's *Black Bull* and at an increasing number of lakeland pubs; **Barngates Brewery** at the *Drunken Duck Inn* (ⓦwww.drunkenduckinn.co.uk) near Hawkshead, serving beers (Cracker Ale, Tag Lag, Chester's Strong and Ugly) named after dogs that have lived at the inn; the **Hesket Newmarket Brewery** (ⓦwww.hesketbrewery.co.uk) whose half-dozen ales are available at the *Old Crown*, Hesket Newmarket, and at other selected northern and western

lakeland pubs; **Hawkshead Brewery** (🌐www
.hawksheadbrewery.co.uk), whose beers are
mostly found in Hawkshead, the southern
and western Lakes; **Yates Brewery** (🌐www
.yatesbrewery.co.uk), from Westnewton,
Aspatria, but widely available, with assorted
bitters, ales and seasonal beers; and the **Tirril Brewery** (🌐www.tirrilbrewery.co.uk), now
based at Brougham Hall near Penrith, but

with its main outlet at the *Queen's Head Inn*
gastro-pub at nearby Tirril. Two classic inns
with their own **micro-breweries** are the *Wasdale Head Inn* (🌐www.wasdale.com) and the
Kirkstile Inn (🌐www.kirkstile.com), while the
Mason's Arms (🌐www.strawberrybank.com)
at Strawberry Bank, Cartmel Fell, produces a
strong fruit-based Damson Beer.

Festivals, shows, sports and annual events

The region maintains its traditions in a unique series of annual festivals, shows
and events held throughout the old lands of Cumberland and Westmorland.
Some date back centuries, while others are modern revivals of past festivals,
but what they all have in common is a shared celebration of rural tradition and
activity. Nearly all are held outdoors and, not surprisingly, the summer months
– particularly August – host the main events.

The month-by-month calendar below picks
out the main highlights: many traditionally take place on fixed days (often fairly
convoluted), so for exact annual dates either
check the websites or contact local information offices, the Cumbria Tourist Board
(☎015394/44444, 🌐www.golakes.co.uk) or
the National Park Authority (☎015394/46601,
🌐www.lake-district.gov.uk).

In addition to the annual festivals and
shows, there are hundreds of other events
held throughout the year in the region
– guided walks, exhibitions, lectures, craft
demonstrations, re-enactments, concerts and
children's entertainments. Many are sponsored by the NPA (which publishes its own
Events brochure) and held at the Lake District
Visitor Centre at Brockhole (p.67) – on bank
holidays there's always guaranteed to be
something good on. You'll come across other
events at museums, churches, halls, farms
and villages throughout the region.

Festivals and events calendar

March

Second week Words By The Water, Literature

Festival, Keswick 🌐www.wayswithwords
.co.uk.
Third or fourth week (Sat & Sun) Daffodil and
Spring Flower Show, Ambleside
🌐www.ambleside-show.org.uk.

April

First week Ulverston Walking Festival
🌐www.ulverston-net.

May

First and second week Ulverston Flag and
Banner Festival 🌐www.ulverston-net.
Second or third week Keswick Jazz Festival.
Fourth week (bank holiday weekend) Cartmel
Races 🌐www.cartmel-steeplechases.co.uk.

June

First week Holker Garden Festival, Holker Hall
🌐www.holker-hall.co.uk.
First week Keswick Beer Festival
🌐www.keswickbeerfestival.co.uk.
Second week Eskdale Beer Festival.
Third week (Sat) Cockermouth Carnival
🌐www.cockermouth.org.uk.
Fourth week (last Sun) Ullswater Country Fair,
Patterdale.

July

First week (Sat) Ambleside Rushbearing Festival.

First week (Sat) Ulverston Carnival
Ⓦ www.ulverston-net.

Second or third week (Fri & Sat) Furness
Traditions Folklore Festival, Ulverston
Ⓦ www.ulverston-net.

Third week (Sat) Cumberland Show, Carlisle.

Fourth week (Thurs before first Mon in Aug)
Ambleside Sports.

Fourth week (Sat) Cockermouth Agricultural
Show Ⓦ www.cockermouth.org.uk.

Fourth week (Sat) Millom and Broughton
Agricultural Show, Broughton-in-Furness.

Fourth week (Sun) Coniston Country Fair
Ⓦ www.conistoncountryfair.com.

August

First week (Wed) Cartmel Agricultural Show
Ⓦ www.cartmelshow.co.uk.

First week (Thurs before first Mon in Aug)
Ambleside Sports.

First week (Thurs) Lake District Sheepdog Trials,
Ings, Staveley.

First week (Fri–Sun) Lowther Horse Trials and
Country Fair, Lowther Castle Ⓦ www.lowther.co.uk.

First week (Sat) Grasmere Rushbearing.

First and second week Lake District Summer
Music Festival Ⓦ www.ldsm.org.uk.

Second week (Thurs) Rydal Sheepdog Trials.

Third week (Wed) Gosforth Agricultural Show.

Third week (Wed) Threlkeld Sheepdog Trials.

Third week (Sat) Skelton Agricultural Show,
Penrith.

Third week (Sun) Langdale Country Fair, Great
Langdale.

Third or fourth week (Sun) Grasmere Lakeland
Sports and Show Ⓦ www.grasmeresports.co.uk.

Third or fourth week (penultimate Tues)
Hawkshead Agricultural Show
Ⓦ www.hawksheadshow.co.uk.

Fourth week (last Wed) Ennerdale and Kinniside
Show.

Fourth week (Sat before bank holiday Mon)
Patterdale Dog Day.

Fourth week (Sat before bank holiday Mon)
Millom and Broughton Agricultural Show.

Fourth week (bank holiday weekend) Cartmel
Races Ⓦ www.cartmel-steeplechases.co.uk.

Bank holiday Mon Keswick Agricultural Show
and Sports.

Bank holiday Mon Muncaster Country Fair,
Muncaster, Ravenglass.

September

First week Wasdale Head Inn Beer Festival.

First week Ambleside Summer Flower Show and
Craft Fair Ⓦ www.ambleside-show.org.uk.

First and second week Ulverston Charter
Festival Ⓦ www.ulverston-net.

Second week (Thurs) Westmorland County
Show, Crooklands, Kendal Ⓦ www.westmorland
-county-show.co.uk.

Second week (Fri) Kendal Torchlight Carnival
Ⓦ www.kendaltorchlightcarnival.co.uk.

Third week (Thurs) Loweswater Agricultural
Show.

Third week (Sat) Egremont Crab Fair and Sports.

Third week (Sun) Borrowdale Shepherds' Meet,
Rosthwaite.

Fourth week (last Thurs) Kentmere Sheepdog
Trials.

Fourth week (last Sat) Eskdale Show,
Brotherilkeld Farm, Hardknott Pass, Boot.

Fourth week (last Sun) Urswick Rushbearing,
Ulverston.

October

Second week (Sat) Wasdale Head Show and
Shepherds' Meet.

Second week (Sat & Sun) Kendal Mountain Film
Festival Ⓦ www.mountainfilm.co.uk.

Second or third week (Sat) Buttermere Show
and Shepherds' Meet.

November

Third week (Thurs) Biggest Liar in the World
Competition, Santon Bridge, Wasdale.

Fourth week (Sat & Sun) Ulverston Dickensian
Christmas Festival Ⓦ www.ulverston-net.

December

First week (Sun) Keswick Victorian Fair.

Festivals and events

The oldest festivals – dating back to medieval times – are the annual **rushbearings**, harking back to the days when church floors were covered in earth rather than stone. The rushes, or reeds, laid on the floors (on which churchgoers knelt or stood) would be renewed once a year. Now the rushes are fashioned into crosses and garlands and carried in symbolic procession around the village and into the church: the most famous rushbearing festivals (with accompanying bands and hymns) are held at Grasmere, Ambleside and Urswick.

Towns such as Kendal, Keswick, Cockermouth and particularly Ulverston host a variety of annual **festivals** concentrating on music, dance, film, drama, processions and other entertainments. And the **Summer Music Festival** brings together an international line-up of talent at venues across the Lake District. In the west, there are a couple of peculiarly Cumbrian affairs. The **Egremont Crab Fair**, held annually since 1267, features such arcane events as greasy-pole-climbing and pipe-smoking competitions and the World Gurning Championship (where contestants stick their head through a horse collar and pull faces). And at a pub in Santon Bridge, Wasdale, the **Biggest Liar in the World Competition** attracts porky-tellers from all over Cumbria to a century-old event. The rules, incidentally, specifically exclude politicians from entering.

Shows, meets and sheepdog trials

As befits a largely rural region, many of Cumbria's annual events take the form of **agricultural shows**, featuring farming equipment, trade and craft displays (including dry-stone walling), food stalls, vegetable-growing and sheep-shearing competitions, and prize-winning animals. The separate Cumberland (Carlisle) and Westmorland (Kendal) shows are the largest examples – relics of the days when they were the annual county shows – but the smaller shows in places such as Gosforth, Coniston, Loweswater and Ennerdale are highly enjoyable affairs where it's still very much a case of local communities coming together.

Some very traditional shows (at Buttermere, Borrowdale, Wasdale and Eskdale) are termed **shepherds' meets**, since that's what they once were – opportunities for shepherds to meet once a year, return sheep belonging to their neighbours, catch up on local gossip and engage in competitions, sporting or otherwise. The mainstay of these events are sheep- and dog-judging competitions, bouts of hunting-horn blowing and displays of decorated shepherds' crooks. In addition, there are several annual **sheepdog trials**, the main ones at Rydal and Patterdale, where border collies are put through their paces, rounding up sheep into pens at the call and whistle of their owner.

Sports, races and pastimes

Some annual shows specifically announce themselves as **Sports**, such as those at Grasmere and Ambleside, the two most important gatherings. At these (but in practice at all of the agricultural shows and meets too) you'll encounter a whole host of special Cumbrian sports and activities, as well as bicycle and track events, carriage-driving, gymkhanas, ferret- or pigeon-racing and tugs-of-war.

Cumberland and Westmorland wrestling is the best-known of the local sports, probably dating back to Viking times: two men, dressed in embroidered trunks, white tights and vests, grapple like Sumo wrestlers and attempt to unbalance each other – if both men fall, the winner is the one on top. It's hugely technical, yet balletic, and has its own vocabulary of holds and grips, like the "hype", the "hank" and the "cross buttock". The winner is declared "World Champion".

Fell-running is basically cross-country running up and down the fells. It's a notoriously tough business, dominated by local farm workers and shepherds who bound up the fells like gazelles. The famous Joss Naylor of Wasdale is typical of the breed: in 1975 he raced over 72 peaks in under 24 hours; in 1986 he ran the 214 Wainwright fells in a week; and to celebrate his 60th birthday he did the sixty highest lakeland peaks in 36 hours. The sports show races are shorter than these trials, but no less brutal.

The other main event is **hound trailing**, derived from the training of fox-hounds for hunting. A trail is set across several miles of countryside using an aniseed-soaked rag and the dogs are then released, with the owners calling them in across a finish line at the show. Trailing (and the heavy betting that accompanies it) also occurs most weeks during spring and summer outside the shows, followed by the **fox-hunting** season proper throughout the winter. This has long been a Cumbrian pastime (on foot in the Lakes, not on horseback), though as in other rural areas it remains to be seen how hunt supporters will react to the eventual ban on fox-hunting that is now proposed by the government.

Walking and climbing

The Lake District was the birthplace of British fell-walking and mountaineering, and hundreds of thousands of people still come to the Lakes every year to get out on the hills. An almost unchartable network of paths connects the lakes themselves, tracks the ridges of the fells, or weaves easier courses through the valleys, around the flanks and onto the tops. So whatever your level of fitness or expertise, you can find a Lake District walk to suit – from an hour's stroll up to a local waterfall on an all-day circuit, or "horseshoe" route, around various peaks and valleys. If you're not confident about being able to find your own way, or simply want someone else to do the organizing, then it's probably best to join a guided walk or a tour. Various operators run Lake District walking holidays, while local schools and instructors can also introduce you to the arts of rock climbing, mountain navigation and winter hill walking.

Footpaths and walks

Of the long-distance paths, Wainwright's Coast-to-Coast – which starts in St Bees, near Whitehaven – spends its first few sections in the northern Lakes, and the Dales Way finishes in Windermere, but the only true Lake District hike is the seventy-mile **Cumbria Way** between Ulverston and Carlisle, which cuts through the heart of the region via Coniston and Langdale. The fifty-mile **Allerdale Ramble**, from Seathwaite (Borrowdale) to the Solway Firth, spends around half its time in the National Park area, running up Borrowdale and across Skiddaw.

The **walks detailed in this guide** – often in special feature boxes – aim to provide a cross-section of lakeland experiences, from

> ### Best walks: the Rough Guide choice
>
> **Horseshoe circuit**: Coledale Horseshoe, p.161.
> **Mountain peaks**: Crinkle Crags and Bowfell, p.106.
> **Pub walk**: Loweswater and Kirkstile Inn, p.187.
> **Round-lake**: Haweswater, p.207.
> **3000-footer**: Helvellyn, p.200.
> **Viewpoint**: Cat Bells, p.153.
> **Waterfall hike**: Stock Ghyll Force, p.76.

valley bottom to fell top. Some of the most famous mountain ascents are included, as well as gentle round-lake perambulations. It's vital to note that the brief descriptions in the Guide are not in any sense to be taken as specific route guides, rather as providing start and finish details and other pieces of local information.

There is any number of local **walking guidebooks** on the market: the best are reviewed on p.251.

Walking equipment, skills and support

Experience isn't always necessary but for any walk you should be properly equipped. Wear strong-soled, supportive walking shoes or boots – you can turn your ankle on even the easiest of strolls. Colourful, warm, wind-and-waterproof clothing, a watch, water (two litres each on hot days) and something to eat are all essential on longer hikes. If you don't have your own, outdoor stores in places such as Ambleside, Coniston and Keswick can rent you a pair of boots and some waterproofs.

Bad weather can move in quickly, even in the height of summer, so before starting out on the fells you should check the **weather forecast** – many hotels, all hostels and most outdoor shops post a daily forecast, or call one of the weather forecasting services listed below. Above all, **take a map** (reviewed on p.27) and, for up on the fells, a **compass** – they're not fashion accessories, so know how to use them. If you're uncertain or inexperienced, you might want to join a guided walk or attend a map-and-compass course – the National Park Authority runs both in spring and summer, while any of the climbing schools and instructors listed in the next section offer instruction courses on all aspects of mountain skills and safety.

For online help, an American website hosted by the **Adventure Network** (ⓦwww .adventurenetwork.com) is invaluable. Nowhere else can you access so much expert, esoteric advice about surviving the great outdoors, from caring for your binoculars to choosing a sports bra.

Hiking support services

Coast-Coast Packhorse ☎017683/42028, ⓦwww.cumbria.com/packhorse. Daily, door-to-door baggage service on the Coast-to-Coast route, plus left-luggage storage for overseas visitors. Service operates Easter until end of Sept.
Sherpa Van ☎0871/520 0124, from abroad ☎00-44-1748/822460, ⓦwww.sherpavan.com. Daily, door-to-door baggage service for walkers and cyclists between overnight stops on the Coast-to-Coast, Sea-to-Sea, Cumbria Way and Dales Way. Service operates from the week before Easter until mid-Oct.

Weather forecasting services

Lake District National Park Weatherline ☎017687/75757. One-day advance forecast for fells and valleys, including hiking conditions.
Met Office ⓦwww.met-office.gov.uk. Three-day regional forecasts and five-day Keswick forecasts available.

Walking holidays

Whatever your level of experience, you can find an organized walking holiday in the Lakes to suit. The tour operators listed below are a good place to start – all are either locally based or have specialist knowledge of the area, and are happy to entertain questions about their holidays. Trips run year-round unless otherwise stated, though there's most choice between Easter and October. Some holidays are self-guided (ie the arrangements are made for you, but you're given a map and walking instructions to follow), while others are fully guided, but there are always baggage transfers and emergency back-up services provided where appropriate. The prices below give an idea of what you can expect to pay for certain types of holiday, but note that transport to and from the Lake District is not included (though some operators may be able to arrange it, if requested).

Specialist walking-tour operators

Cloudberry Holidays ⓦwww.cloudberry.co.uk. Cloudberry runs two-night (£105) and five-night (£260) walking holidays (maximum of 12 people) for the YHA. Trips (graded gentle, moderate or strenuous) are based at Windermere, Elterwater, Borrowdale or Grasmere hostels on a dinner, bed and breakfast, hostel-accommodation basis – contact the hostels direct for details. Trips run from Feb to Nov.
Contours Walking Holidays ☎017684/80451, ⓦwww.contours.co.uk. Large variety of holidays, with self-guided or guided versions of Cumbria Way, Dales Way and Coast-to-Coast walks, running from £300 to £775. Also four-night short breaks (£199) in the north, south, east or west Lakes. The guided walks are fully inclusive, the short breaks on a B&B basis.
Curlew Guided Walking ☎01524/35601, ⓦwww.users.globalnet.co.uk/~curlewgw. Small walking groups tackle six- to twelve-mile hikes a day on seven-night tours in the southern and northern Lakes. Trips cost around £400 B&B, with packed lunch and guide services included. Shorter two- and three-day breaks also available (£150–230).
Discovery Travel ☎01904/766564, ⓦwww .discoverytravel.co.uk. Self-guided walking tours, following the Cumbria Way (seven nights, from £350) or a Lakeland Round circuit (eight nights, £395), though Coast-to-Coast (fifteen nights, £675) or a single-centre Keswick walking holiday (seven nights, £295) are also available. Prices include B&B accommodation, maps and guides, baggage transfer and emergency support.
Knobbly Stick ☎01539/737576, ⓦwww .knobblystick.com. "Take a walk on the wild side, the easy way" – fully guided four- to seven-night (three to six days' walking) holidays, based in comfortable hotels at Ullswater, Keswick, Wasdale, Grasmere and south Lakes, from £350 to £750, including dinner, bed and breakfast, guiding and transport. Operates all year.
Ramblers Holidays ☎01707/331133, ⓦwww .ramblersholidays.co.uk. The sister organization to the Ramblers' Association offers a seven-night walking holiday based at Buttermere (different departure dates are aimed at various abilities), for

£200 to £270, including all meals and daily guided walks. Also fully supported hiking holidays tackling the Allerdale Ramble and Cumbria Way. Trips run from March to Oct and at Christmas/New Year.

Trail Ventures ☎0115/846 0163, 🖰www .trailventures.com. Two-night short breaks (£130–140) in the Lakes, packing in two days' worth of convivial guided walking on routes that change with the seasons. One or two weekly departures all year round. Prices include minibus transfers from northern and midlands towns, B&B accommodation, packed lunches and guide.

Walking Women ☎08456/445335, 🖰www. walkingwomen.com. Women-only guided walking trips to suit all abilities in Borrowdale, Grasmere, Derwent Water and the western Lakes. Two- to five-night tours (£150–300) on a B&B or full-board basis. Trips run from Feb to Nov.

Rock climbing and mountain skills

There's probably no better place in England to learn some **rock climbing and mountain skills**, and certainly no better pool of climbing talent available to teach, at either introductory or advanced level. The schools and instructors listed below offer sessions or courses to individuals, families and groups – it's always best to call first to discuss your requirements. Prices can vary wildly, depending on the number in the group, the level of training and length of the course, but for a guided walk in the company of someone hugely experienced in the mountains you might pay £15 per person. For a day's rock-climbing instruction or abseiling for beginners, you can expect to pay £35–50; while two-day residential courses start at around £150. If all you want is a climbing taster, then the indoor climbing walls at Kendal and Keswick, and at Cockermouth and Penrith Leisure Centres, can offer an hour's unsupervised fun for around £5, or £15 for an introductory training session.

Climbing walls, schools and instructors

Above the Line Wasdale Head Inn, Wasdale ☎019467/26229, 🖰www.wasdale.com. The birthplace of British mountaineering (see feature on p.264) offers a full programme of courses, including hill-walking for softies, guided ascents, mountain navigation courses, mountain first aid, and snow and ice techniques. Women's courses (with women instructors) available too, plus accommodation at the inn.

Harold Edwards Mountaineering Wham Head Lodge, Hutton Roof, Penrith ☎017684/84465, 🖰www.whamheadlodge.co.uk, 🖰www.haroldedw ardsmountaineering.co.uk. Individuals and families of all ages can learn climbing, hill-walking, navigation and abseiling skills, plus introductory and classic rock-climbing courses. Self-catering accommodation available.

Highpoint ☎017684/86731, 🖰www .mountainguides.co.uk. Weekend and five-day courses throughout the year based at Patterdale YHA, concentrating on hill-walking, navigational skills and rock climbing.

Keswick Climbing Wall Southey Hill, Greta Bridge, Keswick ☎017687/72000, 🖰www.keswickclimbingwall.co.uk. Indoor climbing wall, as well as abseiling and ghyll-scrambling days out around Borrowdale. For individuals, families and groups.

Lakeland Climbing Centre Kendal Wall, Mint Bridge Rd, Kendal ☎01539/721766, 🖰www .kendalwall.co.uk. Sessions on the indoor wall for adults and children, plus a full programme of outdoor climbing courses, from introductory sessions and weekend scrambles to five-day in-depth courses.

Graham Watson Low Gillerthwaite, Ennerdale ☎01946/861229, 🖰www.grahamwatson.co.uk. Tailor-made mountaineering instruction and guiding service – beginners' courses, guided ascents, winter skills training and specialist courses. Children and families welcomed. Accommodation also available.

Boating and water sports

There's plenty of water in the Lake District and plenty of ways to get out onto it. Apart from the ferry and cruise services on Windermere, Derwent Water, Coniston Water and Ullswater, a dozen or so outlets and operators rent out all sorts of craft, from rowboats to sailing boats, kayaks to windsurfers. Most places offer instruction as well as rental.

Rowboat piers are detailed in the Guide and prices start at around £2.50 per person per hour; boats usually aren't available in the winter. The main boating and water-sports centres are listed below. Most offer canoes and kayaks (from around £5 an hour), dinghies and sailing-boats (from £50 half-day, £70 full-day), and small, self-drive motor-boats and electric boats (from £35 half-day, £45 full-day). At most places you can expect to pay around £40 for a couple of hours' windsurfing instruction, or £100 a day, and around £70 for a two-hour sailing lesson, or £140 or so for a full day's sailing course – though Windermere Sailing and Adventure School (see listing below) is considerably cheaper than this.

Windermere now has an overall 10mph speed limit (6mph in certain clearly marked zones), as does Coniston Water, Derwent Water and Ullswater. Powerboats are allowed on the lakes (with the exception of Bassenthwaite), but operators must stick to the speed limits. For more information about what you can and cannot do on the lakes, call the Windermere **Lake Wardens** (☏015394/42753), who enforce the restrictions.

Boating and water-sports facilities

Coniston Water

Coniston Boating Centre Lake Rd, Coniston ☏015394/41366. Electric boats, sailing, canoes – rental only, no instruction. Closed mid-Oct to Feb.

Derwent Water

Derwentwater Marina Portinscale, Keswick ☏017687/72912, ⊛www.derwentwatermarina .co.uk. Sailing, kayaking, canoeing, windsurfing.

Nichol End Marine Portinscale, Keswick ☏017687/73082, ⊛www.nicholendmarine .co.uk. Windsurfing, sailing, canoeing and motorboats.

Platty Plus Lodore Boat landings, Borrowdale office ☏017687/76572, waterfront ☏017687/77282, ⊛www.plattyplus.co.uk. Canoeing, kayaking, sailing and dragon-boating. Closed Nov–Feb.

Ullswater

Glenridding Sailing Centre The Spit, Glenridding ☏017684/82541, ⊛www.lakesail.co.uk. Canoes, kayaks and dinghies; introductory sailing lessons, plus weekend and five-day tuition courses. Closed Nov–March.

St Paul's Landing Glenridding Pier ☏017684/82393. Rowboats, motorboats and electric boats. Closed Nov–Feb.

Ullswater Marine Rampsbeck Boatyard, Watermillock ☏017684/86415. Motorboat rental. Closed Nov–March.

Windermere

Low Wood A591, Windermere, a mile south of Ambleside ☏015394/39441, ⊛www.elh.co.uk /watersports. Sailing, kayaking, motorboat rental.

Windermere Canoe & Cycle Hire Ferry Nab Rd, Bowness-on-Windermere ☏015394/44451, ⊛www.windermerecanoecycle.co.uk. Canoe and kayak rental; instruction available.

Windermere Outdoor Adventure Rayrigg Rd ☏015394/447183, ⊛www.southlakelandleisure .org.uk. Canoe, kayak, sailing and windsurfing lessons.

Windermere Sailing and Adventure School Ambleside YHA, Waterhead ☏015394/43789 or 07834/835050. Kayak rental, plus sailing and windsurfing lessons.

43

Organized holidays, courses and outdoor activities

Once you've been out on the fells, climbed the mountains and splashed on the lakes, there's still plenty of scope for an eventful day out. Local tourist offices have details of all sorts of outdoor activities, from horse riding and pony trekking to fishing and go-karting. Individuals and small groups are always welcome, though bear in mind that some of the activity days are aimed at the corporate market, so you may have to fit in around larger groups. Some operators, such as Outward Bound, Pleasure in Leisure and Summitreks, are particularly good for family days out and can tailor their activities to most ages and levels of experience.

Prices vary wildly, though you can expect to pay £15–25 for one-or two-hours' pony trekking, £25–30 for a half-day's activity session, £50–70 for a full-day's activity, and up to £160 for a balloon flight over the Lakes.

Many of the same operators offer residential courses, for those who fancy more than a day's activity, while other businesses offer all-inclusive organized holidays based around various themes, from cycle touring and sketching to cooking and pottery. Note that the prices for organized holidays don't include transport to and from the Lakes, which you'll usually be expected to arrange for yourself.

Arts, crafts and cookery

Gosforth Pottery ☎019467/25296, @www .potterycourses.co.uk. Formal instruction in pottery making (wheel-throwing, handwork and decoration), followed by working at your own pace, or opportunities for local rambling and exploring. The pottery – based in Gosforth, in the western Lakes – runs two-night weekend courses (from £200) and one-week courses (from £455) on a full-board basis, tuition and materials included.

Higham Hall ☎017687/76276, @www.highamhall .com. Residential and day-courses at an adult education centre on Bassenthwaite Lake. A huge variety of courses on offer, from local history talks (£10) to two-day wine-tasting seminars (£190).

Miller Howe ☎015394/42536, @www.millerhowe .com. One of the country's top country-house hotels, on Windermere, offers a four-day, all-inclusive, residential cookery course every November (and perhaps other months too), for between £299 and £550 per person (more for single-room occupancy). Also three-day art courses (each spring, summer,

autumn and winter) for £125 (rooms and food extra), and occasional needlework and embroidery courses. **Rothay Manor Hotel** ☎015394/33605, @www .rothaymanor.co.uk. Five-night themed activity breaks at this agreeable Ambleside hotel include landscape photography, painting (oil and watercolours), music appreciation, gardening, antiques and bridge. Available mainly in winter, spring and autumn, from £375 to £500 per person on a dinner, bed and breakfast basis.

Cycling tour operators

Country Lanes ☎01425/655022, @www .countrylanes.co.uk. Bike-touring specialist offering group tours, day-trips and a three-day "Taste of the Lakes" self-guided circuit (from £295). **Discovery Travel** ☎01904/766564, @www .discoverytravel.co.uk. Self-guided cycle tours: three-night breaks in Langdale (from £150), or a seven-night Lake District circuit (from £385). **Holiday Lakeland Cycling** ☎016973/71871, @www.holiday-lakeland.co.uk. Two five-night cycling tours (including hotel accommodation and baggage transfer): "Nine Lakes Tour" (£300), "Sea to Sea Adventure" (£375; includes two nights in the Lakes). Also tailor-made single-centre cycling breaks based around Keswick or Ambleside, where you choose how long to stay and where to cycle. All tours May–Sept only.

Equestrian centres

Holmescales Riding Centre Holmescales Farm, Old Hutton, near Kendal ☎01539/729388, @www .holmescalesridingcentre.co.uk. Riding instruction, pony trekking and hacking. **Lakeland Equestrian** Limefitt Park, Troutbeck ☎015394/31999, @www.lakelandequestrian .co.uk. Various short rides (1–3hr) in Troutbeck Valley, near Windermere, plus a daily pub ride, full-day excursions, and two and three-day trail rides.

Park Foot Trekking Pooley Bridge, Howtown Rd, Ullswater ☏017684/86696, 🖰 www .parkfootullswater.co.uk. Pony trekking on the northeastern fells. March–Oct only.

Sockbridge Pony Trekking Centre Sockbridge, Penrith ☏01768/863468, 🖰 www.sockbridgeponytrekking.co.uk. One- and two-hour treks in the northeastern fells, near Ullswater.

Fishing

Esthwaite Water Hawkshead Trout Farm ☏015394/36541, ✉trout@hawkshead.demon .co.uk. Boat-fishing on Esthwaite Water, with tuition for beginners, equipment rental, BBQ and picnic areas (cook your own catch), rowboats, bird-watching, a farm shop and café.

Other activities and holidays

Country Adventures ☏01254/690691, 🖰 www .country-adventures.co.uk. A varied programme in the Lakes, from a day's scenic walking or cycling in like-minded company to sailing weekends and activity sessions.

Lake District National Park Authority ☏015394/46601, 🖰 www.lake-district.gov.uk. Organizes a huge programme of day events throughout the year, mostly free though charges are made for some activities. Highlights include mountain-biking with the park rangers, falconry displays, dry-stone-wall building and watersports weekends. Call the events team or check the events diary on the website for forthcoming events.

Outward Bound centres at Watermillock, Penrith, and Eskdale Green, Eskdale; reservations on ☏0870/513 4227, 🖰 www.outwardbound-uk.org. Half- or full-day adventures – canoeing, rafting, zip wire, abseiling – with experienced instructors;

especially good for families (children must be over 8) who qualify for family tickets.

Pleasure in Leisure ☏015394/42324, 🖰 www .pleasureinleisure.co.uk. Huge range of activities organized across the region – archery, ballooning, go-karting, climbing and abseiling, paragliding, kayaking, clay-pigeon shooting, caving and 4x4 driving, to name but a few.

River Deep Mountain High ☏01229/861497, 🖰 www.riverdeepmountainhigh.co.uk. Multi-activity holidays incorporating guided walking, canoeing and mountain biking, plus activity days, river trips and instruction.

Rookin House Farm Troutbeck, A5091, Penrith ☏017684/83561, 🖰 www.rookinhouse.com. Go-karting, quad-biking, horse riding, pony trekking, archery and clay-pigeon shooting, not forgetting "human bowling" (one person strapped into a ball, while the others roll it at pins).

Summitreks ☏015394/41212, 🖰 www.summitreks .co.uk. Established adventure company offering a year-round programme of activities, from climbing to canoeing, aquasailing (abseiling down waterfalls) to canyoning (descending gorges). Children's multi-adventure days in the school holidays usually incorporate mountain biking, gorge scrambling and canoeing; adults can learn orienteering or join guided walks.

Youth Hostel Association ☏0870/770 8868, 🖰 www.yha.org.uk. One of the biggest organizers of holidays in the Lakes, the YHA uses its hostels for weekend breaks or longer holidays, with the emphasis on activities such as hill walking, rock climbing, kayaking, mountain biking and orienteering – though Pudding Nights and Murder Mystery weekends also feature. Accommodation is in bunk rooms (twins and family rooms often available) and most hostels serve budget meals, though self-catering is also available.

Directory

EMERGENCIES Dial ☎999 for all emergencies: in relevant circumstances ask for Mountain Rescue.

ENGLISH HERITAGE PO Box 569, Swindon SN2 2YP ☎0870/333 1181, ⓦwww .english-heritage.org.uk. Historic properties (free to members) are denoted in the Guide by the suffix "EH".

FRIENDS OF THE LAKE DISTRICT Campaigning group, established in the 1930s, dedicated to protecting the region: contact Friends of the Lake District, Murley Moss, Oxenholme Rd, Kendal LA9 7SS ☎01539/720788, ⓦwww.fld.org.uk.

HOSPITALS There are accident and emergency services at the following hospitals:

Barrow-in-Furness: Furness General Hospital, Dalton Lane ☎01229/870870.

Carlisle Cumberland Infirmary, Newtown Rd ☎01228/523444.

Cockermouth: Cockermouth Cottage Hospital, Isel Rd ☎01900/822226.

Kendal: Westmorland General Hospital, Burton Rd ☎01539/732288.

Keswick: Keswick Cottage Hospital, Crosthwaite Rd ☎017687/72012.

Penrith: Penrith New Hospital, Bridge Lane ☎01768/245300.

LAUNDRY Most youth hostels have washing-and-drying facilities of some sort, and B&B owners can sometimes be persuaded (or offer) to help out. There are self-service laundries in Ambleside, Keswick, Penrith, Windermere and other towns (though none in Grasmere or Coniston), with details included in the relevant listings sections.

LEFT LUGGAGE Hotels, B&Bs and hostels will all mind guests' luggage for the day (or longer), but there's a distinct shortage of places where you can simply turn up in town and leave your bag or pack for the day. Tourist offices are understandably reluctant to help, given the number of visitors; the only railway stations in the Lakes (at Kendal

and Windermere) don't have the facilities; and bus stations are usually little more than roadside stops. A couple of willing cafés – in Windermere and Kendal – are picked out in the Guide. Otherwise, your best bet is to ask nicely at local shops, cafés or hotels – buying something first sometimes helps.

MARKETS For local fruit and veg, household goods, cheap clothes and other market staples, check out one of the local markets: Monday, Cockermouth and Kendal; Tuesday, Broughton-in-Furness and Penrith; Wednesday, Ambleside and Kendal; Thursday, Ulverston; Saturday, Kendal, Keswick, Penrith and Ulverston. In addition, there are farmers' markets at Keswick (second Thurs of the month, plus fourth Thurs April–Sept), Ulverston (third Sat), Kendal (last Fri), Whitehaven (first Sat) and Penrith (third Tues).

NATIONAL TRUST Regional Office, The Hollens, Grasmere, Cumbria LA22 9QZ ☎0870/609 5391, membership enquiries ☎0870/458 4000, ⓦwww.nationaltrust.org .uk. The Lake District's largest landowner maintains a series of gardens and properties (free to members), denoted in the Guide by the suffix "NT".

OPENING HOURS Full opening hours are given in the Guide for sights, attractions and tourist offices. Church opening hours vary considerably, though most of those mentioned open daily between 9 or 10am and 4 or 5pm, but you can't count on it. Shops and businesses follow the standard pattern for the UK (Mon to Sat 9am to 5.30pm or 6pm), though you'll find some village stores and local shops open an hour or so earlier or later than these times. Early closing day (when the shops shut for the afternoon) is still observed in many towns and villages, usually on Thursday in the Lakes.

PHARMACIES Those in the main towns and villages (all listed below) are open standard shop hours (see above), though newspapers and all pharmacy windows list the local pharmacies that stay open an hour or two later on some nights of the week (usually on a rota basis).

Ambleside: Thomas Bell, Lake Rd ☎015394/33345; Boots, 8–9 Market Cross ☎015394/33355.

Bowness: Lakeland Pharmacy, 5 Grosvenor Terrace, Lake Rd ☎015394/43139.

Cockermouth: Allison, 31 Main St ☎01900/822292; Boots, 56–58 Main St ☎01900/823160.

Grasmere: Grasmere Pharmacy, 1 Oak Bank, Broadgate ☎015394/35553.

Hawkshead: Collins & Butterworth, Main St ☎015394/36201.

Kendal: Boots, 10 Elephant Yard ☎01539/720180; Highgate Pharmacy, 41 Highgate ☎01539/720461; Lloyd's, Station Yard ☎01539/723988.

Keswick: Boots, 31 Main St ☎017687/72383; Lightfoot's, 25 Main St ☎017687/72108; J.N. Murray, 15–17 Station St ☎017687/72049.

Penrith: Boots, Grahams Lane ☎01768/862735; Lightfoot's, Middlegate ☎01768/862695.

Windermere: Boots, 10–12 Crescent Rd ☎015394/43093; David Carter, 16 Crescent Rd ☎015394/43417.

POLICE There's 24-hour cover at the following regional police stations:

Kendal (☎01539/722611) for Kendal, Windermere, Ambleside and Hawkshead.

Penrith (☎01768/864355) for Penrith and Ullswater.

Workington (☎01900/602422) for Keswick and Cockermouth.

Barrow (☎01229/824532) for Coniston and Ulverston.

The addresses of local police stations are given in the relevant town listings, but you'll have to phone the regional numbers given for assistance. Call ☎999 in an emergency.

RAMBLERS' ASSOCIATION Campaigning organization dedicated to encouraging walking, protecting footpaths and opening up access to the countryside. Contact Ramblers' Association, 2nd Floor, Camelford House, 87–90 Albert Embankment, London SE1 7TW ☎0207/339 8500, ⓦwww.ramblers.org.uk.

SHOPPING AND SOUVENIRS Various interesting art and craft outlets, galleries and museum shops are detailed throughout the Guide, while for specifically lakeland gift ideas consider buying: carved walking sticks; items (house numbers and the like) made from locally quarried slate; embroidered lace (first pioneered by Ruskin); locally produced foodstuffs (see p.35); or Herdwick woolly jumpers. Hiking, camping and climbing equipment is no cheaper in the Lakes than anywhere else, but there is a wider selection available – Ambleside and Keswick are the best places to shop for outdoors gear. Bookshops, for Wordsworthian miscellanea, lakeland tracts, maps and first editions, are listed in individual town and village accounts and on p.250.

SWIMMING The lakes can be very cold for swimming, while steeply shelving sides, water craft and reservoirs put some areas off-limits for bathers. We point out the best places for a dip in the Guide, but you might want to stick to local swimming pools instead: Cockermouth Sports Centre, Castlegate Drive ☎01900/823596; Kendal Leisure Centre, Burton Rd ☎01539/729511; Keswick Leisure Pool, Station Rd ☎017687/72760; Penrith Leisure Centre, Southend Rd ☎01768/863450; Troutbeck Bridge Swimming Pool, Troutbeck Bridge, near Windermere ☎015394/43243; Ulverston Leisure Centre, Priory Rd ☎01229/584110.

Guide

Guide

1

Windermere

CHAPTER 1 # Highlights

✳ **The view from Orrest Head** The summit of Orrest Head, a short climb from Windermere town, provides stunning views up and down the lake. See p.55

✳ **A cruise on Windermere** Spend the day on England's largest lake using a go-as-you-please "Freedom of the Lake" ticket. See p.62

✳ **Lake District Visitor Centre at Brockhole** The National Park HQ, set in acres of gardens, makes a great family day out. See p.67

✳ **Blackwell** Stunning Arts and Crafts house overlooking Windermere, with a handcrafted interior of immense style. See p.68

✳ **The Mason's Arms, Strawberry Bank** A classic country pub that serves a fruity, house-brewed, damson beer. See p.72

✳ **Ambleside Museum** The lowdown on lakeland literary and artistic life – from the writings of John Ruskin to watercolours by Beatrix Potter. See p.75

✳ **Overnight at the Waterhead** Waterfront designer style at the sharpest contemporary hotel in the Lake District. See p.75

✳ **Kentmere** This quiet corner of the southern Lakes boasts some dramatic walking on the Kentmere Horseshoe trail. See p.83

△ Kentmere Tarn

Windermere

he elongated comma that is **Windermere**, England's largest and most famous lake, rarely fails to impress. Its rocky inlets, secluded bays, grassy banks and wooded heights form the very core of most people's image of the Lake District. And on bitingly cold winter days, or in the dappled spring and autumn sun, there are few finer places in England to soak up the scenery. Hardly surprisingly, its manifest attractions make it far too popular for its own good and you're unlikely to find real solitude in any of the three settlements – Windermere, Bowness and Ambleside – which group together on its northeast shore. However, the southern and western reaches of the lake are still remarkably underdeveloped, and their small hamlets, low-key rural attractions and local fells provide some of the most inviting destinations in the southern Lakes.

Windermere town itself (a mile inland of the lake) has been the largest engine of change – literally so, since it was the coming of the railway in the mid-nineteenth century that brought the first mass influx of tourists. Even today, most people approaching the central lakes and fells from the south at least funnel through the town, getting their first glimpse of the lake at nearby Bowness – formerly a medieval lakeside village, though now the National Park's largest resort and boating centre. This also has the pick of the local cultural attractions, most notably the Steamboat Museum, just to the north of Bowness, and Blackwell, a restored Arts and Crafts mansion to the south.

Wordsworth himself thought that "None of the other Lakes unfold so many fresh beauties" and it makes sense to get out on the water as soon as possible. The cruise-boat ride south from Bowness provides access to **Lakeside** and its aquarium, and to the picnic lawns of **Fell Foot Park**, while combined boat-and-train tickets are available for trips on the popular **Lakeside and Haverthwaite Railway**. Heading north from Bowness there are landings at **Brockhole** – whose magnificent gardens form the backdrop for the Lake District Visitor Centre and National Park Headquarters – and at Waterhead for nearby **Ambleside**. This is the northernmost settlement on Windermere, and is a handily sited hiking and touring base with a terrific local museum and a couple of other diverting entertainments.

Away from the lake, the quiet hamlet of **Troutbeck** is strung along a gentle valley that lies between Windermere and Ambleside. There's good walking from here, as there is from the neighbouring **Kentmere** valley, where the River Kent tumbles down through the old mill village of **Staveley** – only four miles east of the hubbub at Windermere but refreshingly unvisited.

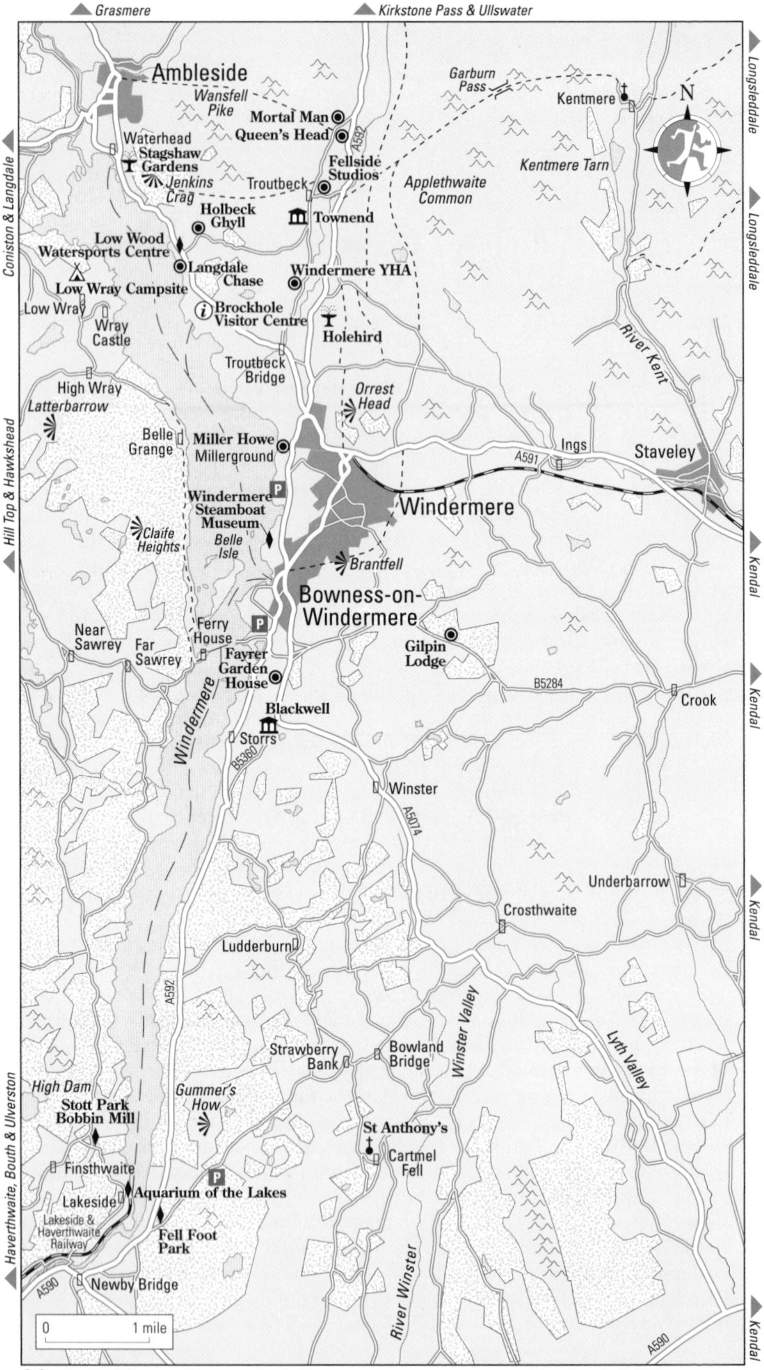
Grasmere
Kirkstone Pass & Ullswater
Longsleddale
Longsleddale
Coniston & Langdale
Hill Top & Hawkshead
Kendal
Kendal
Kendal
Kendal
Haverthwaite, Bouth & Ulverston
Grange-over-Sands
Grange-over-Sands
N
Ambleside
Wansfell Pike
Mortal Man
Queen's Head
A592
Garburn Pass
Kentmere
Kentmere Tarn
Applethwaite Common
Waterhead
Stagshaw Gardens
Jenkins Crag
Troutbeck
Fellside Studios
Holbeck Ghyll
Townend
Low Wood Watersports Centre
Langdale Chase
Windermere YHA
Low Wray Campsite
Low Wray
Brockhole Visitor Centre
Holehird
Wray Castle
River Kent
Troutbeck Bridge
High Wray
Latterbarrow
Orrest Head
Belle Grange
Miller Howe
Millerground
Ings
A591
Staveley
Windermere Steamboat Museum
Windermere
Claife Heights
Belle Isle
Brantfell
Bowness-on-Windermere
Near Sawrey
Far Sawrey
Ferry House
Fayrer Garden House
Gilpin Lodge
B5284
Crook
Windermere
Blackwell
Storrs
B5360
Winster
A5074
Underbarrow
Crosthwaite
Ludderburn
A592
Winster Valley
Lyth Valley
Strawberry Bank
Bowland Bridge
High Dam
Gummer's How
Stott Park Bobbin Mill
St Anthony's
Cartmel Fell
Finsthwaite
Lakeside
Aquarium of the Lakes
Lakeside & Haverthwaite Railway
Fell Foot Park
River Winster
A590
Newby Bridge
0
1 mile
A590

© Crown copyright

Windermere town

The completion of the railway from Kendal in 1847 changed the face of Windermere for ever, providing direct access to the lake for Victorian day-trippers and holiday-makers. The hillside hamlet of Birthwaite, lying a good mile from the water, was entirely subsumed within a newly created town, soon named **WINDERMERE** to emphasize the link with the lake itself. Not everyone welcomed the development. William Wordsworth, ever more conservative in his old age, feared the effects of the railway (while conveniently forgetting that his own *Guide to the Lakes* had done much to popularize the district in the first place). The poet attempted to keep out the hordes by means of a sonnet – "Is then no nook of English ground secure from rash assault?" – and by penning rambling broadsides which must have sorely tested the patience of their recipient, the editor of the *Morning Post*. Wordsworth's defence of the "picturesque" had reason behind it, and he can hardly be said to have been wrong in fearing the "railway inundations [of an] Advance of the Ten Thousand". But (like most gentlemen of his day) his real fear was that of the great unwashed, the "imperfectly educated", sullying his back yard with their "wrestling matches, horse and boat races ... pot houses and beer shops".

Most of the villas and guest houses built for the Victorians still stand, and Windermere town remains the transport hub for the southern and central Lakes, but there's precious little else to keep you in the slate-grey streets. Instead, all the traffic pours a mile downhill to its older twin town, lakeside Bowness, and the only reason for not doing the same is to take time to climb the heights of **Orrest Head** (784ft), just to the north of Windermere town. The bare summit gives a famous 360° panorama, sweeping from the Yorkshire fells to Morecambe Bay, the Langdale Pikes to Troutbeck valley. This was the very first lakeland climb made by a young Alfred Wainwright (see p.214), on his earliest visit to the Lake District in 1930 – one that, in his own words, cast a spell that changed his life. It's an easy twenty-minute stroll up through shaded **Elleray Wood**: the signposted path begins just to the left of the large *Windermere Hotel* on the A591, across from the train station. Ten minutes up the path, in Elleray Wood, you'll pass the cottage-studio of **blacksmith** Steve Hicks, where on most days you can grab a cup of tea and browse over his creative, handcrafted ironwork pieces.

Practicalities

The A591 between Kendal and Ambleside runs across the northern side of town, past the **train station**. Windermere is a major **bus terminus**, with National Express and all local services stopping outside the station – useful routes include the open-top #599 (to Bowness, Brockhole and Grasmere), the #555/556 (Kendal, Ambleside, Grasmere and Keswick), the #618 (Lakeside, Newby Bridge and Ulverston), the #505 (Brockhole, Ambleside, Hawkshead and Coniston) and the #517 (Troutbeck and Ullswater). There are **car parks** inside the train station yard and on Broad Street; on-street parking is limited to thirty minutes. A hundred yards away from the station, in the wooden chalet, opposite the NatWest bank, stands the **tourist information centre** at the top of Victoria Street (Easter–Oct daily 9am–6pm, July & Aug weekends until 6.30pm; Nov–Easter daily 9am–5pm; ☏015394/46499).

Accommodation

Windermere doesn't have the waterside advantages of Bowness, but it does have a lot more **accommodation**. Good first places to look for B&Bs are on High Street and neighbouring Victoria Street, with other concentrations on College Road, Oak and Broad streets. At the bottom of town, halfway to Bowness, Lake Road and its offshoots have a line of mid-range guest houses and hotels, but these are a fair walk (or bus ride) from either Bowness or Windermere. Further out still is a selection of very grand country-house hotels, which

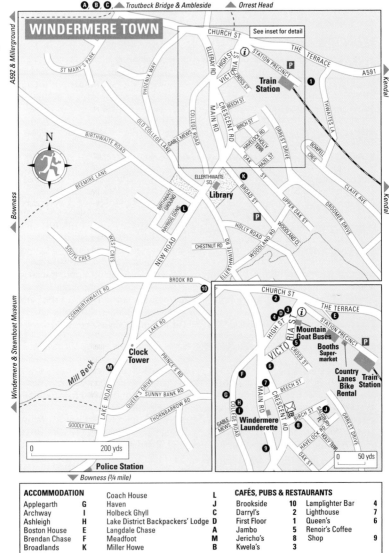

© Crown copyright

ACCOMMODATION				CAFÉS, PUBS & RESTAURANTS			
Applegarth	G	Coach House	L	Brookside	10	Lamplighter Bar	4
Archway	I	Haven	J	Darryl's	2	Lighthouse	7
Ashleigh	H	Holbeck Ghyll	C	First Floor	1	Queen's	6
Boston House	E	Lake District Backpackers' Lodge	D	Jambo	5	Renoir's Coffee	
Brendan Chase	F	Langdale Chase	A	Jericho's	8	Shop	9
Broadlands	K	Meadfoot	M	Kwela's	3		
		Miller Howe	B				

make the most of their secluded locations, lake views and extensive grounds. At the other end of the scale there is a backpackers' hostel in Windermere itself – the nearest YHA youth hostel is at Troutbeck – while for camping you'll have to head down to Bowness.

In Windermere

Applegarth College Rd ⌾015394/43206, Ⓦ www.applegarthhotel.co.uk. Detached hotel that retains its ornate Victorian interior (including a panelled lounge and bar, and stained-glass windows) and terraced garden. The eighteen rooms are well-proportioned – best (fell) views are at the back, at the top – including four singles and five four-poster rooms. Guests have free use of the pool and sauna at a local country club. Parking. ❺

Archway 13 College Rd ⌾015394/45613, Ⓦ www.communiken.com/archway. Four trim rooms (two doubles, two twin) in a non-smoking Victorian house, with the best light and views at the front. Known for its breakfasts (homemade granola, yoghurt, fresh and dried fruit with Scotch pancakes, kippers or traditional full English), served communally in a pine breakfast room; packed lunches (£4) also available. Parking. No American Express.

Ashleigh 11 College Rd ⌾015394/42292, Ⓦ www.ashleighhouse.com. Smart, non-smoking house whose five tasteful rooms (one available as a single) have been furnished in welcoming country pine. Breakfast includes homemade preserves. Parking. No American Express. ❷

Boston House The Terrace ⌾015394/43654, Ⓦ www.bostonhouse.co.uk. Beautifully restored, non-smoking, Victorian Gothic house, down a private drive just off the A591, a minute's walk from the tourist office. Five elegant rooms with four-posters and bright-as-a-button bathrooms, with burnished oak panelling, fresh flowers, scatter rugs and original art adding to the rather refined experience. Off-season discounts available. Parking. No American Express. ❺

Brendan Chase 1 College Rd ⌾015394/45638, Ⓔ brendanchase@aol.com. Popular place with a warm, friendly welcome. Comfortable rooms (some en-suite facilities) are very reasonably priced, especially the spacious, bright family/group rooms which can sleep up to five. Parking. No credit cards. ❷

Broadlands 19 Broad St ⌾015394/46532, Ⓦ www.broadlandsbedandbreakfast.co.uk. In a line of stone-terraced guest houses, *Broadlands* stands out: a cheerily run family home with four rooms (the top one lovely and light), whose owners can provide local walk leaflets. ❷

Coach House Lake Rd ⌾015394/44494, Ⓦ www.lakedistrictbandb.com. Comfort and

contemporary design join hands in this stylish conversion of a Victorian coach house. Five classy rooms with wrought-iron beds, gleaming bathrooms and elegant touches are complemented by a relaxed breakfast with the morning papers, and use of a local leisure club. Off-season specials are a good deal. Parking. ❹

Haven 10 Birch St ⌾015394/44017, Ⓦ www.thehaven.windermere.btinternet.co.uk. Non-smoking corner house whose big windows let the light into its three comfortably appointed rooms (one with a nice Victorian brass bedstead). Two have en-suite showers, the other a pretty private bathroom. Books, maps, drying facilities and packed lunches available. Parking. ❸

Meadfoot New Rd ⌾015394/42610. One of the rooms at this friendly family villa opens directly onto the garden, while the others overlook it – as does the dining room and deck where you take breakfast. It makes for a comfortable touring base, with pine-furnished rooms, patio and summerhouse. Good off-season (Nov–Feb) discounts apply. Parking. ❹

Around Windermere

Holbeck Ghyll Holbeck Lane, off A591, 3 miles north of town ⌾015394/32375, Ⓦ www.holbeck-ghyll.co.uk. A country house that once belonged to the Earl of Lonsdale, now with luxurious rooms either in the main house or in the lodge in the grounds. It's a retreat in every sense – sherry decanter in each room, relaxing lounges, seven acres of gardens and woodland with trails, gym and spa, and jacket-and-tie Anglo-French food of immense refinement (meals are served on the terrace in summer). Room rates start at around £210 (lake view and lodge rooms from £270), but include dinner as well as breakfast. Two-night off-season breaks (Nov–May) offer significant savings. Parking. ❾

Langdale Chase A591, 3 miles north of town ⌾015394/32201, Ⓦ www.langdalechase.co.uk. Lounge on the magnificent lakeside terrace or swoon at the style in this lavish country-house hotel with its stupendous carved-oak interior (including a transplanted seventeenth-century fireplace), gardens, tennis courts and croquet lawn. The Boat House room is right on the water, or there's a secluded stone-built bungalow in the grounds whose six rooms open onto a wide terrace with Windermere views. Deluxe lake-view rooms are priced a category higher, while room rates including dinner in the well-regarded restaurant offer the best value if you intend to eat here. Minimum two-night stay at weekends. Parking. ❼, including dinner ❾

Miller Howe Rayrigg Rd (A592), half-mile west of town ☎ 015394/42536, ⓦ www.millerhowe.com. Gorgeous Edwardian house occupying an elevated position above Windermere. The antique- and art-filled rooms are elegantly furnished, there's a conservatory for year-round use or in summer you can decamp to the terraces and landscaped gardens. Alternatively, sink into a plump armchair in one of the fire-warmed lounges and enjoy the stupendous lake views. Three self-contained suites in a cottage in the grounds provide an alternative to the main house. The price includes a supremely theatrical six-course dinner, plus early morning tea and lavish breakfasts. Rates for rooms (up to £280) and cottage suites (up to £350) vary depending on their size and style or the season. Parking. Closed Jan. ❾

Backpackers' accommodation

Lake District Backpackers' Lodge High St ☎ 015394/46374, ⓦ www.lakedistrictbackpackers .co.uk. Twenty-one beds in small dorms (available as private rooms on request), a laid-back atmosphere and good facilities, including kitchen with washing machine, Internet access, satellite TV, bike storage and lockers. It's a bit of a squeeze when full, but the price includes a tea-and-toast breakfast, and there's information about local tours and work opportunities. Reception open all day. No credit cards. Dorm beds from £12.50, or £15 per person in a private room.

Eating and drinking

You don't need to make the trek down to Bowness as there's plenty of choice of **cafés and restaurants** in Windermere. For the finest local dining, consider the gourmet experience that is *Holbeck Ghyll* (which has a Michelin star) or *Miller Howe* – both open to non-residents (see "Accommodation" above). Dinner costs around £45 a head, plus drinks and service, though lunch is usually half that price, while the **afternoon lakeland tea** at *Miller Howe* (£12.50) is a widely celebrated affair. Good **pubs** are rather harder to come by in town, although a couple of locals will do for a drink after a day's sightseeing. The main **supermarket** is Booths, by the train station, which also has its own café.

Cafés and restaurants

Darryl's 14 Church St (the A591) ☎ 015394/42894. Caff standards – specialities are the all-day breakfast and fish and chips – served from 8am (the earliest start in town). Daytime only; closed Tues & Wed. No credit cards. Inexpensive.

First Floor Lakeland Ltd, behind the train station ☎ 015394/88200. Occupying the impressive first-floor gallery of the kitchen/home-furnishings/design store, this superior café's snacks, lunches and high teas attract peak-period queues. With food by Steven Doherty (of nearby gastro-pub *Punch Bowl Inn*, p.72), you can expect seared scallop salad, salmon on pesto mash and other seasonal delights. Daytime only. Inexpensive.

Jambo Victoria St ☎ 015394/43429. There's warmth in the name (Swahili for "welcome") and in the relaxing decor, and on a weekly changing menu loaded with Mediterranean flavours you might find roast seabass or local lamb on herb mash – meat is free-range and organic where possible, while dessert is a high point for many. Dinner only; closed Thurs. Expensive.

Jericho's Birch St ☎ 015394/42522. With years of *Miller Howe* experience behind them, *Jericho's* owners provide rich, seasonally changing Modern British menus for discerning town diners – five choices, starters and mains, always including a vegetarian option. Dinner only, closed Mon. Expensive.

Kwela's 4 High St ☎ 015394/44954. Unique in the Lakes is this African restaurant, with dishes from across the continent – South African *bobotie* (savoury mince) to Moroccan chicken and chickpea stew – served in a cheerily decorated interior splashed with African art and design. Dinner only; closed Mon, plus closed one week Nov & two weeks Jan. Expensive.

Lamplighter Bar *Oakthorpe Hotel*, High St ☎ 015394/43547. Hugely popular local choice for bistro meals, served in the hotel's bar-cum-dining room. English classics (steaks, gammon and egg, fresh fish and rack of lamb) plus a bit of sophistication (crab mornay, oysters and smoked salmon salad), all in big portions at value-for-money prices; the beer's good too. Closed Sun & Mon lunch. Moderate.

Lighthouse Acme House, Main Rd ☎ 015394/88260. Roomy café-bar that offers a street-side terrace with cane chairs and heaters, seats in the bar, or a first-floor dining room. Drop by either for drinks, cocktails and snacks, or lunch and dinner from the contemporary menu (lamb shanks to seabass). Moderate.

Renoir's Coffee Shop Main Rd ℡015394/44863. Sandwiches, croissants, cakes, baked potatoes and frothy coffees – if the sun's out, eat at the couple of tables outside. Daytime only. No credit cards. Inexpensive.

Pubs

Brookside Lake Rd ℡015394/43541. Nice little local, ten minutes' walk from the centre, which can be relied upon for a decent pint and a yarn at the bar.

Queen's Victoria St ℡015394/43713. The main pub in town, with a fairly youthful clientele taking turns at the pool table and jukebox. Inexpensive meals are served and there's usually Castle Eden cask ale available.

Listings

Banks and exchange NatWest (High St), HSBC, Barclay's and Abbey (all Crescent Rd) have ATMs, and there's an ATM outside Booths supermarket by the station. Travellers' cheques can also be exchanged at the post office.

Bike rental Country Lanes, The Railway Station (Easter–Oct daily 9am–5pm; Nov–Easter weekends and other times by arrangement; ℡015394/44544, ⊛ www.countrylanes.co.uk). Maps and routes provided.

Bookshop Fireside Bookshop, 21 Victoria St ℡015394/45855. Secondhand and antiquarian stockist; good for books on Cumbria and the Lakes.

Car rental Lakes Car Hire, rear of Windermere Social Club, New Rd ℡015394/44408.

Emergencies The nearest hospital is in Kendal: Westmorland General Hospital, Burton Rd; ℡01539/732288.

Internet access Triarom, Birch St (Mon–Sat 9.30am–5.30pm; ℡015394/44639, ⊛ www .triarom.co.uk); Windermere Library, Broad St (Mon

9am–7pm, Tues, Thurs & Fri 9am–5pm, Sat 9am–1pm, closed Wed & Sun; ℡015394/62400).

Laundry Windermere Launderette, 19 Main Rd (Mon–Fri 8.30am–5.30pm, Sat 9am–5pm; ℡015394/42326).

Left luggage Available for £1 at *Darryl's* café, 14 Church St (the A591). Daily 8am–6pm.

Pharmacy Boots, 10–12 Crescent Rd ℡015394/43093; David Carter, 16 Crescent Rd ℡015394/43417.

Police station Lake Rd, just after the war memorial ℡01539/722611.

Post office 21 Crescent Rd (Mon–Fri 9am –5.30pm, Sat 9am–12.30pm; ℡015394/43245).

Swimming pool Troutbeck Bridge Swimming Pool, Troutbeck Bridge, 1 mile northwest of Windermere (daily 7.30am–9.30pm, though public admission hours and sessions vary; ℡015394/43243).

Taxis Bowness Taxis ℡015394/46664; Lakes Village Taxis ℡015394/46777 or 44055; Windermere Taxis ℡015934/42355.

Bowness and the lake

BOWNESS-ON-WINDERMERE – to give it its full title – is undoubtedly the more attractive of the two Windermere settlements, spilling back from its lakeside piers in a series of terraces lined with guest houses and hotels. Set back from the thumbprint indent of Bowness Bay, there's been a village here since at least the fifteenth century and a ferry service across the lake for almost as long. On a busy summer's day, crowds swirl around the trinket shops, cafés, ice-cream stalls and lakeside seats, but you can escape onto the lake or into the hills easily enough and there are several scattered attractions around town to fill a rainy day. And come the evening, when the human tide has subsided and the light fades over the wooden jetties and stone buildings, a promenade around Bowness Bay conjures visions of the Italian lakes.

The Town

What's left of the oldest part of Bowness survives in the few narrow lanes around **St Martin's Church**, consecrated in 1483. The church is notable for its stained glass, particularly that in the east window, now very difficult to make out but sporting the fifteenth-century arms of John Washington, a distant ancestor of first American president George Washington. Outside in the churchyard is the grave of one Rasselas Belfield (d. 1822), "a native of Abyssinia" who was born a slave – and found himself shipped to England – but as a free man became servant to the Windermere gentry.

Most tourists, though, bypass the church and everything else in Bowness bar the lake for the chance to visit **The World of Beatrix Potter**, in the Old Laundry on Crag Brow (daily: Easter–Sept 10am–5.30pm; Oct–Easter 10am–4.30pm; £5, all-year Freedom Pass £10; ☎015394/88444, ⓦwww .hop-skip-jump.com). It's unfair to be judgmental – you either like Beatrix Potter or you don't – but it is safe to say that the displays here find more favour with children than the more formal Potter attractions at Hill Top (see p.128) and Hawkshead (see p.125). All 23 Potter tales are featured in 3D form, and there are virtual walks to the places that inspired the author, plus interactive children's attractions, "emporium" gift shop and themed café.

The other main attraction is the **Windermere Steamboat Museum**, on Rayrigg Road (Easter–Oct daily 10am–5pm; £4.25; ☎015394/45565, ⓦwww.steamboat.co.uk), which displays a variety of water craft in its wet and dry docks. The oldest exhibit is a fragment of an eighteenth-century yacht, the most curious the duck-punt with its mounted blunderbuss, and the most prized the 1850 *Dolly*, claimed to be the world's oldest mechanically driven boat, and extremely well preserved after spending 65 years in the mud at the bottom of Ullswater. An Arthur Ransome exhibition reveals the inspiration behind the boats *Swallow* and *Amazon*, and you're allowed a peek at Captain Flint's houseboat, *Esperance*, as well as take a closer look at Ransome's own boat, *Coch-y-Bondhu*, which became the boat *Scarab* in *The Picts and the Martyrs*. There are also knot-tying and Morse-code-sending games, as well as steam-launch cruises on some of the museum's gleaming specimens (call for times; £5.50). The museum is a fifteen-minute walk north of Bowness centre: bus #505 runs past the entrance every hour.

Out on the lake

All the attractions in Bowness come second-best to a trip on **Windermere** itself – the heavyweight of Lake District lakes, at ten-and-a-half miles long, a mile wide in parts and a shade over two hundred feet deep. As so often in these parts, the name derives from the Norse ("Vinandr's Lake") and since "mere" means lake, references to "Lake Windermere" are tautologous. The only settlements are at Bowness and Ambleside, which means that the views from the water tend towards the magnificent: north to the central fells, or south along a wooded shoreline that is mostly under the protection of the National Trust. The seasons are reflected in the changing colours and tree cover around the lake. Autumn can be a real treat, though global warming has put paid to the spectacular freezing winters of yesteryear – in the 1890s, excursion trains brought astonished sightseers to skate on the lake and marvel at the icicles hanging from the trees. Many of the private lakeside mansions built for Victorian Lancashire mill owners are now hotels, though **Belle Isle** – the largest of eighteen islets in the lake – is still privately owned. For over two hundred years (until the 1990s), its guardians were various members of the Curwen family who built the island's eye-catching Georgian round house, one of the first of its type in England. The current owners don't allow public access to the island, though the house is visible through the trees if you get close enough on a boat.

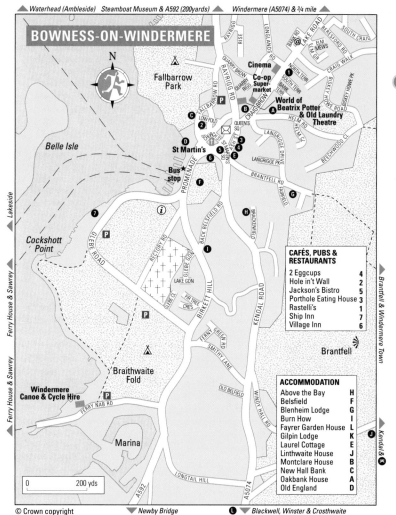

BOWNESS-ON-WINDERMERE

N

Fallbarrow
Park

Belle Isle

St Martin's

Bus
stop

Cockshott
Point

Cinema

Co-op
Super-
market

World of
Beatrix Potter
& Old Laundry
Theatre

**CAFÉS, PUBS &
RESTAURANTS**

2 Eggcups	4
Hole in't Wall	2
Jackson's Bistro	5
Porthole Eating House	3
Rastelli's	1
Ship Inn	7
Village Inn	6

Brantfell

Braithwaite
Fold

Windermere
Canoe & Cycle Hire

Marina

ACCOMMODATION

Above the Bay	H
Belsfield	F
Blenheim Lodge	G
Burn How	I
Fayrer Garden House	L
Gilpin Lodge	K
Laurel Cottage	E
Linthwaite House	J
Montclare House	B
New Hall Bank	C
Oakbank House	A
Old England	D

0　　200 yds

© Crown copyright　　▽ Newby Bridge　　**L** ▽ Blackwell, Winster & Crosthwaite

Bowness is a major **boating** centre and there are more opportunities here than on any other lake just to turn up and pootle about on the water. Row-boats and motorboats are available at **Bowness piers**, with more boating and water-sports outlets further around the bay by the Glebe Road marina. There's a 10mph **speed limit** on the lake (6mph in the more congested areas, where navigation can be hazardous, including Waterhead, and the Bowness Bay and Fell Foot Park areas).

Although it's freezing cold, people also jump in at various spots; indeed, every September there are a couple of **Windermere swims**. The first Thursday of the month sees a cross-lake swim between Wray Castle and Ambleside (which takes between 30 and 45 minutes), while on the first Saturday is the ten-mile endurance route up the lake from Fell Foot Park to Ambleside, which has a nine-hour limit

Windermere boat services and cruises

Windermere Lake Cruises (☎015395/31188, ⊛www.windermere-lakecruises.co.uk) is the main operator on the lake, providing modern cruisers and vintage steamers from Bowness to Brockhole and Ambleside (£6.80 return), as well as to Lakeside at the southern tip (£6.95 return). There's also a direct service from Ambleside to the Lake District Visitor Centre at Brockhole (£5.50 return). A **Freedom-of-the-Lake ticket** is valid on all routes (24hr £12.50; from Nov to March ticket is valid for 48hr).

Services on all routes are very frequent between Easter and October (every 30min to 1hr at peak times and weekends), and reduced during the winter – but there are sailings every day except Christmas Day.

As well as these routes, from mid-May to mid-August the company operates an enjoyable 45-minute circular cruise **around the islands** (£5.25, departs from Bowness), plus a two-hour, summer evening **buffet cruise** (every Wed late-May to early Sept, plus Sat in summer school hols; £22.95), with jazz band accompaniment. There are also **combination boat tickets** available for the Lakeside and Haverthwaite Railway and the Aquarium of the Lakes – more information from the pier-side ticket office – and a Bus-and-Boat ticket (£7; buy on board #599 bus), which gives a day's travel by open-top bus and boat between Bowness, Waterhead and Ambleside. There's discounted **parking** available for customers at Bowness (Braithwaite Fold), Ambleside (Waterhead) and Lakeside.

imposed upon it – the record is under four hours. Many people come here for the **fishing**, hooking perch, pike, roach and brown trout. You can also catch **char**, a reddish lake trout related to the Arctic char and landlocked in the Lakes after the last Ice Age. It thrives in the deep, cold waters of Windermere (and is usually on local menus between May and October). Daniel Defoe recommended potting this "curious fish" and sending it to your best friend.

The traditional **ferry service** is the chain-guided contraption which chugs across the water from Ferry Nab on the Bowness side to **Ferry House**, Sawrey (Mon–Sat 7am–10pm, Sun 9am–10pm, departures every 20min; 40p, cars £2.50). It's a useful service, providing access to Beatrix Potter's former home at Hill Top and to Hawkshead beyond, but as it can take only around eighteen cars at a time queues soon build up in summer. The Ferry Nab pier is a ten-minute walk south of the cruise piers, through the parkland of Cockshott Point (or follow the road signs from the promenade). There's also a useful **launch service** for pedestrians and hikers between Bowness piers and Ferry House, Sawrey (April–Oct daily 10am–5pm every 30min; £1.60 one-way, £2.80 return), saving you the walk down to the car ferry.

Practicalities

The A592 from the south runs into Bowness along the lake, past the piers, and then continues on, meeting the A591 northwest of Windermere town. There's free two-hour parking on Glebe Road, but otherwise you're going to have to put up with the **car park** charges, either at Glebe Park or Braithwaite Fold (both well signposted). **Bus** #599 (Easter–Oct daily every 20min; rest of year hourly) leaves Windermere train station for the ten-minute run down Lake Road to Bowness. The bus stops at the piers, which is also the terminus for the #517 (Troutbeck and Ullswater) and the #618 (Newby Bridge, Haverthwaite and Ulverston). For most other buses you'll have to return to the terminus at Windermere train station, though the useful **Cross-Lakes Shuttle** provides connecting boat-and-minibus services from Bowness pier 3 to Hill Top and

△ Windermere

Hawkshead (daily Easter, bank holidays & July–Sept; weekends only May, June & Oct). For local information, call in at the **Bowness Bay Information Centre**, near the piers on Glebe Road (Easter–Oct daily 9.30am–5.30pm; Nov–Easter Fri–Sun 10am–4pm, though hours may vary; ☎015394/42895).

Accommodation

Budget **accommodation** in Bowness is in short supply, so if you want to spend a night by the lake you should book ahead. And be warned that a lake

---

Walks from Bowness

While Bowness itself gets very busy in summer, there are plenty of other quieter lakeside spots in the vicinity. Even on the east shore, near the town, you can escape the crowds fairly quickly for an hour or two's stroll, while if you cross to Sawrey using the car-ferry or launch, the whole of the wooded west side as far as Wray Castle makes for an easy half- or full-day's circuit.

Rayrigg Meadow and Millerground

A mile north of Bowness (along the A592), past the Steamboat Museum, a path cuts west across **Rayrigg Meadow** to the lakeside and then traces the wooded shore for half a mile to the **Millerground** piers (there's parking here), where you can rejoin the main road. If you're not too muddy, then morning coffee or afternoon tea at nearby *Miller Howe* is a treat. Round-trip from Bowness, including walking along the road, is 2.5 miles, though from Millerground, you can walk up through the woods to Windermere town, a mile away, if you wanted to make a circuit of it.

Brantfell

Best viewpoint is from **Brantfell** (626ft) – "steep hill" – about a mile southeast of Bowness, which takes an hour or so, there and back. Follow Brantfell Road up the hill from St Martin's Square and keep on the path (signposted as the "Dales Way") until you see the diversion up the hillside at Brantfell Farm. The views from the rocks at the top are all-embracing – Belle Isle to Morecambe Bay – and if you rejoin the Dales Way at the farm you could then follow the path east and north all the way into Windermere town (3.5 miles; 2hr, from Bowness) – though it's actually an easier, and nicer, route *from* Windermere to Bowness and the lake, diverting up Brantfell on the way.

Latterbarrow and Claife Heights

The Victorians liked to cross the lake to take tea on the shore below the woods on the west side, and if you're up for an afternoon's walk away from the crowds, this is still the best idea. Cross by car-ferry or launch to Ferry House at Sawrey, from where a gentle path runs two miles north along the shore to Belle Grange. From here you can climb up to **Latterbarrow** (800ft) for lake views before returning along the paths of **Claife Heights** and back to Sawrey. The steep descent through the woods from Far Sawrey to the ferry pier passes the ruins of **The Station**, a castellated viewing platform from which eighteenth-century tourists would view the lake and mountains through a "claude-glass" (named after Romantic landscapist Claude Lorraine), a convex mirror used to "frame" their view. These viewing-stations were very popular until well into the nineteenth century and formed part of any tour of picturesque Lakeland, but the views from this one have been lost to the over-arching trees.

See Basics, p.40, for general walking advice in the Lakes; recommended maps are detailed on p.27.

view itself doesn't come cheap – most places in town with even a glimpse of the water set their prices accordingly, while the local country-house hotels are in uniformly desirable locations. Apart from the places recommended below, Kendal Road has a line of other B&B possibilities. There's no **youth hostel** in Bowness (your best bet for a lakeside hostel is Ambleside), though there are two **campsites** (listed overleaf), both within half a mile of Bowness centre and very popular – book at least a few days ahead in summer.

In Bowness

Above the Bay 5 Brackenfield ☏015394/88658, Ⓦwww.abovethebay.co.uk. An elevated house in a residential area, just off Kendal Rd, a 5min walk from the water. Three spacious rooms (with generously sized bathrooms) open out onto a private terrace with huge lake views. Free entry to local leisure club. Parking. No credit cards. ❸

Belsfield Kendal Rd ☏0870/609 6109, Ⓦwww .corushotels.com. Superbly sited old mansion (once the home of a Barrow steel magnate) in an elevated position above the ferry piers, with an indoor pool and sauna, and sloping lawns where you can have lunch and tea. Rooms are modestly furnished and sized, but those at the front have magnificent lake panoramas (supplement payable), while some garden-view rooms have French windows opening on to the grounds. Two-night minimum stay, but D,B&B and off-season rates can provide big savings. Parking. ❻, weekends ❼

Blenheim Lodge Brantfell Rd ☏015394/43440, Ⓦwww.blenheim-lodge.com. The steep climb from town is rewarded by great lake views (only one room doesn't overlook Windermere) and non-smoking rooms, which vary in size and style from country-pine to Victorian. Guests get use of a nearby leisure club, and there's a restaurant, drying room and parking. Winter rates shave off a few pounds. ❺

Burn How Back Belsfield Rd ☏015394/46226, Ⓦwww.burnhow.co.uk. Upscale chalet units – all family-sized – with sheltered private patios, or smart doubles (some with four-posters) in the main lodge. Breakfast is served in the restaurant, or you can have a continental version served in your room. Summer weekends nudge into the next price category. Parking. ❻

Laurel Cottage St Martin's Sq ☏015394/45594, Ⓦwww.laurelcottage-bnb.co.uk. Three pretty doubles with low ceilings in the seventeenth-century, oak-beamed cottage (once the village school) or more space, for a few extra pounds, in the adjacent Victorian building. Good beds and a public bathroom (the bedrooms have only showers) make this a boon for walkers. Parking. ❹

Montclare House Crag Brow ☏015394/42723. For simple B&B accommodation, these freshly furnished rooms (most with private shower) above

a café are the best value in Bowness. Two family rooms available, sleeping up to four people. Limited parking. No credit cards. ❷

New Hall Bank Fallbarrow Rd ☏015394/43558, Ⓦwww.newhallbank.com. Detached Victorian house with a lake view and a central location (a few yards from the *Hole in't Wall* pub). The en-suite facilities may be tiny, and the dozen rooms themselves not much bigger, but everything is pleasantly decorated, decked out in pine, with better views the higher you go. Parking. No credit cards. ❺

Oakbank House Helm Rd ☏015394/43386, Ⓦwww.oakbankhousehotel.co.uk. Rugs and flowers, scatter cushions and co-ordinated furniture, and a welcoming sherry decanter single out the *Oakbank*, some of whose rooms have lake views – all have TV and video, and there's free use of the pool and facilities at a local country club. Four superior rooms provide a bit more elegance, while parking, packed lunches (£6.95) and good winter discounts are available. Closed Jan. ❺

Old England Church St ☏0870/400 8130, Ⓦwww.macdonaldhotels.co.uk. This lakeside grande-dame with a Georgian kernel sports a small, heated outdoor pool, superb terrace and gardens, and snooker room. Lake-view rooms attract a small premium, though prices drop significantly between November and March. D, B&B rates are priced a category higher. Parking. ❼

Around Bowness

Fayrer Garden House Lyth Valley Rd (A5074), 1 mile south of town ☏015394/88195, Ⓦwww .fayrergarden.com. Quiet Victorian country house overlooking the lake, sporting a yesteryear elegance with heavy drapes, fresh flowers and plump cushions in its rooms and lounges. Standard rooms tend to be small and lacking in outlook, so it's best to go for a pricier garden or lake-view room – the latter all with king-sized beds, whirlpool baths, thick robes and CD players. Rates include a well-regarded four-course dinner. No single-night Saturday reservations. Parking. Closed two weeks Jan. ❼, lake-view ❾

Gilpin Lodge Crook Rd (B5284), 2 miles southeast of town ☏015394/88818, Ⓦwww.gilpin-lodge .co.uk. A luxurious country-house retreat in twenty acres. Its small size ensures personal service and the fourteen elegant rooms are individually styled, some with four-posters, others with whirlpool baths or private patios. It's renowned by foodies for its serious Anglo-French cuisine, and the rates (up to £280) include an extraordinarily lavish breakfast and five-course, seasonally changing dinner. Or sample the food and fine china at more affordable rates with a lunchtime bowl of soup, a superior sandwich or a bistro-style dish. Minimum two-night stay at weekends. Parking. ❾

Linthwaite House Crook Rd (B5284), 1 mile south of town ☎015394/88600, ⒲www.linthwaite .com. Contemporary style has been grafted onto this ivy-covered country house, set high above Windermere. Rooms are superbly detailed – rich muted fabrics, Shaker-style furniture, king-sized beds with canopies, flat-screen TVs, modems and CD players. A conservatory and terrace offer grandstand lake and fell views, and you can work up an appetite for the Modern British dinner with a walk out in the extensive gardens to the hotel's private tarn. Room rates vary according to outlook and size, but run up to £290, suites £330, dinner included. Parking. ❾

Campsites

Braithwaite Fold Glebe Rd ☎015394/42177. A site close to the lakeshore (near the ferry to Sawrey) for caravans and tents; a 10min walk from Bowness. Closed Nov–Easter.

Fallbarrow Park Rayrigg Rd ☎015394/44422 or 0870/774 4024, ⒲www.fallbarrow.co.uk. Caravans and RVs only at this lakeside site with lawns, picnic areas and pub, a 5min walk from Bowness. Van rental (usual period is a week) for up to four people runs from around £120 to £610, depending on season. Closed mid-Nov to mid-March.

Self-catering

Steamboat Flat Rayrigg Rd ☎015394/45565. For an out-of-the-ordinary self-catering option, rent the one-bedroomed flat (sleeps two) above the Windermere Steamboat Museum, which has excellent lake views from its rooms. There's a log-burning stove in the lounge. The flat is available all year (though might be a bit chilly in winter) and costs between £200 and £250 per week. Parking and boat mooring.

Windermere Lake Holidays Afloat Gilly's Landing, Glebe Rd ☎015394/43415, ⒲www .lakewindermere.net. A catamaran houseboat with huge sundeck and barbecue area. It's fully equipped, sleeps up to six people and comes with use of a fishing boat, rowboat and kayak. Three nights cost between £400 and £500, seven nights between £600 and £800.

Eating, drinking and entertainment

There are lots of places in Bowness to get a pizza, a Chinese buffet or a budget **café** meal – a stroll along Ash Street and up Lake Road show you most of the possibilities. Finer dining is available at a couple of local **restaurants**, as well as in the dining rooms of the major hotels – *Gilpin Lodge* and *Linthwaite House* (see "Accommodation" above), in particular, get rave reviews (dinner around £45 plus drinks and service, lunch around half that, reservations advised). The best **pub** by far is the *Hole in't Wall*, though others have their moments, while for morning coffee or sunset drinks you can't beat the terraces of the *Old England* or the *Belsfield* hotels, both open to non-residents.

The Royalty on Lake Road (☎015394/43364, ⒲www.nm-cinemas.co.uk) boasts the Lake District's biggest **cinema** screen; and the *Old Laundry Theatre* on Crag Brow (☎015394/88444, ⒲www.oldlaundrytheatre.com) hosts an annual autumn **Theatre Festival** with two months of music, film and the performing arts.

Cafés and restaurants

2 Eggcups 6a Ash St ☎015394/45979. The best sandwich in Bowness – check the board for spe-cials – in this cute and amiable caff. A couple of outdoor tables catch the sun. Daytime only; closed Thurs. No credit cards. Inexpensive.

Jackson's Bistro St Martin's Sq ☎015394/46264. The local choice for a family dinner or romantic night out, with intimate dining

on two floors and welcoming staff. Mussels, onion tart, poached salmon and grilled duck provide a classic bistro experience, or choose from the good-value £12.95 three-course set menu (avail-able all night). Dinner only. Expensive.

Porthole Eating House 3 Ash St ☎015394/42793. The top restaurant in town serves quality regional Anglo-Italian cuisine in a converted seventeenth-century cottage. Great homemade bread, antipasto, seasonal meat and fish (including locally smoked salmon), operatic warbling, open fires in winter, and a terrific wine list. A rear patio comes into its own in summer. Closed Sat lunch, Tues & mid-Dec to mid-Feb. Very expensive.

Rastelli's Lake Rd ☎ 015394/44227. A favourite for pasta and pizza (the calzone comes smothered with bolognese sauce), so expect to have to wait for a table in summer. Dinner only. Closed Wed. Moderate.

Pubs

Hole in't Wall Fallbarrow Rd ☎ 015394/43488. The town's oldest hostelry, behind Bowness church (and officially the *New Hall Inn*), is named after the hole through which ostlers once had their beer passed to them. Inside are stone-flagged floors, open fires, real ales and bar meals; outside, a terrace-style beer garden that's a popular spot on summer evenings.

Ship Inn Glebe Rd ☎ 015394/45001. Located round by the marina, this has lakeside seats and views of the boats.

Village Inn Lake Rd ☎ 015394/43731. Known for its real ale selection (usually half a dozen on show), though many come for the well-priced bar meals and the chance – in summer – to lounge on the patio opposite the church.

Listings

Banks and exchange NatWest (Lake Rd) has an ATM and there's a Barclays ATM (though no bank) on Crag Brow, Lake Rd. You can also change travellers' cheques at the post office (see below).

Bike rental There's great off-road biking across the lake around Claife Heights. Contact Windermere Canoe & Cycle Hire, Ferry Nab Rd ☎ 015394/44451, ⓦ www.windermerecanoecycle .co.uk.

Emergencies The nearest hospital is in Kendal: Westmorland General Hospital, Burton Rd ☎ 01539/732288.

Internet access Tea Too, 4 Windermere Bank, Lake Rd (Easter–Sept Mon–Fri 9am–6pm, Sat & Sun 9am–5pm; Oct–Easter Tues–Fri 10am–6pm, Sat 10am–5pm; ☎ 015394/45657, ⓦ www .teatoo.co.uk).

Pharmacy Lakeland Pharmacy, 5 Grosvenor Terrace, Lake Rd ☎ 015394/43139.

Post office 2 St Martin's Parade (Mon–Fri 9am–5.30pm, Sat 9am–12.30pm; ☎ 015394/46964).

Taxis Bowness Taxis ☎ 015394/46664; Lakes Village Taxis ☎ 015394/46777 or 44055; Windermere Taxis ☎ 015394/42355.

The Lake District Visitor Centre at Brockhole

The **Lake District National Park Authority** has its main visitor centre at **Brockhole** (Easter–Oct daily 10am–5pm; grounds and gardens open all year; free, though parking-fee charged; ☎ 015394/46601, ⓦ www.lake-district.gov .uk) a late-Victorian mansion set in lush grounds on the shores of Windermere, to the north of Bowness. Besides the permanent natural history and geological displays, the centre hosts a full programme of guided walks, children's activities (including a popular adventure playground), garden tours, special exhibitions, lectures and film shows – the centre, and any local tourist office, can provide a schedule. On a warm day, the **gardens** are a treat, with their little arbours, lakeside paths, grassy lawns, wildflower meadow and picnic areas – the website tells you what's flowering month by month, while woodpeckers, deer, rabbits, foxes and badgers are all regular visitors. The landscaping is among the finest in the Lakes, the work of the celebrated Lancastrian garden architect Thomas Mawson (1861–1933), who also designed the grounds for other Victorian piles at Holehird, Langdale Chase, Holker Hall and Rydal Hall. Inside the former mansion (built originally for a Manchester silk merchant), there's a bookshop – one of the best in the region for local guides and maps – and a café whose outdoor terrace looks down to the lake.

The visitor centre is just off the A591, three miles northwest of Windermere. **Buses** #555/556 and #599 stop outside, though for a more enjoyable ride come by **Windermere Lake Cruises** launch from Waterhead, Ambleside (Easter & May–Sept hourly 9.45am–4.45pm; £5.50 return), or from Bowness (a request stop on any Ambleside service; £6.80 return), which docks at the foot of the gardens. You can also take the launch from Brockhole jetty on a 45-minute circular cruise (£5.50) via Wray Castle, on Windermere's opposite shore, and Waterhead.

Blackwell

A mile and a half south of Bowness, in an elevated position above the lake, stands **Blackwell** (April–Oct daily 10.30am–5pm; mid-Feb to March & Nov to Christmas daily 10.30am–4pm; £5; ☎015394/46139, ⓦ www.blackwell .org.uk), a superbly restored mansion of unique character. It's the masterpiece of Mackay Hugh Baillie Scott (1865–1945) – less celebrated an architect than his contemporaries, Sir Edwin Lutyens and Charles Voysey, but just as influential in the Arts and Crafts Movement that emerged from the ideas of John Ruskin and William Morris. The house is hugely significant as the only major Arts and Crafts house in such remarkable condition open to the public in Britain. Most are still in private hands, and Blackwell itself has had a variety of owners: from World War II until the 1970s the house was a girls' school, and was then leased by English Nature until it was bought and restored by the Lakeland Arts Trust.

Its origins – as with so many houses on the shores of Windermere – lay in the nineteenth-century explosion of wealth in the industrial cities. Given free rein by Mancunian brewer and Lord Mayor Sir Edward Holt, who wanted a holiday home in the Lakes, Baillie Scott grasped the opportunity to design an entire house and Blackwell was completed to his specifications between 1898 and 1900. Taking his cue from Ruskin and Morris, who had championed the importance of traditional handicrafts allied with functionalism, Baillie Scott let Blackwell speak for his ideas and principles – from the almost organic nature of the free-flowing layout to the decorative emphasis on natural motifs and handcrafted designs. The use of natural light, in particular, is revealing, with the family rooms all south-facing, even though this orientates them away from the lake views for which, presumably, Sir Edward had paid a premium. Indeed, there's evidence that the Holts were never entirely comfortable in their designer holiday home. The family (of five children and six servants) soon cluttered Baillie Scott's harmonious interlinked rooms with the paraphernalia of the Victorian gentry – an old photograph shows the main hall encumbered with a heavy chandelier, potted ferns and a stuffed moose's head; and by the end of World War I, as the Arts and Crafts Movement lost its fashionable edge, the Holts visited Blackwell less and less.

The restored house grabs your attention from the very first, as you proceed from the entrance down an oak-panelled corridor, off which is the **main hall**. Baillie Scott's idealized baronial design provides the sort of things you might expect to see in a showpiece country house – vast fireplace, oak-panelling, minstrel's gallery and heraldic crests – but lightens the experience with huge dollops of inventive flair. An open-plan room with nooks and corners of varying proportions sports a peacock wallpaper frieze, a bluebell-and-daisy hessian wall-hanging, copper lightshades, Delft tiles, and – above all – the recurring carved rowan leaves and berries from the family coat of arms. At the end of the corridor, sun streams into the **white drawing room** and here, and elsewhere in the house, you can sit in the cushioned bay windows and enjoy the garden and lake views. The **bedrooms** upstairs contain changing exhibitions of contemporary and historic applied arts and crafts, though the contents of the entire house are display pieces in their own right, from the early twentieth-century carved oak furniture by Simpson's of Kendal to the modern earthenware that is positioned throughout. But it's Baillie Scott's naturalistic touches that perhaps sum up the whole – such as the door handles shaped like leaves or the lakeland birds and flowers that are ever-present in the stained glass and stonework.

The best way to appreciate the overall design is to coincide with one of the informative introductory **tours** of the house, usually on weekday afternoons (call for current times). There's also a pleasant **tearoom**, and a garden terrace where lunches, cream teas and lemonade are served on summer days. A **craft shop** sells works by leading designers, including jewellery, ceramics, scarves and handbags, as well as specialist books on architecture and the Arts and Crafts movement.

Blackwell is on the B5360, just off the A5074, one and a half miles south of Bowness. There's no public transport here, though it's only a 25-minute walk from Bowness.

Lakeside, Finsthwaite and Haverthwaite

From Bowness, boats head five miles down the lake to the piers at **LAKE-SIDE**, where gentle wooded hills frame Windermere's serene southern reaches. This is the quayside terminus of the **Lakeside and Haverthwaite Railway** (Easter–Oct 6–7 services daily; £5 return; ☎015395/31594, ⓦwww .lakesiderailway.co.uk), whose steam-powered engines puff along four miles of track through the woods of Backbarrow Gorge, the only surviving remnant of a line that used to stretch all the way to Ulverston and Barrow. There's parking and a station tearoom at Haverthwaite (closed Jan & Feb) and a chance to look around the engine shed, where (when it's not out on duty) Britain's oldest working standard-gauge loco, built in Manchester in 1863, is kept. Boat arrivals at Lakeside connect with train departures throughout the day and there's a joint boat-and-train ticket available from Bowness (£11.45 return) or Waterhead, near Ambleside (£15.40 return). The annual calendar also incorporates steam gala weekends, Victorian evenings and Santa specials – there's more information on the website. Haverthwaite station itself is on the A590, across the busy main road from the actual village of Haverthwaite – you can reach it on bus #X35 (from Kendal or Ulverston) or #618 (from Ambleside, Windermere, Bowness or Ulverston).

Also on the quay at Lakeside is the **Aquarium of the Lakes** (daily: April–Oct 9am–6pm; Nov–March 9am–5pm; last admission 1hr before closing; £6.25; ☎015395/30153, ⓦwww.aquariumofthelakes.co.uk), an entertaining natural history attraction centred on the fish and animals found in and along a lakeland river. There's a pair of captive otters (Filly and Smudge) and a walk-through tunnel aquarium (with char, perch and diving ducks), while educational exhibits give the low-down on everything from cockles to pike and leeches to lobsters; kids will love it. Afterwards you can grab a drink in the lake-view café and peruse the comings and goings of the boats. There's a joint ticket available with the boat ride from Bowness (£12.25

Bobbins and coppicing

For a time in the nineteenth century the south Lakes' bobbin mills formed an important part of the national economy, supplying up to half of all the bobbins required by the booming British textile mills. There were two reasons for the industry's strength in the Lakes: the fast running water from lakeland rivers to drive the mills and the seemingly inexhaustible supply of wood. To make bobbins and other items, "coppiced" wood was required, from trees cut to stumps to encourage the quick growth of long poles, which were then harvested for use. It's a technique that's been used for over five thousand years, and in more recent times in the southern Lakes, including the area around Stott Park, ash, beech, birch, chestnut, hazel and oak were all grown in this way. The bark was peeled off and used in the tanneries, while coppiced wood was also used widely in charcoal making (another key local industry), thatching and the production of tent pegs, cask bindings, fencing, agricultural implements (such as rakes) and so-called "swill" baskets (cradle-shaped Cumbrian panniers).

return) or Waterhead, near Ambleside (£16.20 return), which includes aquarium entry.

Half a mile up the hill from Lakeside, below Finsthwaite Heights, stands one of England's few working mills, **Stott Park Bobbin Mill** (Easter–Sept daily 10am–6pm; Oct Thurs–Mon 10am–4pm; last tour 1hr before closing; £4; EH; ☏015395/31087). It was founded in 1835 to supply the British textile industry with bobbins – rollers or spools for holding thread – and, as elsewhere when the cotton industry declined, the mill later diversified, manufacturing pulleys, hammers, mallets, spade handles, yo-yos and even duffel-coat toggles. Commercial production finally ceased in 1971, at a time when plastic had replaced wood for most bobbins. Former workers guide visitors on a 45-minute tour through the processes of cutting, roughing, drying, finishing and polishing on machinery that hasn't changed since it was introduced in the mid-nineteenth century. Note that the steam engine driving the waterwheel operates only on Tuesdays, Wednesdays and Thursdays.

From a car park above the mill (follow the road to Finsthwaite) there's a pleasant walk up through the woods to **High Dam**, the reservoir whose water used to drive the mill machinery – allow an hour or so to circle the water and return. Alternatively, if you head for **FINSTHWAITE** hamlet itself, half a mile above the mill, you can clamber up through the woods of **Finsthwaite Heights** to the naval commemorative tower. The only bus to the bobbin mill or Finsthwaite is a twice-a-week service from Lakeside, Newby Bridge or Ulverston, but the half-a-mile walk up from Lakeside is hardly off-putting.

Practicalities

Most people see the southern end of Windermere on a return boat trip from Bowness or Ambleside, but it can make a peaceful overnight stop if you plan ahead. There's limited **accommodation** at Lakeside itself, while just a mile south of the foot of the lake, down the River Leven, the *Swan Hotel* has a fine riverside location. From here, it's another couple of miles southwest along the A590 to the village of Haverthwaite, which also has a selection of B&Bs available. If you're going to stay, it's best not to be reliant upon **public transport**, though for accommodation at Lakeside you only need to step off the boat, while the #618 bus (from Ambleside, Windermere and Bowness) does call at Newby Bridge and Haverthwaite.

Accommodation and food

Boathouse Hotel Lakeside ☎015395/31381, ⓦwww.boathousehotel.co.uk. The nine rooms in this small hotel are very nicely turned out – Shaker-style in look, some with bare boards and rugs, and all with patchwork bedspreads and modern bathrooms with power showers. There's a restaurant and bar attached, and you're just 100 yards from the steamer jetty. Rates drop considerably in winter, when there's also a two-night midweek D,B&B deal. ❻

Coach House Hollow Oak, Haverthwaite ☎015395/31622, ⓦwww.coachho.com. Non-smoking B&B in a 200-year-old former coach house and stables, set in appealing gardens. There are only three rooms, two with en-suite facilities, one with its own bathroom down the corridor. The Haverthwaite village pub is just half a mile away. Parking. No credit cards. ❷

Lakeside Lakeside ☎015395/30001, ⓦwww.lakesidehotel.co.uk. Across from the quayside and aquarium, all the well-appointed hotel rooms have lake views and there's a waterside conservatory, brasserie and bar, gardens and good restaurant with summer terrace-dining. Rates vary considerably, depending on the room, with lake-view suites topping £300, and there's a two-night minimum stay at weekends, though special offers and D,B&B deals can be good value. Parking. ❾

Landing Cottage Lakeside ☎015395/31719, ⓦwww.landingcottageguesthouse.co.uk. Stone cottage offering B&B, lying a hundred yards back from the lake; two of the five rooms have en-suite facilities. There's a wood-burning stove in the lounge, while the garden and patio come into their own in summer. Parking. No American Express. ❷

Swan Newby Bridge ☎015395/31681, ⓦwww.swanhotel.com. This classic old inn, a winding mile or so to the south of Lakeside, has undergone extensive refurbishment to get it up to four-star standard. Stay and you get superior rooms (including king-sized beds, modem points and a sitting room in the executive suites) and comforts (indoor pool, hot tub and sauna). Meals are available in the restaurant or brasserie, or just come for a drink in the traditional bar, where you can take advantage of the riverside tables by the handsome five-arched bridge. Two-night minimum stay at weekends. Parking. ❽

White Hart Bouth, off A590, 1.5 miles northeast of Haverthwaite ☎01229/861229, ⓦwww.whitehartbouth.co.uk. It's a short winding drive off the A590 to this seventeenth-century country inn, non-smoking throughout, with upgraded rooms in the eaves that retain their oak beams and idiosyncratic proportions. Locals know the pub for its food and real ales, both good. Parking. ❹

Fell Foot Park and the Winster and Lyth valleys

Fell Foot Park, on Windermere's southeastern reach (daily 9am–5pm or dusk; free, though parking-fee charged; NT; ☎015395/31273), makes a relaxed picnic spot, where you can lounge on the Victorian landscaped lawns and explore the rhododendron gardens and oak and pine plantations. There was once a private mansion here, to go with the grounds, though that's long gone. But the mock-Gothic boathouse still stands and offers rowboat rental, while doubling as a rather superior tearoom – from the tables outside you can watch the Lakeside and Haverthwaite trains chuff into the station just across the lake. **Launches** run across to the park from Lakeside (Easter–Oct daily 11am–5pm; 80p each way), usually every twenty minutes depending on demand and the weather. By car, access is from the A592 (Bowness road), a mile north of Newby Bridge; bus #618, from Ulverston and Newby Bridge to Bowness, passes close by.

An ancient packhorse route from Newby Bridge to Kendal, now a steep and winding minor road, passes to the northeast behind Fell Foot. A mile up, there's free parking by the start of the footpath to **Gummer's How**, the gorse-topped fell which peers over the southern half of Windermere. It's an easy walk up to the little stone trig-point on the summit – it'll take an hour there and back, including a rest at the top to gaze down at the Fell Foot marina and the snaking River Leven.

Two miles further along the road, the *Mason's Arms* (☎015395/68486, Ⓦwww.strawberrybank.com; ②) at **STRAWBERRY BANK** is impeccably sited overlooking the low stony outcrops and tidy plantations of the **Winster Valley**. The pub's terrace is a great place for a beer – there are hundreds on offer, from all corners of the globe, including a damson beer made on the premises – and the food is especially good too, gastro-pub in style, with a contemporary upstairs dining room as well as tables in the stone-flagged bar. The *Mason's Arms* also has stylish designer accommodation in two cottages (which sleep 4/6) and three two-person suites, all available by the night.

Arthur Ransome moved to the Winster Valley in 1925 and it was here that he wrote *Swallows and Amazons*. His house, known as **Low Ludderburn** (not open to the public), can be seen if you take the tortuous bracken- and bramble-lined road north from the pub for a couple of miles. To the south, exactly a mile from the *Mason's Arms* (follow the signposts), **St Anthony's Church** lies tucked into a hollow on the side of Cartmel Fell. The church dates from 1504 – it was built as an isolated, outlying chapel of Cartmel priory – and despite some brutal modern exterior cladding preserves a characterful seventeenth-century interior: exposed rafters, a triple-decker pulpit and twin "box" pews once reserved for the local gentry.

From Strawberry Bank, the road drops a mile to **BOWLAND BRIDGE**, where the *Hare & Hounds* (☎015395/68333; ④) – right by the bridge – is another nice old inn with a sheltered beer garden. Beyond Bowland Bridge, a minor road makes its way north along the upper Winster Valley as far as **WINSTER** itself (on the A5074), where the *Brown Horse* pub is another pleasant stop for a drink. For food and rooms, though, the most renowned local address is a couple of miles south, down and off the A5074 at **CROSTHWAITE**, where the seventeenth-century *Punch Bowl Inn* (☎015395/68237, Ⓦwww.punchbowl.fsnet.co.uk; ⑤, including dinner ⑦; closed Sun night & Mon), next to the church, nestles in the gentle **Lyth Valley**. There are only three rooms (non-smoking, with king-sized beds), though it's the dining room and summer patio that are the essential draw, serving Steven Doherty's seasonally changing menu (lunch moderate, dinner expensive) that blends traditional lakeland produce with Modern-British flourishes. Lyth Valley damsons are a staple of the local early summer fruit crop, used in these parts in desserts (and to flavour beer) – they are a relic of Lakeland's former textile industry, when the fruit was used to make cloth dyes.

There's an irregular **bus** (#541) from Kendal to Crosthwaite and Winster (not Sun), but no public transport through the rest of the Winster or Lyth valleys.

Ambleside

AMBLESIDE, five miles northwest of Windermere, at the head of the lake, lies at the hub of the central and southern Lakes region. It's a popular, if commercial, base for walkers and tourers, but has lost most of its traditional market-town attributes. The original market square and associated buildings were swept away in a typically vigorous piece of Victorian redevelopment (though the market cross still stands) and today's thriving centre – more a retail experience than a lakeland town – consists of a cluster of grey-green stone houses, shops, pubs and B&Bs hugging a circular one-way system, which loops round just south of the narrow gully of Stock Ghyll.

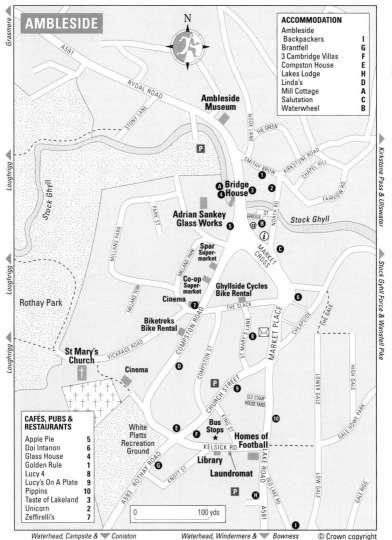

AMBLESIDE

N

ACCOMMODATION
Ambleside
 Backpackers I
Brantfell G
3 Cambridge Villas F
Compston House E
Lakes Lodge H
Linda's D
Mill Cottage A
Salutation C
Waterwheel B

Grasmere

A591

RYDAL ROAD

STONY LANE

NOOK LANE

THE GREEN

SMITHY BROW

KIRKSTONE ROAD

CHAPEL HILL

FAIRVIEW RD

Ambleside
Museum

Loughrigg

Stock Ghyll

PARK ST

MILLANS PARK

A Bridge **3**
4 House **2**

BRIDGE
ST

NORTH RD

Stock Ghyll

**Adrian Sankey
Glass Works** **5**

@ **B**

**Spar
Super-
market**

MILLANS PARK

MILLANS TERR

**Co-op
Super-
market**

Ghyllside Cycles
Bike Rental

Cinema **7**

THE SLACK

MARKET
CROSS

6

THE GATE

Rothay Park

Loughrigg

**Biketreks
Bike Rental**

COMPSTON ROAD

ST MARY'S LANE

MARKET PLACE

CHEAPSIDE

Loughrigg

VICARAGE ROAD

**St Mary's
Church**

COMPSTON ST

Cinema

D

P

CHURCH STREET

KING ST

OLD STAMP
HOUSE YARD

9

10

LOWER GALE

HIGH GALE

GALE HOWE PARK

CAFÉS, PUBS &
RESTAURANTS

Apple Pie	5
Doi Intanon	6
Glass House	4
Golden Rule	1
Lucy 4	8
Lucy's On A Plate	9
Pippins	10
Taste of Lakeland	3
Unicorn	2
Zeffirelli's	7

White
Platts
Recreation
Ground

E

F

Bus
Stops
★

**Homes of
Football**

KELSICK RD

ROTHAY ROAD

G

Library

KNOTT ST

Laundromat

A593

0   100 yds

LAKE ROAD

OLD LAKE RD

LOW GALE

GALE RIGG

P

H

A591

I

Kirkstone Pass & Ullswater

Stock Ghyll Force & Wansfell Pike

The Town

Stock Ghyll once powered Ambleside's fulling and bobbin mills, whose buildings survive intact on either side of Bridge Street, as do a couple of restored waterwheels. Straddling Stock Ghyll is the town's favourite building, tiny **Bridge House** (Easter–Oct daily 10am–5pm; free; ☎015394/35599), a topsy-turvy, two-storey, two-roomed, slate-roofed house, now a National Trust information centre. Scurrilous legend has it that a Scotsman built the house to evade land taxes, but its true origins are as a covered bridge-cum-summer house, used by a local family

73

Harriet Martineau in the Lakes

Harriet Martineau, a delicate child and hard of hearing, was born into a non-conformist East Anglian manufacturing family in 1802. Left penniless by the death of her father in 1826, Harriet began to earn a living by writing, contributing to the Unitarian periodical, *Monthly Repository*, and publishing a gospel history of Palestine, *Traditions of Palestine* (1829), which was well received.

Her forte, though, was the moral and devotional tale, which she called "Illustrations" of current political and economic theory. Martineau produced these on a monthly basis between 1832 and 1834 – and, much to the surprise of her publisher, who expected little from the unknown author, they made her famous overnight. The "Illustrations" were based on her own research and a close reading of the political economists of the day; through these tales, Martineau addressed such weighty matters as slavery, the Poor Laws, taxation, education and emigration. She travelled widely (with ear-trumpet in tow), when it was not easy for a woman of her background to do so, and produced two successful books on America – *Society In America* (1837), lauded by Charles Dickens, and *A Retrospect of Western Travel* (1838). But, never fully well, she collapsed on a visit to Venice in 1839 and remained prone and weak for five years. Often dismissed as an "hysteric", like many Victorian women, Martineau had in fact suffered a prolapse of the uterus, which seriously curtailed her work and travel.

She ascribed an eventual improvement in her health to the powers of mesmerism, a popular "alternative medicine" of the 1840s. Convinced she had been cured – and even appointing a mesmerist, a Mrs Montagu Wynyard, to become part of her household – Martineau was later well enough to tour the Middle East and, on her return, visit the Lake District, where she decided to settle. She ordered the building of a house, The Knoll, in Ambleside, where she was to live for the rest of her life.

Literary England was welcome at The Knoll. Mrs Gaskell and Charlotte Brontë both visited; Matthew Arnold, the future poet, spent his school holidays up the road at his father's house, Fox How. Never an orthodox woman, Martineau cut a notable figure in lakeland society. Smoking a pipe or a cigar, she tramped around the fells in men's boots, picking plants for her garden, much to the amusement of the locals. It was said she bathed in the lake by moonlight; certainly she mixed with the lower orders (lecturing in Ambleside to a working-class audience in the Methodist Chapel) and harried local officials and churchmen. All this, of course, put at her odds with the conservative Wordsworths – with William, she would argue ferociously, while Mary Wordsworth couldn't stand being in Martineau's company and left Rydal Mount every time she came to call. Was there a subconscious prejudice, too? Martineau never married – an early engagement to a cleric was ended by his untimely death – and critics have suggested a latent homosexuality evident in her work and life. Martineau continued to write at The Knoll – her *Complete Guide to the English Lakes* (1855) followed the example of Wordsworth – with later works reflecting her loss of faith and turn to humanism. *Letters on the Nature and Development of Man* (1851) brought her harsh reviews by those who now thought her an atheist (including her own brother).

Her health continued to worry her as she suffered from periodic bouts of illness and after 1855 Martineau rarely left her house. By 1866, poor health had made work impossible and she was taking opium to relieve the pain of an ovarian cyst. She died at The Knoll in 1876 and was buried in Birmingham with members of her family.

to access their orchards across the stream. It's had many other uses over the years, mainly for storage, though records show that in the nineteenth century it was briefly home to a family of eight. Behind the house is **Adrian Sankey** (daily 9am–5.30pm; ☎015394/33039, ⓦwww.glassmakers.co.uk), a contemporary glass and design studio, where you can watch glass being blown (£1), then splash out on one of the finished products in the showroom.

For more on Ambleside's history, stroll a couple of minutes' along Rydal Road to the **Ambleside Museum** (daily 10am–5pm; £2.50; ℡015394/31212, Ⓦwww.armitt.com), the latest and most splendid incarnation of the town's literary museum and library. First founded in 1909 (by local society intellectual Mary Louisa Armitt), the collection catalogues the very distinct contribution to lakeland society made by writers and artists from John Ruskin to Beatrix Potter: others, like the writer Harriet Martineau (author of her own *Guide to the Lakes*; see box) and educationalist Charlotte Mason, made their home in the town, and the museum contains cases full of personal memorabilia – from a life-mask of Martineau to a lock of Ruskin's hair. There's plenty, too, on the remarkable Collingwood family (see p.122), plus displays related to the life and work of Herbert Bell (1856–1946), pharmacist of Ambleside turned pioneering lakeland photographer. And anyone driven to distraction by the bunny-and-hedgehog side of Beatrix Potter should be prepared to revise their opinion on viewing the changing selection of her early scientific watercolour studies of fungi and mosses – a beautifully painted sequence donated by Potter herself.

The old **market cross** still marks the centre of town, reminder that – before the coming of the train and the growth of Windermere – Ambleside was the major commercial and business centre in this part of the Lakes. It was to here, for instance, that William Wordsworth had to travel from his house at Rydal Mount when on official duty as the Distributor of Stamps for Westmorland (a job he acquired in 1813). A plaque on a building at the top of Church Street marks the site of the office he once used. Further down, at the southern end of town, off Compston Road, you reach **St Mary's Church**, whose rocket-shaped spire is visible from all over town. Completed in 1854, it was designed by George Gilbert Scott – the architect responsible for London's Albert Memorial and St Pancras station – and contains a mural of the town's annual rushbearing ceremony, its figures resplendent in their 1940s finery. The ceremony itself dates from medieval times and derives from the custom of replacing the worn rushes (or reeds) on unflagged church floors. In Ambleside, the event takes places on a Saturday in the first two weeks of July, with a procession through town of decorated rushes and the church congregation singing the specially commissioned Ambleside Rushbearers' Hymn. Behind the church, the green pastures of **Rothay Park** stretch down to the River Rothay, while above loom the heights of **Loughrigg Fell** (1101ft), with the climb to the summit signposted from near the humpbacked bridge at the foot of Rothay Park (and see also p.94).

Final port of call is soccer photographer Stuart Clarke's terrific gallery, **The Homes of Football**, 100 Lake Rd (Easter–Oct daily 10am–5pm; Nov–Easter closed Tues; free; ℡015394/34440, Ⓦwww.homesoffootball.co.uk). What started as a peripatetic exhibition, recording games and grounds from the Premier League down to the smallest amateur teams, has blossomed into a permanent archive of over 60,000 images, the massive selection on show all framed and available for sale. It's irresistible for soccer fans, who just might be persuaded to part with £250–350 for a unique memento of their team – or rather less for a soccer-ground postcard.

Waterhead

The rest of town lies a mile south at **Waterhead**, a harbour on the shores of Windermere that's filled with ducks, swans and rowboats and overlooked by the grass banks and spreading trees of **Borrans Park**. Waterhead was the earliest

Walks from Ambleside

Ambleside is impressively framed – Loughrigg Fell to the west, the distinctive line of the Fairfield Horseshoe to the north and Wansfell to the east – and even inexperienced walkers have plenty of choice.

Stock Ghyll

The traditional stroll is up Stock Ghyll Lane (which starts behind the *Salutation Hotel*) and through the leafy woods of Stock Ghyll Park (with wonderful daffs in spring) to the tumbling waterfall of **Stock Ghyll Force**, which drops 60ft through a narrow defile. Allow an hour there and back if you linger on the viewing platform and rest on the benches.

Wansfell

Those with loftier ambitions can regain the lane by Stock Ghyll Park and, a little way further up, look for the signposted path (over a wall-ladder) up Wansfell to **Wansfell Pike** (1581ft) – an hour all told to the top, from where there are superb views of Windermere and the surrounding fells. Circular hikers either cut due south from the summit to Skelghyll and return via Jenkins Crag (2hr), or head east across a clearly defined path to Troutbeck and Townend before cutting back (4hr).

Jenkins Crag and Stagshaw Gardens

The viewpoint of **Jenkins Crag**, a mile from Waterhead, gives a glimpse of the lake as well as the central peaks of the Langdales and the Old Man of Coniston. From Ambleside, walk down Lake Road (though there's a handy car park near Hayes Garden World) and follow the signs up Skelghyll Lane, a thirty-minute walk. On the way back you can detour to the National Trust's woodland **Stagshaw Garden** (Easter–June daily 10am–6.30pm; £1.50), at its best in spring for the shows of rhododendrons, camellias and azaleas.

Fairfield Horseshoe

The classic hiker's circuit from Ambleside is the **Fairfield Horseshoe** (11 miles; 6hr), which starts just out of town, off Kirkstone Road, and climbs up via High Sweden Bridge and **Dove Crag** (2603ft) to the flat top of **Fairfield** itself (2864ft), before dropping back along the opposing ridge to Nab Scar and Rydal, outside Grasmere. From Rydal, you can avoid most of the road back to Ambleside by following the footpath through the grounds of Rydal Hall. This really is a superb walk on a clear day, not too difficult yet encompassing eight different peaks.

See Basics, p.40, for general walking advice in the Lakes; recommended maps are detailed on p.27.

settled part of Ambleside, known as Galava to the Romans, who built a turf-and-timber fort on the lake edge in 90 AD, later superseded by a larger stone structure housing five hundred auxiliary soldiers, which was finally abandoned at the end of the fourth century. The Roman scholar Robin Collingwood first excavated the two forts in separate digs between 1913 and 1920 (the Ambleside Museum holds many of the objects recovered), though there's little left to see *in situ* as the foundations of various buildings, including a large granary with hypocaust, are now largely grass-covered. But it's an emotive spot, backed by glowering fells and with views across the rippling Windermere waters – the perfect place for sunset-watching or star-gazing. Two or three little cafés by the piers have outdoor seats, while the lawns of the *Wateredge Inn* and *Waterhead* hotel also offer lovely views.

Practicalities

Buses (including National Express) all stop on Kelsick Road, opposite the library, with regular local services to and from Windermere, Grasmere and Keswick, plus services to Hawkshead and Coniston (#505), and Elterwater and Langdale (#516). Walking up to town from the **ferry piers** at Waterhead takes about fifteen minutes, though an electric **shuttle bus** service operates from the piers to the *White Lion* pub in the town centre (weather- and ferry-dependent, but usually daily Easter–Oct, weekends only Nov–Easter, 10.30am–5pm, roughly every 30min; £1.50). The A591 runs right through town and drivers are best advised to make straight for the signposted car parks, though be warned that these fill quickly in summer – you may not find a space on your first pass through. The main **tourist office** is in the centre of town in the Central Buildings on Market Cross (daily 9am–5pm; ☎015394/32582); the seasonal **Waterhead Information Centre** (Easter–Nov daily 9.30am–5.30pm; ☎015394/37279) is next to the *Waterhead* hotel, by the piers. For **online information**, consult ⓦwww.amblesideonline.co.uk, a useful community website for the Ambleside area.

Accommodation

Lake Road, running between Waterhead and Ambleside, is lined with **B&Bs**, and there are other concentrations on Church Street and Compston Road, as well as a backpackers just on the edge of town – all these are marked on the main Ambleside map. Fancier places tend to lie out of town, or a mile to the south at Waterhead by the lake (see Around Ambleside: Waterhead map), which is also where you'll find Ambleside's official **youth hostel**. This is one of the most popular in the country – advance reservations are essential during most of the year. The nearest **campsite** is three miles south, by the lake though too far out without your own transport to be used as a base for Ambleside itself.

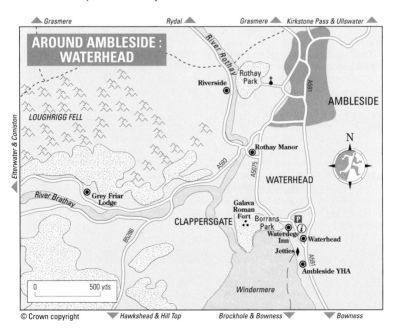

In Ambleside

Brantfell Rothay Rd ☎ 015394/32239, ⓦ www
.brantfell.co.uk. A Victorian house with a friendly
welcome, overlooking the recreation grounds and
encroaching fells on the edge of town. Seven
rooms are available, including a particularly large
one with a four-poster and views, and one single
room. There's a big choice at breakfast – traditional and such alternatives as smoked salmon, hash
browns, pancakes and kippers – while guests get
use of the lounge (with winter log fire) and free
entry to the pool at a local leisure club. Parking. ❹

3 Cambridge Villas Church St ☎ 015394/32307,
ⓦ www.3cambridgevillas.co.uk. The pick of the
bunch on Church Street, the well-kept house hides
a variety of agreeably furnished rooms, including
two singles (these share a bathroom on the same
landing). No credit cards. ❸

Compston House Compston Rd
☎ 015394/32305, ⓦ www.compstonhouse.co.uk.
Inside this traditional lakeland house the owners, Sue and Jerry from New York, have cleverly
created one of the Lakes' most individual B&Bs
–iconic American prints, lovely light (non-smoking) rooms themed after various US states, snazzy
small bathrooms, and (if you wish) pancakes and
maple syrup for breakfast. Free parking permit
provided. No American Express. ❹

Lakes Lodge Lake Rd ☎ 015394/33240, ⓦ www.
lakeslodge.co.uk. The lakeland slate exterior is no
preparation for the changes wrought inside, where
a bold lilac/lavender colour scheme announces
contemporary intent. A dozen spacious rooms have
been stylishly kitted out (room 10 has a glass sink,
and DVD players are standard) and bathrooms
upgraded, with those at the back sporting views
over Loughrigg. A good buffet breakfast (smoked
fish, local ham) is served in the informal café-style
breakfast room, wine and beer are available, and
you can have dinner or use the pool at Waterhead's *Regent Hotel*. Two-night minimum stay.
Parking. No American Express. ❺

Linda's B&B Compston Rd ☎ 015394/32999. The
cheery spirit never flags and the bargain prices
– the lowest in Ambleside – go a long way to
compensating for the simple facilities. Guests can
use the kitchen, while two of the four rooms (all of
which share a bathroom and a top-floor shower-
room) can sleep three or four. A room-only stay
brings the price down to as little as £13 a night.
No credit cards. ❶

Mill Cottage Rydal Rd ☎ 015394/34830. Long
on atmosphere, but with rooms short on space,
this converted sixteenth-century fulling mill (next
to Bridge House) has its moments – particularly
when you can while away time in the downstairs

riverside tearooms. Five rooms available – one
isn't en suite but does have a sink inside the room
and a private bathroom outside. No American
Express. ❸

Salutation Lake Rd ☎ 015394/32244, ⓦ www
.hotelslakedistrict.com. There's not much of its
seventeenth-century origins left, but you couldn't
be much more central. Rooms are pretty compact,
though kept spick-and-span – some "club rooms"
(supplement payable) have balconies and spa
baths, or there's a sauna, steam room and jacuzzi
on site and free use of the pool in Grasmere's *Red
Lion*. Rates drop a bit in winter, while single Saturday-night stays attract a surcharge. Parking. ❼

Waterwheel Guesthouse Bridge St
☎ 015394/33286. The very picture of an old-fashioned Lake District cottage, with its climbing rose
and a waterwheel outside. The owner has been
doing B&B here for over fifty years, and can tell
you a thing or two, and her three "olde worlde"
rooms with big beds and proper bedclothes fill
quickly; there's one shared bathroom. The cottage
is up the cobbled alley off Rydal Road, by the
bridge across Stock Ghyll. No credit cards. ❷

Around Ambleside

Grey Friar Lodge Clappersgate ☎ 015394/33158,
ⓦ www.cumbria-hotels.co.uk. A little over a mile
southwest of Ambleside, the lodge – an old vicarage – makes the most of its commanding position above the River Brathay, and boasts mature
gardens, veranda and terrace. The rooms (some
with antique four-posters) have baths as well as
showers, though prices vary considerably depending on size and aspect – available accommodation
might fall into a price category lower or higher
than shown. Closed mid-Dec to mid-Feb. Parking.
No American Express. ❺

Riverside Under Loughrigg ☎ 015394/32395,
ⓦ www.riverside-at-ambleside.co.uk. Charming,
non-smoking Victorian house on a quiet lane facing the River Rothay, half a mile (10min walk) from
town. Six large, light rooms available (a couple
with whirlpool baths), including a river-facing
four-poster room and a family room (minimum age
5) with bunks and a terrific bathroom. Sit outside
on the garden deck and plan your day's walking
with the library of guides. Parking. No American
Express. ❺

Rothay Manor Rothay Bridge ☎ 015394/33605,
ⓦ www.rothaymanor.co.uk. This Regency-style
mansion, half a mile southwest of the centre, has
been run by the same family for four decades,
offering larger-than-average rooms (including
decent-sized beds and spacious bathrooms, with
baths), stylish decor, appealing grounds and good

food served in a candlelit dining room. The most sought-after "superior" rooms at the front have their own private balcony, while three suites (up to £250) in the grounds provide more space for families. Guests have free use of a nearby leisure centre with pool. No single Saturday-night stays. Parking. ❺, including dinner ❾

Wateredge Inn Waterhead ☏015394/32332, Ⓦwww.wateredgeinn.co.uk. Lakeside inn with rooms either in the main hotel or garden-suites with balcony or patio. There's free use of the pool and sauna at a nearby leisure club, and a good-value brasserie-style menu in the waterside bar and restaurant – the terrace and grassy beer garden (open to non-residents) is a very popular place for lunch, dinner or just a drink, especially with families who can let children run free. Parking. ❻

Waterhead Waterhead ☏015394/32566, Ⓦwww.elh.co.uk. Designer townhouse-style accommodation provides the Lake District's classiest four-star lodgings. White high-ceilinged rooms feature sharp contemporary fabrics and furnishings, with no detail left unattended – king-sized beds with suede headboards, massive flatscreen TVs, monogrammed cups for morning tea and a champagne menu in the sparkling slate-and-marble bathrooms. It's very close to the lake, opposite the Waterhead piers, with a swanky garden-bar (open for lunch and drinks) and positively metropolitan restaurant (dinner £30), both open to non-residents. Guests can use the pool at the nearby Low Wood leisure club. Parking. ❺, including dinner ❾

Youth hostels

Ambleside Backpackers Old Lake Rd ☏015394/32340, Ⓦwww.englishlakesbackpackers .co.uk. This extended and refurbished lakeland cottage, a 5min walk from town, has 72 beds in four- to twelve-bed single-sex dorms. There's not much space in the dorms themselves, though they do have lockers and washbasins and there's a fully equipped kitchen, dining room and lounge with video and Internet facilities – a cereal, tea and toast breakfast is included in the price. Office open 8.30am–1pm & 4–8.30pm, though no curfew. Dorm beds £14, long-stay discounts available.

Ambleside YHA Waterhead, A591, 1 mile south of Ambleside ☏0870/770 5672, Ⓔambleside@yha .org.uk. Impressive lakeside affair with almost 250 beds divided amongst neatly furnished small dorms, doubles and family rooms. There's a licensed café (with Fair Trade coffee), bike rental (and storage), Internet access, laundry facilities and a private jetty (for jumping off). The drawbacks are that it's a 15min walk from Ambleside itself and usually packed with school parties. Reception open 7.15am–midnight; evening meal served. Dorm beds £18, breakfast included.

Campsite

Low Wray Campsite off B5286, 3 miles south of Ambleside ☏015394/32810. National Trust site on the western shore of the lake, where there's a small shop and canoe and bike rental; bus #505 (to Coniston) passes within a mile. No advance reservations – it's first come, first served (so in summer, call to see if it's full first). Closed Nov–Easter.

Eating, drinking and entertainment

There's more choice in Ambleside for eating than just about anywhere else in the Lakes, from **cafés** and takeaways to gourmet **restaurants**, which is one of the reasons the town makes such a good base. Be warned, though, that prices in many are on the high side for what you get, while reservations for the better places are a good idea in the school holidays. **Pubs** are plentiful, too, a couple showing real character, while others have outdoor terraces, which come into their own in summer – though the nicest *al fresco* drinking is done down at Waterhead's *Wateredge Inn*. The two small local **supermarkets**, *Spar* and *Co-op*, are both on Compston Road. *Zeffirelli's* **cinema** (☏015394/33845, Ⓦwww.zeffirellis.co.uk) has four screens at two locations in town; while for details of Ambleside's famous annual **festivals** – the Rushbearing and Ambleside Sports – see p.75 and p.39.

Cafés and restaurants

Apple Pie Rydal Rd ☏015394/33679. Busy café with patio-garden seating and a range of dishes from BLTs and baked potatoes to soup and quiche. The homemade pies come savoury or sweet, the apple variety laced with cinnamon and raisin. Daytime only. Inexpensive.

Doi Intanon Market Place ☏015394/32119. Thai flavours make a welcome change here – all the usual soups and stir-fries, plus specials such as a fiery vegetable jungle curry or a grilled chicken appetizer wrapped in papyrus. There's also warm service and cold Thai beer. Dinner only; closed Mon & Tues. Moderate.

Glass House Rydal Rd ☎015394/32137. A handsome place, housed in a renovated fulling mill with waterwheel and sunny courtyard. The food is Modern British (Caesar salad to braised Herdwick lamb), nicely presented, and at fair prices, especially the light lunch selection or early dinner menu (before 7.30pm, not Sat). It's open all day in summer, otherwise lunch and dinner. Closed Tues Oct–Easter. Expensive.

Lucy 4 2 St Mary's Lane ☎015394/34666. Wine-bar and good-time offshoot of *Lucy's On A Plate*, with a mix-and-match Euro tapas-style menu and decent wines by the glass (there's no need to eat) – there's a no-smoking bar upstairs. Dinner only (from 5pm). Oct–Easter closed Tues & Wed. Moderate.

Lucy's On A Plate Church St ☎015394/31191. Hugely enjoyable stripped-pine bistro offering an inventive, daily-changing, wittily described menu with tons of choice and a varied wine list. Lunch is more snacky and Mediterranean in inspiration; dinner roams the globe, but sources lots of its materials locally (try the char when it's on, or the Cumbrian lamb or Grizedale venison). There's also a very good deli and specialist grocer's next door. Reservations advised. Expensive.

Pippins 10 Lake Rd ☎015394/31338. An easygoing, updated English caff, serving everything from a full breakfast to a steak dinner with a glass of fizz. Other day and night-time eats are pizzas, pasta and burgers – and there's a full drinks list. Moderate.

Taste of Lakeland 1 & 2 Rydal Rd ☎015394/32636. The shop sells all manner of lakeland produce – organic cheese, smoked meats from Brougham Hall, Penrith toffee, Hawkshead relishes, fell-bred lamb – while the small tearoom dishes out coffee and cakes to hikers and passersby. Daytime only. Inexpensive.

Zeffirelli's Compston Rd ☎015394/33845. *Zeff's* is a star – famous for its wholemeal-base pizzas, but also serving a full roster of inventive veggie pastas, salads and homemade cakes. The funky, cavernous downstairs dining room is open for coffee from 10am, lunch from noon and dinner from 6pm, and there's a small sun-trap terrace and upstairs bar. Ask about the dinner-and-cinema special. Moderate.

Pubs

Golden Rule Smithy Brow ☎015394/33363. The long-standing beer-lovers' and climbers' favourite – this is a cosy place for a post-hike pint (six real ales usually available) and a read of the Wainwright, with no jukebox or other playful distractions. A bit of a patio catches the summer sun.

Unicorn North Rd ☎015394/33216. An enjoyable old backstreet inn with hearty bar meals, a selection of real ales and live music nights.

Listings

Banks and exchange NatWest (Cheapside), Barclays and HSBC (both Market Place) have ATMs. You can also change travellers' cheques at the post office (see below).

Bike rental Biketreks, 9 Compston Rd (daily 9.30am–5pm; ☎015394/31505, ⓦwww.biketreks.co.uk); Ghyllside Cycles, The Slack (Easter–Oct daily 9.30am–5.30pm; Nov–Easter closed Wed; ☎015394/33592, ⓦwww.ghyllside.co.uk).

Emergencies Doctors at Ambleside Health Centre, Rydal Rd ☎015394/32693. The nearest hospital is in Kendal (Westmorland General Hospital, Burton Rd; ☎01539/732288).

Internet access Sparks, Central Buildings, Market Cross (Mon–Fri 10am–7pm, Sat & Sun noon–7pm; ☎015394/33762); Ambleside Library, Kelsick Rd (Mon & Wed 10am–5pm, Tues & Fri 10am–7pm, Sat 10am–1pm; ☎015394/32507). Also Internet access at the youth hostels (see p.79).

Laundry Laundromat, Kelsick Rd (Mon–Sat 10am–6pm; ☎015394/32231).

Outdoors stores Ambleside is a good place to pick up walking and climbing gear and camping equipment at reasonable prices. Classic old stores such as F.W. Tyson (Market Place) and Wilf Nicholson (Market Cross) complement specialists such as The Climber's Shop (Compston Corner; walking-boot rental available) and Stewart R. Cunningham (Rydal Rd), while large retailers include Black's and Gaynor Sports (both Compston Rd).

Pharmacy Thomas Bell, Lake Rd ☎015394/33345; Boots, 8–9 Market Cross ☎015394/33355.

Post office Market Place (Mon–Fri 9am–5.30pm, Sat 9am–12.30pm; ☎015394/32267).

Taxis Billy's Taxis ☎015394/31287; Brown's Taxis ☎015394/33263; John's Taxis ☎015394/32857; Kevin's Taxis ☎015394/32371; Sarah's Taxis ☎015394/41171; Steve's Taxis ☎015394/33544.

Troutbeck

Troutbeck Bridge, three miles southeast of Ambleside along the A591 (and just a mile or so from Windermere town), heralds the start of the gentle **Troutbeck valley** below Wansfell, accessed by two roads, one either side of the valley's namesake beck. The main A592 to Patterdale runs north into the valley, passing the Lakeland Horticultural Society's splendid gardens at **Holehird** (daily dawn–dusk; free, though small donation requested; ℡015394/46008), whose four acres encompass various different habitats from rock and alpine gardens to rose gardens and shrubberies.

The better route, though, is up a minor road (Bridge Lane) running high above the west side of **Trout Beck** itself. A mile along here is the youth hostel (see overleaf) and, under a mile further up the road, stands **Townend** (Easter–Oct Wed–Sun 1–5pm, last admission 4.30pm; £3.40; NT; ℡015394/32628), a seventeenth-century house, built in 1626 for George Browne, a wealthy yeoman farmer, one of that breed of independent farmers known in these parts as "statesmen", after the estates they tended. Remarkably, the house remained in the hands of eleven generations of the Browne family, for more than three hundred years, until 1943 when the National Trust took it over. It's an extraordinary relic of seventeenth-century vernacular architecture, with its round chimneys (of the sort admired by Wordsworth) surmounting a higgledy-piggledy collection of small rooms, some added as late as the nineteenth century. The house is well known for its woodcarvings and panelling, and lavishly embellished beds, fireplaces, chests, chairs and grandfather clocks are scattered around the various rooms. You'll also see the surviving laundry room (complete with mangle), dairy, library and parlour.

Townend is at the southern end of **TROUTBECK** village, really just a straggling, though striking, hamlet with a post office (which sells cups of tea and ice cream). Several hikes pass through village and valley, with the peaks of Yoke (2309ft), Ill Bell (the highest at 2476ft) and Froswick (2359ft) on the east side forming the barrier between Troutbeck and Kentmere (see p.83). The most direct route into Kentmere is the easy track over the Garburn Pass, while many use Troutbeck as the starting point for the five-hour walk along **High Street**, a nine-mile range running north to Brougham near Penrith. The course of a Roman road follows the ridge, probably once linking the forts at Brougham and Galava in Waterhead.

North of Troutbeck, the A592 makes a gradual ascent to **Kirkstone Pass**, four miles from the village, at the head of which there's a superbly sited pub, the *Kirkstone Pass Inn*, whose picnic tables (across the road) offer terrific views. A minor road from here cuts down directly to Ambleside – so precipitous that it's known as "The Struggle" – while the A592 continues over the pass and down the valley to Ullswater.

Practicalities

Public transport to Troutbeck is limited to bus #517, which runs from Bowness piers and Windermere train station up the A592 and over Kirkstone Pass three times a day (April to mid-July Sat & Sun; mid-July to early Sept daily), to Ullswater. It makes stops at the *Queen's Head* (see below) and the *Kirkstone Pass Inn*.

The most prominent places to stay in Troutbeck are the two traditional **inns**, the *Mortal Man* and the *Queen's Head*, at the north end of the village, both serving excellent food. As well as the superior B&B option listed below, there are also a couple of cheaper B&Bs in the village – local tourist offices should be able to check on space for you. Budget accommodation is at the valley's self-catering **youth hostel**, confusingly known as the Windermere YHA – a shuttle-bus service for hostellers operates from Windermere train station (meeting arriving trains) and from Ambleside youth hostel.

Inns and B&B

Fellside Studios Fellside, Troutbeck inns ①015394/34000, ⓦwww.bestofthelakes.com. Two non-smoking studios available (one double, one twin), decorated in contemporary style, with oak floors, slate-tiled kitchens and shower-rooms, and sharp-looking living/sleeping areas with TV/DVD players. A generous continental breakfast is brought to your door (cold meats, smoked fish platter, cheese etc), and each studio has an out-side dining terrace. The location is good too, only a 10–15min walk from either inn, with walks start-ing straight from the property. Two-night minimum, with a few pounds off for midweek, off-season or longer stays. Parking. ⑤

Mortal Man Bridge Lane ①015394/33193, ⓦwww.themortalman.co.uk. A cosy spot with a dozen attractive rooms, lording it over the valley – wooden four-posters, hung with drapes, add a touch of romance to some rooms. For non-resi-dents, coffee and biscuits or a meal is a great way to soak up the seventeenth-century surroundings, especially in the timeworn public bar. Or there's a more formal restaurant (D, B&B deals are available at a category higher than the B&B rate). The name, incidentally, derives from the doggerel written on the inn's sign: "O Mortal Man, that lives by bread, What is it makes thy nose so red? Thou silly fool, that look'st so pale, Tis drinking Sally Birkett's ale". Parking. Closed mid-Nov to mid-Feb. ⑤

Queen's Head on the A592 ①015394/32174, ⓦwww.queensheadhotel.com. An old coaching inn that oozes atmosphere, from the slate floors, oak beams and smoky fires to the carved bar fashioned from a four-poster bed. There are eleven rooms in the inn itself (the two largest, with great views, are nos. 10 and 11; the oldest, with an antique four-poster, no. 1) and four more, slightly smaller, in the annexe. Dining is a treat, too, with everything from steak-and-ale cobbler to stuffed pheasant and seared tuna – overnight rates are a category higher if you go for an inclusive din-ner price. Two-night minimum stay at weekends. Parking. ⑥

Youth hostel

Windermere YHA High Cross, Bridge Lane ①0870/770 6094, ⓔwindermere@yha.org.uk. Built originally as a private mansion, the house is now deprived of its turrets, ballroom and boating lake, though it still has magnificent lake views. Rooms are mostly four-bedded, though there is a twin and a triple room. Mountain bikes avail-able for rent; and there's a kitchen and Internet access. Reception closed noon–1pm; evening meal served (note that the nearest pub is *The Sun*, three-quarters of a mile to the south on the A591 – the Troutbeck inns are a mile and a half away to the north). Dec & Jan open Fri & Sat only. Dorm beds £12.50.

Staveley

Four miles east of Windermere, the little village of **STAVELEY** lies tucked away on the banks of the River Kent. The river has powered mills in Staveley for over seven hundred years, and in the eighteenth and nineteenth centuries there was prosperity of sorts as first cotton was produced and then wooden bobbins were manufactured here in sizeable quantities. These wood-turn-ing skills have survived into modern times, with Staveley woodwork still a thing of beauty. **Peter Hall & Son** (Mon–Fri 9am–5pm, Sat 10am–4pm; ①01539/821633, ⓦwww.peter-hall.co.uk), a mile out on the Windermere road, produces renowned handcrafted furniture and household goods, while other cottage industries (including a craft bakery) occupy the old mill buildings themselves in **Mill Yard**, off Main Street.

An easy half-hour stroll around the village starts by the restored tower of **St Margaret's** on Main Street, all that survives of Staveley's original four-teenth-century church. Follow the path at the side of the church tower down to the river, turn left and walk along the riverside path and road to the old bridge, from where you return through the village, passing the replacement nineteenth-century church of **St James** – inside which is a superb Burne-Jones-designed stained-glass window depicting a star-clustered heavenly choir surmounting the crucifixion.

Practicalities

Staveley is bypassed by the A591, which keeps the streets fairly quiet, and you can get here on the train line from Kendal or on the #555/556 bus. Walkers come past on the Dales Way, which follows the River Kent from Kendal, steers just south of the village and then cuts west across the low fells to Bowness.

Accommodation

Burrow Hall Plantation Bridge, A591, 1 mile southeast of Staveley ☎01539/821711, ⓦwww .burrowhall.co.uk. Seventeenth-century farmhouse on the main road (north side) that's been extended to provide four spacious country-style rooms with large bathrooms and rural views. It's very good value for the money, though you'll need a car to stay here. Parking. No American Express. ❸

Eagle & Child Kendal Rd ☎01539/821320, ⓦwww.eaglechildinn.co.uk. The village's nicest inn – right in the centre – has smallish, but tastefully decorated, rooms, some overlooking the River Kent. There's a riverside garden, where you can sip a lakeland beer, and good, moderately priced food, including well-stuffed baguette/ciabatta sandwiches, Kentmere lamb shanks or baked trout. Parking. ❸

Watermill Inn Ings (A591), 1.5 miles west of town ☎01539/821309, ⓦwww.watermill-inn .demon.co.uk. A renowned real-ale pub with a huge choice of beers (there are sixteen on tap at any one time), a garden and popular

bar food. The building was once an old bobbin mill, but has been imaginatively restored, with a bar fashioned from church pews and a beer-cellar viewing area. Seven bedrooms available, six with showers, one with bath and balcony. Parking. ❹

Café

Wilf's Café Mill Yard ☎01539/822239. Housed in the bobbin loft of an old wood mill, with breakfasts, rarebits, chillis, filled baked potatoes and cappuccinos served at locally made tables; an upstairs deck overlooks the river and weir. Speciality dinners held once or twice a month, plus outdoor-themed slide-and-supper nights. Daytime only. Inexpensive.

Campsite

Ashes Lane off the A591, 1 mile southeast of Staveley ☎01539/821119. Bus #555/556 between Kendal and Windermere can drop you off at the local campsite. Closed mid-Jan to mid-March.

Kentmere and Longsleddale

North of Staveley a narrow road runs its dappled way alongside the river, widening out after three miles into the splendid broad valley of **Kentmere**, with its isolated chapel perched on a bluff in the distance. **Kentmere Hall**, a couple of hundred yards up the country lane from the chapel, is the only other prominent building, retaining a remarkably well-preserved fourteenth-century turreted pele tower, which you can see from the lane. The chapel marks the start of the **Kentmere Horseshoe** (12 miles; 7hr), a reasonably strenuous hike along ridges and saddles on either side of Kentmere Reservoir; there's extremely limited parking by the chapel, so get there early. You can walk up instead from Staveley, following Browfoot Lane and then a river path, via **Kentmere Tarn**, or on summer Sundays and bank holidays (June to mid-Sept) take the #519 Kentmere Rambler **bus** from Staveley (with connections from Ambleside, Windermere and Kendal), whose return services are scheduled to allow an all-day hike.

There's **accommodation** at *Maggs Howe* on Lowfield Lane (☎01539/821689; no credit cards ;❷), half a mile or so east of the chapel at Green Quarter. There's either B&B in the house or a mattress on the floor in the bunkhouse next door (£10 per person), which has a couple of showers and a fully equipped kitchen. The nearest shop and pub is down in Staveley, but you can arrange to have breakfast or an evening meal at the B&B.

Both Kentmere and **Longsleddale**, to the east (linked by bridleway), provide the deeply rural environs that inspired the "Greendale" of John Cunliffe's *Postman Pat* stories. There's no lake in either valley, so Cunliffe used Grasmere as his model for "Berkmere". Longsleddale is even less visited than Kentmere, due in part to its harsher upper reaches, but there's a similar parking shortage at graceful **Sadgill Bridge**, which is as far as you can go by car. Beyond here, hikers make their way up to the abandoned Wrengill Quarry and its waterfall and then along the old packhorse trail over Gatesgarth Pass to Haweswater.

Travel details

See Windermere below for stops on the main bus routes #555/556 and #559.

From Ambleside

Bus #505, "Coniston Rambler" to: Hawkshead (20min) and Coniston (35min). Service operates daily: Easter–Oct hourly; Nov–Easter every 1hr 30min–2hr.
Bus #516, "Langdale Rambler" (4–6 daily) to: Skelwith Bridge (10min), Elterwater (17min), Chapel Stile (20min) and Old Dungeon Ghyll (30min).

From Bowness

Bus #517, "Kirkstone Rambler" to: Windermere (8min), Troutbeck Queen's Head (20min), Kirkstone Pass (30min), Brotherswater (45min), Patterdale (50min) and Glenridding (55min). Service operates Easter to mid-July Sat, Sun & bank hols 3 daily; mid-July to early Sept 3 daily.
Bus #618 (4–5 daily) to: Newby Bridge (15min), Haverthwaite (18min) and Ulverston (30min).
Cross-Lakes Shuttle (4 daily): launch from Bowness connects with #525 minibus from Ferry House, Sawrey, to Hill Top (7min) and Hawkshead (15min) – bus may also continue to Coniston (for further connection to Coniston launch) and to

Grizedale. Service operates daily at Easter, bank holidays and July–Sept, weekends only May, June & Oct.

From Windermere

Bus #505, "Coniston Rambler" to: Brockhole (7min), Waterhead (10min), Ambleside (15min), Hawkshead (35min) and Coniston (50min). Service operates Easter–Oct hourly; Nov–Easter Sun only (3 a day).
Bus #555/556 (hourly) to: Troutbeck Bridge (5min), Brockhole (7min), Waterhead (12min), Ambleside (15min), Rydal (21min), Grasmere (30min) and Keswick (50min); also to Staveley (12min) and Kendal (25min).
Bus #599 to: Bowness (10min); also to Troutbeck Bridge (5min), Brockhole (7min), Waterhead (12min), Ambleside (15min), Rydal (21min) and Grasmere (30min). Service operates Easter–Oct every 20–30min; Nov–Easter hourly and only to Bowness or Ambleside.
Bus #618 (4–5 daily) to: Bowness (6min), Newby Bridge (21min), Haverthwaite (24min) and Ulverston (35min).
Train (hourly) to: Staveley (6min) and Kendal (14min).

2

Grasmere and the central fells

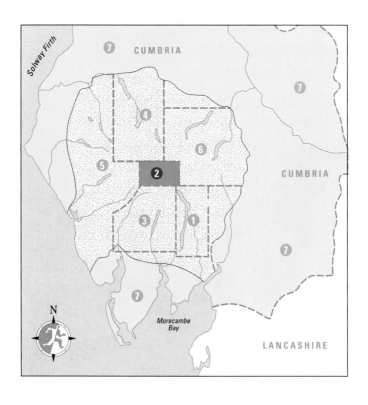

CHAPTER 2 # Highlights

* **Visiting Wordsworth's grave, Grasmere** One of England's most famous literary pilgrimages is to the simple grave of the poet Wordsworth. See p.90

* **Dove Cottage, Grasmere** It's an obvious tourist attraction, but you shouldn't miss Wordsworth's first home in the Lake District. See p.98

* **The walk around Rydal Water** In a region of dramatic, energetic hikes, many visitors will be content with this gentle stroll. See p.102

* **Elterwater** Stay the night in one of the Lake District's most attractive hamlets. See p.104

* **Walking in Great Langdale** Routes up the famous Langdale Pikes, Crinkle Crags and Bowfell could keep serious hikers occupied for a week. See p.106

* **Old Dungeon Ghyll Hotel, Langdale** After a day on the fells, a drink in the stone-flagged hikers' bar of this atmospheric inn never disappoints. See p.107

△ Pavey Ark and Stickle Tarn

Grasmere and the central fells

G rasmere – lake and village – is the traditional dividing line between the north and south Lakes, between the heavily touristed Windermere region and the more rugged fells on either side of Keswick. It lies on the only north–south road through the Lakes (the A591), which cuts through the pass of **Dunmail Raise** (782ft), three miles north of Grasmere – remembered (though with precious little evidence) as the site of the decisive battle in 945 between Dunmail, last independent king of Cumbria, and the Saxon king Edmund, who, in victory, handed Cumbria to Malcolm of Scotland.

Rather than for its own charms (which are considerable), Grasmere owes its wild popularity to its most famous former resident, William Wordsworth, who first moved here in 1799 and lived in a variety of houses in the vicinity until his death in 1850. Two are open to the public: Dove Cottage, where he first set up home in the Lakes with his sister Dorothy; and Rydal Mount, on Rydal Water, the comfortable family home to which he moved at the height of his fame. The influence of other literary lakeland names hangs heavily on Grasmere, too, notably those of Thomas De Quincey, who lived here for more than twenty years and married a local girl; and of the dissolute Coleridges – father Samuel Taylor and son Hartley, whose separate periods of residence often tried the Wordsworths' patience.

The region's other attraction is the proximity of the **central fells**, including some of the Lake District's most famous peaks and valleys. Routes from Grasmere and Ambleside forge west into the superb valleys of Great and Little **Langdale**, overlooked by the prominent rocky summits of hikers' favourites such as the **Langdale Pikes**, **Bowfell** and **Crinkle Crags**. It's not all hard going though: there are easier walks to tarns and viewpoints in the bucolic surroundings of **Easedale** and Little Langdale, while hamlets such as **Skelwith Bridge** and **Elterwater** provide classic inns and country B&Bs for an isolated night's stay.

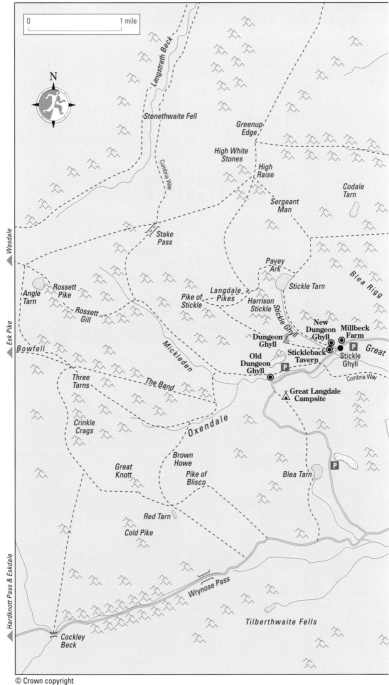

© Crown copyright

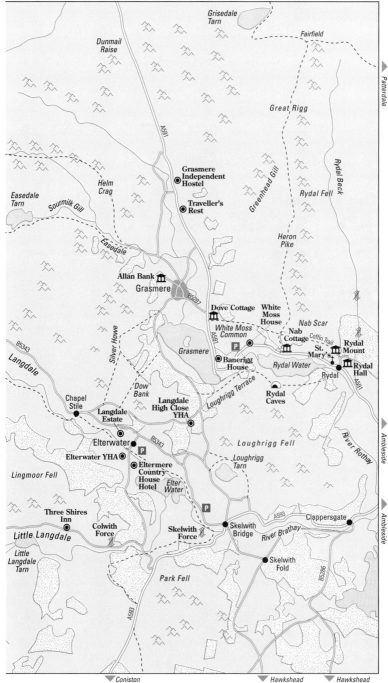

▲ Thirlmere & Keswick   ▲ Grisedale

Grisedale Tarn

Dunmail Raise

Fairfield

► Patterdale

Great Rigg

A591

Helm Crag

Grasmere Independent Hostel

Traveller's Rest

Easedale Tarn

Sourmilk Gill

Easedale

Greenhead Gill

Rydal Fell

Rydal Beck

Heron Pike

Allan Bank

Grasmere

B5287

Dove Cottage   White Moss House

Nab Scar

Nab Cottage   Coffin Trail   Rydal Mount

White Moss Common

St. Mary's

Rydal Hall

Grasmere

P

A591

Silver Howe

Banerigg House

Rydal Water

Rydal

B5343

Langdale

Dow Bank

Loughrigg Terrace

Rydal Caves

► Ambleside

Chapel Stile

Langdale High Close YHA

Loughrigg Fell

River Rothay

Langdale Estate

B5343

Elterwater

Elterwater YHA

Loughrigg Tarn

Lingmoor Fell

Eltermere Country House Hotel

Elter Water

► Ambleside

P

Three Shires Inn

Colwith Force

Skelwith Force

Skelwith Bridge

A593

Clappersgate

River Brathay

Little Langdale

Little Langdale Tarn

Park Fell

Skelwith Fold

B5286

▼ Coniston   ▼ Hawkshead   ▼ Hawkshead

Grasmere

Four miles northwest of Ambleside, the village of **GRASMERE** consists of an intimate cluster of grey-stone houses on an old packhorse road which runs beside the babbling River Rothay. With a permanent population of under a thousand, and just a handful of roads which meet at a central green, it's an eminently pleasing ensemble, set in a shallow bowl of land which reaches down to an alluring lake. Thirty years before Wordsworth put down roots here, the "white village" on the water in this "unsuspected paradise" had also entranced the poet Thomas Gray (of "Elegy" fame) whose journal of his ground-breaking tour of the Lakes did much to bring the region to wider attention. Indeed, if you see Grasmere as being in the "very eye of the Romantic storm" (as does Melvyn Bragg in his novel *The Maid of Buttermere*) you have some idea of its enduring significance as a tourist magnet.

The village

For the most part, Grasmere's assorted gift shops, galleries, cafés and hotels occupy nineteenth-century buildings and houses, though the village is much older than that. St Oswald is reputed to have preached here in the seventh century, while the present church bearing his name dates from the thirteenth century – you can still follow the medieval "**Coffin Trail**" from Rydal over White Moss Common, along which coffin bearers struggled with their load on their way to the church. Other hangovers from medieval times include the village's famous rushbearing ceremony (see p.38) and traditional Sports festival (p.39).

The main point of pilgrimage is the **churchyard of St Oswald's**, around which the river makes a sinuous curl. Here, beneath the yews, Wordsworth is buried alongside his wife Mary and sister Dorothy, his beloved daughter Dora (buried in her married name Quillinan) and two of his much younger children, Catherine and Thomas, whose deaths marred the Wordsworths' early years in Grasmere. A worn Celtic cross behind the Wordsworth plots marks the grave of Hartley Coleridge, Samuel Taylor's son. Like his father, Hartley possessed an addictive personality though – unlike his father – his lapses never produced a formal break with the Wordsworths, with whom Hartley remained a family favourite. Inside, the church's unique twin naves are split by an arched, whitewashed wall. Wordsworth described its "naked rafters intricately crossed" in *The Excursion*; while Thomas De Quincey married a farmer's daughter, Margaret Simpson, here – a match disapproved of by the snobbish Wordsworths. Associations aside, it's a rather plain church, though there is a memorial plaque to Wordsworth ("a true philosopher and poet") on the wall to the left of the altar, as well as his prayer book on display in a small case in the nave. Also in the case is a medallion likeness of **Sir John Richardson**, surgeon, naturalist and Arctic explorer who accompanied John Franklin on the heroic, but futile, expedition of 1819 to discover the North West Passage. Richardson later came into the ownership of a Grasmere country house, Lancrigg in Easedale (now a hotel), where he supervised the laying out of the woods and gardens with specimens collected on his travels. He's buried in Grasmere churchyard (a few paces to the right from the rear entrance).

Right at the rear entrance to the churchyard stands **Sarah Nelson's Gingerbread Shop** (Mon–Sat 9.30am–5.30pm, Sun 12.30–5.30pm; ☎015394/35428, Ⓦwww.grasmeregingerbread.co.uk) – you'll smell the shop before you see it. Grasmere gingerbread has been made on the premises since the mid-nineteenth century and the recipe is a closely guarded secret (kept locked in an Ambleside bank vault). The shop was formerly the village schoolhouse, where Wordsworth taught for a time in 1812.

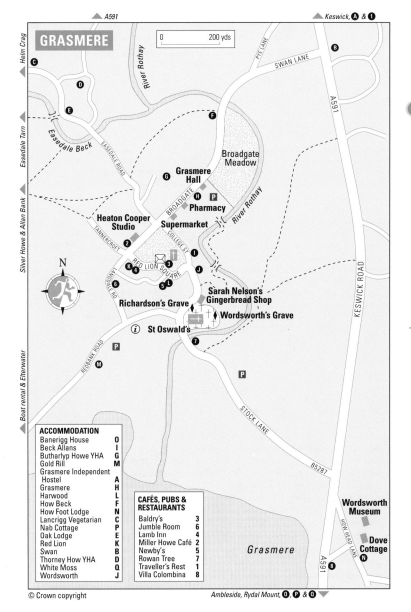

© Crown copyright

Ambleside, Rydal Mount, **O**, **P** & **Q** ▼

Wordsworth spent most of his Grasmere years living in houses outside the village – Dove Cottage and Rydal Mount – but the five years in between these major residences (1808–13) saw the extended Wordsworth family and visiting friends occupying two houses in the village itself. Both are closed to the public, though there's nothing to stop you walking past the **Old Rectory** (opposite St Oswald's) and the more imposing **Allan Bank** – the latter reached up a

Samuel Taylor Coleridge (1772–1834) already knew both Robert Southey and William Wordsworth by the time he moved to the Lake District. With Southey, he shared an enthusiasm for the French Revolution and an unfulfilled plan to found a Utopian community in America; and in 1795 he'd married Sara Fricker, the sister of Southey's fiancée Edith. Later, while living in Somerset, Coleridge and Wordsworth wrote *Lyrical Ballads* together, which contained Coleridge's "The Rime of the Ancient Mariner". Coleridge sang Wordsworth's praises at every opportunity; a favour returned by the enamoured Dorothy, who thought Coleridge a "wonderful man . . . [whose] . . . conversation teems with soul, mind and spirit".

Thus, when Wordsworth moved to Grasmere in 1799, Coleridge needed little prompting to follow. Having toured the Lakes, he settled on the newly built Greta Hall in Keswick, leasing it for 25 guineas a year. The Coleridges – Samuel Taylor, his wife Sara, and four-year-old son Hartley – were installed by July 1800; a third son, Derwent, was born in the house that September (the Coleridges' second son, Berkeley, had died in 1798); and daughter Sara followed in 1802.

Coleridge spent much of his first two years at Keswick helping Wordsworth prepare a new edition of the *Lyrical Ballads*, but found plenty of time to explore. His notebooks detail the walks he took, and in the summer of 1802 he embarked on a nine-day walking tour of the Lakes; see p.265 for more.

But despite his first flush of excitement at lakeland living, Coleridge wasn't happy. He'd been taking opium for years – if *Kubla Khan* didn't spring from an opium-induced dream no poem ever did – and was in poor health, suffering from rheumatism. What's more, his relationship with his wife was deteriorating – spurred by the fact that Coleridge had fallen hopelessly in love with Wordsworth's sister-in-law, Sara Hutchinson (his "Asra"), by now living at Grasmere. Indeed, his last great poem, *Dejection: an Ode*, was originally sent to Sara as a letter in April 1802.

In September 1803, Southey and his wife arrived to share Greta Hall. As the Southeys had just lost a child Coleridge hoped that the two sisters might comfort each other, but he was also looking for a way to escape so that he might regain his health and inspiration. He left for Malta in June 1804 (where for two years he was secretary to the Governor) and never lived with his family again. Southey assumed full responsibility for Coleridge's wife and children who remained at Greta Hall.

When Coleridge returned to the Lakes it was to live with the Wordsworths at Allan Bank in Grasmere, where he produced a short-lived political and literary periodical, *The Friend*, helped by Sara Hutchinson. When she left, to go and live with her brother in Wales, a depressed Coleridge – once more dependent on drugs – departed for London. Wordsworth, sick of having him moping around the house, had described Coleridge to someone else as an "absolute nuisance", which Coleridge came to hear about: after this breach in 1810, Coleridge only ever made perfunctory visits to the Lakes, avoiding Wordsworth (though the two were later reconciled). He died in London on July 25, 1834, and is buried in Highgate cemetery.

signposted path to Silver Howe (see box on p.94). **Samuel Taylor Coleridge** (see box above) was a guest here for almost two years, producing his literary and political periodical, *The Friend*, from a room in the house while sinking ever further into drug-induced decline. Later, Canon Rawnsley of the National Trust (see p.152) owned the house; he left it to the Trust on his death.

The only other place to visit in Grasmere is the **Heaton Cooper Studio**, opposite the green (Mon–Sat 9am–6pm, Sun noon–6pm; winter closes at 5pm; ☎015394/35280, ⊛www.heatoncooper.co.uk). It's a showcase for the works of one of the Lakes' most durable and talented artistic families, headed by the landscapes and village scenes of Alfred Heaton Cooper (1864–1929). Cooper became a well-known illustrator of guidebooks, especially in the first two decades of the twentieth century, and was succeeded in this by his son, William Heaton Cooper (1903–95), who climbed with the pioneering lakeland mountaineers. William produced paintings and sketches for four topographical Lake District guidebooks and then virtually ensured a dynastic succession by marrying the sculptress Ophelia Gordon Bell. Examples of all their work are on show in the gallery, together with those of a rake of contemporary Heaton Coopers – grandson Julian Cooper is the most notable, a climber-artist who produces huge oil paintings of the world's more remote locations.

If you're in the village in summer, you'll be able to see more art at **Grasmere Hall**, up Broadgate from the green, which hosts the annual exhibition of the **Lake Artists Society** (ⓌԜ www.lakeartists.org.uk). The society was founded in 1904 by local writer and artist W.G. Collingwood (see p.122) and its summer exhibition – first held in Coniston, subsequently in Grasmere – has been a lakeland fixture every year since. The work displayed is varied, but the society's members are mostly resident in, and take their inspiration from, Cumbria and the Lake District.

The lake and surrounding fells

It's a ten-minute walk from the centre down Redbank Road to the western side of the fell-fringed **lake** itself. You can rent a rowboat at the *Faeryland Tea Garden* (March–Oct daily 10am–6pm) by the landing stage – and take a picnic out to the wooded islet in the middle of the lake – or continue walking the mile to the southern reaches where **Loughrigg Terrace** sits under the crags of Loughrigg Fell (look for a track off the road through Redbank Woods, signposted "Loughrigg Terrace and YHA"). From the terrace there are tremendous views back up the lake and across the broad valley, culminating in the pass of Dunmail Raise.

Wordsworth composed most of his poetry during long rambles around the lake and up in the surrounding fells, and – clutching a volume of his collected verse – it's still possible to track down the sources of his inspiration. On the east side of the A591, for example, a path rises to the "tumultuous brook" of **Greenhead Gill**, whose surroundings formed the backdrop to the masterful early lyric poem *Michael* (1800), a moving tale of a shepherd abandoned by his wayward son. However, it's **Easedale** and its tarn (northwest of the village) that conjures the most resonant images. The first version of Wordsworth's autobiographical work, *The Prelude*, was partly composed after long hours tramping up and down the valley, while the tragic deaths of George and Sarah Green of Easedale – who died in a blizzard, leaving behind six children – prompted a memorial poem. ("Who weeps for strangers? / Many wept for George and Sarah Green; / Wept for that pair's unhappy fate, / Whose graves may here be seen.") The Wordsworths even took into care one of the orphans, a story exhaustively chronicled by De Quincey (in *Recollections of the Lakes and the Lake Poets*).

A brisk hike (follow Easedale Rd, past the youth hostels), up the tumbling, fern-clad, Sourmilk Gill to **Easedale Tarn** and back, takes around two hours – there's lakeland ice cream available from the *Oak Lodge* B&B teashop (closed mid-Sept to Easter), opposite the bridge across Easedale Beck at the start of the path, or wander up the drive to *Lancrigg Vegetarian Country House Hotel* (see "Accommodation", below), which offers light lunches and afternoon tea for walkers. You also come this way, up Easedale Road, to climb Grasmere's most celebrated peak, **Helm Crag** (1299ft), which takes about an hour from the village – see the box overleaf for route details.

Grasmere makes a good base for a wide selection of walks, from lazy round-the-lake rambles to full-on day-hikes requiring a bit of experience. A decent cross-section is detailed below, while note that you can also walk the Fairfield Horseshoe circuit (see p.76) clockwise from nearby Rydal.

Around Grasmere and Rydal Water

This is an easy circuit (4 miles; 2hr) that skirts the lake and Loughrigg Fell. From Loughrigg Terrace, the route heads east above **Rydal Water**, passing the dripping maw of Rydal Caves, a disused slate quarry (seen in Ken Russell's *The Lair of the White Worm*), before crossing the A591 to Rydal Mount. Above the house the **"Coffin Trail" bridleway** runs back high above the northern shore of Rydal Water, via **White Moss Tarn** (look out for butterflies), and emerges at Dove Cottage.

Loughrigg Fell

There are all sorts of possible ascents of **Loughrigg Fell** (1101ft) – and it's also easily climbed from Ambleside – but the simplest ascent is straight up the hillside from Loughrigg Terrace: the views are fantastic. A six-mile circuit from the terrace, over the undulating top to Ambleside and then back along the lower slopes via Rydal, takes three to four hours.

Silver Howe

The best direct climb from the village is up to the top of **Silver Howe** (1292ft), above the west side of the lake, from where the views take in the Langdale Pikes, Helvellyn and High Street. The easiest signposted route up from the village passes Allan Bank – it's a two-hour walk, climbing to the summit and then circling round via Dow Bank and down to the lakeside road, emerging just outside the village opposite the *Faeryland* tea garden and boat-rental place.

Helm Crag and High Raise

A reasonably tough high-level circuit to the west of Grasmere (10 miles; 6hr) starts with the stiff climb up to **Helm Crag** (1299ft) – follow the signs from the end of Easedale Road – whose distinctive summit crags are known as The Lion and The Lamb, and have thrilled visitors since Wordsworth's day. An undulating ridge walk then runs west to Greenup Edge, and up to **High Raise** (2500ft), popularly regarded as the Lake District's most centrally sited fell. Stay a while for the magnificent views from the summit (marked on maps as High White Stones), before turning back for Grasmere via **Sergeant Man** (2414ft) and then descending past Easedale Tarn.

See Basics, p.40, for general walking advice in the Lakes; recommended maps are detailed on p.27.

Practicalities

Grasmere lies west of the main A591 (Ambleside–Keswick road), with its centre just a few hundred yards down the B5287, which winds through the village. It is served by **buses** #555/556 (between Kendal and Keswick) and the #599 (from Bowness, Windermere and Ambleside), both of which stop on the village green. A **Lakes Day Rider ticket** (£5.75) allows unlimited stops on the return journey between Bowness and Grasmere, allowing you to visit the Wordsworth houses as a day-trip. The **National Park Information Centre** (April–Oct daily 9.30am–5.30pm; Nov–March Fri–Sun 10am–3.30pm, though hours may vary; ☎015394/35245) is five minutes' walk away down

Langdale Road, next to the main **car park** on Redbank Road at the southern end of the village. There's a second car park on Stock Lane, on the east side as you come in from Dove Cottage.

Accommodation

Accommodation can be hard to come by here in summer and you should book well in advance for accommodation in any budget, especially the popular **youth hostels** and **backpackers' accommodation**. You'll be able to walk into Grasmere village and to Wordsworth's Dove Cottage from any of the recommended choices in and around Grasmere. If you stay out at Rydal, you'll be handily placed for the other Wordsworth house, Rydal Mount, though you'll need to drive or catch the bus to the village for food and other services. If the Grasmere hostels are full, try *Langdale High Close* (see p.105), the nearest alternative – though it's a good two miles south of the village. Grasmere has no campsite.

In Grasmere

Beck Allans College St ☏ 015394/35563, ⓦ www.beckallans.com. A quality B&B in a modern but traditionally built house in the centre – the more you pay, the larger the room, but all five are smartly furnished, well-equipped and boast baths. Riverside gardens, parking and self-catering apartments (including a handsome 1930s caravan) are also available, and you can use the pool at the *Wordsworth Hotel*. No credit cards. ❹

Gold Rill Red Bank Rd ☏ 015394/35486, ⓦ www.gold-rill.com. Lakeside accommodation is at a premium in Grasmere, so the *Gold Rill* is a sought-after spot – rooms have lake or fell views, and there are pretty lakeside gardens with a small heated outdoor pool surrounded by deck chairs. A fire in the lounges keeps it nice and snug in winter. Special five-night breaks offer significant discounts. Dinner is included in the room rate. Parking. Closed two weeks in Jan. ❼

Grasmere Broadgate ☏ 015394/35277, ⓦ www.grasmerehotel.co.uk. Elegant Victorian villa, all of whose rooms are named after lakeland literary figures. Refurbishment has brightened the rooms, with fresh flowers and chocolates provided in each, while several of the larger ones have four-posters and baths (as well as showers). A good four-course dinner (included in the price) is served in the ornate dining room, overlooking the gardens and River Rothay. Parking. Closed Jan. ❼

Harwood Red Lion Sq ☏ 015394/35248, ⓦ www.harwoodhotel.co.uk. Eight smallish rooms in a genial, non-smoking, family-run hotel. A makeover had added contemporary colours, co-ordinated furniture and pine or brass bedsteads, while rooms (most with baths) have varied village outlooks. There's a two-night minimum stay at weekends; low-season rates drop a category. ❹

How Beck Broadgate ☏ 015394/35732, ⓔ trevor.eastes@btinternet.com. Two rooms available in this agreeable, non-smoking, family house on the outskirts of the village with a sun lounge that overlooks the garden and fells. It's a great choice for vegetarians – full veggie breakfast (with home-made bread and preserves) and fruit in the room. ❸

How Foot Lodge Town End ☏ 015394/35366, ⓦ www.howfoot.co.uk. The position – a few yards from Dove Cottage – couldn't be better for Wordsworth groupies. The light-filled Victorian villa has six spacious non-smoking rooms (one with its own sun lounge), grand lounge and well-kept gardens. Guests get a discount on dinner at nearby *Villa Colombina*. Parking. Closed Jan. No American Express. ❹

Red Lion Red Lion Sq ☏ 015394/35456, ⓦ www.hotelslakedistrict.com. Sympathetically renovated eighteenth-century coaching inn, with elegance over the village and fells. Most of the attractively decorated rooms have jacuzzi-baths, and wet days are no hardship since there's a very nice indoor pool, plus steam, sauna and spa room, as well as restaurant, conservatory, lounge, bar and next-door pub. Off-season discounts drop the price a category. Parking. ❼

Swan Keswick Rd (A591), by Swan Lane ☏ 0870/400 8132, ⓦ www.macdonald-hotels.co.uk. On the main road, on the edge of the village, this former coaching inn rated a mention in Wordsworth's *The Waggoner* and remodelling hasn't robbed the public rooms at least of their essential eighteenth-century character. Good restaurant (serving lakeland specialities) and a bar. Rates on weekdays are a category lower. Parking. ❽

Wordsworth College St ☏ 015394/35592, ⓦ www.grasmere-hotels.co.uk/wordsworth. The plum hotel choice in the village itself – relaxed, attractive and comfortable, with a heated pool, jacuzzi and gym, gorgeous conservatory and terrace, and good lunches in the Wordsworthian-styled bar (the *Dove & Olive Branch*). The food is also excellent in the *Prelude* restaurant, so D, B&B deals are worth considering. Otherwise, room prices vary according to the type of room, with some available at a category lower than the given rate. Parking. ⑥

Around Grasmere

Banerigg House 1 mile south on A591 ☎015394/35204. A detached lakeside property a 15min walk from the village, past Dove Cottage. It's a non-smoking house, with six doubles and one single – mostly en suite with lake views (though no TVs) – plus drying facilities, good breakfasts and the use of a boat. Parking. No credit cards. ③

Lancrigg Vegetarian Country House Easedale Rd ☎015394/35317, ⓦwww.lancrigg.co.uk. A relaxed gourmet vegetarian retreat half a mile northwest of Grasmere, occupying a secluded country house with connections with Wordsworth (he was a regular visitor and helped in its renovation) and Arctic explorer Sir John Richardson (he owned it at one stage). The house is a beauty, with traditional round lakeland chimneys, trimmed lawns and wildlife-filled woods. A dozen variously sized rooms range from the former library (now with a lace-draped four-poster, free-standing clawfoot bath and private door into the garden) to a one-up, one-down suite; other rooms have whirlpool baths and small sitting areas, with the cheapest option being a room in the cottage annexe in the grounds. An inventive four-course dinner is included in the price (organic wines and beers available), while shiatsu, reiki, therapeutic massage and spiritual healing treatments are available. Parking. ⑧

Nab Cottage 2 miles southeast on A591, Rydal ☎015394/35311, ⓦwww.rydalwater.com. Both De Quincey and Hartley Coleridge lived in this gorgeous seventeenth-century oak-beamed farmhouse facing Rydal Water. It's now a language school, but offers B&B in seven rooms (four en-suite) when space is available – usually *not* between June and September, but call to check. Light suppers and evening meals available on request (£8–15). Parking. No American Express. ③

Oak Lodge Easedale Rd ☎015394/35527, ⓦwww.oaklodge-grasmere.co.uk. Three traditionally furnished B&B rooms in a stone cottage half a mile northwest of town, just by the footpath to Easedale Tarn. It's extremely handy for local walks, with Helm Crag, Silver Howe and the tarn all close by, and from Easter until mid-September the

tea shop here dispenses life-saving lakeland ice cream and cups of tea to thirsty hikers. Parking. No credit cards. ③

White Moss House Rydal Water ☎015394/35295, ⓦwww.whitemoss.com. Look for the sign at the northern end of Rydal Water for the driveway to this secluded early eighteenth-century, ivy-clad house. Longtime owners, the Dixons, preside over five individually styled, antique-filled rooms in the main house (two share a lounge and terrace) and two more in a cottage-suite with lake views. The splendid five-course dinner (included in the room rate, though not available Sunday evening) starts with drinks on the terrace, followed by well-regarded regional and English dishes – the wine list is exemplary. Parking. Closed Dec & Jan. ⑧

Youth hostels and backpackers' accommodation

Butharlyp Howe YHA Easedale Rd ☎0870/770 5836, ⓔgrasmere@yha.org.uk. Closest of the hostels to the centre, this converted Victorian house is just five minutes north of the green. There are modern bedrooms, plentiful showers, carpeting and decent furniture throughout, and a dining room overlooking grassy gardens. There's also a children's play area and outdoor games available. Five of the rooms are available as twins. Reception open all day; evening meal served. Nov–Feb open Fri & Sat only. Dorm beds £14.

Grasmere Independent Hostel Broadrayne Farm, A591 ☎015394/35055, ⓦwww.grasmerehostel .co.uk. Half a mile north of the village (past the *Traveller's Rest* pub), Grasmere's stylishly presented backpackers' hostel has 24 beds, all in small, carpeted en-suite rooms – one available as a twin/family room with private bathroom when space allows. There's an impressively equipped kitchen, plus laundry and drying facilities, bike and luggage storage, even a sauna. Ask advice about local walks, or lounge in the comfortable common room, whose large circular window overlooks the valley. Three self-catering cottages also available (by the week) on the farm, each sleeping between two and five people. Reception open all day. Dorm beds £14.50.

Thorney How ☎0870/770 5836, ⓔgrasmere@yha.org.uk. Grasmere's smaller, simpler YHA hostel is further out of the village, a characterful (ie largely unmodernized) former farmhouse just under a mile along the road past *Butharlyp Howe*: look for the signposted right turn. The road's unlit so bring a torch. Reception opens at 5pm; evening meal served. Closed Sun & Mon, and Nov–Feb. No credit cards. Dorm beds £11.

Eating and drinking

There are plenty of **tearooms and cafés** in Grasmere catering for the mass of tourists that descends every day; the best are picked out below. Good independent **restaurants** are rather thinner on the ground, though there's enough choice to ring the changes over a few days' stay. The most glamorous meals are served in the restaurant of the *Wordsworth Hotel* in the centre or in one of the country-house hotels on the village outskirts. Non-residents are welcome, though you're advised to book well in advance (especially for *Lancrigg Vegetarian* and *White Moss House*). The hotels soak up most of the bar trade as well – the only real **pub** is that attached to the *Red Lion* in the centre, or you can walk out to the *Traveller's Rest* on the A591.

Cafés and restaurants

Baldry's Red Lion Sq ☏ 015394/35301. Tearoom decked out in Provençal colours, serving filled baguettes, homemade cakes (try the sticky gingerbread), scones, tarts and quiche. Daytime only; closed Thurs (and one other day Dec–Feb). Inexpensive.

Jumble Room Langdale Rd ☏ 015394/35188. Funky café-restaurant, festooned with original art, and with an organic touch to its ethnically diverse menu. During the day, come for a slab of gingerbread and fair-trade coffee, or a light lunch; at night there's the likes of Tuscan crostini, chicken and prawn curry, Herdwick lamb kofta or haddock in organic beer batter. Closed Mon & Tues, and occasional other days in winter. Lunch Moderate, Dinner Expensive.

Miller Howe Café Red Lion Sq ☏ 015394/35234. When the sun shines, there's no better spot than the outdoor tables of this refined café overlooking the green. On the menu – crusty breakfast rolls, inventive sandwiches, baked potatoes and a range of tempting mains (baked sausage with apple sauce, salmon with wine and prawn sauce). Daytime only. Moderate.

Newby's Deli and Bakery Red Lion Sq, under the *Harwood* ☏ 015394/35248. Stuffed sandwiches, baguettes and ciabatta to take away, plus a reasonable choice of deli supplies (and Kendal Mintcake) – great for stocking up your picnic hamper. The coffee house at the rear of the deli goes in for toasted paninis, local cheese-and-chutney platters, and home-made pies and quiches. Daytime only. Inexpensive.

Rowan Tree Church Bridge, Stock Lane ☏ 015394/35528. Mainstream vegetarian dining, enhanced by its outdoor terrace in a gorgeous position on a lazy bend in the river, opposite the church. The daytime tearoom menu gives way to Mediterranean-style dining at night, including pizza and pasta choices. Moderate.

Villa Colombina Town End ☏ 015394/35268. The old *Dove Cottage Tearooms* now sports an authentic Italian menu, but it's the same informal set-up – hardwood floors and terracotta-coloured walls, with sofas on the upper gallery. Open throughout the day, and then serving dinner (6–9pm; reservations recommended), with a menu of pizzas, pastas, steak and chicken, plus wild mushroom and red pepper risotto and other specials. Closed Jan, and other days in winter; call for details. Moderate.

Pubs

Lamb Inn Red Lion Sq ☏ 015394/35456. The public bar of the *Red Lion* is the best choice in Grasmere for a drink, and consequently is packed to the rafters at weekends. Theakston's and guest beers on tap, and a queue of local Fast Eddies waiting to drub you at pool.

Traveller's Rest Half a mile north on the A591 ☏ 015394/35604. A popular place for real ales and bar meals, though the thundering main road does the pub's outdoor tables no favours. Big breakfasts set you up for the day, while there's a warming log fire in winter for anyone just off the fells.

Listings

Banks and exchange There's no bank in Grasmere, though there is an ATM inside the post office (where you can also exchange travellers' cheques).

Bike rental The nearest bike-rental outlets are in Ambleside.

Emergencies The nearest doctors' surgery is at Ambleside Health Centre (Rydal Rd ☏ 015394 /32693), the nearest hospital is in Keswick (Keswick Cottage Hospital, Crosthwaite Rd; ☏ 017687/72012).

Laundry Apart from the facilities at the hostels and backpackers', the nearest laundry is in Ambleside.

Outdoors stores Outdoor equipment and walking gear from Outdoor World (Red Lion Sq) and Summitreks (College St).
Pharmacy Grasmere Pharmacy, 1 Oak Bank, Broadgate ☎ 015394/35553.

Post office Red Lion Sq (April–Sept Mon–Fri 9am–5.30pm, Sat 9am–12.30pm; Oct–March Mon–Wed & Fri 9am–12.30pm & 1.30–5.30pm, Thurs & Sat 9am–12.30pm; ☎ 015394/35261).
Taxis Grasmere Taxis ☎ 015394/35506.

Dove Cottage

On the southeastern outskirts of Grasmere village, in the former hamlet of Town End, stands **Dove Cottage** (daily 9.30am–5.30pm; closed mid-Jan to mid-Feb; £5.95, museum only £4, though prices may increase; ☎ 015394/35544, ⊛ www.wordsworth.org.uk), home to William and Dorothy Wordsworth from 1799 to 1808 and where Wordsworth wrote some of his best poetry. The house stands just off the A591 and buses #555/556 and #599 stop close by on the main road.

Wordsworth first saw the house in November 1799 while on a walking tour with his friend Samuel Taylor Coleridge, with whom he had published *Lyrical Ballads* the previous year. Keen for a base in the Lakes, Wordsworth negotiated a rent of £8 a year for what had originally been an inn called the *Dove & Olive-Bough*; he and his sister moved in just before Christmas of that year. It was a simple stone house with a slate roof – Wordsworth at this time was far from financially secure – where the poet could live by his guiding principle of "plain living but high thinking". But its main recommendation as far as Wordsworth was concerned was one that is no longer obvious: the views he had enjoyed to the lake and fells were lost when new housing was erected in front of Dove Cottage in the 1860s. When the Wordsworths left in 1808, their friend Thomas De Quincey took over the lease and Dove Cottage is as much a monument to his happiest days in Grasmere (he married from here) as it is to Wordsworth's plain living; the house has been open to the public since 1917.

The **cottage** forms part of a complex administered by the Wordsworth Trust, whose guides, bursting with anecdotes, lead you around the rooms, little changed now but for the addition of electricity and internal plumbing. There's precious little space and and – downstairs, at least – very little natural light: belching tallow candles would have provided the only illumination. William, not wanting to be bothered by questions of a domestic nature, kept to the lighter, upper rooms or disappeared off on long walks to compose his poetry. De Quincey later reckoned that Wordsworth had walked 175,000 to 180,000 miles in the course of his poetry writing – "a mode of exertion which, to him, stood in the stead of wine, spirits, and all other stimulants whatsoever to the animal spirits". Wordsworth married in 1802 and his new wife, Mary Hutchinson, came to live here, necessitating a change of bedrooms for everyone; three of their five children were later born in the cottage (John in 1803, Dora in 1804 and Thomas in 1806). Sister Dorothy kept a detailed journal of daily life and the endless comings and goings of visitors, notably Coleridge and his brother-in-law Southey, but also Walter Scott, William Hazlitt and, once he'd plucked up the nerve to introduce himself, Thomas De Quincey (see box below). The garden behind the cottage was tamed, while William chopped wood for the fire, planted runner beans, built a summerhouse and hid the disliked cottage whitewash behind a train of roses and honeysuckle. And with all this going on, Wordsworth produced a series of odes, lyric poems and sonnets that he would never better, relying on Dorothy and Mary to make copies in their painstaking handwriting. After eight years at Dove

Cottage it became clear that the Wordsworths had outgrown their home and, reluctantly, the family moved to a larger, new house in Grasmere called Allan Bank – Wordsworth had watched it being built and referred to it as a "temple of abomination". They were never as happy there, or in the Old Rectory to which they later relocated, and it wasn't until 1813 and the move to Rydal Mount that the Wordsworths regained the sense of peace they had felt at Dove Cottage.

Thomas De Quincey in the Lakes

The direct object of my own residence at the lakes was the society of Mr Wordsworth.

Thomas De Quincey, *Recollections of the Lakes and the Lake Poets.*

The young **Thomas De Quincey** (1785–1859) was one of the first to fully appreciate the revolutionary nature of Wordsworth's and Coleridge's collaborative *Lyrical Ballads*, and as a student at Oxford in 1803 he had already written to Wordsworth praising his "genius" and hoping for his friendship. In reply, Wordsworth politely invited him to visit if he was ever in the area. It took De Quincey four years (and two abortive visits, abandoned out of shyness) to contrive a meeting, eventually through the auspices of Coleridge, a mutual friend.

De Quincey first came to Dove Cottage in November 1807 to meet his hero, trembling at the thought: the meeting is recorded in one of the more self-effacing chapters of his *Recollections*. When the Wordsworths moved to Allan Bank the following year, De Quincey – by now a favourite with the Wordsworth children – went too, staying several months. His small private income enabled him to take over Dove Cottage in February 1809, which he filled full of books (in contrast to Wordsworth, who had very few). He also demolished the summerhouse and made other changes in the garden which annoyed the Wordsworths, while the relationship further cooled after 1812 following the deaths of young Catherine and Thomas Wordsworth. De Quincey was particularly badly affected by the loss of Catherine, his "sole companion", and for two months after her death passed each night stretched out on her grave in Grasmere churchyard.

The truth is, De Quincey wasn't a well man. Since his university days, he had been in the habit of taking opium in the form of laudanum (i.e. dissolved in alcohol), and at Dove Cottage he was taking huge, addictive doses – the amount of alcohol alone would have been debilitating enough. He closeted himself away in the cottage for days at a time, complaining that Wordsworth was spoiling the books he borrowed from him, and began an affair with Margaret (Peggy) Simpson of nearby Nab Cottage, a local farmer's daughter who bore him an illegitimate child. The drug-taking was bad enough for the upright, snobbish Wordsworths, but when De Quincey married Peggy in 1817 (at St Oswald's Church, Grasmere) any intimate relationship was at an end.

De Quincey was never suited to regular employment and following a disastrous stint as editor of the *Westmorland Gazette* he became a freelance critic and essayist for various literary periodicals. His *Confessions of an English Opium-Eater* (1821) first appeared in the *London Magazine* and made his name, and he had sufficient resources to take on another house (Fox Ghyll, south of Rydal) for his growing family (he eventually had eight children), retaining Dove Cottage as a library. Growing success meant De Quincey spent less and less time in the Lakes, giving up Fox Ghyll in 1825 and finally abandoning Dove Cottage in 1830 to move to Edinburgh, where he lived for the rest of his life. It was only between 1834 and 1839 – long after he'd left the area – that De Quincey started writing his Lake "recollections", offending Wordsworth all over again.

Most of the furniture in the cottage belonged to the Wordsworths, while in the **upper rooms** are displayed a battered suitcase, a pair of William's ice skates and Dorothy's sewing box, among other possessions. There are surprisingly few reminders of De Quincey's long tenancy, save a pair of opium scales, yet he lived here far longer than did the Wordsworths. In the adjacent **museum** there's much to be learned about Wordsworth's life and times. It's full of paintings, portraits, original manuscripts (including that of "Daffodils"), pages from Dorothy's journals and more memorabilia, most poignantly Mary's wedding ring. The museum ticket allows entry to any special exhibitions currently running (see below), while in good weather the **garden** is open for visits as well.

Wide-ranging as the museum is, it can only present a fraction of the complete collection held by the Wordsworth Trust, which amounts to some 70,000 manuscripts, books, letters, portraits and other items. These are stored in the adjacent **Jerwood Centre**, a £3-million facility opened in late 2004, which is accessible to scholars and researchers. The Rotunda here acts as an "interpretation space", hosting various related displays and events, while Dove Cottage is the headquarters of the **Centre for British Romanticism**, which together with the Wordsworth Trust sponsors special annual exhibitions, residential conferences and summer poetry readings attracting some top names – call for details or check the website.

Rydal Mount

Following the deaths of their young children Catherine and Thomas in 1812, the Wordsworths couldn't bear to continue living in Grasmere's Old Rectory. In May 1813 they moved a couple of miles southeast of the village to the hamlet of Rydal (see opposite), little more than a couple of isolated cottages and farms set back from the eastern end of Rydal Water. Here William rented Rydal Mount from the Flemings of nearby Rydal Hall, where he remained until his death in 1850. Buses #555/556 and #599 stop on the A591 at Rydal Church, 200 yards from the house.

Rydal Mount (March–Oct daily 9.30am–5pm; Nov–Feb Mon & Wed–Sun 10am–4pm; closed last 3 weeks in Jan; £4.50, garden only £2; ☎015394/33002, ⓦ www.rydalmount.co.uk) is a fair-sized family home, a much-improved-upon Tudor cottage set in its own grounds, and reflects Wordsworth's change in circumstances. At Dove Cottage he'd been a largely unknown poet of straitened means, but by 1813 he'd written several of his greatest works (though not all had yet been published) and was already being visited by literary acolytes. More importantly, he'd been appointed Westmorland's Distributor of Stamps, a salaried position which allowed him to take up the rent of a comfortable family house. Wordsworth, Mary, the three surviving children (John, aged 10; Dora, 9; and William, 3) and Dorothy arrived, plus his wife's sister Sara Hutchinson, by now living with the family. Later the household also contained a clerk, a couple of maids and a gardener. Dances and dinners were held, the widowed Queen Adelaide visited, and carriage-loads of friends and sightseers came to call – a far cry from the "plain living" back at Dove Cottage.

Wordsworth only ever rented the property, but the house is now owned by descendants of the poet, who have opened it to visitors since 1970. It's a much less claustrophobic experience than visiting Dove Cottage and you're free to wander around what is still essentially a family home – summer concerts feature poetry readings by Wordsworth family members, and there are recent family pictures on the sideboard alongside more familiar portraits of the poet and his circle. In the light-filled **drawing room** and **library** (two rooms in Wordsworth's day) you'll find the only known portrait of Dorothy, as an old lady of 62, and also Mary's favourite portrait of Wordsworth, completed in 1844 by the American portraitist Henry Inman. Memorabilia abounds: Wordsworth's black-leather sofa, his ink-stand and despatch box, a brooch of Dorothy's and, upstairs in the attic, their beloved brother John's sword (recovered from the shipwreck in which he drowned) and the poet's own encyclopedia and prayer book. **William and Mary's bedroom** has a lovely view, with Windermere a splash in the distance; in daughter **Dora's room** hangs a portrait of Edward Quillinan, her Irish dragoon, whom she married in 1841, much against Wordsworth's will. The couple spent their honeymoon at Rydal Mount, while the delicate Dora – often ill and eventually a victim of tuberculosis – later came home to die in the house in 1847. The other bedroom was Dorothy's, to which she was virtually confined for the last two decades of her life, suffering greatly from what was thought to be a debilitating mental illness – an underactive thyroid is the current opinion. She died at Rydal Mount in 1855; Mary died there in 1859.

Many people's favourite part of Rydal Mount is the four-and-a-half-acre **garden**, largely shaped by Wordsworth who fancied himself a gardener. He planted the flowering shrubs, put in the terraces (where he used to declaim his poetry) and erected a little rustic summerhouse (for jotting down lyrics), from which there are fine views of Rydal Water. Lining the lawns and surrounding the rock pools are rhododendrons and azaleas, maples, beeches and pines. If you're looking for an unusual souvenir, head for the Rydal Mount **shop**, which sells fell-walking sticks fashioned from the wood found in the garden.

Rydal and Rydal Water

RYDAL, as the name suggests, sits at the foot of its own valley, whose beck empties into the River Rothay. As a hamlet, it's hardly any bigger than it was in Wordsworth's day; though, having seen the poet's house of Rydal Mount, you may as well wander back down the road for the other local sights – namely Rydal's lake, church and hall and, under a mile west, Nab Cottage, the former home of Hartley Coleridge.

There was no local church in Rydal until **St Mary's** (at the foot of Rydal Mount on the main A591) was built in 1824 – Wordsworth was churchwarden here for a year in the 1830s. A swing gate by the church entrance leads into **Dora's Field** (always open; free; NT), a plot of land bought by Wordsworth when he thought he might have to leave Rydal Mount because the owners, the Flemings, wanted it back. Wordsworth planned to build a house here instead, but when the Flemings changed their minds, he gave the land to his daughter. On Dora's death in 1847, the heartbroken Wordsworths planted the hillsides with daffodils.

Across from the church, a driveway leads to **Rydal Hall**, erstwhile home of the Flemings. The hall has a sixteenth-century kernel but was considerably renovated during Victorian times; it's now a residential conference centre. The formal gardens to the front (open dawn to dusk; donation requested) were laid out by Thomas Mawson on classical lines in 1909 and there are captivating views of Rydal Water from the terrace. Around the back of the hall, a summer **tearoom** (daily 11am–5.30pm) has picnic tables from where you can watch Rydal Beck tumble under a moss-covered packhorse bridge. There's a series of small falls a few hundred yards up Rydal Beck, while a footpath runs south through the estate grounds to join the A591 road just outside Ambleside.

Few people bother much with **Rydal Water**, one of the region's smallest lakes at under three-quarters of a mile long and only fifty feet deep in parts. It's handsome enough – though it was considerably quieter before the A591 traced its northern shore – and there's a nice walk along the southern shore, back to Grasmere past Rydal Caves. For the best views of the water itself, follow the original route to Grasmere, along the "**Coffin Trail**", which starts directly behind Rydal Mount and runs west under the craggy heights of Nab Scar (1450ft). Medieval coffin bearers en route to St Oswald's would haul their melancholy load along this trail, stopping to rest at intervals on the convenient flat stones.

Nab Cottage, less than a mile west of Rydal on the A591, overlooks Rydal Water. This was the family home of Margaret Simpson before she married Thomas De Quincey; and it was rented much later by the sometime journalist and poet Hartley Coleridge, a Wordsworth family favourite ("O blessed vision! happy child!") despite his trying ways. Abandoned by his father and effectively brought up in Robert Southey's Keswick household (see p.142), Hartley was a frail, precocious child who took to the demon drink and failed to live up to his early promise. But Wordsworth always retained a soft spot for him and when Hartley died in Nab Cottage in 1849 Wordsworth picked out a plot for him in Grasmere churchyard. The cottage is now a language school, with B&B usually available outside the summer months (see p.96).

Skelwith Bridge and Little Langdale

Langdale is a byword for some of the region's most stunning peaks, views and hikes, and the route there starts at **SKELWITH BRIDGE**, around three miles south of Grasmere and the same distance west of Ambleside. Here, a cluster of buildings huddles by the bridge over the River Brathay, prime among them **Touchstone Interiors** (daily 10am–6pm; ☎015394/34711, Ⓦwww.touchstoneinteriors.com), a contemporary design studio specializing in, among other things, items made from Westmorland green slate. There's terrace seating here outside *Chesters Café By The River* (daily 10am–5.30pm; ☎015394/32553), which serves lunch from noon until 3pm and makes excellent cakes, while the *Skelwith Bridge Hotel*, on the main road, has restaurant meals and a public bar. **Bus** #505 from Ambleside or Coniston stops at Skelwith Bridge, as does the #516 "Langdale Rambler" between Ambleside and the *Old Dungeon Ghyll* in Great Langdale.

From the bridge, there's a riverside stroll along a signposted footpath to Elterwater, a mile away, passing the fairly unimpressive gush that is **Skelwith Force**. For a finer waterfall altogether follow the hilly footpath west of Skelwith Bridge (it starts on the south side of the river) the mile or so to **Colwith Force**, hidden in the woods off the minor road to Elterwater. A circuit taking in both falls and Elterwater won't take more than a couple of hours. There's another local walk from Skelwith, north through Neaum Woods to pretty **Loughrigg Tarn**, where there's basic **camping** (toilets and a cold tap) at Tarn Foot Farm on the south side.

Heading west, a very narrow minor road off the A593 twists into **Little Langdale**, a bucolic counterweight to the dramatics of Great Langdale to the north. The bedrooms at the *Three Shires Inn* (☎015394/37215,

△ Rydal Water

Ⓦwww.threeshiresinn.co.uk; Ⓞ), about a mile west of Colwith Force, make the most of the valley views, and the inn is the traditional starting point for local walks, notably the stroll down to the old packhorse crossing of Slater Bridge and to Little Langdale Tarn. A longer route – shadowed by a very minor road – runs north over **Lingmoor Fell** (1530ft) via **Blea Tarn** (where there's parking) into Great Langdale – the eight-mile circuit, returning to the *Three Shires Inn* via Elterwater, takes around four hours. The name of the inn, incidentally, is a reference to the fact that it stands near the meeting point of the old counties of Cumberland, Westmorland and Lancashire. West from Little Langdale, the ever-narrower, ever-hairier road climbs to the dramatic **Wrynose Pass** (1270ft), before dropping down to Cockley Beck for the Duddon Valley or on to the Hardknott Pass.

Elterwater and Chapel Stile

ELTERWATER village lies half a mile northwest of its water, named by the Norse for the swans that still glide upon its surface. It's one of the more idyllic lakeland beauty spots, with its riverside setting, aged inn, spreading maple tree and aimless sheep getting among the sunbathers on the pocket-sized green. Historically, the village made its living from farming, quarrying and lace-making, though these days it's almost entirely devoted to the passing tourist trade: only around a quarter of the houses here are lived in, the rest are used as holiday cottages. There are no sights here, as such, just the quiet comings and goings of a country hamlet, albeit one inundated on fine summer days and bank holidays with vehicles disgorging hikers. Before you head off, you might spare some time first for **Judy Boyes' Studio** (Easter–Oct Wed–Sat 10am–5pm; Nov & Dec Thurs–Sat 10am–4pm; ℡07071/780533, Ⓦwww.judyboyes.co.uk; free), near the inn, which displays a changing exhibition of the artist's locally inspired watercolours.

Elterwater sees its fair share of Langdale-bound hikers – not least because of the two local youth hostels – and numerous fell or riverside walks start straight from the village. Everyone should make the easy half-mile stroll northwest up the river – through the slate-quarry workings, still in use after over 150 years – to **CHAPEL STILE**, where a simple quarrymen's chapel sits beneath the crags. There's a pub and café for those that need a target and, suitably refreshed, you can push on from Chapel Stile; either on the level walk alongside the beck into the lower reaches of Langdale or up through the crags to the north and across Silver Howe (see box on p.94) to Grasmere.

Practicalities

The #516 "Langdale Rambler" **bus** stops by Elterwater village green. There's **parking** on the common outside the village and more limited space close to the bridge in the centre. Overnight **accommodation** is relatively thin on the ground, though there are plenty of **self-catering cottages** available by the week (sometimes less during winter); contact the Langdale Estate (see below) or Wheelwright's (℡015394/37635, Ⓦwww.wheelwrights.com), who should be able to fix you up with something in the vicinity. The **village shop** and **post office**, Maple Tree Corner (open daily), opposite the inn, has basic grocery supplies and can sell you a newspaper or a map. In nearby Chapel Stile, the **Langdale Co-operative** (open daily), in business since 1884, has everything else – from cornflakes to hiking boots.

Hotels

Britannia Inn Elterwater ☎015394/37210, ⓦwww.britinn.co.uk. The hugely popular pub on Elterwater's green has nine rooms available, and while not overly spacious (the inn is over 500 years old) they are comfortable following refurbishment – one or two may still be on the old-fashioned side, but are priced a few pounds cheaper (as are midweek stays). It's known for its wide range of beers and good-value food – from homemade pies, lamb shanks and Cumberland sausage to tuna steaks and vegetarian specials – served either in the dining room (booking advised) or cosy front bar. The simple back room bar is where the hikers congregate, while the merest hint of good weather fills the outdoor tables on the slate-covered terrace. Two-night minimum stay at weekends. Parking. ⑥

Eltermere Country House Elterwater ☎015394/37207, ⓦwww.eltermere.co.uk. An imposing country house just a little way past the *Elterwater YHA* with grounds stretching down to the lake. Its seventeenth-century origins are well hidden, though some of the eighteen rooms still sport exposed oak beams. Many also have uninterrupted lake views. If you're going to eat in the restaurant D, B&B rates (a category higher than those given) offer the best deal. Special deals are often available, even in summer. Parking. ⑥

Langdale Estate Elterwater ☎015394/37302, ⓦwww.langdale.co.uk. Spreading up the valley, north of the village, this luxurious complex blends in well with its surroundings. Set in the grounds of a former woollen mill and gunpowder works it contains a variety of very comfortable hotel rooms, well-equipped self-catering Scandinavian-style lodges, a superb pool, gym, games room, squash court, two restaurants and a café-bar – plus a pub within walking distance. It's never anything less than pricey, though there are good off-season discounts and other special offers. Parking. ⑧

Youth hostels

Elterwater YHA ☎0870/770 5816, ⓔelterwater@yha.org.uk. A converted farmhouse and barn, just across the bridge from the pub, provides simple hostel facilities in two- to eight-bedded rooms. There's mountain-bike rental available, too, plus cycling weekends and other activities. Hostel parking is extremely limited and while you can unload here, you'll probably have to park overnight in the village car park. Reception opens at 5pm; evening meals are served. Open daily July, Aug & school/bank holiday periods, otherwise flexible opening – call to check availability. Dorm beds £11.

Langdale YHA High Close, Loughrigg, 1 mile northeast of Elterwater ☎0870/770 5908, ⓔlangdale@yha.org.uk (bookings through *Ambleside YHA*). This large Victorian mansion set in its own grounds sits high on the road over Red Bank to Grasmere. It's popular with schools and groups. Reception opens at 5pm; evening meal available. Closed Nov–Feb. Dorm beds £11.

Café

Brambles Langdale Co-operative, Chapel Stile ☎015394/37500. The store's upstairs café serves large breakfasts as well as filled rolls and picnic lunches for hikers (who can get their flasks filled with tea or coffee). Daytime only. Inexpensive.

Pub

Wainwrights Inn Chapel Stile ☎015394/38088. Welcoming slate-floored pub with local beers on tap and popular bar meals – the house speciality is braised lamb shanks, though there are plenty of other choices. The terrace outside is a good spot to rest weary feet.

Great Langdale

Beyond Chapel Stile you emerge into the wide curve of **Great Langdale**, flanked by some of the Lake District's most famous peaks – Crinkle Crags, Bowfell and the Langdale Pikes. It's a dramatic, yet sobering, valley, one of the few in the Lakes where you get a real sense of scale from the lie of the land. It's also one of the oldest occupied parts of the region, the evidence in the shape of Stone Age axes found in "factory" sites in the upper valley. A footpath from Elterwater (signposted as the Cumbria Way) runs up the valley to its head – eight miles from Ambleside – from where there are popular onward hiking routes over the passes to Wasdale and Borrowdale. Parking by the side of the B5343 road is discouraged, and drivers should make for either of the valley's main (signposted) car parks, depending on their target for the day.

Walks in Great Langdale

Walking in Great Langdale isn't necessarily an expeditionary undertaking, but you do need to be more aware than usual of time, weather conditions and your own ability before setting off on a hike. Once you leave the valley bottom there's nothing much that's simply a stroll – then again, of the classic routes picked out below, all save Jack's Rake are within the average walker's ability.

Pavey Ark

Behind Stickle Tarn stands the fearsome cliff-face of **Pavey Ark** (2297ft), which can actually be climbed relatively easily if you approach it up the grassy path to its rear (north). Gung-ho walkers make the more dramatic climb up **Jack's Rake**, which ascends the face right to left and is the hardest commonly used route in the Lake District – in parts it's effectively rock-climbing and requires a head for heights and steady nerves. An alternative climb, up Easy Gully (it isn't), starts from near the base. However you get up, count on it taking an hour from Stickle Tarn.

The Langdale Pikes

From the top of Pavey Ark it's a straightforward walk on to **Harrison Stickle** (2414ft), down to the stream forming the headwaters of Dungeon Ghyll and then slowly up to **Pike of Stickle** (2326ft). To make a long walk of it, aim then for **Stake Pass** to the northwest and return down the old Langdale packhorse route. You could of course walk the Pikes the other way round, finishing with a descent from Stickle Tarn. Either way, the walking is around seven miles and takes about five hours.

Pike o'Blisco

For a short(ish), sharp climb out of Langdale, **Pike o'Blisco** (2304ft) is a tempting target – you can see its summit cairn from the valley floor, and you'll be on the top in ninety minutes glorying in the views. The easiest route follows the path from the *Old Dungeon Ghyll* road-end, through Stool End farm, and then crosses Oxendale Beck to climb up via Brown Howe to Red Tarn (1hr) for the final push to the pike. Total walk is five miles, a three-hour round trip, but experienced hikers won't find it any problem to incorporate Pike o'Blisco in a full-day Crinkle Crags and Bowfell circuit (see below).

Crinkle Crags, Bowfell and Esk Pike

The orthodox route up to the distinctive **Crinkle Crags** (2816ft) – the name, as you'll see, is deserved – is via Oxendale and Red Tarn. From the summit, an exciting ridge walk north along the "crinkles" drops down to Three Tarns (from where there's a possible descent down The Band to Langdale) or you continue north instead up to the rocky, conical summit of **Bowfell** (2960ft) – one of Wainwright's half-dozen favourite fells. From Bowfell, descend via Ore Gap to **Angle Tarn**, and then back to the *Old Dungeon Ghyll* down Rossett Gill and Mickleden Beck. This is a nine-mile (6hr) circuit, though determined peak-baggers will also want to add **Esk Pike** (2903ft) to the route, after Bowfell (total 11–12 miles, 7–8hr), before swinging back round and down to Angle Tarn.

See Basics, p.40, for general walking advice in the Lakes; recommended maps are detailed on p.27.

From the car park at **Stickle Ghyll**, where the Langdale Pikes and Pavey Ark form a dramatic backdrop, most walkers aim no further than **Stickle Tarn**, an hour's climb up Stickle Ghyll itself, following a wide stone-stepped path that's been put in place to prevent further erosion of the hillside. Another easy target is the dramatic sixty-foot waterfall of **Dungeon Ghyll**, less than half an hour away – the "dungeon" in question is a natural cave. The other car park, a mile further west up the road by the **Old Dungeon Ghyll Hotel** is the starting-point for a series of more hardcore hikes (see box below), though there's the option of an easier walk south over Lingmoor Fell (see p.104).

Practicalities

The #516 "Langdale Rambler" **bus** from Ambleside runs via Skelwith Bridge, Elterwater and Chapel Stile to the road end at the head of the valley. It passes all the **accommodation** reviewed below en route and turns around by the *Old Dungeon Ghyll*. The local **campsite** is immensely popular with climbers and hikers, so book in advance if you can. **Eating and drinking** in Langdale isn't a problem – all the hotels and pubs serve food – though for groceries and **supplies** of any kind you'll have to head back down to Elterwater or Ambleside.

Hotels and B&B

Millbeck Farm ☎015394/37364, ⊛www .millbeckfarm.co.uk. "What you see is what you get", says the owner – basically, three small, country-style rooms in the farmhouse (all sharing a bathroom and toilet), a big breakfast and glorious valley views. A nourishing evening meal (not Sun) costs £12. The farm is up the narrow lane by the bridge, just before the *New Dungeon Ghyll*. Parking. No credit cards. ❷

New Dungeon Ghyll ☎015394/37213, ⊛www .dungeon-ghyll.com. Victorian-era hotel near Stickle Ghyll, beneath the Langdale Pikes. It's a more modern experience than the "Old DG", a mile up the road, and though rooms are a few pounds pricier they've all got nice bathrooms, up-to-date furnishings and expansive views. There's a restaurant and bar, open to non-guests (good bar meals available on the outdoor terrace), while off-season and multi-night deals offer real savings. Parking. ❻, with dinner ❼

Old Dungeon Ghyll ☎015394/37272, ⊛www .odg.co.uk. Langdale's most famous inn is decidedly old-school in character and appearance – well-worn oak, floral decor and assorted watercolours – but walkers have long appreciated its comfortable beds and the huge armchairs in the somnolent lounge.

The en-suite rooms (not all are) offer the best value. Dinner (£20, reservations essential) is served in the dining room at 7.30pm, but all the action is in the barebones, stone-flagged *Hikers' Bar*, which has a range of real ales and filling chips-with-everything meals (the bar is also open summer weekends from 9am for hikers' breakfasts). Minimum two-night stay at weekends. Parking. ❻

Campsite

Great Langdale ☎015394/37668. The National Trust's very popular campsite lies about a quarter of a mile south of the *Old Dungeon Ghyll* (which is where everyone goes at night). It has a laundry and drying room, a well-stocked shop and a children's playground.

Bunkhouse and pub

Sticklebarn Tavern ☎015394/37356. Langdale's budget choice is next to the *New Dungeon Ghyll*, with a sunny terrace for drinks with views. There are sixteen beds available in the bunkhouse – which is centrally heated and carpeted – and one simple room suitable for couples. Big breakfasts are served every day and bar meals available all year round, plus *glühwein* and hot chocolate for those chilly days. Parking. Dorm beds £10.

Travel details

From Grasmere

Bus #555/556 (hourly) to: Dove Cottage (2min), Rydal (5min), Ambleside (20min), Brockhole (30min), Windermere train station (35min), Kendal (1hr); or to Keswick (20min).

Bus #599 to: Dove Cottage (2min), Rydal (5min), Ambleside (20min), Brockhole (30min), Windermere train station (35min), Bowness piers (45min). Service operates Easter–Oct every 20–30min.

To Langdale

Bus #516, "Langdale Rambler" from Ambleside (4–6 daily) to: Skelwith Bridge (10min), Elterwater (17min), Chapel Stile (20min), *Old Dungeon Ghyll* (30min).

3

Coniston Water, Hawkshead and the south

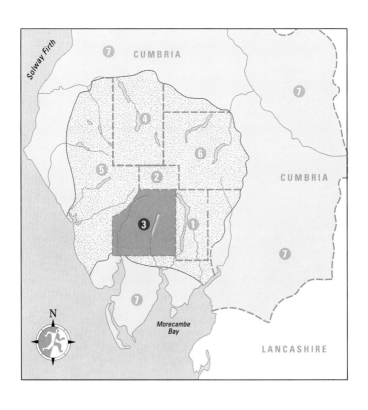

CHAPTER 3 # Highlights

✳ **Climbing the Old Man of Coniston** The finest single climb in the area for anyone who wants to say they've been up a classic Lake District mountain. See p.114

✳ **Ruskin Museum, Coniston** The best of Coniston – its history, trades, pastimes and personalities – all under one roof. See p.116

✳ **Steam Yacht Gondola** The sumptuous way to cruise Coniston Water and reach Ruskin's Brantwood home is on the elegant nineteenth-century steam yacht. See p.119

✳ **Swallows and Amazons cruise** See the locations that inspired Arthur Ransome to write his famous children's books. See p.119

✳ **Go Ape in Grizedale Forest** The high-wire adventure course in the trees of Grizedale Forest brings out the Tarzan in visitors young and old. See p.130

✳ **The Duddon Valley** Drive – or better still, walk – the Duddon Valley, celebrated in sonnet form by Wordsworth, but often overlooked today. See p.133

△ Beatrix Potter's house, Near Sawrey

3

Coniston Water, Hawkshead and the south

Coniston Water – five miles west of Windermere as the crow flies – is not one of the most immediately imposing of the lakes, yet it's one of the oldest settled parts of Lakeland. For as long as there has been human habitation, there has been industry of sorts around Coniston, whether fishing in the lake by the monks of Furness Abbey, copper-mining and slate-quarrying in the northwestern valleys and fells, or coppicing and charcoal-making in the forests to the south and east. The lake's understated beauty – and very possibly its association with these traditional lakeland trades – attracted the Victorian art critic, essayist and moralist John Ruskin, who moved here in 1872. **Brantwood**, his isolated house on the lake's northeastern shore, provides the most obvious target for a trip, though boat rides on the National Trust's elegant steam yacht, *Gondola*, or on the lake's wooden motor-launches, also provide a powerful incentive for a visit.

Those wanting to stay in the area usually look no further than the cute cottages and cobbled streets of **Hawkshead**, three miles east of Coniston Water, with its connections to the big two literary lakeland names of William Wordsworth (who went to school here) and Beatrix Potter (whose husband's former office has been turned into an art gallery). Certainly, the former mining village of **Coniston** itself has to work hard to keep visitors in the face of such stiff competition, but it grows on some after a while and is the usual base for an ascent of the **Old Man of Coniston**, the distinctive peak that backs the village. Wherever you stay, there are easy side trips: to the renowned local beauty spot of **Tarn Hows**, the woodland paths and sculptures of **Grizedale Forest**, or Beatrix Potter's former house of **Hill Top** – the latter one of the most visited attractions in the Lake District. Routes south towards the Furness peninsula take you through the pretty **Duddon Valley** – immortalized by Wordsworth in a series of sonnets – and to the quiet market town of **Broughton-in-Furness**, on the southern edge of the National Park.

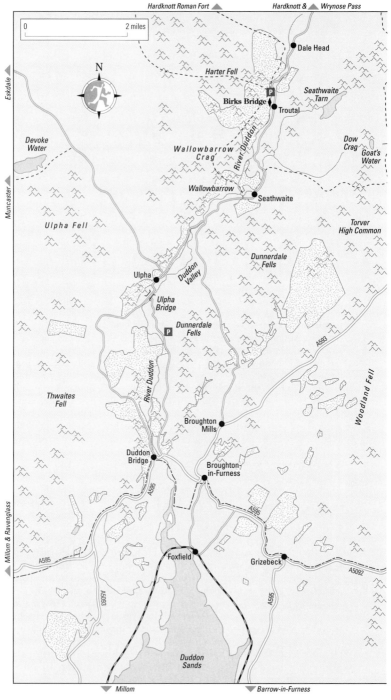

3

Hardknott Roman Fort ▲   Hardknott & ▲ Wrynose Pass

0   2 miles

N

Dale Head

Harter Fell

Eskdale ◀

Seathwaite Tarn

P

Birks Bridge

Troutal

Devoke Water

Dow Crag

Goat's Water

Wallowbarrow Crag

River Duddon

Muncaster ◀

Wallowbarrow

Seathwaite

Ulpha Fell

Torver High Common

Dunnerdale Fells

Ulpha

Duddon Valley

Ulpha Bridge

P

Dunnerdale Fells

A593

Thwaites Fell

River Duddon

Woodland Fell

Broughton Mills

Duddon Bridge

Broughton-in-Furness

A595

A595

Millom & Ravenglass ◀

Foxfield

Grizebeck

A5092

A595

A595

A5093

Duddon Sands

▼ Millom   ▼ Barrow-in-Furness

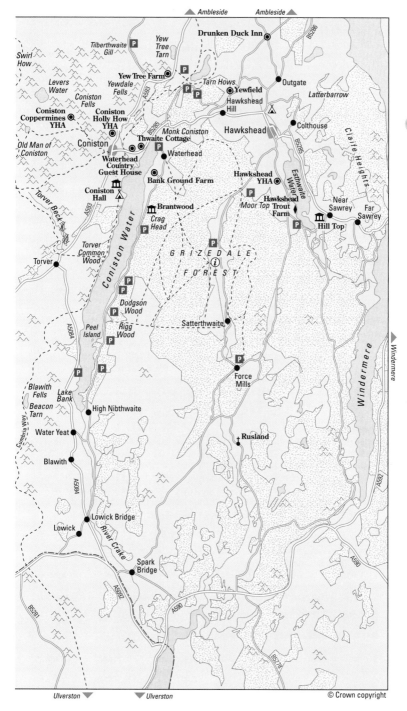

Ambleside Ambleside

Drunken Duck Inn

Swirl How

Tilberthwaite Gill

Yew Tree Tarn

Levers Water

Yewdale Fells

Tarn Hows

Yew Tree Farm

Yewfield

Outgate

Latterbarrow

Coniston Fells

Hawkshead Hill

Coniston Coppermines YHA

Coniston Holly How YHA

Old Man of Coniston

Coniston

Thwaite Cottage

Monk Coniston

Hawkshead

Colthouse

Claife Heights

Waterhead

Hawkshead YHA

Esthwaite Water

Torver Beck

Waterhead Country Guest House

Bank Ground Farm

Hawkshead Trout Farm

Moor Top

Near Sawrey

Far Sawrey

Coniston Hall

Brantwood

Crag Head

Hill Top

Coniston Water

G R I Z E D A L E

F O R E S T

Torver Common Wood

Torver

Dodgson Wood

Satterthwaite

Peel Island

Rigg Wood

Windermere

Windermere

Force Mills

Blawith Fells

Lake Bank

Beacon Tarn

Cumbria Way

High Nibthwaite

Water Yeat

Rusland

Blawith

Lowick Bridge

River Crake

Lowick

Spark Bridge

Ulverston Ulverston

© Crown copyright

Coniston

Its dimensions are nothing out of the ordinary – five miles long, half a mile across at its widest point – and its only village is the plainest in the Lakes, but the glassy surface of **Coniston Water** weaves a gentle spell on summer days.

Walks from Coniston

The classic walk from Coniston village is to the top of the Old Man of Coniston, which is tiring but not overly difficult – Wainwright's flippant reference to ascending crowds of "courting couples, troops of earnest Boy Scouts, babies and grandmothers" isn't that far wide of the mark. Other Coniston walks are similarly accessible to most abilities, ranging from lakeside strolls to ghyll scrambles.

Old Man of Coniston

Most walkers can reach the summit of the **Old Man of Coniston** (2635ft) in under two hours from the village, following the signposted path from Church Beck. It's a steep and twisting route, passing though abandoned quarry works and their detritus, but there's a pause on the way up at Low Water tarn while the views from the top are tremendous – to the Cumbrian coast and Morecambe Bay, and across to Langdale and Windermere.

Old Man circular routes

Hardier hikers combine the Old Man in a ridge-walk loop with **Swirl How** (2630ft) and **Wetherlam** (2502ft) to the north – a seven- or eight-mile walk (5–7hr). Wetherlam, too, is pitted with caves, mines and tunnels, requiring caution on the various descents to Coppermines Valley. Or instead of heading north you can loop around to the south, descending via **Goat's Hause** and Goat's Water tarn, under the fearsome **Dow Crag** (a famed lure for rock climbers). This eventually deposits you in Torver (see below), with the full circuit back to Coniston being something like eight miles (5hr).

Lakeside walks

From Coniston village the Cumbria Way footpath provides access to Coniston Water's west side. The route runs past sixteenth-century Coniston Old Hall (note its traditional circular chimneys) and through Torver Common Wood to **Torver**, where there are a couple of pubs and the possibility of climbing up Torver Beck to see its waterfalls. There are also several park-and-walk spots on the lake's **east side** – nearest to the village is the northern pier of Monk Coniston – with trails and picnic tables in the National Trust woodland.

Tilberthwaite Gill and Yewdale

North of Coniston the crags, beck and tarn of **Yewdale** offer a multitude of short walks. **Tilberthwaite Gill** is a quiet, narrow glen set among dramatic old quarry workings – there's free parking up a signposted lane off the Ambleside road (one-and-a-half miles from Coniston), or you can walk here from Coppermines Valley via Hole Rake. **Yew Tree Tarn**, right on the Ambleside road (two miles from Coniston), is another pretty spot – there's parking back down the road, and a footpath to Tarn Hows, as well as a useful tearoom at *Yew Tree Farm* (11am–4pm: daily July, Aug & school hols, weekends rest of the year).

See Basics, p.40, for general walking advice in the Lakes; recommended maps are detailed on p.27.

Wooded on its eastern shores (and traced by a minor road from the south), with much of the western side accessed only by the Cumbria Way footpath, it's easy to lose the worst of southern Lakeland's crowds around the lake. At the end of the nineteenth century, **Arthur Ransome** spent his childhood summer holidays at the still serene southern end, near Nibthwaite, and was always "half-drowned in tears" when it was time to leave. His vivid memories of messing about on the water, camping on the islets, making friends with the local charcoal-burners and playing make-believe in the hills surfaced later in his children's classic, *Swallows and Amazons*, when **Peel Island** became the "Wild Cat Island" of the book (for more on Ransome, see p.131). The sheltered waters also attracted speed-adventurers **Sir Malcolm and Donald Campbell**, father and son, who between them set a series of records on Coniston Water, starting with Sir Malcolm's world water-speed record of 141mph in 1939. After raising the record in successive years, Donald reached 260mph here in 1959 (and 276mph in Australia five years later) but on January 4, 1967, having set out once again to better his own mark, his jet-powered *Bluebird* hit a patch of turbulence at an estimated 320mph, which sent the craft into a somersault. Campbell was killed immediately, and his body and boat lay undisturbed on the lake bed until both were retrieved in 2001.

Coniston village

Copper has been taken from the Coniston fells since the Bronze Age, though the Romans were the first to mine it systematically. The industry again flourished in the seventeenth century, and by the nineteenth century hundreds of workers were employed in the local copper mines – producing ore used for the "copper-bottoming" of the wooden hulls of ships. Together with slate-quarriers – first recorded here in the seventeenth century – Coniston's industrious miners established themselves in the village of **CONISTON** (a derivation of "King's Town"). That it was originally a mining village, pure and simple, is clear from the rather drab, utilitarian, rows of cottages and later Victorian shopfronts which make up the slate-grey/green settlement. By the late nineteenth century the copper-mining business was in terminal decline and the railway, built in 1859 to remove the mined copper and quarried slate, began to bring the first tourists, who then, as now, nearly all made time to ascend the craggy, mine-riddled bulk of **The Old Man of Coniston**, which looms to the northwest. It may sound an odd name, but "Man" is a common fell term hereabouts, signifying a peak or summit, while "Old" is merely a corruption of the Norse "alt", or high. Even if you're not game for the climb, it's worth the initial stroll from the village up Church Beck and over the old Miner's Bridge – along what's known as **Coppermines Valley** – to get a glimpse of the scars and gouges from the industrial past.

The village itself is a functional kind of place, with just enough shops, pubs and cafés to kill an hour or two. It keeps to itself to such an extent that some first-time visitors are surprised to find it has a lake – the water is hidden out of sight, half a mile southeast of the village. Before you leave, though, don't miss the few sights that Coniston village does muster: Ruskin's and Campbell's graves and the excellent local museum.

The church and cemetery

St Andrew's church, by river and bridge, sits right in the centre of the village. The **grave of John Ruskin** lies in the churchyard beneath a beautifully worked Celtic cross, and most people spare a minute or two here before proceeding to the lake or museum. The other person inextricably linked with the village is, of course, Donald Campbell and a memorial plaque set in a slate

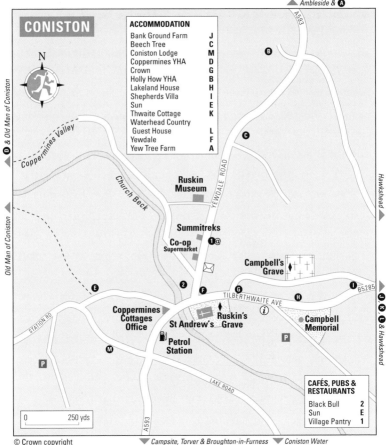

CONISTON

ACCOMMODATION

Bank Ground Farm	J
Beech Tree	C
Coniston Lodge	M
Coppermines YHA	D
Crown	G
Holly How YHA	B
Lakeland House	H
Shepherds Villa	I
Sun	E
Thwaite Cottage	K
Waterhead Country Guest House	L
Yewdale	F
Yew Tree Farm	A

CAFÉS, PUBS & RESTAURANTS

Black Bull	2
Sun	E
Village Pantry	1

0 — 250 yds

© Crown copyright

Campsite, Torver & Broughton-in-Furness   Coniston Water

---

wall and dedicated to Campbell (and his chief mechanic, Leo Villa) dominates the small green in the centre. When his body was eventually retrieved from the lake in 2001, Campbell's funeral was held at the church, before the blue coffin (the colour of his boat) was carried through the village by horse and carriage to the small church cemetery behind the *Crown Hotel*. Here you can view the **grave of Donald Campbell** (1921–67).

Ruskin Museum

Coniston's **Ruskin Museum**, on Yewdale Road (Easter to mid-Nov daily 10am–5.30pm; mid-Nov to Easter Wed–Sun 10am–3.30pm; £3.75; ☏015394/41164, ⓦwww.ruskinmuseum.com) – named after its most famous resident but devoted to all aspects of local life and work – is the most thought-provoking in the Lakes. The village's first museum had its genesis in the memorial exhibition held following John Ruskin's death in 1900. Organized by his long-time secretary and literary assistant W.G. Collingwood (for more on whom, see p.122), the exhibition appropriated manuscripts and mementoes from Ruskin's house at Brantwood and raised sufficient funds for a permanent museum, largely devoted to Ruskin himself. This was housed in Coniston's Mechanics Institute, a local cultural society supported by Ruskin during his life. The latest building stands at the back of this, and is still first port of call for anyone interested in tracing Ruskin's life and work. In relating his ideas and theories to local trades and pastimes the museum also doubles as a highly effective record of Coniston's history through the ages.

The museum begins with a walk-through timeline, placing the village and Ruskin within the wider historical context. Stone and Bronze Age artefacts give way to an exposition of the local geology, essential for an understanding of why Coniston became an important mining and quarrying district. The slate quarried locally has been used for centuries to roof buildings and build bridges and walls – here in the museum, it flags the floors. You'll learn about dry-stone walling (there's a fine example outside the museum) and sheep farming, as well as about the traditional trades that Ruskin himself promoted as a means of sustaining local employment, notably woodcarving and the making of **Langdale linen** and the famous **Ruskin lace** – examples of these are contained in slide-out panels and drawers. In the museum's separate **Ruskin Gallery** are found artefacts from the original memorial exhibition (including a pair of his socks and his matriculation certificate from Oxford), alongside a mixed bag of letters, manuscripts, sketchbooks and a series of Ruskin's own watercolours. Most enterprisingly of all, an interactive side-gallery lets you view pages of Ruskin's sketchbooks at the click of a mouse.

The museum is also the place to track the latest developments in the reconstruction of Donald Campbell's powerboat **Bluebird**, whose wreckage was lifted from the bottom of Coniston Water. The boat will eventually be displayed here in a purpose-built gallery, though for now photographs of Campbell, his funeral and the recovery of the craft are on display, along with related mementoes. For the full story you can visit Ⓦ www.bluebirdproject.com.

Coniston Water

It's a ten-minute walk down Lake Road from the village to **Coniston Water** and its piers, where a second Campbell memorial plaque is sited. The pebble shoreline and grassy verges are very popular on sunny summer days, as is the **Coniston Boating Centre** (Ⓣ015394/41366; free parking available), which can provide the wherewithal for fooling around on the water in rowboats, sailing dinghies, canoes, electric launches or motorboats. Also right by the lake is the *Bluebird Café*, a nice place with outdoor tables, serving meals, snacks, ices and drinks.

Ruskin linen and lace

Encouraged by Ruskin, who had his own theories about the sanctity of traditional labour (see "Brantwood", p.121), a local woman, Marion Twelves, revived the trade of flax hand-spinning in Elterwater in 1884. It had almost died out in the Lake District, and the flax itself had to be imported from Ireland. The linen trade flourished, assisted financially by Ruskin's own Guild of St George, though contemporary tastes dictated that the finished article would be more attractive to purchasers if it was embroidered. Ruskin provided a series of designs inspired by those of Renaissance ruffs, and the hand-cut lace was attached to the plain linen to make cushion and sideboard covers and bedspreads. Ruskin's own name was used to promote the work after 1894; and his funeral pall (displayed in the museum) was a particularly fine example. The industry continued until the 1930s, though by then few were relying upon it as a principal means of income.

△ Slate carver, Coniston

Boat speeds are limited to 10mph, a graceful pace for the sumptuously uphol-stered and quilted **Steam Yacht Gondola** (Easter–Oct hourly departures 11am–4pm; ℡015394/35599, ⓦwww.nationaltrust.org.uk/gondola), first launched in 1859 but fully restored by the National Trust. This leaves Coniston Pier for hour-long circuits of the lake (£6 round trip), though you can stop off at Ruskin's Brantwood if you prefer. Evening cruises are also sometimes available – call for current details.

The other lake service is the **Coniston Launch** (Easter–Oct hourly depar-tures 10.30am–4.30pm; Nov–Easter up to 4 daily depending on demand and weather; ℡015394/36216 or 0797/108 0370, ⓦwww.conistonlaunch.co.uk), whose two solar-electric-powered wooden vessels operate on two routes around the lake – north to Monk Coniston, Torver and Brantwood (£4.60 return) and south to Torver, Lake Bank and Brantwood (£6.80 return). You can stop off at any pier on either route. Special **cruises** once or twice a week (Easter–Oct; call for details) concentrate on the various sites associated with *Swallows and Amazons* (£8) and the speed-racing Campbells (£7), or show you the lake at sundowner time (£8.50, includes wine).

Practicalities

Most **buses** – principally the #505 "Coniston Rambler" (from Kendal, Windermere, Ambleside or Hawkshead) and the #X12 (Ulverston) – stop by the *Crown Hotel*, on the main road (B5285) through the village. A **Ruskin Explorer ticket** (£11.50) gets you return bus travel on the #505 from any point between Windermere and Coniston, plus use of the Coniston Launch and free entrance to Brantwood – buy the ticket on the bus. In previous years, the Cross-Lakes Shuttle service from Bowness has extended to Coniston (via Hill Top, Hawkhead and Tarn Hows) – if it's still in operation, the bus stops at the Coniston Launch pier at the *Waterhead Hotel*, at the head of Coniston Water, half a mile out of the village. Drivers will come in on either the A593 (Ambleside road) or the B5285 (from Hawkshead) – the latter runs through the village as Tilberthwaite Avenue. The main **car park** is signposted; it's right in the centre (off Tilberthwaite Ave), next to **Coniston Information Centre** on Ruskin Avenue (Easter–Oct daily 9.30am–5.30pm; Nov–March daily 10am–3.30pm, though hours may vary; ℡015394/41533). For **online information**, consult the useful ⓦwww.coniston-net.com.

Accommodation

Accommodation is plentiful and, for the most part, reasonably priced. Holiday **cottages** are fairly thick on the ground, too, though none so intri-cately linked with the area's heritage as *The Coppermines* (℡015394/41765, ⓦwww.coppermines.co.uk), a series of converted dwellings in the old saw mill in Coppermines Valley, behind the Coppermines **youth hostel**; note that the road up here is largely unsurfaced.

In Coniston

Beech Tree Guesthouse Yewdale Rd
℡015394/41717. Coniston's former vicarage, 150 yards north of the village, makes a charming, non-smoking, vegetarian base. Decorated with zest, half of the eight rooms have their own showers, the others (priced a pound or two less) share a bright bathroom; and there's a garden, with fell views, where you can have tea. Parking. No credit cards. ❸

Coniston Lodge Sunny Brow, Station Rd
℡015394/41201, ⓦwww.coniston-lodge.com. Six immaculate cottage-style rooms (with bath as well as shower) occupy the extension of the Robinsons' comfortable, non-smoking family home, just a minute or two from the village centre. There's a very cosy feel inside – the lounge is stuffed full of antiques and mementoes – while a veranda over-looks the garden. Parking. ❻

Crown Tilberthwaite Ave ☎ 015394/41243, ⓦ www.crown-hotel-coniston.com. The nicely refurbished rooms at the *Crown* offer a fair amount of space for your money, and many have both baths and showers, a boon for aching walkers. There's a traditional bar downstairs (with meals) and an outdoor terrace. Two- and four-day breaks (including dinner and a packed lunch for your day on the fells) are a steal. Parking. ⑤

Lakeland House Tilberthwaite Ave ☎ 015394/41303, ⓦ www.lakelandhouse.com. A centrally located option accustomed to walkers and their ways, with an attached café, laundry, Internet service, bike storage and drying facilities. Half the rooms are en suite, with squeezed-for-space shower-and-toilet facilities. No American Express. ③

Shepherds Villa Tilberthwaite Ave ☎ 015394/41337, ⓦ www.shepherdsvilla.co.uk. One of Coniston's most popular B&Bs has a decent sense of space, an approachable owner and nine comfortable rooms, some of which retain their original fireplaces – only two aren't en suite, and these are priced a category lower. Packed lunches and parking available. No American Express. ③

Sun ☎ 015394/41248, ⓦ www.thesunconiston .com. This sixteenth-century inn – 200 yards uphill from the bridge in the centre of the village – has its guest rooms in an Edwardian country-house-style adjunct with fell views. Three family rooms offer the most space. There's an informal atmosphere, with a cosy lounge, restaurant and conservatory, while the public bar is Coniston's most enjoyable drinking spot. Two-night minimum stay at weekends. Parking. No American Express. ⑥

Yewdale Yewdale Rd ☎ 015394/41280, ⓦ www .yewdalehotel.com. A notch up from a B&B, the eight rooms at the *Yewdale* – bang in the village centre – make an agreeable base. The Victorian building was once a bank, with the old counter now pressed into service as the bar. There's also a restaurant and a little street patio. Parking. ⑤

Around Coniston

Bank Ground Farm Coniston Water, east side, north of Brantwood ☎ 015394/41264, ⓦ www .bankground.com. The model for Holly Howe Farm in *Swallows and Amazons* (and used in the 1970s film), sixteenth-century *Bank Ground Farm* has its own shoreline, plus seven country-style rooms in the main house, and six more in a barn annexe, many with lake and fell views. Rooms without a lake view, or without en suite facilities, tend to be a category cheaper. Also on the farm, four self-catering holiday cottages and a converted barn have log fires and share laundry facilities. Parking. ④

Thwaite Cottage Waterhead, B5285 ☎ 015394/41367, ⓦ www.thwaitcot.freeserve .co.uk. Half a mile (10min walk) east, set back from the Hawkshead road up a little lane. There are three well-appointed rooms available in this peacefully located slate-flagged house, with plenty of atmosphere supplied by the oak beams and panelled walls, plus a log fire in the guests' lounge and a couple of acres of gardens. Parking. No credit cards. ③

Waterhead Country Guest House Waterhead, B5285 ☎ 015394/41442, ⓦ www.waterheadguesthouse.co.uk. Less than ten minutes from the village, just 200 yards from the north end of the lake and with views to the Old Man of Coniston, it's easy to see why this small guesthouse fills quickly. The five rooms aren't huge, but they are decently furnished and there's a garden, bar and parking. No American Express. ④

Yew Tree Farm A593, 2 miles north of Coniston ☎ 015394/41433, ⓦ www.yewtree-farm.com. Hiker-friendly accommodation in a historic seventeenth-century farmhouse with tea room – Beatrix Potter bought the house in 1930 and furnished it for the tenants. Three atmospheric rooms with valley views (one en suite) are tucked away amid the oak beams and panelling. Tea and coffee are provided on arrival, and there are walks straight from the farm gates (Tarn Hows is only half a mile away). Parking. No credit cards. ②

Youth hostels

Coniston Coppermines YHA Coppermines Valley ☎ 0870/770 5772, ⓔ coppermines@yha.org.uk. The hikers' favourite (perfectly placed for ascents of the Old Man and Wetherlam) has a dramatic mountain setting a steep mile-and-a-quarter from the village – follow the "Old Man" signs past the *Sun Hotel* or take the small road between the *Black Bull* and the Co-op; both routes lead to the hostel. It's simpler than *Holly How*, with 26 bunks in four-, six-and eight-bedded rooms. Reception opens at 5pm; evening meal available. Sept & Oct closed Sun & Mon; also closed all Nov–March. Dorm beds £11.

Coniston Holly How YHA Far End, A593 ☎ 0870/770 5770, ⓔ conistonhh@yha.org.uk. The closest hostel to the village is in a slate house (with some four-bedded rooms) set in its own gardens just a few minutes' walk north of Coniston on the Ambleside road. It's popular with schools and families (it's open every school and bank holiday) and only has limited weekend opening outside the main summer-holiday period. Reception opens at 5pm; evening meal and bike rental available. Closed Nov to mid-Jan. Dorm beds £12.50.

Campsite

Coniston Hall Campsite Haws Bank, off A593 ☎015394/41223. The most convenient campsite for the village is a mile south of town, set in spacious grounds by the lake, with showers, toilets, laundry facilities and a small shop. Booking is essential. Closed Nov–Easter.

Eating, drinking and entertainment

Eating opportunities outside Coniston's **pubs** are fairly limited, but then the two main pubs – the *Sun* and the *Black Bull* – are both excellent in any case, so there's no hardship in spending a night in either. During the day, a few **cafés** and a couple of bakeries take care of lunch and snacks, while the *Jumping Jenny* tearoom at nearby Brantwood (see below) is worth a special trip. The Co-op **supermarket** on Yewdale Road has basic supplies, but for anything more exotic you'll have to go to Ambleside. Annual festivals include Coniston **Water Festival Week** in May and the **Coniston Country Fair** in July, when all manner of country trades, crafts, contests and entertainment take place in the grounds of Coniston Hall.

Café

Village Pantry 16 Yewdale Rd ☎015394/41155. Bakery-café and sandwich bar with a few counter stools in the window. All-day breakfasts are popular, or try the homemade pies or hot steak sandwiches. Daytime only. Nov–March closed Sun. Inexpensive.

Pubs

Black Bull Yewdale Rd ☎015394/41335. By the bridge in the centre, this is the oldest pub in the village and has outdoor tables in the former coachyard – perfect for a pint after a day in the fells. Inside, it fills quickly at lunch and dinner for its bar meals, while the Coniston Brewing Company out back produces its own Bluebird bitter among other fine ales. Moderate.

Sun ☎015394/41248. Very good, nicely presented pub food – rack of local lamb, Cumberland sausage, heaped pasta plates, grilled organic trout – served in either the traditional bar (which has a roaring winter fire) or the hotel restaurant. It's a cosy pub of the old school (low lighting, no jukebox) with half a dozen real ales on tap at any one time; summer drinkers can take advantage of the outdoor terrace, which looks onto the fells. Donald Campbell stayed here during his attempts on the water-speed record and contemporary photographs and newspaper accounts are on display inside the bar. Moderate.

Listings

Banks and exchange There are ATMs in the petrol station and post office (fee charged at both), but not one at the bank (Barclays, Bridge End; open Mon, Wed & Fri only). Otherwise, the nearest facilities are in Ambleside.

Bike rental Ask at Summitreks, Yewdale Rd (daily 9am–5pm; by arrangement only in winter; ☎015394/41212, ⊛www.summitreks.co.uk) – though the bikes themselves (for adults only) are available from the unit down Lake Rd.

Emergencies The nearest hospital is in Kendal (Westmorland General Hospital, Burton Rd; ☎01539/732288).

Internet access Available at the *Village Pantry*, 16 Yewdale Rd (April–Oct Mon–Sat 8.30am–5pm, Sun 10am–4pm; Nov–March Mon–Sat 8.30am–5pm).

Outdoor stores Two or three places in the village sell all the walking gear you might need; the best is Summitreks, which also rents out boots, rucksacks and waterproofs.

Pharmacy The nearest pharmacy is in Hawkshead (Collins & Butterworth, Main St ☎015394/36201).

Post office Yewdale Rd (Mon–Fri 9am–5.30pm, Sat 9am–12.30pm; ☎015394/41259).

Taxis Coniston Taxi ☎015394/41683.

Brantwood

Nestling among trees on a hillside above the eastern shore of the lake sits **Brantwood** (mid-March to mid-Nov daily 11am–5.30pm; mid-Nov to mid-March Wed–Sun 11am–4.30pm; house £5.50, gardens £3.75, ☎015394/41396,

The Collingwoods

Few families have had as sure a feel for the Lake District as the **Collingwoods**, whose home was at **Lanehead** at the northern end of Coniston Water. Local scholar, historian and artist William Gershorn **(W.G.) Collingwood** (1854–1932) was born in Liverpool, but visited the Lake District on holiday as a child and moved here as soon as was practicable. He became an expert on lakeland archeology, the Vikings and early Northumbrian crosses (his *Northumbrian Crosses of the Pre-Norman Age*, published in 1927, is a classic), writing his own guide to *The Lake Counties* (1902) and even a lakeland saga, *Thorstein of the Mere*, largely set around Coniston. While at Oxford University, Collingwood had studied under John Ruskin (who was Professor of Fine Art) and was immediately impressed by his mind and ideas; later, Collingwood became Ruskin's trusted secretary and literary assistant. It was W.G. who designed Ruskin's memorial cross and established the first Ruskin Museum in Coniston. The family befriended the young Arthur Ransome, who was of a similar age to W.G.'s son **Robin Collingwood** (1889–1943). Robin was later to become an Oxford professor of philosophy, influential historiographer and an authority on Roman Britain – he excavated the Galava site and fortifications at Waterhead near Ambleside. W.G.'s wife **Edith** and two daughters, **Barbara** and **Dora**, were also highly talented: Edith and Dora as painters, Barbara as a sculptor. Barbara's bust of the elderly Ruskin is on display in the Ambleside Museum. The family graves all lie, with Ruskin's, in Coniston's churchyard.

ⓦ www.brantwood.org.uk), the magnificently sited home of **John Ruskin** (1819–1900). It's only two and a half miles by road from Coniston, off the B5285, though the approach is greatly enhanced if you arrive by either the Steam Yacht *Gondola* or Coniston Launch (see p.119), in which case you can claim 50p discount off entry. The Ruskin Explorer ticket (see Coniston's "Practicalities" above) combines bus and launch travel and Brantwood entry.

Ruskin lived here from 1872 until his death: at first sight he was captivated, though by the stunning mountain and lake views and not by the house itself which he complained was "a mere shed". Indeed, the house today bears little resemblance to the eighteenth-century cottage bought for £1500 in 1871 from Radical engraver William James Linton. Ruskin spent the next twenty years expanding it, adding another twelve rooms and laying out its gardens. Thus adapted, Brantwood – "brant" is a Cumbrian dialect word meaning steep – became Ruskin's lair, where the grand old eminence of Victorian art and letters gardened, wrote, painted and pontificated.

The precocious only child of a wine merchant, Ruskin was from a wealthy background and could afford to indulge his passion for art from an early age, travelling in Europe with his parents and maintaining diaries and sketchbooks. He went up to Oxford in 1836, publishing his first book, *The Poetry of Architecture*, a year later when he was just 18. He made his name as an art critic with the publication of the first part of his celebrated *Modern Painters* (1843), conceived as a defence of J.M.W. Turner, whose work he had admired (and collected) since his student days. Later a champion of the Pre-Raphaelites and, after his wide European travels, a proponent of the supremacy of Gothic architecture, Ruskin came to insist upon the indivisibility of ethics and aesthetics. He was appalled by the conditions in which the captains of industry made their labourers work and live, while expecting him to applaud their patronage of the arts. "There is no wealth but life," he wrote in his study of capitalist economics, *Unto the Last* (1862), elaborating with the observation: "That country is richest which nourishes the greatest number of noble and happy human beings."

Drawing a distinction between mere labour and craftsmanship, he intervened in the lakeland economy by promoting a revival of woodcarving, linen and lace-making, and ventures like this as well as his architectural theories did much to influence such disparate figures as Proust, Tolstoy, Frank Lloyd Wright and Gandhi. Nonetheless, not all Ruskin's projects were a success, partly because of his refusal to compromise his principles. A London teashop, established to provide employment for a former servant, failed since Ruskin refused to advertise; meanwhile, his street-cleaning and road-building schemes, designed to instil into his students (including Arnold Toynbee and Oscar Wilde) a respect for the dignity of manual labour, simply accrued ridicule. Perhaps more relevant today is the very Ruskinian notion of ecological conservation – some see him as the first "Green" – espoused in his opposition to the expansion of the railways and the creation of Thirlmere reservoir.

House and gardens

Once you've paid to go in the **house**, you're free to wander around the various rooms. Ruskin's study (hung with handmade paper to his own design) and dining room boast superlative lake views; they are bettered only by those from the Turret Room where Ruskin used to sit in later life in his bathchair – itself

Ruskin's life and death at Brantwood

Ruskin was certainly looking for something other than mere bricks and mortar when he acquired **Brantwood** in 1871. Following his father's death in 1864 he was independently wealthy, lauded for his works, and regarded as the country's foremost authority on art and achitecture – indeed, he had just been appointed **Slade Professor of Fine Art** at Oxford University. But Ruskin's personal life was complicated by two singular relationships, which perhaps led him to seek simplicity and harmony in the lakeland fells. His **marriage** to Euphemia (Effie) Gray in 1848 – they honeymooned in the Lakes – had been annulled in 1854, with the **divorce** a cause-célèbre of the day, sensationally alleging Ruskin's impotence. Euphemia eventually married the artist John Everett Millais, which – given Ruskin's unflinching support of the Pre-Raphaelites – was a hard blow. Ruskin later formed a long attachment with the young **Rose La Touche**, who was almost thirty years his junior. Her parents disapproved (a proposal in 1866 came to nothing) and when Rose died in 1875, Ruskin was affected badly. Retreating to his lakeland house, he suffered the first of a series of mental breakdowns in 1878. **At Brantwood** he was looked after by his married cousin Joan Severn and her husband Arthur, whose family moved into the house in the early 1880s, supervising Ruskin's visits from the Victorian great and good. **W.G. Collingwood**, for one, was always suspicious of the Severns' influence and it's clear that they eventually restricted the number of Ruskin's visitors. The Severns would argue it was to protect Ruskin's health and they had a point, since the last years of his life were punctuated by bouts of depressive illness and mental breakdown. From 1885, he began to produce sections of his **autobiography**, *Praeterita* and, eventually, it was the only thing Ruskin would work on. Tellingly selective in content, there was no mention of his former wife, Effie. Ruskin broke down again in 1889 and fell into silence, writing nothing after this time, rarely receiving visitors or even speaking. He caught influenza and died at Brantwood on January 20, 1900. **The Severns** inherited Brantwood, ignored Ruskin's wishes that the house be open to the public for a set number of days each year and sold off many of his paintings. Joan died in 1924, Arthur in 1931, following which the house and its remaining contents were sold to **J.H. Whitehouse**, founder of the Birmingham Ruskin Society, who began the task of restoration.

on display downstairs, along with a mahogany desk and Blue John wine goblet, amongst other memorabilia. A twenty-minute video expands on the man's philosophy and whets the appetite for rooms full of his watercolours, as well as for the surviving Turners from Ruskin's collection that weren't sold off after his death. Other exhibition rooms and the Coach House Gallery display Ruskin-related arts and crafts, while there's also a well-stocked **bookshop** for those who want to bone up on the Pre-Raphaelites or the Arts and Crafts Movement. There's a summer **theatre** season here, too, held in the grounds; and various other lectures, recitals and walks scheduled throughout the year – call the house for a brochure.

The 250-acre estate surrounding the house boasts a nature trail, while paths wind through the lakeside meadows and into eight distinct **gardens**, some based on Ruskin's own plans. You can potter about, as did Ruskin, among the native flowers, fruit, herbs, moorland shrubs and ferns – his slate seat is sited in the Professor's Garden – or climb the heights behind the house to Crag Head for some splendid views.

The *Jumping Jenny* **tearoom** (☎015394/41715; open same days as the house) – named after Ruskin's boat – serves very nice (mostly veggie) food, especially its cakes and flans, and there are more fine views from the outdoor terrace. You can eat here without paying to go inside either house or gardens.

Hawkshead

HAWKSHEAD, midway between Coniston and Ambleside, wears its beauty well, its patchwork of whitewashed cottages, cobbles, alleys and archways backed by woods and fells and barely affected by modern intrusions. This is partly due to the enlightened policy of banning traffic in the centre. Huge car parks at the village edge take the strain and when the

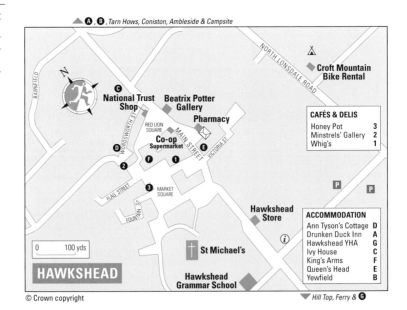

© Crown copyright

crowds of day-trippers leave, Hawkshead regains its natural tranquillity. The village sits at the head of **Esthwaite Water**, a skinny lake less than two miles long that empties into Windermere. This isn't troubled by too many visitors, though it's renowned for its trout-fishing and Wordsworth is known to have rambled and splashed around its perimeter as a boy. Best view of the water is from the car-park access point on the far southwestern shore, two miles from Hawkshead.

The Village

The Vikings were the first to settle the land here, Hawkshead probably founded by and named after one Haukr, a Norse warrior. In medieval times it became an important wool market, the trade controlled by the monks of Furness Abbey, whose last remaining manorial building – **Hawkshead Courthouse** (key available from National Trust shop, Main St) – is sited half a mile north of the village, where the Ambleside and Coniston roads meet.

This early wealth explains the otherwise puzzling presence in such a small community of **Hawkshead Grammar School** (Easter–Sept Mon–Sat 10am–12.30pm & 1.30–5pm, Sun 1–5pm; Oct same days, but closes 4.30pm; £2), whose entrance lies opposite the tourist office. This was founded in 1585 and – even by Wordsworth's day, when the wool trade had much declined – was considered to be among the finest schools in the country. Wordsworth and his brother Richard were sent here following the death of their mother in 1778 to acquire an expensively bought education; "grammar" of course being Latin grammar, knowledge of which was the mark of every gentleman. In the simple, yet rather forbidding, school room the Wordsworth boys were taught geometry, algebra and the classics at time-worn wooden benches and desks (some date back to the school's foundation); you'll be shown the desk on which the rapscallion William carved his signature – a foolhardy stunt given the anecdote that miscreants were suspended from a pulley in the centre of the room to be birched. He also wrote his first surviving piece of poetry, a paean to the bicentenary of the school's foundation, before leaving in 1787 to go up to Cambridge. The only other things to see are the headmaster's study upstairs, a small exhibition on the history of English grammar schools and a few quills and nibs. The school closed in 1909.

During his schooldays Wordsworth attended the fifteenth-century church of **St Michael's** above the school, which harks back to Norman and Romanesque designs in its rounded pillars and patterned arches. It's chiefly of interest for the 26 pithy psalms and biblical extracts illuminated with cherubs and flowers, painted on the walls during the seventeenth and eighteenth centuries. Wordsworth's other connection with the village is that during term-times he lodged with a local woman, **Ann Tyson** – someone he remembered kindly as "my old Dame" in *The Prelude*. Her Hawkshead cottage is now a guest house (see below), though the Tyson family, and Wordsworth, actually lived for longer in another (unknown) house after 1783 when they moved half a mile east to Colthouse.

From its knoll the churchyard gives a good view over the village's twin central squares, anchored by a couple of pubs and several cafés. Past the *Queen's Head* on Main Street, the **Beatrix Potter Gallery** (mid-March to Oct Mon–Wed, Sat & Sun 10.30am–4.30pm; £3.50; NT; ☏015394/36355) hoovers up all Hawkshead's remaining visitors; in summer, its popularity is such that timed-entry tickets are issued. The gallery occupies rooms once used by Potter's solicitor husband, William Heelis, whom she met while purchasing land in the Hawkshead area. There had been a Heelis law firm in the village since 1861 and William was a partner in the family firm from 1900 until he died in 1945, when the building passed to the National Trust (Heelis's prewar office is maintained downstairs). If you were ever going to crack the enduring mystery of his wife's popularity you'd think this would be the place, since the upstairs rooms contain an annually changing selection of Potter's original sketchbooks, drawings, watercolours, letters and manuscripts. Although never formally schooled, she had drawn fossils, fungi and pet animals since childhood and her work is certainly closely observed. Her animals aren't caricatures, but neither are they "art" in any meaningful sense (Potter herself thought it "bosh" to think so) and to a non-Potterite, the paintings and drawings are pleasant without ever being more than mere fluff: the less devoted will find displays on her life as a keen naturalist, conservationist and early supporter of the National Trust more diverting. Potter bought eighteen fell farms and large parcels of Lake District land, which she bequeathed to the Trust on her death.

Practicalities

The main **bus service** to Hawkshead is the #505 "Coniston Rambler" between Windermere, Ambleside and Coniston. This is complemented by the seasonal **Cross-Lakes Shuttle** (bus #525), whose minibuses run from Hawkshead down to the Beatrix Potter house at Hill Top and on to Ferry House, Sawrey, for boat connections back to Bowness. The B5285 between Coniston and Sawrey skirts the eastern side of Hawkshead; no traffic is allowed in the village itself. The **National Park Information Centre** is at the main **car park** off Main Street (daily: Easter–Oct 9.30am–5.30pm; Nov–Easter 10am–3.30pm; ☎015394/36525); everything lies within five minutes' walk of here.

Accommodation

Book a long way ahead if you want to stay in Hawkshead during the peak summer season. The information centre can help if the places recommended below are full. For **cottages**, barn and farm conversions in Hawkshead and the surrounding area, contact Hideaways Cottages in the *Minstrels' Gallery* tearoom on The Square (☎015394/42435, ⓦ www.lakeland-hideaways.co.uk).

In Hawkshead

Ann Tyson's Cottage Wordsworth St ☎015394/36405, ⓦ www.anntysons.co.uk. Wordsworth briefly boarded here, and the street and house have changed little since. Choose between variously sized rooms in the main house (oak beams, low ceilings) – ask for the room with Ruskin's bed in it – the adjacent barn conversion, or the two self-catering cottages (one was formerly a chapel). ❸

Ivy House Main St ☎015394/36204, ⓦ www .ivyhousehotel.com. Elegant Georgian house whose rotunda lights up the country-house-style interior. There are six rooms in the main house (some with four-poster beds, supplement charged), five more in the lodge behind. Rates include a good four-course dinner, though B&B is available on request (except at weekends) for £10 less per person. Parking. No American Express. ❻

King's Arms Market Sq ☎015394/36372, ⓦ www.kingsarmshawkshead.co.uk. There are bags of character in this venerable inn, with nine rooms retaining their oak beams and idiosyncratic proportions; bathrooms and furnishings, though, are reassuringly up-to-date. A snug little bar with a fire and a fine beer selection does the honours when you're thirsty, while good-value meals include sarnies, salads and hot lunches and a wider-ranging dinner menu featuring the likes of local trout, venison and vegetarian specials. Free parking provided in the village. ❺

Queen's Head Main St ☎015394/36271, ⓦ www.queensheadhotel.co.uk. Guest rooms in the old inn have been thoroughly modernized, with good beds and repro antique furnishings. Though not huge, the family rooms can sleep three or four. Downstairs, the sixteenth century reasserts itself in the oak-and-panel interior, and the wide-ranging menu takes some beating, from a lunchtime *croque monsieur* or tortilla wrap to dinner specials celebrating the versatility of Herdwick lamb. Lake trout, sea bass and halibut are other choices. Of course, you can just have a pint and a sandwich at an outdoor table; beers are by Hartley's. ⑥

Around Hawkshead

Drunken Duck Inn Barngates crossroad, 2 miles north of Hawkshead off B5285 ☎015394/36347, Ⓦwww.drunkenduckinn.co.uk. This 400-year-old inn is more a restaurant-with-rooms these days. The sixteen bedrooms mix antiques and cool colours with bold contemporary design; the more spacious annexe accommodation includes a deluxe Garden Room with sensational views and a balcony. Food is the main event, with the likes of pigeon with licorice and venison and chocolate challenging traditional lakeland tastes. Add sharp service, a great selection of wines by the glass, homebrewed ales, a suntrap garden with private tarn, and glorious valley views and it's easy to see why this is many people's favourite country inn. Rates vary per room, include afternoon tea and increase £25–30 at weekends; most fall within the category given, though midweek standard rooms are priced a category lower. Parking. ⑦

Yewfield Hawkshead Hill, 2 miles west of Hawkshead off B5285 ☎015394/36765, Ⓦwww .yewfield.co.uk. Non-smoking vegetarian guest house set amongst organic vegetable gardens, orchards and wildflower meadows. The owners make stylish use of the spacious Victorian Gothic interior, and breakfast is a real treat – either a full cooked veggie or a wholefood continental buffet. Best views are from the "luxury" room at the front of the house (priced a category higher), while the old coach house and stables in the grounds are also rented out as self-catering apartments. Parking. Closed mid-Nov to Jan. ③

Youth hostel

Hawkshead YHA Newby Bridge Rd ☎0870/770 5856, Ⓔhawkshead@yha.org.uk. The local hostel is a mile to the south, on Esthwaite Water's west side, housed in a Regency mansion which retains many of its original architectural features. There are over 100 beds and, with 14 three- or four-bedded rooms, and a separate family annexe, it's very popular with families and small groups. Reception opens at 1pm; evening meals are served. Closed mid–Dec to Jan; also closed Nov to mid-Dec Mon–Thurs & Sun, and Feb Sun & Mon. Dorm beds £12.50.

Campsites

Croft Caravan and Campsite North Lonsdale Rd, beyond the car parks on the edge of the village ☎015394/36374, Ⓦwww.hawkshead-croft.com. The closest campsite to the centre is this busy (and relatively expensive) spot with full facilities, including coin-op laundry, games/TV room and bike rental, and caravan rental (by the week, from £205). Closed Nov to mid-March.

Hawkshead Hall Farm half a mile north of Hawkshead on the Ambleside road ☎015394/36221. Escape some of the crowds at this basic, tap-and-toilet campsite; bus #505 passes the farm on the way into Hawkshead. Closed Dec–Feb.

Eating, drinking and entertainment

Apart from the daytime **cafés** and small local **supermarket**, Hawkshead's **pubs** provide the main eating options, the top choices being the *King's Arms* and *Queen's Head* (see "Accommodation" above), both of which have bar meals and outdoor tables as well as more formal dining rooms. The best local dining, however, is at the *Drunken Duck Inn* (see "Accommodation", above), where wonderfully inventive meals run to around £30 a head, excluding drinks and service (reservations essential). Rural activities and entertainment are offered each August during the **Hawkshead Agricultural Show**.

Honey Pot Market Sq ☎015394/36267. This is the best place for takeaway sandwiches for hikers and picnickers. The deli also sells good bread, local produce (sausage, smoked meats and cheese, chutneys, etc) and other food supplies. Daytime only. Inexpensive.

Minstrels' Gallery Market Sq ☎015394/36423. Cosy tearoom in a fifteenth-century building with a menu that satisfies traditionalists (tea, soup and sticky toffee pudding) and the fashion conscious

(espresso, bagels and lemon drizzle cake) alike. Daytime only. Inexpensive.

Whigs Café Market Sq ☎015394/36614. Tearoom whose eponymous speciality is a chewy white roll flavoured with caraway seeds; try one toasted with garlic butter, or as a rarebit with cheese. The café is also the HQ of the Hawkshead Relish Company, so grilled sausages and other dishes are accompanied by homemade relishes, chutneys, mustards and pickles. Daytime only; closed Thurs. Inexpensive.

Banks and exchange There's no bank in Hawkshead. The nearest ATM is in Ambleside, though the post office will exchange travellers' cheques.

Bike rental Croft Mountain Bike Hire at *Croft Caravan and Campsite*, North Lonsdale Rd (available daily when site is open; closed Dec & Jan; ☎015394/36374, ⓦwww.hawkshead-croft.com). Bikes also available at nearby Grizedale Forest and in Coniston.

Emergencies The nearest hospital is in Kendal (Westmorland General Hospital, Burton Rd; ☎01539/732288).

Fishing Hawkshead Trout Farm (☎015394/36541, ⓔtrout@hawkshead.demon .co.uk) offers loch-style day-fishing from boats (including for beginners) on Esthwaite Water (southwest side), catching wild rainbow and brown trout. Barbecue and picnic facilities available.

Outdoor stores The village is the home of the country-and-outdoor-wear store Hawkshead (ⓦwww.hawkshead.com). There are now forty branches nationwide, but the first is still trading here on Main Street.

Pharmacy Collins & Butterworth, Main St ☎015394/36201.

Post office At Hawkshead Newsagents, Main St (Easter–Oct Mon–Sat 9am–5.30pm, Sun 10am–3pm; Nov–Easter Mon–Fri 9am–5.30pm, Sat 9am–12.30pm; ☎015394/36911).

Tarn Hows

A minor road off the Hawkshead–Coniston road (B5285) winds the couple of miles northwest to **Tarn Hows**, a body of water surrounded by spruce and pine, circled by paths and studded with grassy picnic spots. The land was donated to the National Trust by Beatrix Potter in 1930 – one of several such grants – since when the Trust has carefully maintained it. It takes an hour to walk around the tarn, during which you can ponder on the fact that this miniature idyll is in fact almost entirely artificial – the original owners enlarged two small tarns to make the one you see today, planted and landscaped the surroundings and dug the footpaths. It's now a Site of Special Scientific Interest – keep an eye out for some of the Lakes' (and England's) few surviving native **red squirrels**.

Tarn Hows is one of the Lake District's most popular beauty spots, and the best way to appreciate it is to walk there, so that its charms are gently unveiled as you approach. It's about two miles on paths and country lanes from either Hawkshead or Coniston, with a half-mile or so detour possible from the tarn to the tearoom at *Yew Tree Farm* (see p.120). Drivers will have to pay to use the designated National Trust car park. In previous years, a seasonal bus service has dropped day-trippers and walkers off at Tarn Hows, but it may no longer be in operation – local tourist offices will have the latest details.

Hill Top

It's two miles down the eastern side of Esthwaite Water from Hawkshead to the twin hamlets of Near and Far Sawrey, overlooked by the woods and tarns of Claife Heights. Near Sawrey in particular – a cluster of flower-draped whitewashed cottages in a shallow vale – receives an inordinate number of visitors since it's the site of Beatrix Potter's house, **Hill Top** (mid-March to Oct Mon–Wed, Sat & Sun 10.30am–4.30pm; £5; garden entry free on Thurs & Fri when house is closed NT; ☎015394/36269). The seasonal Cross-Lakes Shuttle service runs directly here from Bowness.

Hill Top is an almost mandatory stop on many tours of England (London, Stratford, Hill Top) and the house furnishings and contents have been kept as they were during Potter's occupancy – a condition of her will. The small house is always thronged with visitors, so much so that numbers are often limited. In summer, expect to have to pick up a timed ticket and wait in line. The carved oak bedstead and sideboards, the small library of bound sets of Gibbons and Shakespeare, and the cottage garden are all typical of well-to-do, if unexceptional, Edwardian taste – though the few mementoes and curios do nothing to throw light on Potter's character. But if you love the books then Hill Top and the Sawrey neighbourhood will be familiar (the *Tower Bank Arms*, next door, for instance, is the inn in *The Tale of Jemima Puddle-Duck*). And where better to buy a Mrs Tiggy-Winkle salt-and-pepper shaker or a Peter Rabbit calendar?

A Londoner by birth, **Beatrix Potter** (1866–1943) spent childhood holidays in the Lakes, first at Wray Castle on Windermere and later in houses with grand gardens, at Holehird (Troutbeck) and Lingholm (Derwent Water). Her landscape and animal sketching was encouraged by Canon Rawnsley, a family friend, who inspired her to produce her first book, *The Tale of Peter Rabbit*, published in 1901. With the proceeds, Potter – remembering her happy holidays – bought the lakeland farmhouse at Hill Top in 1905. Half a dozen of her later books are set in and around Hill Top, though she still lived for much of the year in London. Following her marriage to a local solicitor in 1913, when she was 47, Potter retained the house as her study but installed a manager at Hill Top to oversee the farm. Only known locally as Mrs Heelis the farmer (rather than Beatrix Potter the author), she lived down the road in another house, Castle Cottage (not open to the public), but visited Hill Top most days, usually to work on business associated with her increasing portfolio of farms, which took up more and more of her time. She actually wrote very few books after her marriage, preferring to develop her interest in breeding the local Herdwick sheep, for which she won many prizes at local shows. When she died, her ashes were scattered locally by the Hill Top farm manager: the place has never been identified and there's no other memorial to her, save the house.

Near and Far Sawrey

The little hamlet of **NEAR SAWREY** maintains its equilibrium once the Beatrix Potter house of Hill Top has closed for the day. It makes a lovely overnight stop if you can find a room, and if you can't, you can console yourself with a drink in the pub, the *Tower Bank Arms*, the very model of an English country inn. A mile or so away, across the hay fields, lies **FAR SAWREY**, an equally miniature hamlet, though this time with a church, shop and post office, and also with a pub, the *Sawrey Hotel*, which has a beer garden. From here, tracks fan out across **Claife Heights**, past its little tarns and down through the woods to the western shore of Windermere – the most direct route runs steeply downhill to Sawrey ferry pier, where you can catch the car-ferry or passenger launch across to Bowness. It must be the only route in England signposted in Japanese (the Japanese have a special fondness for Beatrix Potter). Coming from the lake, it takes about an hour to walk from the ferry pier to Near Sawrey and Hill Top; going back downhill, slightly less.

Accommodation

Buckle Yeat Near Sawrey ☎015394/36446, ⓦwww.buckle-yeat.co.uk. Gorgeous seventeenth-century cottage close to the Potter house (and illustrated in Potter's *The Tale of Tom Kitten*), offering six non-smoking double/twin rooms and one single (this one doesn't have private facilities). There's always a colourful display of flowers and baskets outside the cottage; inside, the cosy guest lounge has a slate-flagged floor, big armchairs and a log fire. Packed lunches available (£4). Parking. ❹

Ees Wyke Near Sawrey ☎015394/36393, ⓦwww.eeswyke.co.uk. Georgian country house – Beatrix Potter stayed here on childhood holidays – most of whose eight elegant rooms have matchless views across the fields to Esthwaite Water. Dinner (included in the price) is the highpoint, with more lovely views accompanied by five courses served from a refined daily changing menu. Parking. No American Express. ❼

Sawrey House Near Sawrey, overlooking Esthwaite Water ☎015394/36387, ⓦwww.sawrey-house.com. Victorian grace and comfort in this country house, with panoramic views of Esthwaite Water and three acres of grounds. The ten, traditionally decorated rooms are variously sized and priced (the best have king- or queen-size beds). Breakfast specials include wild mushrooms and smoked haddock, while D, B&B rates are also available for another £20 or so a head. Parking. ❼

Tower Bank Arms Near Sawrey, next to Hill Top ☎015394/36334, ⓦwww.towerbankarms.co.uk. The cosy pub – thankfully untouched by modernization – has three rooms available (two doubles, one twin); totter downstairs for good sandwiches, lakeland game pie and local lamb, trout and sausages, washed down by an acclaimed array of beers. In summer, the outdoor tables make the best perch for observing the comings and goings at Hill Top. Parking. ❹

Grizedale Forest

Historically, much of the land between Coniston and Windermere was thickly forested, as indeed it is today, though by the eighteenth century successive generations of charcoal-making, coppicing and iron-smelting had taken their toll and stripped the fells and dales virtually bare. Regeneration by the Forestry Commission has restored thick oak, spruce, larch and pine woodland to **Grizedale Forest**, whose picnic spots, open-air sculptures, cycle trails and high-wire adventure course make a great day out in good weather. Red deer are seen here occasionally and the forest also provides a habitat for badgers and squirrels, grouse, woodcock and woodpeckers.

The best starting point is the visitor centre (see "Practicalities" below), which is the hub of the waymarked trails that spread across both sides of the Grizedale Valley. These extend for between two and fourteen miles on undulating tracks, with the longest, the **Silurian Way**, linking the majority of the ninety-odd remarkable stone and wood **sculptures** scattered amongst the trees. Since 1977 artists have been invited to create a sculptural response to their surroundings using natural materials. Some of the resulting works are startling, as you round a bend to find pinnacles rising from a tarn, sculpted wooden ferns, a hundred-foot-long wave of bent logs or a dry-stone wall slaloming through the conifers. On a bike (available for rent at the forest centre, see below), you can see much of Grizedale in a day, and while there are climbs involved on every route you'll be rewarded on occasion by some excellent fell views. Off the trails, two miles south down the road from the visitor centre, the forestry hamlet of **Satterthwaite** has a pub, the *Eagle's Child*, while some clever route-finding in the narrow lanes the same distance beyond brings you to rustic **Rusland church**. Surrounded by undulating grazing land, it's a serene setting for the simple graves of children's writer **Arthur Ransome** and his wife Eugenia. (See opposite for more on Ransome's life and work).

The more adventurous forest activity is the excellent **Go Ape** (Easter–Sept daily; Oct, Nov & March weekends only; closed Dec–Feb; £18; advance booking essential ℡0870/444 5562, ⓦwww.goape.co.uk), an exhilarating aerial assault course through the Grizedale trees, starting near the visitor centre. After a full safety briefing participants are let loose to follow the inter-linked rope bridges, Tarzan swings, aerial ladders, tree platforms, scramble nets and zip slides, and as you're attached to a safety line at all times the experience turns even the most vertiginous visitor into Spiderman without too much

Arthur Ransome

Arthur Ransome (1884–1967) was born in Leeds and spent early childhood holidays with his brother and sisters at Nibthwaite by Coniston Water. His boyhood holiday pursuits were all put to use in his books, though it was the friendship he made with the outgoing Collingwood family as a young man of 20 which cemented his love affair with the Lakes – sailing with them on Coniston Water, picnicking on Peel Island, and visiting the local copper mines.

Ransome's first job was with a London publisher, though he was soon published in his own right, producing critical literary studies of Edgar Allan Poe and Oscar Wilde, and an account of London's bohemia. He met and **married** Ivy Constance Walker and they had one daughter, Tabitha, in 1910, but the marriage was never happy. In part this prompted a bold solo move to Russia in 1913, after which his marriage was effectively at an end. Ransome was keen to learn the language and had a special interest in Russian folklore – a well-received translation and adaptation of various fairy tales (*Old Peter's Russian Tales*) appeared in 1916.

During World War I, ill health prevented him joining up and he was hired as a **war correspondent** by the *Daily News*. Consequently, when the Russian Revolution broke out, he was well placed to report on events. Ransome clearly knew his Russian politics and was a sympathetic but critical observer of the Bolshevik Revolution, producing two books of on-the-spot reportage. He interviewed Lenin and other leading figures, and was introduced to Trotsky's secretary, Eugenia, who – on the final break-up of his first marriage – became his second wife.

Ransome spent much of the following ten years in Russia and the Baltic states, latter-ly as special correspondent for the *Manchester Guardian*, for whom he travelled widely. In 1925 he bought his first lakeland house at **Low Ludderburn**, in the Winster Valley and, having eventually abandoned journalism, it was here he wrote **Swallows and Amazons** (published in 1930). This was the first of twelve books he produced in the series (the last in 1947), most, but not all, set in the Lake District – spells in Norfolk and Suffolk provided the background for *We Didn't Mean To Go To Sea* and *Coot Club*.

Ransome was inspired to write for and about the five children of the **Altounyan family**, whose father, Ernest, brought them to the Lake District on holiday in 1928. Ernest Altounyan, married to Dora Collingwood, a long-time Ransome family friend, bought two boats (one called *Swallow*) and he and Ransome first taught the children to sail. That the Altounyan children were models for the "Swallows" is now accepted – the first edition of the book was dedicated to them – though when the relation-ship cooled in later years, Ransome denied this and withdrew the dedication. Other friends and local characters appeared in the books, while Coniston locations figured heavily – Peel Island as "Wild Cat Island", the Coniston fells and mines in *Pigeon Post* and the Old Man of Coniston as "Kanchenjunga". Ransome and Eugenia lived in Coniston itself between 1940 and 1945, but settled in retirement at a house called **Hill Top** in Haverthwaite. He died on June 3, 1967.

Eugenia donated various effects and mementoes of her husband's to Abbot Hall in Kendal, which maintains an Arthur Ransome exhibition and doubles as the HQ of The Arthur Ransome Society (TARS), whose zealous members keep his flame alive by means of literary events, publications and activities. For more information, contact the museum or visit the expansive Arthur Ransome website: ⓦwww.arthur-ransome.org/ar.

effort. The high point on the Grizedale course is at an adrenaline-inducing 59ft above floor level. It takes a good two hours to complete the course, while friends and family can follow on foot – there's a minimum age of 10 and a minimum height of 4ft 7in, but apart from that anyone can undertake the course.

Practicalities

Access to the forest is easiest from Hawkshead, which is just two-and-a-half miles northeast of the visitor centre, while you can walk through the forest from the east side of Coniston Water, from Monk Coniston and from Brantwood. In previous years, the seasonal Cross-Lakes Shuttle launch-and -bus service from Bowness, via Hill Top and Hawkshead, has been extended to Grizedale – local tourist offices will have the latest service information. Otherwise, the only public transport is on the weekday postbus or schoolbus from Ulverston to the south, though the timings on either aren't much use for day trips.

Buses stop by the **Grizedale Visitor Centre** (daily: March–Nov 10am –5pm; Dec–Feb 10am–4pm; free; ℡01229/860010, Ⓦwww.forestry.gov.uk /grizedaleforestpark), where there's also plenty of parking (fee charged). Opposite the centre is a **tearoom** with very nice food at reasonable prices, while occupying another nearby building is **Grizedale Mountain Bikes** (March –Oct daily 9am–5.30pm; Nov–Feb weekends only 9am–4.30pm, though hours/days may vary; ℡01229/860369, Ⓦwww.grizedalemountainbikes.co.uk), which provides a wide variety of rental bikes, plus trail maps and cycling gear.

Broughton-in-Furness

Southwest of Coniston Water, a quiet triangle at the southern edge of the National Park is anchored by the small market town of **BROUGHTON-IN-FURNESS**. It dates back to medieval times, though its aspect is pure Georgian. Tall houses surround an attractive square, complete with spreading chestnut tree, commemorative obelisk, stone fish slabs and stocks. In the eighteenth century the market was a staging post for wool, wood and cattle, shipped out of the area from the nearby Duddon estuary. Follow Church Street to the edge of town and you'll reach the **church of St Mary Magdalene**, originally twelfth century though now much restored. The town's only literary connection is a slight one: the scapegrace Brontë brother, Branwell, taught here briefly before terminally pickling himself in Haworth.

Just ten miles from Coniston, Broughton makes a handy local walking base. It's also well-sited for touring the **Furness peninsulas**, which lie just south of the National Park: it's only ten miles south to Dalton-in-Furness (burial place of the artist George Romney) and the South Lakes Animal Park, and another four to Furness Abbey (p.225), the medieval powerhouse of the lakeland economy. The most direct route here is along the A593 from Coniston, via Torver, through the gentle charms of the **Woodland Valley** – the way the branch railway line (now dismantled) used to run. **Cumbria Way** hikers cut through an even less-frequented sector of the park, as their route takes them above the **Crake Valley**, through the bracken and heather of Blawith Fells, past Beacon Tarn. The A5084 parallels the path, sticking closer to the River Crake as it falls away from Coniston Water; turn west at Lowick for the main road to Broughton.

Practicalities

The most frequent **bus services** to Broughton are from the south on the #511 (not Sun), from Ulverston, every hour and a half, or twice a day from Millom. The **tourist office** is in the old town hall on The Square (Easter–June & Oct daily 10am–12.30pm & 1.30–4pm; July–Sept daily 10am–12.30pm & 1.30–5pm; Nov–Easter Mon–Sat 10am–12.30pm; ℡01229/716115, ⊛www .broughton-in-furness.co.uk). Other facilities are scarce (the nearest ATM is in Millom), but there's a post office/store, bakery and grocer's shop among others.

Accommodation is available in a couple of the local pubs – most notably, the *Manor Arms* on The Square (℡01229/716286; ❸), a pleasant old local with a large real ale selection, and breakfast (and drinks) served in your room, though no other meals available. Broughton's best **tearoom**, the *Square Café*, at Annan House on The Square (℡01229/716388, ⊛www .thesquarecafe.co.uk; ❷), also has three cosy B&B rooms available (one with en-suite facilities, ❸), furnished with old oak furniture and original fireplaces. For **bar meals**, the *Black Cock Inn* (℡01229/716529), around the corner from the square on Princes Street, is the town favourite – you'll need to book ahead for dinner at weekends. The best country-pub choice is the venerable *Blacksmiths Arms* (℡01229/716824) at **Broughton Mills**, just over two miles to the north off the A593, with a good beer selection and fine, moderately priced food.

The Duddon Valley

A mile west of Broughton, from Duddon Bridge, the minor road up the stunning **Duddon Valley** – marked **Dunnerdale** on some maps – twists and turns its increasingly dramatic way northeast to the foot of the Wrynose and Hardknott passes. Wordsworth wrote a sequence of 34 sonnets about the valley (published as *The River Duddon* in 1820), his conclusion "Still glides the Stream, and shall for ever glide"– a comment on the ephemeral nature of man. Lofty thoughts indeed as you navigate around the rocky outcrops and through the wandering sheep crowding the road.

On warm days cars line the verges at **Ulpha Bridge**, five miles north of Broughton, as picnics are spread on the riverbanks and kids plummet from the bridge into the water. A small post office/shop a little way up from the bridge sells ice cream. At **SEATHWAITE**, another three miles along the road, there's a pub and a church, and a popular short walk to Wallowbarrow Crag, below which the river tumbles through a gorge. The pub, the highly attractive *Newfield Inn* (℡01229/716208), was visited by Wordsworth on his ramblings, and today features Coniston's Bluebird bitter on tap and a beer garden which looks up onto the fells. Good food (organic trout, home-roast chicken and the like) is served daily between noon and 9pm.

Beyond Seathwaite the road is ever more tortuous, though there's parking a couple of miles further north close to **Birks Bridge**, an ancient bridge which spans a twenty-foot-deep chasm. People picnic here, too, or climb through the forestry land to the west to ascend **Harter Fell** (2140ft), whose summit is a jumble of rocky outcrops with excellent views. A good circular walk from Birks Bridge (7 miles; 4hr) climbs first to Hardknott Pass and then down to the Roman fort there (see p.180), before climbing again to Harter Fell for a final descent through the plantation land to the River Duddon.

Shortly after Birks Bridge the head of the valley widens dramatically at Dale Head, whose "Big Sky" perspective is quite out of keeping with the confined Lakes – more New Zealand than Cumbria. The river is at its widest here, and at the bridge and junction of **Cockley Beck** you can debate the dubious pleasures of attempting your onward route: west over Hardknott Pass into Eskdale or east over Wrynose Pass to Little Langdale; both passes require careful driving or, in the case of out-of-condition cyclists, an oxygen tent. *Cockley Beck Farm* (℡01229/716480) by the bridge has a farmhouse tearoom.

There's a very slow early-morning **postbus** once a day (not Sun) from Broughton-in-Furness to Cockley Beck, via Ulpha and Seathwaite; a quicker afternoon service (Mon–Fri) only goes as far as Seathwaite. Realistically, though, you need your own transport to see much of the Duddon Valley or be prepared to walk.

Travel details

From Broughton

Bus #511 (Mon–Sat every 1hr 30min) to: Ulverston (30min).

Postbus #523 (Mon–Sat 1–2 daily) to: Duddon Valley (circular service to Ulpha, Duddon Bridge, Seathwaite and Cockley Beck).

From Coniston

Bus #505 "Coniston Rambler" to: Hawkshead (16min), Ambleside (35min), Brockhole (41min), Windermere (47min). Service operates Easter–Oct

roughly hourly; Nov–Easter frequency is much reduced.

Bus #X12 (Mon–Sat 8–9 daily) to: Torver (7min), Ulverston (30min).

From Hawkshead

Cross-Lakes Shuttle (4 daily): minibus #525 to Hill Top (7min) and Ferry House, Sawrey (15min, for launch connection to Bowness) – bus may also operate to Tarn Hows, Coniston and Grizedale Visitor Centre. Service operates daily at Easter, bank holidays & July–Sept, weekends only May, June & Oct.

4

Keswick, Derwent Water and the north

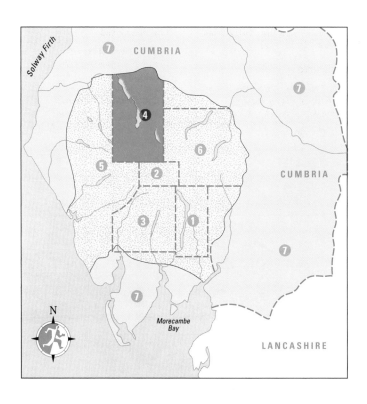

CHAPTER 4 # Highlights

✳ **Castlerigg Stone Circle**
The mysterious standing
stones above Keswick
are a brooding presence.
See p.144

✳ **Evening cruise on Derwent Water** Sit back
and enjoy the sunset as
the shadows fall across
the lake. See p.151

✳ **Climbing Cat Bells** This
celebrated climb and
viewpoint above Derwent Water is a real family favourite. See p.153

✳ **The #79 bus route** The
"Borrowdale Rambler"
runs through some of
England's most spectacular valley scenery.
See p.154

✳ **Honister Slate Mine** A
thrilling tour explores the
tunnels and caverns dug
deep into the mountains
above Honister Pass.
See p.159

✳ **St John's in the Vale**
This hidden valley has
some splendid walking
and you can stop for ice
cream at Low Bridge
End Farm. See p.159

✳ **View the ospreys, Bassenthwaite** Between
April and August, you
can usually see wild
ospreys on Bassenthwaite Lake. See p.162

✳ **Caldbeck** Most come to
see the grave of huntsman John Peel, but this
attractive old village also
boasts a restored riverside mill housing a caférestaurant. See p.164

△ Rosthwaite

Keswick, Derwent Water and the north

Keswick – main town in the lakeland north – has one of the region's most advantageous settings: standing on the northern shores of beautiful Derwent Water, backed by the imposing heights of Skiddaw and Blencathra, and lying at the junction of the main north–south (A591) and east–west (A66) routes through the Lake District. Despite its long history as a market and mining town, it's now almost entirely devoted to the tourist trade, though most of Keswick's visitors are the type who like to rock-hop in the dramatic surroundings rather than clamber from tour-bus to gift shop. Consequently, there's slightly less of the themed lakeland packaging that afflicts the southern towns, and rather more of an outdoors air, with walkers steadily coming and going from their peregrinations. The town also has solid literary connections – not with Wordsworth for a change, but with the other members of the poetical triumvirate, Samuel Taylor Coleridge and Robert Southey, who both settled in Keswick in the early years of the nineteenth century.

Derwent Water lies just a few minutes' walk from the town centre, its launch service providing easy access to long-famed beauty spots such as Ashness Bridge, Watendlath and the Lodore Falls. And even with just a day in town you should make the effort to take in the charms of **Borrowdale**, the glorious meandering valley to the south of Derwent Water that's been a source of inspiration to artists and writers over the centuries. There are fellside scrambles, isolated tarns and waterfalls, riverside walks and tranquil farming hamlets, while the lonely settlements of Rosthwaite, Seatoller, Stonethwaite and Seathwaite are the jumping-off points for the many walking routes to the peaks around **Scafell Pike**, the Lake District's (and England's) highest mountain.

Keswick also makes a good base for climbing either of its shadowing northern bulks, **Skiddaw** or **Blencathra** – the first, one of the four Lakes' mountains that clocks in at over the magic 3000-feet mark, but easy to conquer; the second, a couple of hundred feet lower but with several rather more challenging approaches. Also north of town lies **Bassenthwaite Lake**, from where minor roads and footpaths head northeast into the region known locally as **Back o' Skiddaw**, a little-visited neck of the lakes hidden behind Skiddaw itself. This is as off-the-beaten track as it gets in the National Park, though handsome villages such as **Caldbeck** and the unsung heights of **Carrock Fell** make a trip worthwhile. East

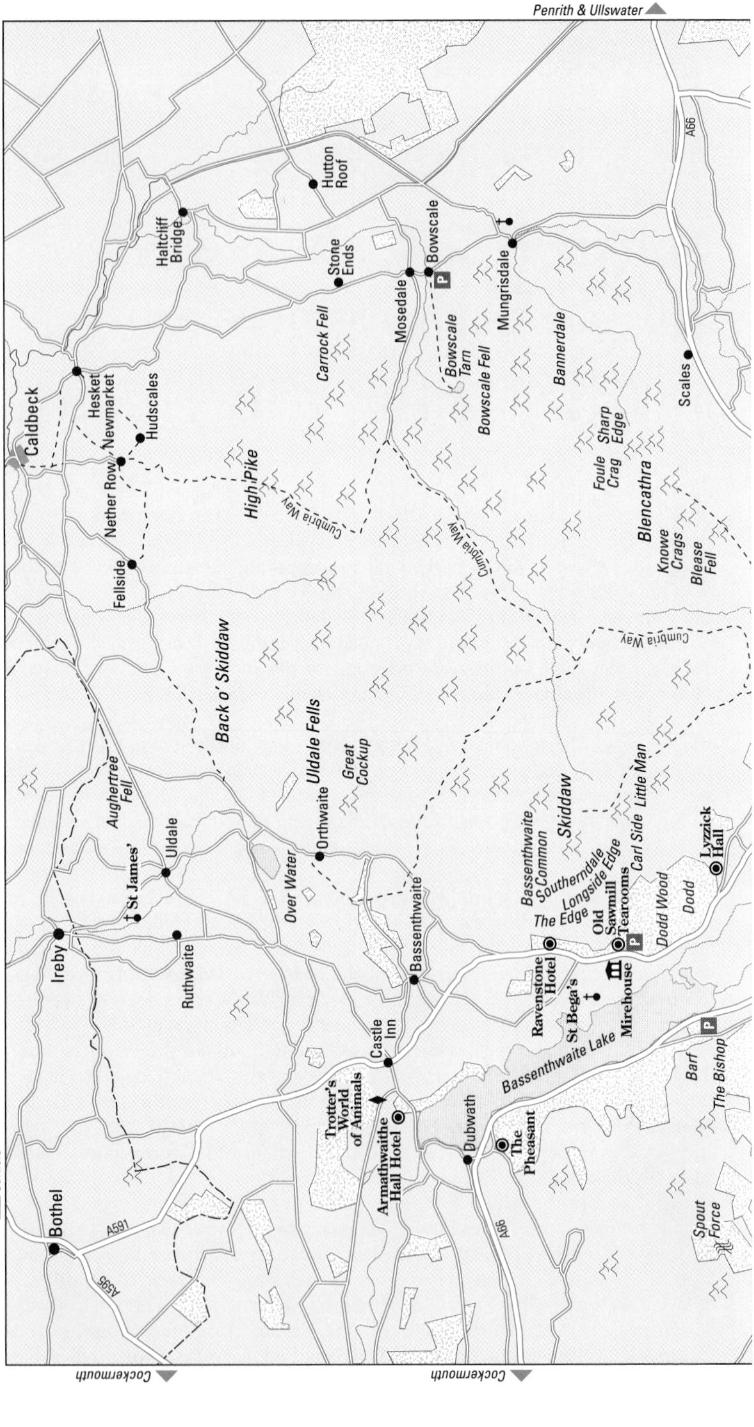

Penrith & Ullswater

Hutton
Roof

Bowscale

Haltcliff
Bridge

Stone
Ends

Mosedale

Bowscale Tarn

Mungrisdale

A66

Carrock Fell

Bowscale Fell

Bannerdale

Scales

Caldbeck

Hesket
Newmarket

Hudscales

Sharp
Edge

Foule
Crag

Blencathra

Fellside

Nether Row

High Pike

Cumbria Way

Knowe
Crags

Blease
Fell

Cumbria Way

Cumbria Way

Back o' Skiddaw

Aughertree
Fell

Uldale Fells

Great
Cockup

St James'

Uldale

Orthwaite

Skiddaw

Little Man

Ireby

Over Water

Bassenthwaite
Common

Southerndale

Longside Edge

Carl Side

Lyzzick
Hall

Ruthwaite

Bassenthwaite

The Edge

Old
Sawmill
Tearooms

Dodd Wood

Dodd

Castle
Inn

Ravenstone
Hotel

St Bega's

Mirehouse

Trotter's
World
of Animals

Bassenthwaite Lake

Barf

The Bishop

Dubwath

Bothel

A591

Armathwaite
Hall Hotel

The
Pheasant

Spout
Force

A66

A595

Carlisle

Carlisle

Cockermouth

Cockermouth

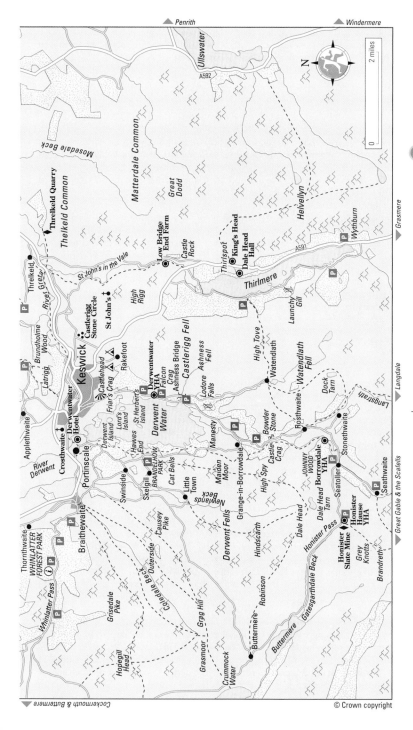

▲ Penrith ▲ Windermere

Ullswater

A592

N

2 miles

0

Mosedale Beck

Matterdale Common

Great Dodd

▶ Grasmere

Helvellyn

Thelkeld Common

Threlkeld Quarry

King's Head

Thirlspot

Dale Head Hall

Low Bridge End Farm

Castle Rock

Wythburn

P

Threlkeld

River Greta

St John's in the Vale

Thirlmere

A591

Castlerigg Stone Circle

St John's †

High Rigg

P

Keswick

Rakefoot

Derwentwater YHA

Castlerigg Fell

Launchy Gill

P

Brundholme Wood

Castlehead

Falcon Crag

Ashness Bridge

Ashness Fell

High Tove

Watendlath

Latrigg

Friar's Crag

Lodore Falls

Watendlath Fell

Applethwaite

P

Derwentwater Hotel

St Herbert's Island

Derwent Water

Dock Tarn

P

Crosthwaite

Lord's Island

Hawes End

Bowder Stone

Rosthwaite

Portinscale

Derwent Island

Manesty

Castle Crag

Langstrath

▶ Langdale

River Derwent

Swinside

Skelgill

BRANDELHOW PARK

Cat Bells

High Spy

Stonethwaite

Seathwaite

P

Braithwaite

Little Town

Newlands Beck

Maiden Moor

Grange-in-Borrowdale

JOHNNY WOOD

Borrowdale YHA

P

Seatoller

▶ Great Gable & the Scafells

WHINLATTER FOREST PARK

i

P

Causey Pike

Dale Head

Dale Head Tarn

Thornthwaite

P

Grisedale Pike

Coledale Beck

Outerside

Derwent Fells

Hindscarth

Honister Hause YHA

P

Whinlatter Pass

P

Grag Hill

Robinson

Dale Head

Honister Pass

Honister Slate Mine

Grey Knotts

Brandreth

Hopegill Head

Grasmoor

Buttermere

Gatesgarthdale Beck

Buttermere

Crummock Water

▲ Cockermouth & Buttermere

© Crown copyright

of Keswick, the old railway line footpath makes a fine approach to the little village of **Threlkeld**, from where some are drawn south through bucolic **St John's in the Vale** to **Thirlmere**, the Lake District's largest reservoir.

Keswick

The modern centre of **KESWICK**, a town of around 5000 people, sits south and east of the River Greta, though its origins lie around an early medieval church just over the river in Crosthwaite. Scattered farms probably provided its first local industry, if the town's name (*kes*, meaning cheese, and *wic*, meaning dairy farm) – is anything to go by. Granted its market charter by Edward I in 1276 – **market day** is still Saturday – Keswick became an important centre for trading wool and leather until around 1500, when these trades were supplanted by ore-mining and, later, the discovery of local graphite, which formed the mainstay of the local economy until the late eighteenth century. The railway (long defunct) arrived in the 1860s, since when Keswick has turned its attention fully to the requirements of tourists. There's plenty of accommodation and some good cafés aimed at walkers, while several bus routes radiate from the town, getting you to the start of even the most challenging hikes. For those not up to a day on the fells, the town remains a popular place throughout the year, with its handsome park, three interesting museums and several old pubs – and you're only ever a short stroll away from the shores of Derwent Water.

The Town

The centre of Keswick fills the space between Main Street and the wide River Greta, which makes a lazy curve through town and park. Most of the main sights – including the Pencil Museum, Crosthwaite church, and Castlerigg stone circle – lie outside this area, but don't abandon the centre without a quick walk around. Many of the buildings are Victorian, including the **Moot Hall** (1813), marooned in the middle of Market Place; formerly the town hall and prison, it now houses the tourist office. Down St John's Street, sandstone **St John's Church** dates from the same year, notable only for its handsome spire (a landmark from all over town) and for the fact that the novelist Sir Hugh Walpole – who set his Herries novels in Borrowdale and the Back o' Skiddaw – is buried in the churchyard: follow the sign to where the "Man of Letters, Lover of Cumberland, Friend of his fellowmen" lies beneath a Celtic cross, looking towards the west side of Derwent Water, where his house still stands. By way of quite extraordinary contrast, the **Cars of the Stars Motor Museum**, on Standish Street (Easter–Nov daily, weekends only in Dec, plus Feb school hols, 10am–5pm; £4; ☎017687/73757, ⓦwww.carsofthestars. com), does no less than its name suggests. James Bond's Aston Martin DB5, the Batmobile, Emma Peel's Lotus Elan, Mad Max's Ford Falcon, the *Back to the Future* Delorean, Mr Bean's Mini – all of these and more are displayed in glorious incongruity in a restored garage in a Keswick back street.

Keswick Museum and Art Gallery

Some of Sir Hugh Walpole's original manuscripts are on display in Keswick's terrific **Museum and Art Gallery** on Station Road (Easter–Oct Tues–Sat 10am–4pm; free; ☎017687/73263), at the edge of the riverside **Fitz Park**. Founded in 1780, the museum is a classic of its kind, its elderly glass cases preserving singular archeological, mineral and butterfly collections, as well as stuffed birds, a set of

Keswick

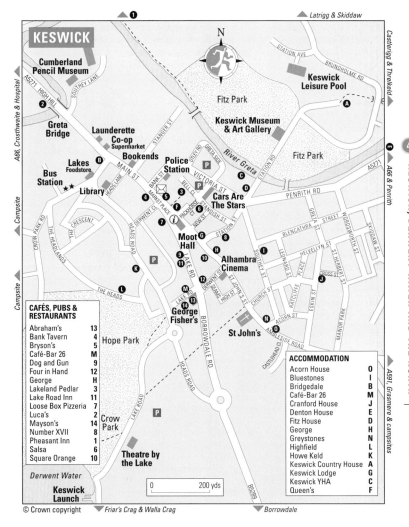

KESWICK

Latrigg & Skiddaw

N

Cumberland Pencil Museum

Keswick Leisure Pool

Fitz Park

Greta Bridge

Launderette

Co-op Supermarket

Keswick Museum & Art Gallery

Fitz Park

River Greta

Lakes Foodstore

Bookends

Police Station

Bus Station

Library

Cars Are The Stars

Moot Hall

Alhambra Cinema

CAFÉS, PUBS & RESTAURANTS

Abraham's	13
Bank Tavern	4
Bryson's	5
Café-Bar 26	M
Dog and Gun	9
Four in Hand	12
George	H
Lakeland Pedlar	3
Lake Road Inn	11
Loose Box Pizzeria	7
Luca's	2
Mayson's	14
Number XVII	8
Pheasant Inn	1
Salsa	6
Square Orange	10

Hope Park

George Fisher's

St John's

Crow Park

Theatre by the Lake

Derwent Water

Keswick Launch

0   200 yds

ACCOMMODATION

Acorn House	O
Bluestones	I
Bridgedale	B
Café-Bar 26	M
Cranford House	J
Denton House	E
Fitz House	D
George	H
Greystones	N
Highfield	L
Howe Keld	K
Keswick Country House	A
Keswick Lodge	G
Keswick YHA	C
Queen's	F

Friar's Crag & Walla Crag

Borrowdale

lions' teeth, antique climbing equipment, cock-fighting spurs, packhorse bells and a massive set of Victorian "musical stones" – cordierite-impregnated slate – which bong in tune when you hit them. Under protective covers in the literary room sits a huge array of letters, manuscripts and poems by Southey, Wordsworth, De Quincey, (Hartley) Coleridge, Walpole and Ruskin. There's interesting memorabilia too: a cheque for thirty pounds drawn on Ruskin's account, Southey's gloves and leather chair, and a desk filched from Greta Hall (see p.143).

Cumberland Pencil Museum

For the town's industrial history, you need to pop along to the **Cumberland Pencil Museum** (daily 9.30am–4pm, July & Aug until 5pm; £2.50; ☏017687/73626, ⓦwww.pencils.co.uk), west along Main Street by Greta

Bridge. For centuries Borrowdale shepherds marked their sheep with a locally occurring substance they knew as wadd and, later, as plumbago or black lead. It was, of course, graphite (a pure carbon) from the Borrowdale fells and after about 1500, when it was discovered that it could also be carved and cut to shape, graphite mining became commercially viable. In the early days, graphite was used in several ways – rubbed on firearms to prevent rusting, to make cannon-ball moulds and as a medicinal cure for stomach disorders. With the idea of putting graphite into wooden holders (prototype pencils were used by Florentine artists), Keswick became an important pencil-making town – the mines and shipments were so valuable that they were put under armed guard to thwart smugglers. The town prospered until the late eighteenth century, when the French discovered how to make pencil graphite cheaply by binding the common amorphous graphite with clay. Keswick's monopoly was quickly broken, though its major pencil mills by the River Greta – first established in 1832 – continued to thrive. Today, only the factory which owns the museum still survives and even that is under persistent financial pressure. Its future is far from certain and although pencils are still made here, the graphite is now imported from the Far East and the wood used is American cedar. All this, and more than you'll ever need to know about the pencil-producing business, is explained inside, where a mock-up of the long-defunct Borrowdale mine heralds multifarious examples of the finished product, including the world's

Robert Southey in the Lakes

Few better or more blameless men have ever lived, than he; but he seems to lack colour, passion, warmth.

Nathaniel Hawthorne, *English Notebooks*, 1855

Robert Southey (1774–1843) – his surname, incidentally, pronounced "Sow-thee" and not "Suh-thee" – first visited the Lake District in 1801 at the request of his brother-in-law, Samuel Taylor Coleridge. The two poets already had a spiky relationship – a failed plan to form a Utopian society abroad dwindled into recriminations later as, having married Edith Fricker in 1795, Southey was accused of pushing Coleridge into an unhappy marriage with her sister, Sara. Moreover, Southey was already a published poet when Coleridge and Wordsworth produced their *Lyrical Ballads* (1798), which Southey reviewed, infamously, for the *Critical Review*. He was harsh about Wordsworth's efforts and dismissive of Coleridge's "Rime of the Ancient Mariner" ("a poem of little merit").

Reconciliation came with the deaths of Coleridge and Sara's second son Berkeley, and Southey and Edith's first child, Margaret Edith. Coleridge, unhappy with his life at Greta Hall, repeated the invitation to Southey, who accepted thinking the visit might alleviate Edith's grief. The Southeys arrived in September 1803 and Edith soon became pregnant again. Southey enjoyed the landscape and when Coleridge suggested leaving for Malta for his health, Southey agreed to stay on and pay the rent. With Sara Coleridge now effectively a lodger in her own home, Edith's other sister (and widow), Mary Lovell, also arrived to stay – soon the family joke was that Greta Hall was the "Aunt Hill".

Coleridge himself never returned to live there, but Sara Coleridge now had three children at Greta Hall; Mary Lovell, one son; plus the Southeys' eventual brood – Edith May, Herbert, Emma, Bertha, Kate, Isabel and Cuthbert. Emma, Isabel and Herbert died before adulthood, but there were still up to ten childen in the house at any one time, who Southey entertained with stories and poems, including his *Tale of Three Bears*. All the children were taught languages, music and drawing at home, though the boys were eventually sent to Ambleside school.

largest (six-foot-high) pencil, duly acknowledged as such by the *Guinness Book of Records*.

Crosthwaite

Over Greta Bridge, it's a fifteen-minute walk down High Hill and Church Lane to the edge of town and **Crosthwaite Church**, dedicated to St Kentigern (or Mungo), the Celtic missionary who founded several churches in Cumbria. Evidence suggests that Kentigern passed through in 553 AD and planted his cross in the clearing ("thwaite") here, though it's unlikely a permanent church was built on this site until the twelfth century, while the present structure dates from 1523. The poet **Robert Southey** is buried in the churchyard, alongside his wife and children; his quasi-imperial marble effigy (inscribed by Wordsworth, who attended the funeral) stands inside the church, as does a plaque honouring Canon Hardwicke Drummond Rawnsley, one of the co-founders of the National Trust (see p.152). Both men had strong links with Keswick. Rawnsley was the vicar at Crosthwaite between 1883 and 1917, while Southey moved into his brother-in-law Samuel Taylor Coleridge's house in the town in 1803 and, after Coleridge moved out, continued to live there for the next forty years. Southey was Poet Laureate from 1813 until his death in 1843 and his house, a Georgian pile known as **Greta Hall**, played its part in the Lakes' literary scene: it had a library stuffed with 14,000 books, which

Southey's poetry sold slowly and most of his income was derived from journalism and other works. Early visits to an uncle in Portugal had sparked an interest in the Portuguese empire and a *History of Portugal* was planned on a huge scale, though only the volumes on Brazil (1810–19) were completed. This was the work Southey considered his best, though it was his *Life of Nelson* (1813) – only moderately successful during his life – that later became the work most associated with him.

Although never in financial difficulty, Southey was not well off, certainly given the size of his household, and he was compelled to accept the Poet Laureateship in 1813 (the best of the sinecures offered to him over the years). This opened him up to attack from the likes of a young Shelley, who came to stay at Keswick and rather ungratefully belittled Southey as the "paid champion of every abuse and absurdity". It's true Southey had long outgrown the radicalism of his youth, but perhaps the greater irony is that, with the assumption of the laureateship, he gave up on large-scale poetry altogether. *Roderick*, the last of his epic poems, appeared in 1814.

At home, Edith was suffering bouts of depression, brought on by the steady loss of her children. After Isabel died in 1826 (the fourth of the Southeys' eight children to die), Edith was sent to a progressive retreat in 1834 in York, but never really regained full mental health. She died in November 1837 and within a year Southey had married an author, Caroline Bowles, twelve years his junior, with whom he had corresponded for almost twenty years.

Southey, ill by now, never consummated the marriage and suffered a stroke. Caroline's arrival at Greta Hall had upset everyone, especially the Southey girls, and when their father died on March 21, 1843 – a silent invalid for the last two years – the family was divided. Son Cuthbert was left in charge of the literary estate, which Wordsworth and others felt he wasn't up to – a point on which they felt vindicated following the poorly received publication of Southey's *Life and Correspondence*. And Southey's vast library – his pride and joy, catalogued by Sara Coleridge and his daughters – was broken up and sold.

Southey delighted in showing to his visitors – Wordsworth (who tended not to hold with libraries) laments in his memorial inscription, "Loved books, no more shall Southey feed upon your precious lore." Greta Hall is now part of Keswick School (closed to the public) whose playing fields lie across from the church.

Castlerigg Stone Circle

Keswick's most mysterious landmark, **Castlerigg Stone Circle** (always open; free) can be reached by path along the disused railway line to Threlkeld (sign-posted by the *Keswick Country House Hotel*, at the end of Station Road) – after half a mile, look for the signposted turning to the right. The site is a mile further on atop a sweeping plateau, dwarfed by the encroaching fells. Thirty-eight hunks of Borrowdale volcanic stone, the largest almost eight feet tall, form a circle a hundred feet in diameter; another ten blocks delineating a rectangular enclosure within. The array probably had an astronomical or timekeeping function when it was erected four or five thousand years ago, but no one really knows. Whatever its origins, it's a magical spot – and particularly stunning in winter when frost and snow blanket the surrounding fells.

The Stone Circle is signposted off both the A66 and A591 on the way into Keswick. The "Caldbeck Rambler" bus #73/73A runs here twice a day in summer school holidays and on Saturdays all year, or town bus #87 comes this way twice a day (not Sun).

Practicalities

Buses (including National Express services) use the terminal at The Headlands, behind the Lakes Foodstore, off Main Street. The town is a major transport hub, with regular services to and from Grasmere, Ambleside, Windermere and Kendal (#555/556), Borrowdale (#79), Caldbeck (#73/73A), Buttermere (#77/77A), and Bassenthwaite, Cockermouth and Penrith (#X4/X5/X50), among others – see "Travel details" at the end of the chapter for full routes. Parking is easier than in many places: large **car parks** down Lake Road near the lake, and on either side of Market Place, soak up most of the visiting and shopping traffic; while there are no restrictions in the streets off Southey Street (where most of the B&Bs are) or on Brundholme Road behind the park.

The **National Park Information Centre** is in the Moot Hall on Market Place (daily: July & Aug 9.30am–6pm; April–June, Sept & Oct 9.30am–5.30pm; Nov–March 9.30am–4pm; ☎017687/72645). **Guided walks** – from lakeside rambles to mountain climbs – depart from the Moot Hall (Easter–Oct daily 10.15am; £6; ☎017687/71292, ⓦwww.keswickrambles.co.uk); just turn up with a packed lunch. There's **online information** for the Keswick area at ⓦwww.dokeswick.com and ⓦwww.keswick.org.

Accommodation

B&Bs and guest houses cluster around Southey, Blencathra, Church and Eskin streets, in the grid off the A591 (Penrith road). Smarter guest houses and hotels line The Heads, overlooking Hope Park, a couple of minutes south of the centre on the way to the lake, and there's also a clutch of guest houses and hotels out at **Portinscale**, a small village a couple of miles west of town around the lake. Nearly all the town **pubs** offer accommodation too – the best are picked out below – while if you're in the mood for an upmarket country house-hotel experience, Keswick's rugged environs have plenty of choice. The town's riverside **youth hostel** and out-of-town **backpackers** are open all year and usually have space; hostels at nearby Derwent

Keswick walks fall into three categories: strolls down by the lake or up to scenic viewpoints, and the considerably more energetic peak-bagging of Skiddaw and Blencathra. If you've got time to make only one local hike, there's a case for making it up Cat Bells (see Derwent Water, p.153), which forms the distinctive backdrop to many a Keswick view.

Latrigg

Latrigg (1203ft), north of town, gets the vote for a quick climb (45min) to a fine viewpoint – up Bassenthwaite Lake and across Derwent Water to Borrowdale and the high fells. Driving first to the Underscar car park gets you even closer, within twenty minutes of the summit. For a circular walk (4–6 miles; 2–3hr), follow the eastern ridge to Brundholme, returning through Brundholme wood or along the railway line path.

Walla Crag

South of town, the best half-day walk is to **Walla Crag** (1234ft) and back (5 miles; 4hr), approaching via Friar's Crag and Derwent Water. At Calf Close Bay you cross the Borrowdale road (B5329) and climb through Great Wood to the summit, which provides terrific views of the lake, St Herbert's Island and the fells beyond. The descent back to town is via Rakefoot, with a possible diversion to Castlehead (530ft) for lesser, but still attractive, lake views.

Skiddaw

Easiest of the true mountain walks is the hike up the smooth mound of splintery slate that is **Skiddaw** (3053ft). From the Underscar car park it's a steady (and, it has to be said, boring) walk up a wide eroded track, with a possible diversion up Skiddaw **Little Man** (2837ft), before reaching the High Man summit. Straight up and down is around five miles and takes about five hours, but there's a much better route back, descending to the southwest, along the ridge above Bassenthwaite formed by Longside Edge, **Ullock Pike** (2230ft) and The Edge, before dropping down into Dodd Wood (8 miles; 7hr). Either catch the bus along the A591 back to Keswick, or keep off the road on the signposted Keswick path from Dodd Wood.

Blencathra

Blencathra (2847ft) – also known as Saddleback – could keep hikers occupied for a fortnight. Wainwright details twelve possible ascents of its summit and though made of the same slate as Skiddaw, it's a far more aggressive proposition. Many use Threlkeld as the starting point: easiest route is via Blease Fell and Knowe Crags (an ascent that Wainwright pooh-poohs as too dull); the path starts from the car park by the Blencathra Centre. The more adventurous steer a course up any of the narrow ridges, whose names (Sharp Edge, Foule Crag) don't pull any punches – for most of these, the best starting point is the *White Horse* pub at Scales, another mile-and-a-half up the A66 (towards Penrith) from Threlkeld.

See Basics, p.40, for general walking advice in the Lakes; recommended maps are detailed on p.27.

Water and in Borrowdale really require advance reservations in summer. The same applies to the main **campsites**, which are all very popular. For self-catering **cottages** in the area, call local specialists Keswick Cottages (☏017687/73895, Ⓦwww.keswickcottages.co.uk) or Lakeland Cottages (☏017687/71071, Ⓦwww.lakelandcottages.co.uk).

In Keswick

Acorn House Ambleside Rd ☎017687/72553, ⓦwww.acornhousehotel.co.uk. The handsome eighteenth-century house offers nine generously sized rooms with period furniture, including a couple of antique four-posters. Nice touches proliferate – bedside choccies, and corkscrew and wine glasses provided – and it's a quiet, friendly, non-smoking base, just 5min from the centre. Breakfasts are good too. Parking. ④

Bluestones 7 Southey St ☎017687/74237. A welcoming guest house that's used to families (check out the classic Dinky car collection) and groups of walkers – three of the reasonably spacious rooms have three or four beds; though all bar one share a bathroom. And there's fresh fruit and yoghurt at breakfast. No American Express. ②

Bridgedale 101 Main St ☎017687/73914, ⓦwww.insiteswd.co.uk/bridgedalecottage. Keswick's most amenable landlady, Mrs Taylor, makes her half-dozen rooms suit all requirements. The Shirley Bassey-style lamé shower curtain aside, there are few frills, but whether you're looking for an early breakfast before a day on the fells (weather forecast and packed lunch provided), a room-only deal, or a discount for a longer stay, you'll find it here – with rates often dropping a category accordingly. There's a summer tea garden out back, left-luggage and bike storage facilities, and parking. No credit cards. ②

Café-Bar 26 26 Lake Rd ☎017687/80863. Three stylishly decorated rooms on the first floor above the café offer a chintz-free base right in the town centre. They're all nice and light, with pretty tiled shower rooms. ②, weekends ③

Cranford House 18 Eskin St ☎017687/71017, ⓦwww.cranfordhouse.co.uk. Classy town-house B&B, whose appealing rooms feature large comfortable beds, ethnic throws and scatter cushions. The six rooms include two singles (these share a bathroom), while the two rooms at the top have rooftop views and exposed beams. Breakfast (English, vegetarian or continental) is taken in front of the open fire. No American Express. ③

Fitz House 47 Brundholme Terrace, Station Rd ☎017687/74488, ⓦwww.fitzhouse.co.uk. Beautiful Victorian house overlooking the park, glowing with restored pine, lovely furnishings and artwork. One room has a private terrace, another has window seating with park views, while all share use of a stunning tiled conservatory (where glasses and corkscrew are provided for that post-walk sundowner). No credit cards. ③

George St John St ☎017687/72076, ⓦwww.georgehotelkeswick.co.uk. Old town-centre coaching inn with bags of character in its venerable public bars. The rooms themselves have been modernized (ask if you want a bath instead of a shower), and are comfortable enough, though you'll be easily tempted downstairs to sample the food and ales. Limited parking. ④

Greystones Ambleside Rd ☎017687/73108, ⓦwww.greystones.tv. Non-smoking terrace house opposite the church. Seven spick-and-span rooms (one single available) have fell views and there's parking. ③

Highfield The Heads ☎017687/72508, ⓦwww.highfieldkeswick.co.uk. Beautifully restored non-smoking Victorian stone hotel whose eye-catching feature rooms include two perky turrets and a converted chapel, the latter with lots of space and a four-poster bed. Some front rooms have balconies and lake views, all have comfortable beds, and there's garden seating, parking, a bar and an inventive restaurant with a daily changing menu (dinner included in the price). ⑦

Howe Keld 5–7 The Heads ☎017687/72417, ⓦwww.howekeld.co.uk. The Fishers' non-smoking guest house has a reputation for great breakfasts, including organic bread, pancakes and syrup, fishcakes, veggie rissoles and other homemade specialities. Rooms have fell views and pretty fabrics, plus compact bathrooms with power showers and thoughtful toiletries. There's also a view-laden lounge supplied with walking books. Good-value evening meals are available (£14.75) by prior arrangement on certain nights. Parking. ④

Keswick Country House Station Rd ☎017687/72020, ⓦwww.thekeswickcountryhousehotel.co.uk. Grand hotel, built for the nineteenth-century railway trade and sitting in landscaped grounds beneath Latrigg Fell. The conservatory is a beauty, and rooms provide a bit more space than usual in town for the money. Guests get free entry to the adjacent Keswick Leisure Pool. One-night B&B rates are available, but you get much better value if you stay at least a couple of days and take dinner. Parking. ⑦

Keswick Lodge Main St ☎017687/74584, ⓦwww.keswick-lodge.co.uk. Old coaching inn with decently priced rooms, and good beer downstairs in one of Keswick's jollier hostelries, warmed in winter by an open fire. Ask about the three-for-two-night offers (not available over weekends or throughout August). ③

Queen's Main St ☎017687/73333, ⓦwww.queenshotel.co.uk. The traditional central hotel has a very cosy bar and a huge variety of rooms, all reasonably sized, many with good views. Some have been upgraded more recently than others, so ask to see first – the cheapest are priced a category lower. Parking (fee charged) and free pass to Keswick pool. ⑥

Around Kewick

Derwentwater Portinscale, 2 miles west of town, off the A66 ☎017687/72538, ⓦwww .derwentwater-hotel.co.uk. Superior lakeside retreat with very comfortable rooms – nice enough in the standard range and positively luxurious at the de luxe level (priced a category higher), where you also get lounge areas, sherry decanter, CD and video players. The public lounges, conservatory and restaurant all rate highly too, while guests get free use of a nearby health spa and pool. Two-night D,B&B rates are a good deal, while self-catering one- and two-bedroomed apartments and cottages are available at adjacent Derwent Manor. Parking. ⑦

Lyzzick Hall Under Skiddaw, A591 ☎017687/72277, ⓦwww.lyzzickhall.co.uk. A couple of miles northwest of town, this relaxed country-house hotel is a bit heavy on the floral decor but is set in its own lovely grounds with sweeping views, plus an indoor pool, lounges warmed by log fires and a very good restaurant. Having dinner here as well pushes the price up into the next category. Parking. ⑥

Youth hostels and back-packer accommodation

Denton House Penrith Rd ☎017687/75351, ⓦwww.vividevents.co.uk. Keswick's cheapest bed is at the independent backpackers housed in a former station master's house and cadet barracks, a 10min walk from the centre (by the railway bridge, just after the ambulance/fire station). A rolling refurbishment is in hand, but all the basics are in place (kitchen, bike storage, drying room, free tea and coffee), while single-sex/mixed dorms range in size from four to twelve beds (56 in total). Sign up for outdoor activities and tours at reception; office open at least Mon–Fri 9am–1pm. Parking. No credit cards. Dorm beds £10.

Derwentwater YHA Barrow House, 2 miles south of Keswick on the B5289 (Borrowdale) road ☎0870/770 5792, ⓔderwentwater@yha.org.uk. Based in a 200-year-old mansion with fifteen acres of grounds sloping down to the lake. It's a bit far to walk in and out for the shops and pubs, but bus #79 runs past and the Keswick Launch stops at a nearby pier. There are 88 beds, mostly in four- to eight-bedded rooms, and a drying room and laundry. Reception open all day; evening meals are served. Parking. Open Fri & Sat only Nov–Jan. Dorm beds £12.50.

Keswick YHA, Station Rd ☎0870/770 5894, ⓔkeswick@yha.org.uk. A converted woollen mill by the river, across from the park, which has 91 beds available but still fills quickly in summer. Most of the rooms have just three or four beds (though there is one ten-bedded dorm), so it's hardly institutional and suits families. There's Internet access, drying room, laundry, plenty of local hiking and biking info, a lounge with pool table and balcony overlooking the river, and free tea and coffee on arrival. Reception open all day; evening meal served. Dorm beds £12.50.

Campsites

Castlerigg Farm Rakefoot Lane, off A591, Castlerigg ☎017687/72479. Mainly for tents (with showers and a small shop), just over a mile south-east of the centre. Closed Nov–Easter.

Castlerigg Hall Rakefoot Lane, off A591, Castlerigg ☎017687/74499, ⓦwww.castlerigg.co.uk. Large tent-and-caravan site; it's the first one you reach up this road, just over a mile southeast of the centre. Van rental is available by the week (£180–390), and there's a shop, campers' kitchen, laundry, lounge and games room, plus a breakfast room (open mornings only) supplying cooked breakfasts. Closed Nov–Easter.

Derwentwater Camping and Caravan Club Site Derwent Water ☎017687/72392. Less than a 10min walk from the centre, down by the lake (which means it's always busy); turn off Main Street and head past the bus terminal. Closed Dec & Jan.

Eating, drinking and entertainment

Keswick is a real metropolis compared to anywhere else in the National Park, which means for once that there's no shortage of places to eat and drink, especially down Lake Road, which is fast becoming Keswick's "food street". Daytime **cafés** are firmly aimed at the walking and shopping crowd – you won't want for a big bowl of soup or a cream tea – and there are some decent **restaurants** and lots of **pubs**. The two **supermarkets**, Lakes Foodstore and the Co-op, are near the bus station, off Main Street.

If you're planning to be around for any length of time, it's worth a call to see what's on at the **Theatre by the Lake**, whose full repertoire of performances, concerts and events makes Keswick something of a cultural centre for the Lake District. Otherwise, the biggest events in town are the annual **jazz festival** each May, the June **beer festival**, and the traditional **Keswick Agricultural Show** (August bank holiday), which is the place to learn more about sheep-shearing and other rural pursuits.

Cafés and café-bars

Abraham's Tearooms George Fisher, 2 Borrowdale Rd ☎017687/72178. The top-floor tearoom of the outdoors store (housed in the former quarters of the Abraham's lakeland photography studio, hence the name) comes to your aid with warming mugs of *glühwein*, home-made soups, big breakfasts with free-range eggs and daily specials. Daytime only. No credit cards. Inexpensive.

Brysons 42 Main St ☎017687/72257. Top-notch bakery and tearoom with breakfasts, traditional main dishes, cream teas and speciality plum bread. Daytime only; closed Sun Jan–March. No credit cards. Moderate.

Café-Bar 26 26 Lake Rd ☎017687/80863. Contemporary café-bar – all bold colours and leather sofas – serving lunch (noon–2pm), dinner (6–8pm), good coffee, and a range of wines and continental beers. On the short but appealing menu are things like shared Mediterranean platters, smoked chicken salad, and steak with potato wedges, while a patio out the back catches the sun. No food Mon. Moderate.

Lakeland Pedlar Henderson's Yard, Bell Close Car Park ☎017687/74492. Keswick's best caff – a (licensed) wholefoood veggie experience – has fell views from its outdoor tables, great coffee, inspired breakfasts (burritos, muffins with scrambled eggs) and a Mediterranean/Tex-Mex menu featuring nachos, pizzas, veggie specials and sandwiches. Daytime only (till 8pm July & Aug). Moderate.

Number XVII Coffee Shop 17 Station St ☎017687/71171. Five small tables at the back of the deli provide intimate seating for "light bites" (spicy beanburgers, mozzarella melts), stuffed bagels and wraps, grilled sandwiches and all-day brunches. Daytime only. Inexpensive.

Square Orange 20 St John's St ☎017687/73888. A relaxed little café-bar with a nice line in authentic stone-baked pizzas, served lunch and dinner. Otherwise, it's coffee and muffins over a read of the paper. Inexpensive.

Restaurants

Loose Box Pizzeria King's Arms Courtyard, Main St ☎017687/72083. Popular pizza-and-pasta joint – the house special is *spaghetti rustica* (tomato, garlic, chilli and prawns) – with an outdoor deck in the courtyard. It's nothing fancy, but does the job for a budget night out. Moderate.

Luca's Greta Bridge ☎017687/74621. Riverside Italian bistro (housed in the old Keswick School of Industrial Arts) offering upmarket pastas, pizzas and mains – monkfish wrapped in pancetta or roast lamb shoulder on olive-oil mash are typical dishes. Closed Mon. Expensive.

Mayson's 33 Lake Rd ☎017687/74104. Under the tumbling houseplants is a licensed, self-service restaurant serving lasagne, moussaka, pies, curries and stir-fries, accompanied by brown or spicy rice or baked potatoes and salad. Choose from the menu or make up your own stir-fry combo. May–Oct open until 9pm; daytime only rest of the year. No credit cards. Inexpensive.

Salsa 1 New St ☎017687/75222. Keswick's best night out –Tex-Mex tapas and drinks downstairs, and restaurant upstairs (reservations recommended) serving fajitas, tacos, ribs, wraps, grilled fish and steaks. Moderate.

Pubs

Dog and Gun 2 Lake Rd ☎017687/73463. Retains its old slate floor and oak beams, and shows off a series of classic Abraham brothers' climbing pictures. A changing selection of guest ales is available.

Bank Tavern 47 Main St ☎017687/72663. Currently has a local reputation for its bar meals, which means that every table is often filled. The beer's good too (Jennings and guest ales), while a terrace at the back looks up Market Square.

Four in Hand Lake Rd ☎017687/72069. An old coaching inn whose racehorse-owning landlord has festooned the interior with racing pictures. The bar meals here get a lot of takers.

George St John's St ☎017687/72076. Keswick's oldest inn certainly looks the part, its snug bars lined with historic portraits, pictures and curios, and featuring wooden settles in front of the fire. Jennings' beers accompany classic bar meals, or there's a fancier menu available in the restaurant – where dinner might be anything from lamb shanks on mash to grilled halibut.

Lake Road Inn Lake Rd ☎017687/72404. An intimate Jennings' pub known for its good-value food, particularly the homemade pies and local Borrowdale trout. There's also a small courtyard beer garden.

Pheasant Inn Crosthwaite Rd ☏017687/72219. A 10min walk out of town (up the road on the west side of the park) is rewarded by a drink in Keswick's nicest local, festooned in rural and country-life cartoons. You can fill up here too on basic pub grub.

Theatre and cinema

Alhambra St John's St ☏017687/72195, ⓦwww.keswick-alhambra.co.uk. The cinema shows mainstream releases, but Keswick Film Club (ⓦwww.keswickfilmclub.org) puts on arthouse and other screenings on Sundays (Oct–April) and hosts an annual Film Festival (in Feb), featuring the best of world cinema.
Theatre by the Lake Lake Rd ☏017687/74411, ⓦwww.theatrebythelake.com. England's newest repertory theatre company hosts a full programme of drama, concerts, exhibitions, readings and talks. "Words By The Water", a literature festival, takes place here in the spring, while on selected mornings there's a guided backstage tour of the theatre (advance booking required; £3).

Listings

Banks and exchange There are ATMs at Barclays and HSBC (both on Market Sq); Lloyds-TSB (4 Main St); and NatWest (28 Main St). You can exchange travellers' cheques at the post office.
Bike rental Keswick Mountain Bikes, Southey Hill, Greta Bridge (daily 9am–5pm; ☏017687/75202, ⓦwww.keswickmountainbikes.co.uk).
Bookshop Bookends, 66 Main St ☏017687/75277, has a good selection of local-interest books and hiking guides, plus discounted books and novels.
Car rental Keswick Motor Company, Lake Rd ☏017687/72064.
Hospital Keswick Cottage Hospital, Crosthwaite Rd, Keswick ☏017687/72012.
Internet access Northern Lights, 22 St John St, upstairs in the gallery (Mon–Sat 10am–5pm, Sun 10.30am–5pm; ☏017687/75402, ⓦwww .northernlightsgallery.co.uk); U-Compute, 48 Main St, upstairs at the post office (Mon–Sat 9am–5.30pm, Sun 9.30am–4.30pm; ☏017687/75127, ⓦwww .ucompute.net). Also available at Keswick YHA.
Laundry Keswick Laundrette, Main St, next to the Co-op (daily 7.30am–7pm; ☏017687/75448).
Left luggage There's no official place to leave luggage, but you can try Bridgedale guest house,
101 Main St, which sometimes obliges for non-residents (£2–3 a day).
Outdoor stores George Fisher, 2 Borrowdale Rd (☏017687/72178, ⓦwww.georgefisher. co.uk), is perhaps the most celebrated outdoors store in the Lakes, with a full range of equipment and maps, a daily weather information service and café. Needle Sports, 56 Main St (☏017687/72227, ⓦwww.needlesports.com), is the local climbing and mountaineering specialist. But Keswick also has a dozen other outdoors stores, most found along the western half of Main Street, between the post office and the bus station.
Pharmacies Boots, 31 Main St ☏017687/72383; Lightfoot's, 25 Main St ☏017687/72108; J. N. Murray, 15–17 Station St ☏017687/72049.
Police station Bank St ☏01900/602422.
Post office 48 Main St (Mon–Fri 8.30am–5.30pm, Sat 8.30am–1pm; ☏017687/72269).
Swimming pool Keswick Leisure Pool, Station Rd (Easter–Sept daily 9am–5pm; winter limited hours, call for details; ☏017687/72760).
Taxis Davies Taxis ☏017687/72676; Derwent Taxis ☏017687/75585; Skiddaw Taxis ☏017687/75600 or 0800/654321.

Derwent Water

Derwent Water may not be that big – three miles long and, at most, a mile wide – but it's among the most attractive of the lakes. What's more, it's only five minutes' walk south of the centre of Keswick, down Lake Road and through the pedestrian underpass, and is fully served by a launch service that circles the lake at regular intervals. Standing on the northern shore, headed by the grassy banks of **Crow Park** and ringed by glowering crags, you look down the lake to its islets. One of these, **Derwent Island**, was settled by sixteenth-century German miners brought to Keswick to mine its ores. Another, **St Herbert's Island**, in the middle of the lake, is thought to be the site of the seventh-century hermitage's cell of St Herbert, disciple and friend of St Cuthbert of

Lindisfarne. Derwent Water is also a relatively shallow lake, eighty feet at its deepest point but averaging more like twenty feet deep; so shallow in fact that roe deer from the surrounding woods sometimes swim across to **Lord's Island**. There's a mysterious floating island, too, which appears only after sustained periods of dry weather.

Derwent Water marks a geological divide, where the slate of Skiddaw gives way to the volcanic rock of Borrowdale, something you'll notice at jutting

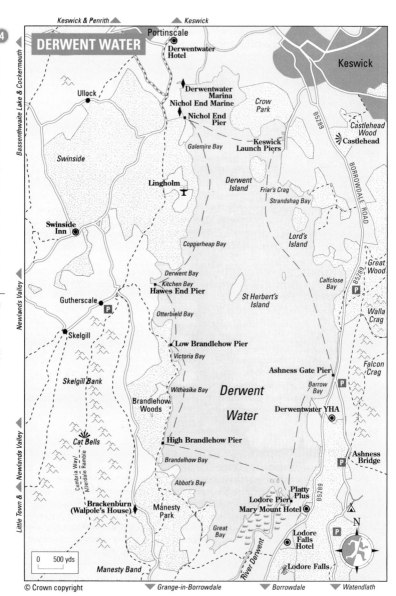

Keswick & Penrith ◣ ◣ Keswick

DERWENT WATER

Portinscale

Derwentwater Hotel

Keswick

Derwentwater Marina

Nichol End Marine

Ullock

Nichol End Pier

Crow Park

Castlehead Wood

Castlehead

B5289

Galemire Bay

Keswick Launch Piers

BORROWDALE ROAD

Swinside

Lingholm

Derwent Island

Friar's Crag

Strandshag Bay

Swinside Inn

Copperheap Bay

Lord's Island

Great Wood

B5289

Derwent Bay

Kitchen Bay

Hawes End Pier

Calfclose Bay

P

Gutherscale

P

Otterbield Bay

St Herbert's Island

Walla Crag

Skelgill

Low Brandlehow Pier

Victoria Bay

Ashness Gate Pier

Falcon Crag

Skelgill Bank

Barrow Bay

P

Withesike Bay

Derwent

Brandlehow Woods

Water

Derwentwater YHA

Cat Bells

Cumbria Way/ Allerdale Ramble

High Brandlehow Pier

Ashness Bridge

P

Brandelhow Bay

Abbot's Bay

Platty Plus

B5289

Brackenburn (Walpole's House)

Manesty Park

Lodore Pier

Mary Mount Hotel

Great Bay

N

Lodore Falls Hotel

P

0   500 yds

River Derwent

Lodore Falls

© Crown copyright

▽ Grange-in-Borrowdale   ▽ Borrowdale   ▽ Watendlath

Falcon Crag, halfway down the east side. Falcons still nest and breed here; indeed, Derwent Water supports several **wildlife** habitats, including those of the sandpiper and yellow wagtail, as well as Britain's rarest fish, the plankton-eating vendace (like the char, an Ice Age survivor). But the otters and wild cats remembered in place names around the lake are long gone.

Human interaction has shaped the lakeside: you can still see the scars from the old mines on the west side, though further damage has been prevented by the intervention of the National Trust, whose first purchased parcel of land in the Lake District was that of **Brandlehow woods and park** in 1902. During the eighteenth and early nineteenth centuries, the lake saw regular **regattas**, orchestrated initially by Joseph Pocklington, a wealthy banker, for whom the word eccentric seems woefully inadequate. He built himself a house, church and fortress on Derwent Island (the house is still there, owned and rented out by the National Trust; tours from June–Aug, ☎015394/35599) and appointed himself "Governor and Commander-in-Chief", blasting off brass cannons at the boats. The house that's now Derwentwater YHA was also his; he had the rocks behind it dynamited to fashion an artificial waterfall.

The ferry service around the lake is provided by the **Keswick Launch** (see box, below), whose piers are just a few minutes' walk from Keswick town centre on the northeastern edge of Derwent Water. You can also rent **rowboats** and self-drive motorboats at the Keswick Launch piers, though for kayaking, canoeing, sailing and windsurfing you'll need to contact one of the other **water-sports outlets** on the lake, at Portinscale or Lodore (see next page). The launch departures during the day are frequent enough to combine a cruise with a walk and picnic, though you can also **walk** around the entire lake from Keswick (9–10 miles; 3–4hr); the path around the western side forms part of the Cumbria Way and Allerdale Ramble long-distance routes. **Bus services** to points around the lake involve catching either the #79 "Borrowdale Rambler" (operates all year; day rider ticket £4.50) down the B5289 from Keswick to Seatoller, or the seasonal (Easter–Oct) #77A "Honister Rambler" (day rider ticket £5.90), which runs along the western shore via Portinscale, Cat Bells (for Newlands Valley) and Grange.

Friar's Crag and Castlehead

The most popular short walk on the lake – no more than ten minutes from the launch piers – is to **Friars' Crag**, a wooded peninsula on the northeastern shore from where medieval pilgrims left for St Herbert's Island to seek the hermit's blessing. The Friar's Crag land was acquired by the National Trust in 1922, and is held in memory of its founder Canon Rawnsley (see next page), though

---

Keswick Launch

Keswick Launch (☎017687/72263, ⊛www.keswick-launch.co.uk) runs services right around the lake calling at six points en route (£1.10p per stage; £6 round trip). Between Easter and the end of November, services run hourly from 10am until 4pm, both clockwise and anticlockwise around the lake (ie a service leaves every 30min in one direction or another). Services are extended into the early evening from the Spring bank holiday until mid-September, with the last departure at 7pm (8pm in summer school holidays). From December until Easter services depart on Saturdays and Sundays only, three times daily in each direction. There's also a one-hour **evening cruise** (£7) from May Day bank holiday until mid-September; pop down earlier in the day to buy a ticket and ensure a place.

Hardwicke Drummond Rawnsley (1851–1920) was ordained in 1875, gained his first living in the Lakes (at Wray, near Ambleside) two years later, and was appointed vicar at Crosthwaite, Keswick, in 1883. It was a period of rapid industrial development and the conservation-minded Canon Rawnsley found himself opposing the proposed Braithewaite and Buttermere Railway, fighting footpath disputes and lining up with Ruskin (an old Oxford college friend) against the creation of Thirlmere reservoir – though Rawnsley later accepted the needs of the northern cities for water and even attended Thirlmere's official opening. His time served on the County Council and the newly formed Lake District Defence Society convinced him of the need for a preservation society with money and teeth. In 1893, together with Octavia Hill and Sir Robert Hunter, and the backing of the Duke of Westminster, he established the **National Trust**. This received its first piece of donated land (in Wales) the following year and encouraged subscriptions to buy endangered property elsewhere: between 1902 and 1908 the Trust acquired much of Derwent Water and Borrowdale and is now easily the largest landowner in the Lake District.

Rawnsley remained an active part of the Trust while continuing to preach and write – he produced many collections of lakeland sonnets, poems, histories and guides, including an entertaining book of "reminiscences" of Wordsworth by the local peasantry (none of whom thought the Poet Laureate's poetry was any good). After Rawnsley's wife died in 1916 he retired to Wordsworth's old house at Allan Bank in Grasmere. He married again in 1918, but died only two years later on May 28, 1920.

it's long been a beauty spot. Ruskin's childhood visit to Friars' Crag famously inspired "intense joy, mingled with awe", which is a bit over the top, but the grass banks and little rocky coves nearby are very attractive. For a longer walk, return to Keswick via the **Castlehead** (530ft) viewpoint, from where you can look straight down Derwent Water to Castle Crag, with Scafell Pike rising in the distance. Castlehead is reached from the lake by cutting up to and crossing the B5289 – a round-trip of three miles or one and a half hours from town.

Ashness Bridge and Watendlath

The pier at **Ashness Gate** (or bus #79) provides access to a narrow road branching south off the B5289 that climbs a steep half-mile to the photogenic **Ashness Bridge**, an old dry-stone packhorse bridge providing marvellous Derwent Water views. The minor road past Ashness Bridge (and a well-used footpath) ends two miles further south at **WATENDLATH**, an isolated farmstead, tearoom and tarn which can be hopelessly overrun at times in summer. Watendlath – the Norse "end of the lake" – provided the setting for Hugh Walpole's most famous episode of his Herries Chronicles, *Judith Paris* (1931). You can buy a copy in the tearoom and lounge about for an hour or two on the grass, or rent boat and rod from the farm for a trout-fishing trip on the tarn.

From Watendlath tarn, walkers have a few options, all pleasant, all easy: south via smaller Dock Tarn to Stonethwaite in Borrowdale; southwest over the tops to Rosthwaite; or east, up and over High Tove, to the western shore of Thirlmere.

Lodore and Lodore Falls

At **Lodore** landing stage there are rowboats for rent and other water sports available at Platty Plus. The #79 bus stops nearby, from where a path heads to the **Lodore Falls**, much visited in Victorian times by the romantically inclined though only really worth the diversion after sustained wet weather.

Then, you'll be able to appreciate Robert Southey's magnificent, alliterative evocation of the falls in "The Cataract of Lodore": "Collecting, projecting, receding and speeding, and shocking and rocking, and darting and parting", and so on, for line after memorable line. However, even in dry weather there's some lovely woodland clambering to be done around here and with a keen sense of direction (or a map) you'll be able to find the Watendlath path and road, east of the falls.

The most prominent **accommodation** at this end of the lake is the *Lodore Falls Hotel* (℡017687/77285, Ⓦ www.lodorefallshotel.co.uk; Ⓦ), which has lake or fell views from all rooms, gardens, a bar and restaurant, and all manner of other facilities including a leisure centre and two pools (one indoor, one outdoor). Even closer to the lake – just a few yards from the Lodore piers – is a more intimate and modest family-run affair, *Mary Mount Hotel* (℡017687/77223, Ⓦ www.marymounthotel.co.uk; Ⓦ, superior rooms Ⓦ), nestling under the crags in four acres of lakeside and woodland gardens. The twenty rooms are either in the main house or the lodge-style bungalow in the grounds, with half-a-dozen rated "superior" (room 25, for example, has bay windows and big lake views). There's a nice oak-panelled bar serving lunch (available outside on the terrace), a moderately priced restaurant with picture windows, and they'll pack you a picnic lunch and fill a flask if you ask.

Cat Bells, Lingholm and Portinscale

Asked to pick a favourite Lake District walk and climb, many would plump for **Cat Bells** (1481ft), a renowned vantage-point above the lake's western shore. It's not difficult (possible for all the family), the views from the top are stupendous, and it's easy to combine with the launch to or from Keswick. The name derives from the age-old belief that the fell once harboured a wild cat's den (*bield*, the Norse word for den, was later corrupted to "bells"). Most people climb up and down the path from Hawes End (launch pier), near where there's also a small car park (Gutherscale), though the longer haul up from Manesty to the south (High Brandlehow launch) has its merits. Return to either launch pier along the lakeside path through Manesty Park and Brandlehow woods and park, allowing, say, two-and-a-half hours for the entire walk. Walpole fans should note that Sir Hugh lived and worked for many years in the lee of Cat Bells, at the house he called **Brackenburn**, by Manesty Park.

The *Swinside Inn* (see "Newlands Valley" below) is only a mile from Hawes End, a welcome stop for a post Cat Bells pint, while a signposted path from Hawes End pier runs all the way back to Keswick, which is only a couple of miles away through the woods and round the top of the lake. Under a mile north of Hawes End you'll pass the entrance to **Lingholm Gardens** – now sadly closed to the public, but featuring fabulous rhododendron displays. Beatrix Potter spent many childhood holidays at the grand house at Lingholm and, hardly surprisingly, the surroundings here and in the lovely Newlands Valley to the southwest (see below) appeared in several of her later stories. Just beyond, there are refreshments at hand at the lakeside café (℡017687/73082 daily until 5pm, 8pm July & Aug) at **Nichol End**, a marine store and boat rental place. The name is a corruption of "St Nicholas' Ending", as the site was once an embarkation point for medieval pilgrims crossing to St Herbert's Island (St Nicholas being the patron saint of sailors). After Nichol End, the path joins the main road as it snakes through the village of **Portinscale**, a satellite of Keswick, where you can relax with a drink in the conservatory-bar and lakeside gardens of the *Derwentwater* hotel (see p.147), before striking off over the River Derwent and through the fields to emerge by Greta Bridge in town.

Newlands Valley

A valley for connoisseurs unfolds along Newlands Beck, to the west of Cat Bells and Derwent Water. Save for the very minor road over Newlands Hause to Buttermere, there's little in the isolated farms and sparse hamlets of the **Newlands Valley** to lure touring drivers. But hikers have the choice of two fine circuits, one following the pastoral valley lowlands, the other tracing the encircling ridges and peaks. The **valley walk** (5 miles; 3hr) follows a path from the Cat Bells (Gutherscale) car park to Little Town – the main valley hamlet, with an isolated chapel – beyond which can be made out the old Goldscope lead mines. These have been long abandoned, but were a hive of activity as far back as the sixteenth century when German miners were brought here to work the seams. Better, if you (and the weather) are up to it, is the exhilarating **Newlands Horseshoe** (11 miles; 6–7hr), which begins with the ascent of Cat Bells (see above) and then links Maiden Moor (1887ft), High Spy (2143ft), Dale Head (2473ft) and Hindscarth (2385ft) in a terrific circular walk above and around the valley. The views, needless to say, are magnificent.

Either walk can be done from Keswick, via the launch to Hawes End, and should culminate in a visit to the valley's only **pub**, the excellent *Swinside Inn* (℡017687/78253, ⓦwww.theswinsideinn.com; ➌), three miles from Keswick, whose beer garden gazes up to the encroaching fells. There are comfortable rooms here, or mattresses provided in a basic **camping barn** (℡017687/72645; £5, breakfast available) a mile or to the south at Skelgill.

Borrowdale

Beautiful **Borrowdale** stretches beyond the foot of Derwent Water, south of Keswick, and it's difficult to overstate the attraction of its river flats, forested crags, oak woods and yew trees. Early visiting writers and poets, including Thomas Gray who marvelled at the prospect in 1769, saw it as an embodiment of their Romantic fancy; Turner and Constable came to paint it; and Wordsworth praised its yews, "those fraternal Four of Borrowdale, joined in one solemn and capacious grove". But the dale's sonorous place names suggest a more prosaic heritage. The numerous "thwaites" were the site of Norse clearings, while by the thirteenth century the monks of Furness Abbey were farming the valley from their "grainge" (an outlying farmhouse), grazing sheep and smelting iron-ore along the becks. The valley's higher reaches were later extensively mined and quarried, activities that impinged upon the indigenous wood cover. Borrowdale's oak woods once, effectively, formed part of a temperate rainforest – the surviving fragments are still known for their mosses, ferns, liverworts and lichens, and provide cover for a wide range of berries and birds, including warblers and flycatchers.

In summer there's a fairly steady stream of traffic taking hikers to the head of the valley, overshadowed by the peaks of Scafell and Scafell Pike (the two highest in the Lakes) and Great Gable, the latter one of the finest-looking mountains in England. Public transport access is by **bus** #77A (along the minor road on the west side of Derwent Water) and the highly scenic #79 "Borrowdale Rambler" (along the B5289), which runs south to Grange and Seatoller, dropping day-trippers and hikers at points of interest and walk-access points all the way down. A **Borrowdale Day Rider** (£4.50) gives a day's unlimited travel between Keswick and Seatoller on the #79 service; buy it from the driver.

Grange and around

The riverside hamlet of **GRANGE-IN-BORROWDALE**, four miles south of Keswick, sits back from an old twin-arched packhorse bridge, under which the River Derwent tumbles from the narrower confines of Borrowdale and runs across the flood plain to the lake. And flood it does on occasion, which is why the raised wooden walkways snake across the flats between here, Lodore and Manesty. It's always nice to stop for a drink at the **tearoom** at *Grange Bridge Cottage* (☎017687/77201; closed Nov–Feb, though open in school holidays), which is in a great spot, right by the bridge.

South of Grange, the valley narrows at a crag-lined gorge known as the **Jaws of Borrowdale**. Until the eighteenth century, the route beyond was considered wild and uncertain, and there was no permanent road through until the mid-nineteenth century, when travellers other than locals first began to venture into the valley. The views are famed from **Castle Crag** (985ft), possibly the site of an ancient fort and one of the western "teeth" of the Jaws, which you can reach on paths from Grange or Rosthwaite. Across the valley from the crag, also around a mile from Grange, stands the 1870-ton **Bowder Stone** (there's a car park on the B5289), a house-sized lump of rock scaled by wooden ladder and worn to a shine on top by thousands of pairs of feet. Controversy surrounds the origin of this rock, pitched precariously on the edge. Some say it came from the fells above, others contend it was brought by glacier movement during the last Ice Age. The crag behind the Bowder Stone, **King's How**, is named in memory of Edward VII. It's a fair climb to the top, but the views are worth it.

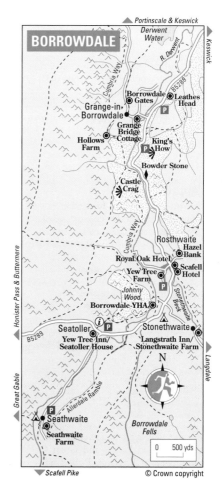

© Crown copyright

Accommodation

Borrowdale Gates Grange ☎017687/77204,
🌐www.borrowdale-gates.com. The traditional
choice hereabouts is this superbly sited country-
house hotel in two acres of wooded gardens, 200
yards up the western shore road, past the church.
It has a deserved reputation for its food, and dinner (included in the price) is accompanied by fine
views from the restaurant. Closed Jan. ❽

Hollows Farm ☎017687/77298. Three B&B
rooms set on a working farm, half a mile from
Grange; you can camp here too. Closed mid-Dec
to end Jan. No credit cards. ❷

Leathes Head B5289, 1 mile north of Grange
☎017687/77247, 🌐www.leatheshead.co.uk.
Welcoming family-run, non-smoking hotel with a
dozen spacious rooms, all with fell views – two
in particular (supplement payable) have windows
on two sides, making them lovely and light. The
elegant, polished Edwardian house has three
interlinked lounges, including a conservatory
with telescope, while dinner (included in the
price) is the main event every night – there's
plenty of choice from a changing *table d'hote*
menu that always has a fish and vegetarian
selection. ❼

Rosthwaite

The riverside path and the B5289 lead on to the straggling hamlet of **ROS-
THWAITE**, two miles south of Grange. Its whitewashed stone buildings,
backed by the encroaching fells, sustain the most concentrated batch of accommodation in the valley (see below), while at the Rosthwaite **village shop**
(open daily) – the only one in the valley – you'll be able to put together a
basic picnic and buy a map or a postcard. Both hotels on the road, the *Royal
Oak* and the *Scafell*, offer drinks and teas to non-guests, while the *Scafell* is also
the starting point of the annual **Borrowdale Fell Race** (first Sat in Aug),
an eighteen-mile gut-buster that takes in the peaks of Scafell Pike and Great
Gable. The winners clock in at well under three hours, their names immortalized on an honours board displayed in the hotel's *Riverside Bar*. Tortoises can
reflect on these hare-like exploits while seated on the memorial bench in the
hotel grounds dedicated to Walter ("W.A") Poucher (1891–1988), author, fellwalker and photographer, whose classic *Lakeland Peaks*, first published in 1960,
is the only serious rival in scope and breadth to the Wainwright guides.

Hotels and B&B

Hazel Bank 200 yards from the road, over the
bridge ☎017687/77248, 🌐www.hazelbankhotel
.co.uk. Victorian-era country house (non-smoking)
set in its own serene gardens, with magnificent fell
views to all sides. There are eight elegant rooms,
often full, since guests return year after year,
drawn by the seclusion and the well-regarded food
– a daily changing four-course dinner is included
in the price. Parking. ❽

Royal Oak On the main road ☎017687/ 77214,
🌐www.royaloakhotel. co.uk. The hikers' favourite
– an expanded eighteenth-century farmhouse with
barn annexe, where a hearty lakeland dinner (no
choice, but vegetarian alternative available) is served
promptly at 7pm, a bacon-and-eggs breakfast at
8.30am. Weather conditions are posted daily, packed
lunches and filled flasks supplied, but if the rain
comes down you may prefer to repair to the firelit
sitting room for tea and scones, or to the stone-
flagged bar. Rates include dinner. Parking. ❻

Scafell On the main road ☎017687/77208,
🌐www.scafell.co.uk. Set back from a trimmed

lawn, with period furnished rooms in the main
building and more modern, slightly less spacious
ones in the annexe, all with baths and showers.
Food is traditional country-house "fayre" (prawn
cocktail, silver service, meet-and-greet owner),
but despite the formalities it's a friendly, relaxed
place to stay. The four-course *table d'hote* dinner is £24, though the attached *Riverside Bar*
– the only local pub – serves cheaper bar meals,
including smoked trout and grilled salmon. Special hotel breaks and last-minute rates are good
value. Parking. ❻

Yew Tree Farm 200 yards up the narrow road
opposite the shop ☎017687/77675, 🌐www
.borrowdaleherdwick.co.uk. Traditional farmhouse
B&B that has the unofficial royal seal of approval,
since Prince Charles once stayed overnight on an
incognito walking trip. Three non-smoking rooms
available. The farm also has a tearoom, the *Flock-
In*, where you can sit in the garden with a tea or
coffee (available in pints for thirsty walkers) and
gaze across the valley fields. Parking. Closed mid-
Dec to late Jan. No credit cards. ❸

Youth hostel

Borrowdale YHA Longthwaite, 1 mile south of Rosthwaite ☎0870/770 5706, ✉borrowdale@yha .org.uk. Located right on the riverside footpath to Seatoller, this has some rooms available for couples and families, as well as dorms. It's a peaceful place to stay, with riverside picnic tables in the grounds. Reception opens 1pm. Closed Jan. Dorm beds £14.

Campsite

Chapel House Farm B5289, half-mile south of Rosthwaite ☎017687/77602. A simple farm field site, with toilets and showers available. Closed Nov–Feb.

Stonethwaite

STONETHWAITE, a place of some antiquity just to the southeast of Rosthwaite and half a mile up a side road, is the trailhead for those aiming to walk into Langdale via Langstrath and the watershed of Stake Pass. There's more foot traffic than you might expect, since it's on the route of both the Cumbria Way and the Coast-to-Coast walk. Pretty whitewashed stone cottages huddle around the sixteenth-century *Langstrath Country Inn* (☎017687/77239, ⓦwww.thelangstrath.com; ❹), an upmarket pub with ten rooms, a pretty little beer garden and cosy bar. The food is mostly locally sourced – trout, sausages, lamb, beef – but you'll need to reserve in advance if you want to eat, which doesn't make it the most convenient stop for hikers. There's always farmhouse **B&B** and basic **camping** facilities (toilets and cold water; campsite closed Nov–March) a couple of doors up at *Stonethwaite Farm* (☎017687/77234; no credit cards; ❸). The inn, incidentally, features in the Lake District section of Ian McEwan's Booker prize-winning novel *Amsterdam* (1998), which is short enough to read overnight if you've come armed with a copy, before tackling the bleak Langstrath valley – "one long frown set in stone".

Seatoller and Seathwaite

Another mile or so up the valley from Rosthwaite, and eight miles from Keswick, lies the old farming and quarrying settlement of **SEATOLLER**. Most visitors stop long enough to call in at the **Borrowdale Tourist Information Centre** at Seatoller Barn (Easter–Oct daily 10am–5pm; ☎017687/77294) to check the programme of events, craft displays, talks and local walks; there are also drinks and snacks on sale, and a good book, map and guide selection. Outside, you can walk from the car park into **Johnny Wood** to see the moss-covered boulders and lichen-draped trees. Opposite, a few slate-roofed houses cluster around a moderately priced **café-restaurant**, the *Yew Tree* (☎017687/77634; no food Mon evening; closed Jan), fashioned from seventeenth-century stone-flagged quarrymen's cottages. During the day you can get good sandwiches, omelettes and the like, while at night it becomes a grill restaurant and bar, serving steaks, gammon and homemade pies.

For local **accommodation**, you can't beat *Seatoller House* (☎017687/77218, ⓦwww.seatollerhouse.co.uk; ❹, including dinner ❻; closed Dec–Feb) next door to the restaurant, a well-maintained seventeenth-century farmhouse with plenty of original panelling, a library, parlour and fire, and an honesty bar. Very popular communal meals (not Tues) using local produce are served at 7pm in the former kitchen. The house is owned by the family of the historian G.M. Trevelyan, who first visited a century ago as a Cambridge undergraduate and later organized "hare and hound" hunts on the fells above – stalking people rather than animals – which are still held here each year.

A minor road south runs to **SEATHWAITE**, twenty minutes' walk away, where there's limited parking and a fine café (Easter–Sept daily 10am–6.30pm), serving fresh and smoked salmon and trout, cakes and sandwiches. This is a major departure point for walks up the likes of Great Gable and Scafell Pike

In good weather, the minor road to Seathwaite is lined with cars by 9am as hikers take to the paths for the rugged climbs up the three major peaks of Scafell, Scafell Pike and Great Gable. Technically, they're not too difficult; as always, though, you should be well-prepared and reasonably fit.

Scafell and Scafell Pike

The summit of Scafell Pike (3205ft), the highest point in England, is close to Scafell (3163ft), the second highest point in the Lakes; an eight-mile (six-hour) loop walk taking in both leaves Seathwaite via Stockley Bridge to the south, branching up Styhead Ghyll to Styhead Tarn. This is as far as many get, and on those all-too-rare glorious summer days the tarn is a fine place for a picnic.

Great and Green Gable

A direct but very steep approach to Great Gable (2949ft) is possible from Styhead Tarn, though most people cut west at Seathwaite campsite up Sourmilk Ghyll and approach via Green Gable (2628ft), an eight-mile (six-hour) return walk. However, the easiest Great Gable climb is actually from Honister Pass (see below), following a six-mile (four-hour) route past Grey Knotts and Brandreth to Green Gable, before rounding Great Gable and returning along an almost parallel path to the west.

See Basics, p.40, for general walking advice in the Lakes; recommended maps are detailed on p.27.

(see box above), and *Seathwaite Farm* (☎017687/77394; no credit cards) at the end of the road has a popular if basic **campsite** (toilets, and hot and cold water) as well as a **camping barn** (£3.50 per person). Prospective campers might like to know that Seathwaite has a reputation for being the wettest inhabited place in England, with an average of over 120 inches of rain recorded a year.

Honister Pass and Slate Mine

Overlooked by the steep Borrowdale Fells, the B5289 cuts west at Seatoller, up and over the dramatic **Honister Pass**, dominated by the dread thousand-foot heights of Honister Crag. From the top of the pass the road down to Buttermere is an absolute beauty, following tumbling Gatesgarthdale Beck. Bus #77A comes this way, making the initial, steep mile-and-a-quarter grind from Seatoller to the car park at the top of Honister Pass. Nearby is the supremely isolated **youth hostel**, *Honister Hause YHA* (☎0870/770 5870, ✉honister@yha.org .uk; closed mid-Nov to March, also closed certain days Sept to mid-Nov; dorms £11), with all accommodation in two- to four-bedded rooms (reception opens at 5pm). An evening meal is served here, which is just as well if you're on foot since it's a fair slog down into Borrowdale to the nearest pub.

Slate has been quarried on the pass since Elizabethan times, and by the eighteenth century the local green roofing slate was much sought after. Miners – living in wooden huts on the mountainside and working by candlelight – hand-dug eleven miles of tunnels and caverns within the bulk of Fleetwith Pike, leaving vicious scars, slate waste piles and old workings that are visible even today. Until well into the nineteenth century, the finished slate was either carried down the severe inclines in baskets on men's backs, or guided on heavy hand-pulled wooden sledges, since pit ponies couldn't get a foothold on the scree. Needless to say, this was ridiculously dangerous work. Full commercial quarrying ceased in 1986, but **Honister Slate Mine** (℡017687/77230, ⓌWwww.honister-slate-mine.co.uk) is now in operation again as a heritage enterprise, with ornamental and roofing slate for sale, and a visitor centre (daily 10.30am–5pm), where you can buy souvenirs and browse the slate stone garden. Best of all, you can get an idea of what working life was like by donning a hard hat and lamp and joining one of the hugely informative **guided tours** (daily at 10.30am, 12.30pm & 3.30pm; £8.50; booking recommended), which start by showing you the "riving" (hand-shaping) process and then lead you through narrow tunnels into illuminated, echoing, dripping caverns. A more extreme version of the tour takes you around "The Edge", a high-level shortcut into one of the most extensive mine workings.

Threlkeld to Thirlmere

The A591 between Keswick and Grasmere runs directly past **Thirlmere**, and this is the way the buses go. But if you're in no particular hurry, it's more pleasant to detour east to **Threlkeld** first and then turn south along the minor road through **St John's in the Vale**. You can come this way entirely on foot too – it's an extremely attractive route (7 miles; 4hr) – and pick up the #555/556 bus back up the A591 to complete the circuit back to Keswick.

Threlkeld
Keswick's disused railway path (signposted by the *Keswick Country House* hotel on Station Road) runs straight to **THRELKELD** ("Thrall's Spring"), three miles east of Keswick; or it's a quick ride on bus #X4/X5/X50 or the #73/73A. The riverside walk's a delight, enhanced by the promise of a drink in one of Threlkeld's charming old pubs at the end, either the *Horse & Farrier* or the *Salutation*. Threlkeld is the starting point for many of the strenuous hikes up Blencathra (see box on p.145) and there's parking at a couple of places up the signposted road to the Blencathra Centre. Across the A66 (follow the signs) you can delve further into the mechanics of the local mining industry at **Threlkeld Quarry** (March–Oct Tues–Sun 10am–5pm; Nov–Feb usually weekends only, call for times; £3; ℡017687/79747, ⓌWwww.threlkeld-mine .co.uk), which produced granite for road- and railway-making until 1982. The entrance price gets you into the museum of mining artefacts and minerals, as well as the locomotive shed and machine shop, while for another £5 you can descend into a recreated mine for a forty-minute hard-hat-and-torch tour.

St John's in the Vale
A bucolic walk from Threlkeld cuts south from the railway path, across Threlkeld Bridge and through the fields into **St John's in the Vale**; the B5322 shadows the same route. The old chapel of St John's and views of the Blencathra ridges behind are the draws, with the southward path hugging the base of **High Rigg** (1163ft) and eventually following the river to **Low Bridge End Farm** (℡017687/79242, ⓌWwww.campingbarn.com). This is a little local hive of activity, with a rustic tea garden (serving homemade lemonade and local ice cream), a woodland trail and pottery. The range of overnight **accommodation** options includes a small campsite, and self-catering available in the old stable and hayloft, either by the week in the flat (sleeps 2–4; £175–270, call the farm) or overnight in the camping barn (£5 per person; reservations on

ⓣ017687/72645). From the farm the A591 is under a mile away – on the way, keep an eye out for climbers scaling **Castle Rock** across the river, Walter Scott's model for the fairy castle in his poem "Bridal of Triermain".

Thirlmere

Thirlmere, a five-mile-long reservoir at the southern end of St John's in the Vale, was created from two smaller lakes at the end of the nineteenth century when Manchester's booming population and industry required water. Over a hundred miles of gravity-drawn tunnels and pipes still supply the city with water from here. In an ultimately unsuccessful campaign – but one that fore-shadowed the founding of the National Trust – the fight against the creation of Thirlmere was led by Ruskin and other proto-environmentalists, outraged at a high-handed raising of the water level, which drowned the hamlet of Armboth and various small farms. No one was best pleased either by the subsequent regimental planting of thousands of conifers around the edge (to help prevent erosion), which dramatically changed the local landscape. The century since the creation of the reservoir has softened the scene – these are among the oldest planted trees in the park – and you'd be hard pushed now to tell that Thirlmere was man-made.

The only side served by public transport (take any bus along the A591 between Grasmere and Keswick) is the eastern one, from which some visitors choose to make the climb up Helvellyn and back – in which case, you'll be pleased at the thought of a pint in the roadside *King's Head* at **THIRLSPOT** (ⓣ017687/72393, ⓦwww.lakedistrictinns.co.uk; ❺, weekends ❻). Nearby *Dale Head Hall* (ⓣ017687/72478, ⓦwww.daleheadhall.co.uk; ❼) – an Eliza-bethan building with a Victorian adjunct – has a lakeside location, with gardens that run right down to the shores of Thirlmere.

To enjoy fully the waterside paths, forest trails (through planted conifers and mixed woodland) and viewpoints, you need to be on the minor road that hugs the western shore. There are several small car parks, with trails leading off from each, like at **Launchy Gill**, an oak and birch woodland Site of Special Scien-tific Interest. Alternatively, the #555/556 bus can drop you at the foot of the reservoir for the six-mile walk up the western side and around to Thirlspot.

Braithewaite, Thornthwaite and Whinlatter Pass

Just under three miles west of Keswick, the cottage gardens of **BRAITHE-WAITE** (bus #X5 from Keswick) line the banks of Coledale Beck, with the distinctive Grisedale Pike towering above. As an alternative walking base to Keswick, the village provides immediate access to the fells between Derwent and Crummock waters, notably on the stupendous Coledale Horseshoe circuit (see below). There's B&B **accommodation** in and around Braithewaite (par-ticularly along the minor Thornthwaite road), but the most atmospheric lodg-ings are at the fine *Coledale Inn* (ⓣ017687/78272, ⓦwww.coledale-inn.co.uk; ❹) on the hillside above the village. Once a mill, this is now a cosy lakeland inn with a dozen (mostly upgraded, reasonably spacious) rooms, a sheltered garden and good-value bar meals. They'll make you up a packed lunch for your day's walking. The other pub choice is the *Royal Oak* (ⓣ017687/78533, ⓦwww .royaloak-braithewaite.co.uk: ❹), down in the village itself, with modernized rooms, Jennings beers and a wide bar meal menu. Or you can splash out a bit on the Modern British food at nearby *Ivy House* (☎017687/78338; dinner only; advance reservations required; closed Sun), a private members' hotel and **restaurant** whose dining room is open to non-residents.

A mile north up the minor road shadowing the A66, pretty **THORN-THWAITE** looks across the Derwent basin to the Skiddaw range. There's parking a mile or so further up the road, from where you can climb (yes, really) **Barf** (1536ft), whose distinctive craggy protuberance – usually painted white – is known as "The Bishop". Back in the village, the refined **Thornthwaite Galleries** (March–Oct Mon & Wed–Sun 10.30am–5pm; Nov to mid-Dec Fri–Sun 10.30am–5pm; free; ☎017687/78248, ⓦwww.thornthwaite.net) exhibit a good range of lakeland arts and crafts – from paintings and sculpture to jewellery and fabrics – and some of the artists demonstrate their work during special sessions in the summer. The tearoom is open until 4.30pm, though muddy boots and their owners will have to give it a miss.

The B5292 climbs west past Braithewaite to the **Whinlatter Pass** (1043ft), on the way to Buttermere or Cockermouth. A couple of miles up are the extensive woodland plantations of **Whinlatter Forest Park**, England's only true mountain forest, whose excellent visitor centre (daily: April–Oct 10am–5pm; Nov–March 10am–4pm; free; parking fee; ☎017687/78469, ⓦwww .whinlatterforestpark.co.uk) can put you on track for a day's exploration. Bus #77/77A runs here directly from Keswick. Seasonal exhibitions concentrate

Walks from Braithewaite

The great advantage of basing yourself in Braithewaite is that you can walk straight out of the door and on to the fells. Grisedale Pike is the traditional climb, which can be incorporated into a much longer circular, or "horseshoe", walk. It's one of the Lakes' best one-day hikes, and dedicated Wainwright peak-baggers can knock off up to ten summits on the one circuit. The start of the route up Cat Bells (see p.153) is only two miles to the south of the village, as well, which means you could also walk the Newlands Valley (p.154) from Braithewaite.

Grisedale Pike

From the small quarry car park on the Whinlatter road, just above the village, it's 90min to the top of **Grisedale Pike** (2593ft), along a very well-worn route. Moving on to **Hopegill Head** (2525ft) – from where the Isle of Man can be seen on the best days – you then drop to the head of the valley at Coledale Hause for the straightforward valley return to the village (total trip 5 miles; 3hr).

Coledale Horseshoe

Unless you're pushed for time, on a clear day you'd be mad not to complete the circuit since, having gained the height at Grisedale Pike and Hopegill Head, there's a relatively small amount of extra climbing involved to return to Braithewaite via **Sail** (2530ft), **Outside** (1863ft) and **Barrow** (1494ft) – with a possible diversion to **Grasmoor** (2791ft, superb Crummock Water views) en route, and an alternative return via **Scar Crags** (2205ft) and **Causey Pike** (2035ft, Newlands Valley views). It's a hugely satisfying circuit, with changing panoramas all the way round. Depending on your peak choices, it's nine to twelve miles, six to eight hours, on clearly defined paths and ridges, with just the odd bit of scrambling.

See Basics, p.40, for general walking advice in the Lakes; recommended maps are detailed on p.27.

on the area's wildlife, most notably Bassenthwaite's wild **ospreys** (see below), which can be seen on the visitor centre's live video nest-cam link (April–Sept only). In addition, there are walks (up to Spout Force falls, for example) and viewpoints, plus waymarked trails for hikers and cyclists, a permanent orienteering course and adventure playground. The centre's *Siskins Café* is worth a stop in any case, with really good food, proper coffee and a terrace that looks over the plantations and down the valley.

④ Bassenthwaite Lake

Pub-quiz bores love **Bassenthwaite Lake** as it's the only lake in the Lake District (all the others are known as waters or meres). It's also the northernmost of the major patches of water, but it doesn't receive much attention otherwise, partly because of the difficulty in actually reaching its shores. Although just three miles from Keswick, and linked by the River Derwent which flows across the broad agricultural plain between the two, most of the shoreline is privately owned. Powerboats are banned and there are no-boating zones, restrictions that are intended to preserve the lake's rich variety of plants and animals. The shoreline habitat is the best-preserved example in the National Park, where over seventy species of birds and wildfowl (including ospreys) winter and breed, while Bassenthwaite is one of the only two places in Britain (with Derwent Water) where the vendace, a nine-inch fish related to other Arctic species, is found.

There's a three-mile path up the west shore as far as Dubwath, but as this is paralleled by the busy A66 the noise of traffic is ever present. The main interest is really on the **east shore** of the lake, though again access is restricted to certain sections, all clearly marked on maps; buses #X4, #73/73A and #555 run this way from Keswick.

Dodd Wood

The only permitted parking places close to the east shore are at the heavily planted Forestry Commission land of **Dodd Wood**. Starting from the *Old Sawmill Tearooms* (mid-March to Oct daily 10am–5pm; ☎017687/74317) there are four marked trails of varying length. Some of the crowded pines, planted in the 1920s, are now 120ft high, which makes the climb (3 miles; 3hr return) to the heights of **Dodd** (1612ft) itself a rather disorienting experience. Keep an eye out: roe deer and some of the Lakes' few surviving red squirrels are occasionally seen around here. However, the main interest in recent years has been the arrival of **wild ospreys** to nest and breed on the shores of Bassenthwaite, below the woods. A quarter-mile path (15min uphill climb) from the tearooms leads to an open-air **viewing platform** (telescopes provided, staffed April–Aug daily 10am–5pm; free; ⓦwww.ospreywatch.co.uk) from where, on most days, you'll be able to see the ospreys fishing and feeding, hovering over the lake, then plunging feet first to catch roach, perch, pike and trout. The birds usually arrive in April or May; the eggs hatch in June, and the ospreys leave for Africa in August or September. For an even closer look, don't miss the live video feed from the nests shown over at Whinlatter Forest Park (see previous page).

Mirehouse

The bus stop and parking by the *Old Sawmill Tearooms* also provides access to **Mirehouse** across the road (April–July, Sept & Oct Sun & Wed 2–4.30pm; Aug Wed, Fri & Sun 2–4.30pm; gardens same days 10am–5.30pm; house &

gardens £4.60; gardens only £2.20; ☎017687/77287, ⓦwww.mirehouse.com). This lakeland home of the Spedding family has been passed down the generations for three hundred years (Sir James was a friend of Tennyson, who is supposed to have sought inspiration for his *Morte d'Arthur* here) and the current members open up the interior a couple of days a week for a view of the contents and portraits. The terraced lawns, gardens, orchard, wildflower meadow and lakeside walk are more worthwhile – there are adventure playgrounds for the kids – while you don't need to pay for the best sight of all, the glorious chapel on the shores of Bassenthwaite. Look for the footpath to the side of the entrance, which runs down through the fields in twenty minutes to the **church of St Bega**, originally Norman, heavily restored and completely serene, protected by the flanks of Skiddaw.

Trotters World of Animals

Signs from the head of the lake direct you to **Trotters World of Animals** at Coalbeck Farm (mid-Feb to Oct 10am–5.30pm; Nov to mid-Feb 11am–4.30pm; £5.25; ☎017687/76239, ⓦwww.trottersworld.com), home to hundreds of animals, from baby goats to a family of gibbons. As you can imagine, children love this place, since handling the animals is encouraged (even the snakes) and there are feeding programmes, play areas, bird of prey displays, tractor and pony rides, a tearoom and picnic sites.

Practicalities

There's a renowned inn on the west side of Bassenthwaite Lake (the *Pheasant*) and another pub in the small village of **Bassenthwaite** (bus #73/73A), a couple of miles east of the top end of the lake. Other than that though, the *Old Sawmill Tearooms* is the best place for a snack or a meal.

Accommodation

Armathwaite Hall B5291, northern end of Bassenthwaite Lake ☎017687/76551, ⓦwww .armathwaite-hall.com. Live the noble life at one of the Lake District's most glamorous country-house hotels, a restored sixteenth-century hall set in 400 acres of deer park and woodland and with terraces overlooking lawns that sweep down to the lakeside. Rooms (up to £260) are every bit as gracious as you might imagine; there's wood panelling and log fires throughout, plus pool and spa, steam room and gym. Two-night breaks include dinner, which softens the considerable bill a little. Parking. ❾

Pheasant Off the A66, just before Dubwath ☎017687/76234, ⓦwww.the-pheasant.co.uk. This handsome old coaching inn features a carefully preserved period bar and comfortable lounges festooned with flowers where superior bar lunches and afternoon tea are served. Dinner is a more formal affair in the restaurant, after which you can repair to one of the thirteen characterful rooms, all tastefully decorated – three suites offer a bit more space (priced a category higher). Parking. ❼

Ravenstone A591, 5 miles northwest of Keswick ☎017687/76240, ⓦwww.ravenstone-hotel .co.uk. A Victorian hotel in two acres of grounds, with terrific views over Bassenthwaite Lake and enough decorative oak to denude a small forest. There's a handsome firelit lounge, full-sized snooker table, restaurant and bar – a lakeland dinner is included in the price. Parking. ❼

Pub

Sun Bassenthwaite village ☎017687/76439. Retains its seventeenth-century air – oak beams, open fires – and serves good bar meals from noon to 2pm and 6 to 9pm. You can sit outside on a warm day too.

Back o' Skiddaw

People often complain that the Lake District is too crowded, that tourists (including themselves) have overwhelmed the infrastructure and transformed the villages – none of which, happily, is true of the **Back o' Skiddaw**, the local name for the arc of fells and valleys that stetches around the back of Skiddaw mountain, tucked into the northernmost section of the National Park. For the most part it's countryside that really does deserve the epithet "rolling", with farmland tumbling down from Skiddaw's gentle humps to encircle small hamlets and villages that see little tourist traffic. The only **public transport** is the #73/73A "Caldbeck Rambler" bus, which runs daily in the school summer holidays, on selected Sundays and bank holiday Mondays, and on Saturdays throughout the year (see "Travel details" at the end of the chapter).

Uldale and Ireby

From the *Castle Inn* junction, half a mile from the northern edge of Bassenthwaite Lake, the sweeping road into Uldale ends three miles further on at **ULDALE** village where the cow dung on the road announces its farming credentials. Farming in the Lakes is a precarious business at the best of times: what it must have been like in the past in "wolf's dale" doesn't bear thinking about. Walpole used the quiet village and moorland surroundings as the backdrop in the middle two Herries novels, *Judith Paris* and *The Fortress*, with the fictional Fell House as the Herries family lair. There's a pub – the *Snooty Fox* (☎016973/71479) – and a tearoom in the old Victorian school, now *Mike's Eye Gallery* (Tues–Sun 10am–5pm; closed Jan & Feb; ☎016793/71778, ⓦwww.mikes-eye.com), which displays locals arts and crafts, and shows specially filmed Lake District videos. A mile and a half south of the village lies tiny **Over Water**, the northernmost splash of water in the Lake District, with the farms of Orthwaite beyond. Only bad things await, surely, on the heights of **Great Cockup** (1720ft), an easy two-mile walk east from Orthwaite.

In the other direction, Uldale's **St James church** lies a full mile from the village on the Ireby road, a pretty building with some interesting old gravestones and uninterrupted fell views. Another mile beyond is sleepy **IREBY**, with its lion's head drinking trough. You can eat well in the venerable beamed-and-nooked *Sun Inn* (☎016973/71346), whose small beer garden is a restful spot on a sunny day.

Caldbeck

Prosperity came easily to **CALDBECK**, six miles east of Ireby and just twelve from Carlisle, and it remains one of lakeland's most appealing villages. The fast-flowing "cold stream" from which it takes its name provided the power for the rapid expansion in the number of mills here in the seventeenth and eighteenth centuries. Corn, wool and wooden bobbins flowed out, lead and copper from the fells was carted in; and the many surviving contemporary buildings (look for the dates carved on the lintels above the doors) attest to its wealth. A signposted quarter-mile walk from the car park up to the limestone gorge known as **The Howk** shows you the river in all its rushing glory, as well as the restored ruins of one of the old bobbin mills.

The village is anchored by its **church of St Kentigern**, dedicated to the sixth-century saint better known as Mungo, who journeyed from Scotland through Cumberland to Wales to preach the gospel to the heathen Saxons and Celts. The well he is supposed to have used for baptism lies by the packhorse bridge, next to the churchyard. The first stone church here was built in the twelfth century and although a medieval tombstone survives in the chancel, today's church bears the brunt of heavy nineteenth-century restoration. No matter, since all the interest is outside in the churchyard, where you'll easily find the ornate tombstone of **John Peel** of Ruthwaite (d. 1854),

IN Memory OF
JOHN PEEL OF
RUTHWAITE, who died
Nov.13th 1854. aged 78 Years.
Also MARY, his wife, who
died Aug! 9th 1859, aged 82,
Also JONATHAN their Son
who died Jan.21st 1806,
aged 2 Years.
Also PETER their Son, who
died Nov.r 15th 1840,
aged 27 Years.
Also MARY DAVIDSON their
DAUGHTER who died Nov 50
1865. aged 48 Years.
Also JOHN their Son who died
Nov: 22nd 1887. aged 90 Years.

△ Johan Peel's grave, Caldbeck

emblazoned with reliefs of hunting horns and his faithful hound. Peel's is a name synonymous with fox-hunting, yet he was just one of several hardened and hard-drinking nineteenth-century hunting men of local repute; his fame today derives squarely from the song ("D'ye ken John Peel") written about him by one of his friends. Eighteen paces from his grave, walking away from the church, is the tombstone of the Harrisons of Todcrofts: Richard was a simple farmer; it's his wife Mary (d. 1837) who is better known – as Mary, the Maid of Buttermere, the most celebrated beauty of her day (see p.189). These days, Caldbeck's most famous resident is mountaineer and writer Chris Bonington. **Priest's Mill** (mid-Feb to Oct Tues–Sun 11am–5pm, Nov & Dec Tues–Sun noon–4pm), near the church, has been turned into a little arts centre, with a jeweller and co-operative woolshop among the outlets.

For a stretch of the legs, Caldbeck's most favoured local walk is the climb up **High Pike** (2157ft), the fell to the south, mined for its minerals in the nineteenth century. The most obvious route is from Nether Row, a mile south of Caldbeck – count on five miles, three hours, there and back. Views from the cairn and bench at the summit sweep from the Solway Firth to the Yorkshire hills, with Blencathra and Bowscale Fell in the foreground.

Practicalities

Caldbeck makes a peaceful night's stop and, although there's no tourist office, you can check local **information** online at Ⓦ www.caldbeckvillage.co.uk. The **bus** drops you by the churchyard, there's free **parking** near the river, and a choice of local accommodation (including several farmhouse B&Bs, which are listed on the website). A very well-kept village **B&B**, *The Briars* (Ⓣ 016974/78633; no credit cards; ❷), near the car park and next to the doctor's surgery, has one single and a twin sharing a nice large bathroom, while an en-suite double at the back looks on to the local hillside. The **pub**, the *Oddfellows Arms* (Ⓣ 016974/78227; Ⓦ www.oddfellows-caldbeck.co.uk; ❸), boasts good-value trim rooms in a converted mill at the back. The bar meals here are very popular (restaurant bookings advised at weekends), or you can eat at the riverside *Watermill* vegetarian **restaurant** at Priest's Mill (Ⓣ 016974/78267; closed Jan to mid-Feb), open throughout the day for snacks, meals, organic hot

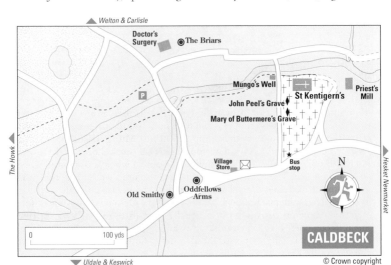

Welton & Carlisle

Doctor's Surgery — ◉ The Briars

Mungo's Well

St Kentigern's — Priest's Mill

John Peel's Grave

Mary of Buttermere's Grave

P

The Howk

Hesket Newmarket

Village Store — ✉

Bus stop

N

Old Smithy ◉ — ◉ Oddfellows Arms

0 — 100 yds

CALDBECK

Uldale & Keswick

© Crown copyright

chocolate and herbal teas, and serving dinner by arrangement (usually once a month on Fri). The *Old Smithy* (℡016974/78246; closed Wed, plus all Jan & Feb) on the river, behind the pub, also serves tearoom favourites, while for a drive out to a country pub, there's the attractive *Royal Oak* at **Welton**, about four miles to the north.

Hesket Newmarket

There's a path from Caldbeck a mile-and-a-half southeast through the fields to the small eighteenth-century village of **HESKET NEWMARKET**, which straddles a long village green. Markets were long held here, though the last was a century ago, and the prosperous village once supported half a dozen inns, yet the *Old Crown* (℡016974/78288, ⓦwww.theoldcrownpub.co.uk) by the green is the only survivor. It's a cosy local of great charm, owned by a local co-operative, and brewing a variety of excellent ales out the back in the Hesket Newmarket Brewery. The food is very popular, too, with many coming for the speciality curries. There's a tearoom at *Fellside Stores*, the local grocer's and post office, while the other way, past the pub, *Denton House* (℡016974/78415, ⓔdentonhnm@aol.com; no credit cards; ❷) has half a dozen rooms available. A mile or so southwest of the village, on the flank of the fells, Hudscales Farm **camping barn** (℡017687/72645; £5) offers simpler overnight accommodation for hikers.

Incidentally, if Caldbeck can boast John Peel and Chris Bonington as local famous names, Hesket Newmarket is not to be outdone – road haulage king and spotter's cult hero Eddie Stobart started out here in the family firm.

Carrock Fell, Mosedale and Mungrisdale

The road south from Caldbeck and Hesket Newmarket winds the eight miles back to the A66, effectively down the eastern boundary of the Lake District. Away to the east lie fields not fells, and beyond is the Eden Valley and Yorkshire. The bulk looming to the west, behind Blencathra and Bannerdale, is **Carrock Fell** (2174ft), best climbed from Stone Ends Farm – you can park by the road – three miles from Hesket Newmarket. The fell is riddled with abandoned mines (keep back – exploration is dangerous), while a huge tangle of fallen rocks litters the hillside: Charles Dickens and Wilkie Collins had a particularly disastrous time climbing Carrock Fell in mist, described in *The Lazy Tours of Two Idle Apprentices* (1857).

The broad valley of **Mosedale**, another mile or south down the road, has a minor road running up to meet the Cumbria Way at the valley's head. Day walkers usually head instead for **Bowscale Tarn**, 1600ft up, scooped dramatically out of Bowscale Fell and ringed by crags. It's an easy walk (1hr) from the roadside parking at nearby Bowscale, following a clear bridleway for much of the route. The summit of **Bowscale Fell** (2306ft) itself is reached from the tarn by a further, gut-busting, 45-minute climb, and to make a circular walk of it (5 miles; 4hr) you can then drop down into **Mungrisdale**, a narrower valley whose foot embraces a few stone houses, a small church and the *Mill Inn* (℡017687/79632, ⓦwww.the-millinn.co.uk; ❹) where a stone mill wheel props up the bar. The rooms have been nicely refurbished and there's good, moderately priced food in the bar or restaurant – homemade pies are a speciality, celebrated at the pub's annual Pie Festival every October. Almost next door – and not to be confused with it – the *Mill Hotel* (℡017687/79659, ⓦwww.themillhotel.com; no credit cards; ❺, including dinner ❼; closed Nov–Feb) is a more intimate, highly personalized country-house experience – the two cheaper rooms here share a bathroom.

Travel details

From Keswick

Bus #73/73A "Caldbeck Rambler" circular route to: Castlerigg Stone Circle (6min), Threlkeld (13min), Mungrisdale (25min), Mosedale (30min), Hesket Newmarket (45min), Caldbeck (50min), and around to Mirehouse (1hr 20min) and back to Keswick; or to Mirehouse (14min), Uldale (30min), Ireby (35min), Caldbeck (50min), and around to Mungrisdale (1hr 10min) and back to Keswick. Service operates mid-July to end-Aug 2–3 daily; plus Sun & bank hols from end-May to mid-July, & Sat all year.

Bus #77/77A "Honister Rambler" circular route to: Cat Bells (11min), Grange (20min), Seatoller (30min), Honister Pass/YHA (40min), Buttermere (50min), Lorton (1hr 10min) and Whinlatter Pass (1hr 20min); or to Whinlatter Pass (15min), Lorton (25min), Buttermere (45min), Honister Pass (1hr), Seatoller (1hr 5min) and Grange (1hr 15min). Service operates Easter–Oct 4 daily.

Bus #79 "Borrowdale Rambler" (every 30min–1hr) to: Lodore (15min), Grange (20min), Rosthwaite (25min) and Seatoller (30min).

Bus #86 Keswick Town Service: to Portinscale (Mon–Sat 4 daily; 15min).

Bus #87 Keswick Town Service: to Castlerigg Stone Circle (9min), Threlkeld (14min); Mon–Sat 2 daily.

Bus #208 to: Aira Force (25min), Glenridding (35min) and Patterdale (40min). Service operates mid-July to end-Aug 5 daily, plus Sat, Sun & bank hols end-May to mid-July.

Bus #555/556 (hourly service) to: Thirlspot (10min), Grasmere (25min), Ambleside (45min), Windermere (1hr) and Kendal (1hr 30min); and also (3 daily) to Carlisle (1hr 10min).

Bus #X4/X5/X50 (Mon–Sat every 30–60min, Sun every 2hr) to: Threlkeld (12min), Rheged (30min) and Penrith (35min); and also to Mirehouse (10min), Bassenthwaite (15min) and Cockermouth (30min).

5

The western fells
and valleys

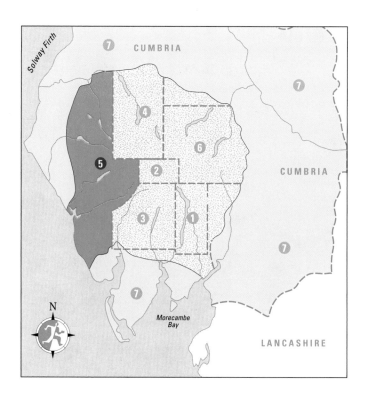

CHAPTER 5

Highlights

✳ **Silecroft beach** The only stretch of beach within the National Park extends for miles, providing a habitat for wildlife. See p.174

✳ **Ravenglass & Eskdale Railway** The finest approach to quiet Eskdale is in the toy-town carriages of the Ravenglass & Eskdale Railway. See p.175

✳ **Muncaster** A great family day out – gardens, ghosts and owls. See p.176

✳ **Viking cross, Gosforth** The finest reminder of the Norse influence on the Lakes is this intricately carved stone cross. See p.182

✳ **Wasdale Head Inn** Relive the old days in the atmospheric rural inn, where walkers and climbers congregate over drinks and dinner. See p.185

✳ **Haystacks** The favourite peak of avid fellwalker, Alfred Wainwright, whose ashes are scattered here. See p.190

△ Muncaster Castle

5

The western fells and valleys

Great Gable and the Scafells stand as a formidable last-gasp boundary between the mountains of the central lakes and the mostly gentler land to the west, which smooths out its wrinkles as it descends to the Cumbrian coast. Here, in the **western fells and valleys**, lies some of the National Park's most diverse scenery – the stunning lakeland vistas you'd expect around Wast Water and Buttermere, tempered by the forested swaths of Ennerdale, the deeply rural hamlets of Wasdale and Eskdale, and a little-known coastline. Indeed, it's the west Cumbrian coast that impinges most upon this part of the region. The old industrial ports of Whitehaven, Workington and Maryport all lie outside the National Park but their influence is felt in subtle ways: for one hundred and fifty years water has been drained from Ennerdale to supply the towns and only a spirited defence in the late 1970s by environmental protesters prevented a scheme to build a higher weir at Ennerdale Water and raise the water level. The driving force behind the proposed increase in water extraction was the Sellafield nuclear reprocessing plant, a major local employer that lurks on the coast just north of Ravenglass. It's changed its name twice, from Calder Hall to Windscale and then to Sellafield, in what might seem, to a cynic, an attempt to hide its manifest dangers.

The main road, the **A595** between Broughton-in-Furness and Workington, is the principal means of approach for the western fells and valleys. It runs along the coastal plain, with minor roads striking off north and east into the valleys, and it's this limited access that preserves the region's relative isolation – only Eskdale and Buttermere can be reached by road from the central fells. **Eskdale**, for that reason, is among the most popular targets, though the narrow-gauge **Ravenglass & Eskdale Railway** has as much to do with it. **Wast Water**, which points its slender finger towards Great Gable, remains one of the most isolated of the lakes and a night at the inn at **Wasdale Head** is unlikely to be forgotten. "No part of the country is more distinguished by sublimity", claimed Wordsworth, who – no mean walker himself – thought Wasdale "well worth the notice of the traveller who is not afraid of fatigue". It's actually a toss-up whether Wast Water or **Ennerdale Water** is the better-looking lake, though Ennerdale is, if anything, even more remote. En route north to Cockermouth, a few interested visitors are drawn to tiny **Loweswater** and its excellent inn, though the biggest attractions are the twin lakes of

Crummock Water and **Buttermere**. These are situated on a well-defined circuit from Keswick but there's enough grandeur in the surrounding fells to make the summer crowds bearable.

Public transport is limited. You can reach Ennerdale Water and Loweswater by public bus, but only on summer weekends and public holidays, while the daily Buttermere service from Keswick is also seasonal (Easter–Oct). At all

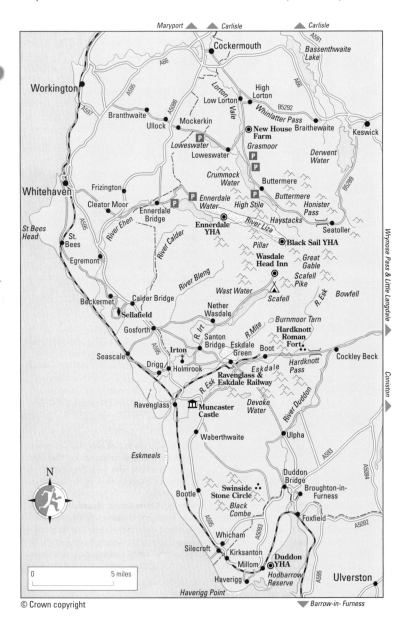

© Crown copyright

other times, you're going to find yourself walking between the lakes and villages, over mountain passes and across fells whose names (Pillar, Great Gable, the Scafells) are among the most resonant in the region.

Millom, Black Combe and the coast

The short section of the **west Cumbrian coast** that falls within the National Park – the twenty miles between Silecroft and Ravenglass – is neither particularly dramatic nor appealing. Its one unique feature is the bulky **Black Combe**, which dominates the southern part of the coast, the only Lake District fell to fall straight to the sea. This gives climbing it a certain appeal, since the views are tremendous and, unusually for the Lakes, only run out with the horizon. To the southeast, just outside the National Park boundary, the former iron-ore mining town of **Millom** tries hard to capture some of the passing traffic, though more are drawn to the fine duned beaches out of town at **Haverigg** or to the long sandy stretches from **Silecroft** northwards.

Millom and around

Road and rail shadow the coast from **MILLOM** (which lies just outside the National Park), the small, plain town split by the railway line and flanked to the south and east by the shifting sands of the Duddon Channel. A late-medieval settlement here – to the north of the current town – focused on the castle and church of the local lords, the Hudlestones, whose seat is now largely in ruins (there's no regular public access to the castle ruin or church). It wasn't until the mid-nineteenth century – and the local discovery of high-grade iron ore – that Millom itself was established around the mining and ore-processing operations on the neighbouring Hodbarrow peninsula. In its day, it was a massive operation, with millions of tons of iron ore extracted by thousands of workers housed in drab, company-built streets. Their employment came to an end in 1968 when the mine finally closed, but working and living conditions are graphically recalled in Millom's excellent **Folk Museum** (Easter–Oct Mon–Fri 10am–1pm & 2–4.30pm; £2), sited with the tourist office at the

Black Combe and Swinside Stone Circle

The A595 makes a V-shape around the **Black Combe** massif, with the angle at the hamlet of **Whicham**, near Silecroft, where there's a path up to the **summit** (1857ft) that starts from the minor Kirkbank road, behind the church. It's not a particularly demanding climb (approx. 3 miles there and back; 2hr 30min), and the views from the top are hugely rewarding, stretching out to sea to the Isle of Man, up the coast to St Bees Head and south to Morecambe Bay. It's traditionally claimed that you can see up to fourteen English and Scottish counties from here, plus Snowdon and the Irish coast, but that would require one of those all-too-rare crystal-clear days and Clark Kent-like vision.

The fell's northeastern side shelters the **Swinside Stone Circle**, though this is best reached from back up the A595 towards Broughton-in-Furness: look for the minor Broadgate turnoff, park by the farm buildings and walk the mile up the rough fell track to the ancient standing stones. They stand in a natural amphitheatre, with the local name for the stones, Sunkenkirk, reflecting the belief that the devil struck (or sunk) the stones of an ancient church (kirk) into the ground. A pagan winter solstice ceremony is held here each year.

town's train station. There's a recreation of one of the old mines, using original items from the last pit to close, as well as other reassembled shop and domestic interiors, and any number of local finds, photographs, relics and memorabilia.

The museum is also the place to discover something about Millom's famous son, the poet **Norman Nicholson** (1914–87). An only child, he contracted TB at 16 and spent two years in a Hampshire sanatorium before returning to Millom, where it was another twelve years before he was considered cured. His wide reading in convalescent isolation was one of the main factors, he considered, that made him a reflective poet; that, and his deep attachment to his Cumberland roots, whose industry, landscape, people and history informed all his work. Nicholson spent his life in Millom. His house, at 14 St George's Terrace, just off the small market square, two minutes from the train station, is marked by a blue plaque – it's now a health-food store and tearoom. In **St George's Church**, up the drive opposite the square, a beautiful contemporary stained-glass window celebrates Nicholson's life and work – ask about access at the tourist office – while he is buried with his wife in the new part of St George's churchyard. The grave lies beyond the church and down to the right, in front of a wooden bench by a wooden fence, and is inscribed with a moving line from his last published work, *Sea to the West*: "Let our eyes at the last be blinded/Not by the dark/But by dazzle."

Respects paid, the local beach at **Haverigg** beckons. A mile to the south, it's typical of what's to come – a lengthy, duned stretch that leads a quiet existence, even in summer. There's a children's playground and a beach café. The nearby **Hodbarrow RSPB Reserve**, two miles from Millom (always open; free; ⑩ www.rspb.org.uk) – sited around a freshwater lagoon formed from flooded mine workings – is a good place to spot wading birds and waterfowl. The lagoon is of national importance for wintering waterfowl such as wigeon, goldeneye, red-breasted merganser and pintail, while in summer three species of tern nest on the reserve and can be viewed from the hide on the sea wall. The number and variety of orchids at Hodbarrow also catch the eye in summer – not just the plentiful marsh, spotted and pyramidal orchids but the largest colony of bee orchids in Cumbria.

Practicalities

In town, practical matters are easily dealt with. The **train station** is on Station Road, while the **tourist office** next door (Easter–Oct Mon–Fri 10am–1pm & 2–4.30pm; ☎01229/774819) has local **accommodation** details. There are a few town B&Bs, but if you are going to stay you might as well immerse yourself in Millom's estuarine surroundings. From the station, follow St George's Road then Devonshire Road to find the friendly, no-smoking *Duddon Pilot Hotel* (☎01229/774116; ❹), under a mile out of town by the estuary and old iron works. There's a nautical theme throughout – family members were once ships' pilots on the River Duddon, hence the name. Three hundred yards further on, closer to the river and sands, the *Duddon Estuary YHA* (☎0870/770 6107, ⓔduddon@yha.org.uk; advance bookings essential; £10), at Borwick Rails, is a small, eighteen-bed cottage **youth hostel** perched on the edge of the peninsula, with terrific views. It's self-catering only, with the nearest shops back in Millom, though the *Duddon Pilot* has bar meals.

Silecroft, Bootle and Eskmeals

Next decent sweep of beach is at **SILECROFT**, four miles northwest of Millom. The coastal scrub here is a habitat for the natterjack toad; and, as elsewhere along the Cumbrian coast, terns, oyster-catchers and ringed plovers nest and breed, scraping the shingle over their camouflaged eggs. There's a pub at Silecroft (near the station, not the beach), where you can get a lunchtime sandwich, though some prefer the *King William IV* at **KIRKSANTON**, a mile back down the A5093 towards Millom. At **BOOTLE**, five miles up the A595, the sandstone-faced church is split from its cemetery by the road. Bootle's nearest beach is three miles to the northwest, at **ESKMEALS**, which has a stony foreshore, though when the tide is out a large expanse of sand is exposed, from which you can admire the views as far north as St Bees Head. North of here, as far as Ravenglass, the coastline itself is off limits – red flags fly over an experimental firing range – while beyond lie the hard-to-miss towers and buildings of Sellafield. Whether you'd choose to swim anywhere in the vicinity of a nuclear-reprocessing plant is, of course, entirely a matter for you.

Ravenglass and around

The principal coastal stop before the headland of St Bees is **RAVENGLASS**, a sleepy village at the estuary of three syllabically challenged rivers, the Esk, Mite and Irt. The village is the starting point for the narrow-gauge Ravenglass & Eskdale Railway (see below), but it merits a closer look before you take the train or visit nearby Muncaster Castle. Its single main street preserves a row of plain nineteenth-century cottages. These back on to estuarine mud flats and dunes, which are accessible when the tide's out – the northern section, across the Esk, is a nature reserve where black-headed gulls and terns are often seen. The Romans, who used the estuary as a harbour, established a supply post at Ravenglass in the first century AD for the northern legions manning Hadrian's Wall. Nothing remains of what the Romans knew as Glannaventa save the remarkably complete buildings of their **bathhouse**, part of a fort that survived in Ravenglass until the fourth century. It's on the road out of the village, just past the station, 500 yards up a (signposted) single-track lane.

Ravenglass & Eskdale Railway

The **Ravenglass & Eskdale Railway** (known affectionately as La'al Ratty) opened in 1875 to carry iron ore from the Eskdale mines to the coastal railway. Long converted to tourist use and running on a 15-inch-gauge track, the tiny train takes forty minutes to wind its way through seven miles of forests and fields, first along Miterdale under Muncaster Fell and then into the valley of the River Esk, where it terminates at Dalegarth station, near Boot. You can break your journey with an "Explorer" ticket, allowing you to get off and walk from one of the half-dozen stations en route; the full return journey, without a break, takes an hour and forty minutes. Or take your bike up on the train and cycle back from Dalegarth down the traffic-free **Eskdale T-Rail** (8.5 miles; one-way ticket plus bike carriage £8.20); it takes around two hours and a route guide (£2) is available from stations at either end. There's parking at Ravenglass station, a small **railway museum** (same days and times as rail service), a short video showing you the route, a café on the platform and a shop, where budding engine drivers can buy an all-important driver's cap. The station **café** serves drinks and light meals, while over by the main station, the *Ratty Arms* (☎01229/717676) has real ales, daily specials and sandwiches, served on a sunny terrace.

In summer school holidays (mid-July to end-Aug), trains run daily from 9am to 5.30pm, with **departures** roughly every twenty minutes. At Easter, and in

June/mid-July and September, hourly departures run from 9am to 4.50pm; while between November and March, trains tend to run at weekends only (but daily in school holidays) hourly from 10.30am to 3.50pm. An **Explorer Ticket** (£8.60) gives one day's unlimited travel on the line, while special days out, involving Thomas the Tank Engine and the like, are held throughout the year. For more **information**, contact the Ravenglass & Eskdale station (℡01229/717171, ⍟www.ravenglass-railway.co.uk), adjacent to the Furness coastal line station.

Muncaster Castle

A mile east of Ravenglass, on the A595, spreads the estate of **Muncaster Castle**, whose house, grounds and attractions are billed as the Muncaster Experience (Feb half-term hols to first week Nov: castle Mon–Fri & Sun noon–5pm; gardens, owl centre and maze daily 10.30am–6pm or dusk; £9, £6 without castle entrance; ℡01229/717614, ⍟www.muncaster.co.uk) – one of the region's best days out. There's parking at the castle, or bus #6/X6 runs daily from Whitehaven (and on Sundays from Millom). Or you can walk here (30min) on the path from Ravenglass, up past the Roman bathhouse and across the fields.

The **castle** itself was built around a medieval pele tower, and has been home to the Pennington family since the thirteenth century; family members still live here today, as photographs throughout and contemporary portraits in the Drawing Room attest. An audio tour points out the family treasures (a Gainsborough here, a Reynolds there), and leads you through various rooms, notably the impressive octagonal library and the Tapestry Room, with its Flemish wall hangings and mighty Elizabethan fireplace. An electro-magnetic "spectre-detector" provides evidence to back up Muncaster's claim to be one of the most haunted houses in Britain – sceptics and others can test their nerve with an all-night vigil in the Tapestry Room (Ghost Sit, from £350 for up to six people, breakfast included). The seventy-acre **grounds and gardens** win plaudits too (best in spring and autumn), with a stupendous view straight up Eskdale from the Terrace Walk, and half a dozen other marked trails, including one winding through a hilly Sino-Himalayan Garden. The plants here, all grown from seeds from Bhutan, Vietnam, and Yunnan and Sichuan provinces in China, thrive in conditions apparently similar to those 11,000 feet up a Far Eastern mountain – which doesn't say a lot for Cumbrian weather patterns.

The castle is also the headquarters of the World Owl Trust, whose excellent **Owl Centre** (℡01229/717393, ⍟www.owls.org) in the grounds acts as a breeding centre for endangered species (including England's own barn owl). The aviaries contain birds from fifty different owl species, some of which are put through their paces on the castle lawns at the informative daily "Meet the Birds" display (2.30pm); the wild herons feed at 4.30pm (3.30pm in winter). Finally, the **meadowvole maze** is a lighthearted look at mole-sized life in the wildflower meadows, where escaping being eaten by an owl is the challenge for younger visitors.

The castle is closed in winter, though the grounds, owl centre and maze remain open most weekends (Nov, Dec & Feb; £4), when you can also experience **Darkest Muncaster** (£5, or £1 with general admission; call for details), an illuminated walk through the grounds, packed with interactive surprises.

Refreshments are provided by the **café**, *Creeping Kate's Kitchen*, in the stable yard, while smart B&B **rooms** in the former coachman's quarters (see above for contact details; ➌) offer a comfortable night's stay (not all are en suite). No meals are served other than breakfast, though guests have the use of a lounge and kitchen, and it's only a mile's walk down the path to Ravenglass and the *Ratty Arms* – or stick a bottle of bubbly in the fridge and toast yourself on the Muncaster lawns. Guests also get free access to the gardens and owl centre, and a discount on the Ravenglass & Eskdale railway.

Eskdale

Eskdale, accessed most easily from the Cumbrian coast, is just twelve miles long from start to finish, but what a finish it provides – in the dramatic high-fell surroundings of Hardknott Pass. It's a fairly gentle valley in its early stages, with various approach roads (from Ulpha in the Duddon Valley, from Wasdale or along the River Esk itself) meeting at the elongated hamlet of **Eskdale Green** (a stop on the Ravenglass & Eskdale Railway), on a rise above the valley. From Eskdale Green, the valley road continues east, passing **Dalegarth station** (terminus of the Ravenglass & Eskdale Railway), which lies just a short walk from the valley's isolated church and from Eskdale's other hamlet, **Boot**. Here there's an old mill to explore, an excellent inn and several more local hikes, not to mention the walk or drive up and out of the valley to the superbly sited **Hardknott Roman Fort**.

Eskdale Green

First village stop on the Ravenglass & Eskdale Railway is **ESKDALE GREEN**, where you can access short walks into nearby Miterdale Forest and up to the valley head, or even plan on hiking back along the spine of Muncaster Fell to Ravenglass. This is around four miles and shouldn't take more than a couple of hours. Nearest **pub** to the station (200 yards away, by the turnoff to Boot) is the ivy-strewn *King George IV* (☎019467/23262, ⓦwww.kinggeorge-iv.co.uk; ❹), a traditional hostelry with an impressive collection of real ales and malt whiskies. The local **campsite** isn't far from here, 400 yards up the Boot road, at *Fisherground Farm* (☎019467/23349, ⓦwww.fishergroundcampsite.co.uk; closed Dec–Feb), where as well as camping there are stone **cottages** and log **cabins** available for rent (£255 –525 per week; weekend and short lets available off-season), all well

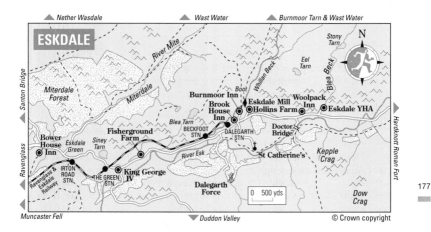

© Crown copyright

Eskdale is a great choice for a walk at any time of year: you'll rarely come across many other people on the routes outlined below, even on the shorter strolls. There's parking at Dalegarth station and in Boot, and as the train runs year-round the valley makes a fine off-season day out.

Dalegarth Force and the River Esk

Footpaths along both sides of the **River Esk** between Eskdale's St Catherine's church and Doctor Bridge (near the *Woolpack Inn*) allow an easy two-mile (1hr) riverside walk – in low water you can cross the river below the church by stepping stones, or there's a bridge further up. You can combine this with the steep climb up the wooded ravine that holds the impressive sixty-foot falls of **Dalegarth Force** (also known as Stanley Ghyll Force), in full spate for much of the year.

Hardknott and the Esk Falls

It's harder going east of Doctor Bridge, where a path to the foot of the **Hardknott Pass** keeps to the south side of the River Esk beneath Birker Fell, before cutting up, via the farm at Brotherikeld, to the Roman fort. Keeping to the Esk, you can hike on up the narrow valley between overhanging crags to **Lingcove Bridge**, beyond which tumble the **Esk Falls** – an eight-mile (5hr) round-trip that requires fine weather and good visibility, otherwise you risk getting bogged down and lost.

The Woolpack Walk

The most strenuous hike from Eskdale is the **Woolpack Walk** (18 miles, 10–12hr), a tough high-level circuit topping the two highest mountains in England (the Scafells) and several others (Bowfell, Crinkle Crags, Harter Fell) that aren't much lower. It is not easy going and a certain amount of scrambling is required, but the views and the varied terrain make this one of the finest lakeland walks. Traditional start- and finishing-point is the *Woolpack Inn*, where full route details are available.

See Basics, p.40, for general walking advice in the Lakes; recommended maps are detailed on p.27.

equipped and south facing to soak up the sun. The campsite has its own station on the Ravenglass & Eskdale Railway.

Heading the other way, west, through Eskdale Green, you'll pass a small post office-general store and *Forest How Guest House* (☏019467/23201, ⓦwww .foresthow-eskdale-cumbria.co.uk; no credit cards; ❷), with seven country-style bedrooms (three en suite) and a lovely patio with rural views. Finally, at the Santon Bridge turnoff, there's the *Bower House Inn* (☏019467/23244, ⓦwww.bowerhouseinn.co.uk; ❺), a cut above the usual rural inn, with a selection of real ales (some local), bar **meals** and a restaurant serving a table d'hôte dinner for £25.

Dalegarth station and Boot

By the time the valley road and train line reach **Dalegarth station**, two miles east of Eskdale Green, the fells beyond can be seen more clearly and eyes are drawn ever upwards to the singular skyline. Passengers pile off the train for the walk to Dalegarth Force (see p.178), heading down a track opposite the station, which leads in a couple of hundred yards to Eskdale's **St Catherine's church**. Its riverside location is handsome in the extreme and in the small cemetery you can't miss the distinctive gravestone of Thomas Dobson

(d. 1910), former hunt Master of the Eskdale and Ennerdale Hounds whose likeness grins from the top of the stone, above a carved fox and hound. Dobson actually died in the *Three Shires Inn* in Little Langdale, which involved his coffin being carted to Eskdale over the gruelling Wrynose and Hardknott passes. If he hadn't already been dead the bearers would probably have killed him for his thoughtlessness. It's another 350 yards up the valley road from Dalegarth station to the turning for the dead-end hamlet of **BOOT**. The few stone cottages and pub, cowering beneath the fells, mark the last remnant of civilization before the road turns serious. The mines near Boot that supplied ore for the railway to Ravenglass never really paid their way and closed in 1913. But there's been industry of sorts here for centuries, since the Furness Abbey monks first introduced a corn mill into Eskdale. Over the packhorse bridge at the back of the hamlet, the sixteenth-century **Eskdale Mill** (April–Sept Tues–Sun 11am–5pm; £1.50; ☎019467/23335) preserves its wooden machinery and you can picnic near the waterfalls that power the wheels. For a stretch of the legs, follow the signposted path up the heights to **Eel Tarn**, a mile away.

Boot has a fair smattering of **accommodation and services**, which makes it the obvious base for extended walks in the valley. All the overnight options are covered below, from rooms in old inns to bunkhouse and youth hostel accommodation. A small **general store–post office** in Boot sells lakeland ice cream and rents out hiking boots. Local **information** is available online at Ⓦwww.eskdale.info. The **Boot Beer Festival** each June splits its festivities between the three inns, while the **Eskdale Show** (last Sat in Sept) is the annual valley celebration of traditional ways and sports.

Inns and B&B

Brook House Inn 350 yards east of Dalegarth station, at the Boot road junction ☎019467/23288, Ⓦwww.brookhouseinn.co.uk. Cheery family-run hotel with eight rooms, which serves morning coffee and meals in its bar (real ales always available) and also has a separate, moderately priced restaurant with a varied menu. Parking. ❹

Burnmoor Inn Boot ☎0845/130 6224 or 019467/23223, Ⓦwww.burnmoor.co.uk. The traditional hikers' choice is a genial place, right in the centre of the hamlet, whose nine rooms (several with baths, not showers) have lashings of hot water (but no TVs). There's a peaceful beer garden, and the food's good and not particularly expensive – game stew, wienerschnitzel and the Boot Pie (steak and Guinness) are all favourites. Parking. ❹

Dale View The Post Office, Boot ☎019467/23236, Ⓦwww.booteskdale.co.uk. The post office has two doubles, a twin and a single, all sharing a bathroom, and can pack you a lunch (£4) for a day's walking – while the *Burnmoor Inn* is right over the road for meals. Advance reservations recommended in winter, when B&B not always available. No credit cards. ❸

Woolpack Inn Eskdale, Hardknott Pass road, 1 mile east of Boot ☎019467/23230, Ⓦwww.woolpack.co.uk. The friendly inn provides all the essentials, including a well-kept selection of real ales, a fell-view garden and mountainous portions of inexpensive home-cooked food. There are eight cosy rooms (three en suite, priced a category higher), and there may also be bunkhouse beds available – call for details. You'll get good hiking advice, wherever you're heading, and if residents complete the infamous Woolpack Walk in less than nine hours, they get a free pint. Parking. No American Express. ❸

Youth hostel

Eskdale YHA Eskdale, Hardknott Pass road, 200 yards east of Woolpack Inn ☎0870/770 5824, Ⓔeskdale@yha.org.uk. A secluded, detached house nestling under Eskdale Fell, with some rooms available to couples and families. Laundry facilities and drying room available. Reception opens at 5pm; evening meals available. Closed Nov–Feb; also closed 1 or 2 days a week March–June & Oct. Dorm beds £11.

Campsite

Hollins Farm Eskdale, Hardknott Pass road, 200 yards east of Boot ☎019467/23253. Small campsite, beautifully sited in the Esk valley.

Hardknott Fort and Pass

Three miles beyond Boot and 800ft up the twisting road, the remains of **Hardknott Roman Fort** (always open; free access) – known as Mediobocdum to the Romans – command a strategic and panoramic position just below Hardknott Pass. If ever proof were needed of how serious the Romans were about keeping what they had conquered, then Hardknott proves the point. This full-scale fortification was built during the reign of Hadrian by a cohort of Dalmatian (Croatian) troops, who gave it walls twelve feet thick and a double-towered gateway, and endowed it with granaries, bathhouses and a plush, stone-built *praetorium* or commandant's quarters. The troops had to endure the discomforts of timber barracks, though since the *praetorium* was built along Roman lines – rooms ranged around an open courtyard – the commandant probably cursed his luck at his assignment every time the wind blew (about every ten seconds up here). Much of the lower part of the defensive wall is original Roman work; elsewhere, the foundations of the granaries and various other buildings have been re-erected to indicate their scale. Needless to say, the views back down into Eskdale and up to the Scafells are stunning.

Past the fort, after negotiating the narrow switchbacks of **Hardknott Pass**, the road drops to Cockley Beck (for the Duddon Valley, see p.133), before making the equally alarming ascent of Wrynose Pass, gateway to Little Langdale (p.102).

Wast Water and around

Nothing prepares you for the first sight of **Wast Water**, England's deepest lake, and certainly not the gentle approach from the southwest through the forestry plantations and farmland between the Wasdale hamlets of **Santon Bridge** and **Nether Wasdale**. Bracken-covered walls hide the fields from view, while the roads cross little stone bridges and pass farm shops selling jars of bramble jelly or bags of new potatoes. A mile and a half east of Nether Wasdale the lake comes into view and the initial glimpse of the water brings gasps – not for the lake itself (just three miles long and less than three hundred feet deep), but for the crowding fells that surround it and the awesome screes that plunge to its eastern shore. These tumble 1700ft from Illgill Head, separating Wast Water from Eskdale to the south, while the highest peaks in England – Great Gable and the Scafells – frame **Wasdale Head**, the tiny settlement at the head of the lake. You'll have seen the view up the lake to Great Gable, unwittingly, countless times already since the National Park Authority uses the outline as its logo on every publication, signpost and notice board. For a true measure of your own insignificance, take a walk along the eastern lakeshore path, approaching the impassable, implacable screes and look up. Thomas Wilkinson, an overawed eighteenth-century Quaker, fancied that he was gazing upon "the Pyramids of the world, built by the Architect of the Universe".

Isolated Wasdale Head and its famous *Wasdale Head Inn* are very much the main events in Wasdale, though on the way you should also make time to see the ancient cross in **Gosforth**, a village just off the A595. There's currently no **public transport** to Wasdale Head, save a limited-service, pre-booked taxi from Gosforth via Nether Wasdale and *Wasdale Hall YHA* (Thurs, Sat & Sun only; call Gosforth Taxis ☎019467/25308). Drivers should note that the road beyond Nether Wasdale is single-track for the most part and hugs Wast Water's western shore, with occasional parking spots by bosky groves, stony coves and little promontories.

△ Wast Water

Dry-stone walls

A dry-stone wall
Is a wall and a wall,
Leaning together
(Cumberland and Westmorland
champion wrestlers),
Greening and weathering,
Flank by flank,
With filling of rubble
Between the two.

From "Wall", by Norman Nicholson

The hundreds of miles of **dry-stone walls** that crisscross the Lake District are one of the region's most characteristic sights. Although the earliest farmers had identified boundaries and enclosed fields, these tasks assumed greater significance with the medieval expansion of sheep farming. As early as the thirteenth century the monks of Furness Abbey were enclosing extensive tracts of moorland within stone-built walls, traces of which can still be seen in upper Eskdale. Walls provided the means of converting unproductive high land into enclosed sheep farms: separating grazing areas, providing flocks with shelter (and preventing them straying), and facilitating sheep-driving and collection (by means of stone-built "pounds"). At first built on an ad hoc basis, walls tended to follow irregular patterns to suit local needs – often they were no more than dumping grounds for stones cleared from new pastures.

Irregularly walled enclosures gave way to systematic patterns during the eighteenth and nineteenth centuries as the Enclosure Acts (1801) prevailed – basically, statutes sanctioning the grabbing of once common or wild land by the bigger, richer landowners. Not only was common land seized, but small farmers were deprived of traditional grazing, cropping and wood-gathering rights, forcing them either to become tenants or to move. Behind this larceny was a rapidly increasing demand for food and wool, driven by the mushrooming population of the newly industrialized cities and the effect of the blockades during the Napoleonic War which kept food prices high. For many, the resulting walls – now an integral part of the landscape, but then a novelty – symbolized the growing hardship of the

Gosforth and around

At the Wasdale turnoff from the A595, **GOSFORTH** ("ford of geese") – a large if unremarkable village, with a couple of pubs, a bank and petrol station – has one extraordinary attraction: the tall, carved **stone cross** in the churchyard of **St Mary's** on the eastern edge of town. Signposted as the "Viking" cross, it's a rare example in Cumbria of the clash between pagan and Christian cultures, with the four faces of the slender shaft carved with Norse figures from the Sagas, which are surmounted by a Christian cross. There's been a church on this site since at least the tenth century, though it's been rebuilt many times since: nineteenth-century restoration revealed the church's other treasures, the two Viking "hogback" **tombstones**, found buried in the foundations. If your imagination is captured by the Gosforth cross, you should really drive the three miles south back down the A595, through Holmrook, and take the left turn signposted to Santon Bridge. A mile up the ruler-straight road, a signposted track – accessible with care for cars – leads to isolated **St Paul's**, Irton, which has a worn tenth-century stone cross in its churchyard.

More on the crosses and tombs can be found if you delve through the second-hand and antiquarian books in Archie Miles's **bookshop**, on small farmer. Nineteenth-century English "peasant poet" John Clare wrote bitterly that: "Enclosure came, and trampled on the grave of labour's rights, and left the poor a slave."

The increased demand for walls outstripped the capabilities of most farmers and inspired a new trade, undertaken by bands of itinerant craftsmen (not strictly masons, but skilled nonetheless). Sleeping on the fells and using the stone they found *in situ* – which explains the homogeneous, almost organic quality of lakeland walls – these "wallers" would set about erecting what are known locally as "dykes". A good waller could build seven yards of wall a day, though often less as many walls in the Lakes are unnecessarily thick – surplus stone had to be used up to maximize the grazing land. Tools and methods varied: shovel or spade, pick and stone hammer were common utensils; many wallers preferred to rely on sight rather than use builder's "lines"; others used a "walling frame" (two boards fastened with crosspieces) to establish the height of the wall and the slope of its sides.

As its name makes clear, a dry-stone wall has no mortar to hold it together. Instead, it's built on the cavity-wall principle – that is, as a double wall with the space between packed with small stones (guts). Ideally a two-person job (someone working alone has to keep changing sides), the wall starts off at anything up to 3ft wide, narrowing to around a foot wide at the top. Long stones (throughs) are placed at intervals through the width for stability; while the walls are topped by slanted stones (cams) so that the rain drains off. To allow sheep access from one pasture to another, a space (hogg hole) might be left in the base of a wall. A waller requires a good eye, both for the line of the wall and the selection of stones, which must either have a smooth side or be suitable for corners. The finished product is remarkably hardy: dry-stone walls might last fifty or one hundred years without shifting or collapsing, often longer.

While not exactly a growth industry these days, new dry-stone walls are still needed on modern sheep farms and existing walls require maintenance. The old skills have been kept alive by a dedicated band of wallers: you'll see them in action at annual agricultural shows, while there are also dry-stone wall-building demonstrations every summer, co-ordinated by the Lake District Visitor Centre at Brockhole.

Gosforth's main street on the way to the church; it's also good for first editions and rare copies of old Lakeland guides. The two old **pubs** in the centre, the *Lion & Lamb* and the *Globe*, can provide a bite to eat, as can the *Lakeland Habit Café* (℡019467/25232) above the village shop and post office. Gosforth also has a bakery, farm grocery shop and an ATM, which makes it the most reliable place for services and supplies in this neck of the woods.

Nether Wasdale and Santon Bridge

East of Gosforth, the hamlet of **NETHER WASDALE**, a mile and a half before the lake, has a clutch of useful accommodation options. Two attractive, traditional hotels by the green are under the same management: five rooms and a nice public bar at the *Screes Inn* (℡019467/26262, ⓦwww.thescreesinnwasdale .com; ❸), and more rooms, plus bar, lounge and restaurant over at *Strands Hotel* (℡019467/26237, ⓦwww.strandshotel.com; ❹). Or there's nearby *Low Wood Hall* (℡019467/26100, ⓦwww.lowwoodhall.co.uk; ❹), a restored Victorian country house whose gardens look toward the fells. Budget accommodation is either at *Murt Barn* (℡017687/72645; £5), a basic **camping barn** 250 yards from the village on the Wast Water road, or at the **youth hostel**, *Wasdale Hall*

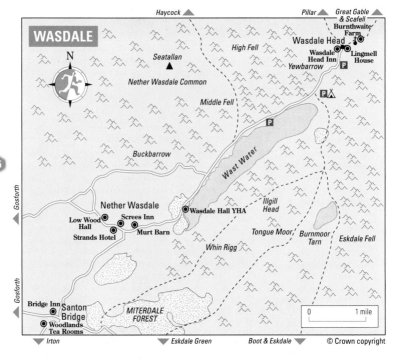

YHA (☎0870/770 6082, ✉wastwater@yha.org.uk; Sept–Easter closed 1–2 days a week; £11), another mile and a half to the east, at the foot of the lake. It's a converted country house in a wooded hollow, set in its own grounds, with bunks in largish rooms, and an evening meal offered. From the hostel, it's just under three miles to the inn at the head of the lake.

In the other direction, two miles to the southwest of Nether Wasdale, **SAN-TON BRIDGE** has the *Bridge Inn* (☎019467/26221, ⓦwww.santonbridgeinn .com; ➍), a modest country pub by the River Irt, with bistro meals and week-end walkers' breakfasts. It also hosts the annual "**Biggest Liar in the World**" competition every November, a tradition started by Will Ritson of Wasdale Head (see below) who told famously tall tales of country life to his guests and neigh-bours. A few hundred yards away (on the Irton road, to the A595), there are teas, meals and cakes at the *Woodlands Tea Rooms* (☎01946/726281), attached to a country gift shop.

Wasdale Head

The Wast Water road ends a mile beyond the lake at **WASDALE HEAD**, a Shangri-La-like clearing between the mountain ranges, where you'll find the **Wasdale Head Inn**, one of the most celebrated of all lakeland inns. British mountain-climbing was born here in the days when the inn's landlord – and champion liar – was the famous Will Ritson (1808–90): black-and-white photographs pinned to the panelled rooms inside show Victorian gents in hobnailed boots and flat caps scaling dreadful precipices with nonchalant ease (for more on the birthplace of British mountain climbing, see p.264). The inn's gone a bit upmarket since those days, but still attracts a genuine walking and climbing crowd.

What's reputed to be England's smallest church, **St Olaf's** lies a couple of hundred yards from the inn, encircled by evergreens and dwarfed by the surrounding fells. The small cemetery contains graves and memorials to several of those killed while climbing them. There's been a church at Wasdale since medieval times and though no one knows quite how old this plain chapel is, its current appearance – moss-grown slate roof and all – dates from a complete overhaul in 1892.

Pillar, the Scafells and Great Gable are popular hiking targets from Wasdale Head, as are the routes over the various passes, into Borrowdale, Ennerdale or Eskdale. That over Eskdale Moor, via **Burnmoor Tarn**, was the former "corpse road" along which the dead were carried for burying in Eskdale church, since St Olaf's had no consecrated churchyard until 1901.

The Wasdale Web (Ⓦwww.wasdaleweb.co.uk) is the best source of local **information**, including **accommodation** listings – the farm and B&B listed below are only a short walk from the inn, while other farmhouse B&Bs lie scattered down the valley. For supplies, the **Barn Door Shop** (Ⓣ019467/26384) next to the inn has basic foodstuffs, Kendal Mintcake, and outdoor clothes and equipment; check in here before pitching a tent at the adjacent field, tap-and-toilet **campsite** (no reservations; open all year). The other local campsite is the **National Trust campsite** (Ⓣ019467/26220; open all year), a mile to the south at the head of the lake, which provides tent space, showers and a laundry room beneath the trees.

Accommodation and food

Burnthwaite Farm Ⓣ019467/26242, Ⓦwww
.burnthwaitefarm.co.uk. A handsome old working sheep farm with six traditional B&B rooms, with and without en-suite facilities. Also a self-catering apartment (sleeps four, from £300/week, or £50 a night when available). Packed lunches available. Parking. Closed mid-Nov to Jan. No credit cards. ❸

Lingmell House Ⓣ019467/26261, Ⓦwww
.wasdalehead.co.uk. This was once the vicarage and now has three rooms sharing a couple of bathrooms, all glorying in fine fell views. Tim, the owner, can point you in the right direction for a hike and pack you a lunch. Closed Jan. No credit cards. Parking. ❸

Wasdale Head Inn Ⓣ019467/26229, Ⓦwww
.wasdale.com. The compact rooms (no TV reception) all have supremely comfortable beds, while for more space, ask for one of the "superior rooms" in the adjacent cottage conversion, which have a kitchenette, lounge area and full bathroom (though breakfast is not included with these). There are also six self-catering apartments in a converted barn (sleeps two to four). Local hiking information and a daily weather forecast are on hand, and there's a drying room for wet gear. The inn brews its own beer, the breakfasts are legendary and, though there are good bistro meals in the lively bar, the imaginative four-course dinner (£25) in the oak-panelled dining room is one of the Lake District's best buys. Parking. ❻

Ennerdale

Ennerdale, the next major valley north of Wasdale, is about as far off the beaten track as you can get in the western fells and valleys. There's only one very small village, limited public transport and no road at all around Ennerdale Water, which makes it one of the most inaccessible of the lakes – or one of the best for walkers, depending on how you look at it. Having made the effort, you'll find that Ennerdale Water is among the most alluring of the lakes, its quiet two-and-a-half-mile length (fiddle-shaped according to Coleridge) ringed by crags and dominated at the head by the dramatic heights of **Pillar**. If you haven't seen this peak before, you'll not recognize it from the name alone – the bulky fell takes its name instead from one of its northern crags, the devilish Pillar Rock, the proving-ground of British mountaineers for over a century.

There's nothing new about conifer plantations in the Lake District. Wordsworth was already complaining about the spread of larch and fir plantations in his *Guide to the Lakes*; a "vegetable manufactory" he called it, which thrust every other tree out of the way. In the early days afforestation was carried out as much for aesthetic reasons as for profit, though once the battle for Thirlmere was lost (see p.160) another was joined as the water authorities planted the shores of the new reservoir with regimented conifers to prevent erosion. With the formation of the Forestry Commission in 1919, the planting of soft woods for profit picked up pace, with Ennerdale, Bassenthwaite and the Duddon Valley heavily forested by the 1930s. Only local resistance prevented Eskdale, Wast Water and Buttermere going the same way.

The problem is the very nature of the forests. In England's mild climate, larch, spruce and pine plantations grow quickly, blocking out the light and carpeting the valley floors with slow-decomposing acidic needles. As a consequence, wild plants (and therefore animals) are forced out of their natural habitat. However, almost a century of commercial planting has taught the Forestry Commission several lessons and its planting policy has changed accordingly over the years. Its information centres are keen to explain matters and to point out that plantations imposed upon previously bare fellsides help soil conservation and encourage animal and bird shelter. Managed forests, moreover, help preserve the surviving indigenous broadleaved woods, which were increasingly threatened by the local practice of wintering sheep among the trees (the animals ate the seedlings). Behind the mission to explain is the undeniable economic sense of afforestation: Britain currently imports eight percent of the timber it uses and in a bid to even out the figures, over £1 billion has been invested in timber-processing over the last decade.

The village, **ENNERDALE BRIDGE**, straddles the River Ehen, a mile and a half west of the lake, encircled by a bowl of rounded fells and tucked just inside the National Park boundary. It's only ten miles from Cockermouth (from where there's a regular bus service) and seven from the coast, but seems much further from anywhere, especially in the peaceful shaded churchyard; still "girt round with a bare ring of mossy wall", as Wordsworth described it at the beginning of *The Brothers*. A small post office-shop and a couple of pubs provide what few facilities there are, though the village sees a fair amount of foot traffic as it's the first overnight stop on the Coast-to-Coast walk from St Bees.

Car parks on **Ennerdale Water** provide access for walkers, with two at the western end of the lake, near the village, and a third at **Bowness Knott**, midway along the northern shore, this also the terminus of the summer-only "Ennerdale Rambler" bus #263 from Cockermouth, Buttermere and Loweswater. Cars aren't allowed any further than Bowness Knott – though there is a track for vehicle access to Ennerdale YHA (see below) and a couple of nearby lakeside picnic areas.

A series of forest trails at Bowness Knott announces the start of Ennerdale's thick blanket of **Forestry Commission** land, either side of the River Liza. It may now be an accepted part of the landscape but before 1930 the upper part of Ennerdale was a desolate, rocky wilderness, devoid of trees. The mass imposition of uniform conifer plantations irrevocably changed the landscape, and though time and more enlightened planting policies (mixing in broad leaved trees and following the contours instead of straight lines) have softened the scenery, many still wish Ennerdale had been left untouched.

Ennerdale walks soon escape the tree cover in any case. The **circuit of the lake** (8 miles; 4hr) is an enjoyable low-level walk, with the option of a scramble up **Angler's Crag** on the southwestern promontory. Sterner tests are provided by any of the peaks on the valley's southern side, though unless you're staying at either of the Ennerdale youth hostels you've got to add the valley walk-in and return to Bowness Knott car park to your day's hike. For that reason, you won't see too many others en route (most choose to climb Pillar, say, from Wasdale), which is a recommendation in itself: an **Ennerdale peaks circuit** (12 miles; 7hr) from Bowness Knott, taking in Haycock (2618ft), Scoat Fell (2760ft), Steeple (2687ft) and Pillar (2927ft), is one of the most exhilarating fell walks in the region.

Accommodation and food

Black Sail YHA 6 miles east of Bowness Knott ☏07711/108450. The Lakes' most isolated and basic hostel (no road access – only foot visitors), a former shepherd's bothy with just sixteen beds and no heating in the bedrooms. But evening meals are served and the walking is marvellous, either up the local peaks, or over the passes into Buttermere or Wasdale. Reception opens 5pm. Closed Nov–March, plus Sun & Mon in Sept & Oct. Dorm beds £11.
Ennerdale YHA 2.5 miles east of Bowness Knott ☏0870/770 5820, ✉ennerdale@yha.org.uk. Gas-lit hostel converted from two old forestry cottages, pro-viding 24 beds for hostellers. Evening meals served. Reception opens 5pm. Closed Nov–March, plus Tues & Wed in Sept & Oct. Dorm beds £11.

Low Cockhow 1.25 miles south of Ennerdale Bridge ☏01946/861354, ⓦwww .walk-rest-ride.co.uk. The farm is right on the Coast-to-Coast walk, and has three B&B rooms, as well as a twelve-bed bunkhouse (£11, £16 with breakfast) with cooking and shower facilities. Evening meals, packed lunches and horse-riding available. Parking. **❸**
Shepherd's Arms Ennerdale Bridge ☏01946/861249, ⓦwww.shepherdsarmshotel .co.uk. Cosy old inn that is a popular Coast-to-Coast stopover, with hearty bar meals and a good choice of beers. There's a daily weather forecast posted, and plenty of hiking advice to hand. Parking. **❹**

Lorton Vale and Loweswater

Southeast of Cockermouth the B5292 rolls into the pastoral **Lorton Vale**, turning east to tackle the Whinlatter Pass on the way to Keswick. The scattered settlement of **LORTON** – divided into Low and High – has a twelfth-century church, St Cuthbert's, of minor interest, but there's also a pub and post office-general store, and some gentle walking in the fields near the River Cocker. The Quaker, George Fox, preached to a seventeenth-century Lorton crowd under a spreading yew tree, which Wordsworth later commemorated ("pride of Lorton Vale") in his poem "Yew-trees" (1803).

Keeping south on the B5289, the fells – and Buttermere – are beckoning but a diversion to **Loweswater**, six miles from Cockermouth, provides an oppor-tunity to see one of the region's smallest, shallowest and least-known lakes. The water only averages a depth of sixty feet, and the reeds and lily pads that cling to the shores are a habitat for many species of insects and birds. You'll never be bothered by crowds here. There's no village to speak of, rather a collection of houses, a church and a telephone box, with a couple of signs pointing you towards the *Kirkstile Inn* (see overleaf). Loweswater itself is a mile beyond the inn and really the only thing to do is to walk around it, on a gentle low-level route (4 miles; 1hr 30min) that stays under a woodland canopy for much of the duration. A detour in Holme Wood up to **Holme Force** adds a bit of interest after sustained rain; while the best views of the water are from Water-end, at the northern end of the lake. The distinctive volcano-shaped peak that towers above the southern end of Loweswater is **Mellbreak** (1676ft), fairly easily climbed from the *Kirkstile Inn* in around an hour or so.

There are a couple of small **parking** places at Waterend, and a National Trust car park (unmarked on most maps) near Watergate Farm at the southern end. The "Ennerdale Rambler" **bus** from Buttermere also passes Loweswater, running along the northern shore road past Waterend. For Lorton and the Whinlatter Pass, the service is the #77A from Buttermere, which runs up the B5289 before turning east along the B5292 towards Keswick.

Accommodation and food

Kirkstile Inn Loweswater ☏01900/85219, ⓦwww.kirkstile.com. The welcoming sixteenth-century riverside inn has given its non-smoking rooms a contemporary makeover, retaining the beams and country furniture but adding smart bathrooms, crisp linen and very comfortable beds. There are seven rooms in the main inn and two self-contained family suites in the adjoining buildings, which can accommodate up to four adults – one also has a kitchen and lounge. On-the-ball staff deliver quality bar meals (smoked sausage salad, salmon en croute, fellbred steak) and you can take in the sunsets in the beer garden and sink a pint of their exclusive own-brew beer. Parking. ⑤ suites ➐

New House Farm B5289, 1 mile south of Low Lorton ☏01900/85404, ⓦwww.newhouse-farm.co.uk. Six hugely attractive rooms, either in the meticulously restored seventeenth-century farmhouse or its period outbuildings – the old dairy room (the largest) has an extraordinary carved four-poster bed and a stunning bathroom with free-standing bath and hanging tapestry. Seventeen surrounding acres include mown grass walkways, ponds, gardens and an outdoor hot tub, while the barn tearoom (closed Dec–Easter) provides all-day meals and snacks – dinner is available too. Parking. ⑤, 4-poster rooms ➐

Old Vicarage Church Lane, Low Lorton ☏01900/85656, ⓦwww.oldvicarage.co.uk. Wooded grounds surround this non-smoking Victorian property, and it's just as impressive inside where a mahogany staircase ascends to the rooms. There's also a family suite in an old coach house, priced a few pounds lower than rooms in the main house. Afternoon tea is served in the garden in good weather and the pub is only five minutes' walk away (they'll lend you a torch for evening visits). Dinner available (£29.50) if you prefer to stay put. Parking. ⑤

Wheatsheaf Inn Low Lorton ☏01900/85268, ⓦwww.wheatsheafinnlorton.co.uk. Lorton's local pub has a pleasant beer garden, substantial bar meals (prices are very reasonable), Jennings' ales and jazz nights every week through the summer. Out the back, there's a campsite (closed Dec–Feb) with shower, toilet block and drying facilities (enquiries at the inn).

Winder Hall Low Lorton ☏01900/85107, ⓦwww.winderhall.co.uk. There's been a house here on the banks of the River Cocker since the fifteenth century, though the hall has been extended and modernized since then to incorporate seven spacious rooms, most filled with antiques (two have four-posters), though one is contemporary in style. Despite the undoubted elegance, it is friendly and informal, with Wainwright guides and maps provided, free entry to a nearby spa and pool, and children welcome. Room rates include afternoon tea, pre-dinner sherry and dinner (not served Tues), though B&B might be possible at quieter times, for about £20 less per person. The pub is almost opposite. Parking. ⑧

Crummock Water and Buttermere

A glance at the map shows that **Crummock Water** and **Buttermere** – separated by only a half-mile of slightly elevated flood-prone land – were once joined as one lake. In the main, they're visited as one, with nearly all the day-traffic concentrated in and around **BUTTERMERE** village, a small settlement in the middle of the two lakes with an outlying church, two inns and the rest of the local facilities.

The two lakes, however, have entirely different aspects: small Buttermere ("Boethar's lake") is ringed by crags and peaks, culminating in the desolate heights of Gatesgarthdale; more expansive Crummock Water ("crooked lake") is almost twice as long (at two and a half miles) and half as deep again, yet peters out in the gentle flat lands of Lorton Vale. It's a contrasting beauty that brought back that most obsessive of fell walkers, Alfred Wainwright, again and again. A plaque in the small parish **church of St James**, on a hillock above Buttermere village, asks you to pause and remember him and then lift your eyes to Haystacks, his favourite peak (see box overleaf), where his ashes are scattered. In *Fellwanderer*, his account of the writing of his famous *Pictorial Guides*, he's typically and playfully brusque: "If, dear reader, you should get a bit of grit in your boot as you are crossing Haystacks in the years to come, please treat it with respect. It might be me."

The grandeur of the locality was well-known even before Wainwright gave it his seal of approval. With the Lakes in vogue amongst travelling men in the late-eighteenth century, many made their way over the passes to what was then a remote hamlet with a reputation for good fishing in the twin lakes. A certain Captain Budworth – resident at the *Fish Inn*, the only inn in those days – waxed lyrical about the beauty of the landlord's daughter in his bestseller, *A Fortnight's Ramble in the Lakes*. Within a couple of years, curious sightseers – Wordsworth and Coleridge included – were turning up to view **Mary Robinson, the Maid of Buttermere**. One such visitor was Alexander Augustus Colonel Hope, Member of Parliament and brother to an earl. Flush with money and manners, he wooed and married Mary – only to be revealed as the bigamous impostor, John Hatfield, whose whole life had been one of deception and fraud. Arrested and tried for forgery (franking letters as an MP without authority was a capital offence), Hatfield was hanged at Carlisle in 1802 – the entire scandal recorded for the *Morning Post* by Coleridge in investigative journalist mode. Mary became a cause célèbre, the subject of ballads, books and plays, before retiring from the public gaze at the *Fish* to become wife to a Caldbeck farmer. She died there, as Mary Harrison, in 1837.

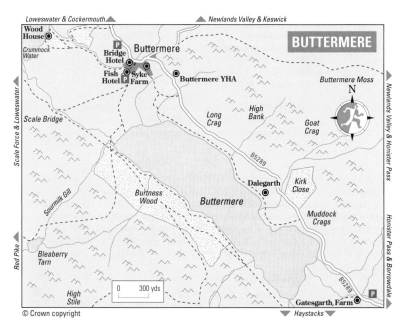

© Crown copyright

Practicalities

There's a **car park** behind the *Fish Hotel* and another is 300 yards up the road to Crummock Water; other parking places are signposted on the Crummock Water lakeshore road. The main **bus** service is the #77/77A, which runs between Easter and October (4 daily) on a circular route from Keswick, either via Whinlatter Pass and Lorton or Borrowdale and Honister Pass. There's also the seasonal weekend #263 "Ennerdale Rambler" service, which connects Buttermere with Loweswater, Ennerdale Bridge and Cockermouth.

There's no tourist office in Buttermere, though Ⓦwww.buttermere-lorton.com gathers together some useful local listings and **information**. The village also has no shops, but there are two **hotels**, the *Bridge* and the *Fish* (and no TV reception in either), plus a **youth hostel** and various local farms and houses offering **B&B** and **camping**. The popular bar and beer garden at the *Bridge* is the best place to eat, though there's a wide restaurant menu too. Alternatively you could sit on the benches outside the *Croft House Café* and munch on filled rolls – and don't forget an ice cream from *Syke Farm*, made from the milk from their Ayrshire cows. *Dalegarth* campsite and B&B has **rowboats** for rent, and there are more available from *Wood House* on Crummock Water (Easter–Oct only), where the day-rate includes a fishing permit.

Walks from Crummock Water and Buttermere

Many hikers have their fondest memories of the fells around Buttermere and Crummock Water, and one – Haystacks – is the final resting place of the greatest walker of them all, Alfred Wainwright. It's easy to gain height quickly around here for some terrific views, though the low-level circuits of the two lakes are also very rewarding.

Crummock Water and Scale Force

Any circuit of **Crummock Water** should include the diversion to the 170ft drop of **Scale Force**, among the most spectacular of Lake District waterfalls. You can then either regain the western shore and stick close to the lake for the rest of the circuit (8 miles; 4hr), or climb past the falls and follow the Mosedale valley path to Loweswater (where there's a pub, the *Kirkstile Inn*) before completing the circuit (10 miles; 5–6hr).

Around Buttermere

The four-mile stroll circling **Buttermere** shouldn't take more than a couple of hours – in wet weather, the waters tumbling a thousand feet down Sour Milk Ghyll are amazing. And you can always detour up **Scarth Gap** to **Haystacks** (see below) if you want more of a climb and some views. It's worth knowing that, in summer, there's usually an ice cream van parked by Gatesgarth Farm at the southern end of the lake.

Red Pike to Haystacks

The classic Buttermere circuit (8 miles; 6hr 30min) climbs from the village up **Red Pike** (2479ft) and then runs along the ridge, via **High Stile** (2644ft), **High Crag** (2443ft) and **Haystacks** (1900ft), before descending to the lake – either by backtracking and heading down Scarth Gap or by picking your way down off Haystacks, rounding Inominate Tarn and descending via **Warnscale Bottom**. For a fuller experience, add another hour to the beginning of the hike by first climbing up Scale Force from Buttermere (see above) and working your way across to Red Pike from there.

See Basics, p.40, for general walking advice in the Lakes; recommended maps are detailed on p.27.

Hotels

Bridge Hotel Buttermere ☎017687/70252, ⓦwww.bridge-hotel.com. As well as the standard rooms – perfectly fine – there's a selection of cheerfully decorated superior rooms with large bathrooms, some with balconies; and there are south-facing, self-catering apartments available across the beck (sleeps 2–6, £310–650 per week). The room price includes afternoon tea and dinner, but you might be able to negotiate a B&B price. Non-guests can settle for filling Cumbrian specials (including home-made soups and casseroles) and Black Sheep beer in the oak-beamed Walkers' Bar. Parking. ❽

Fish Hotel Buttermere ☎017687/70253, ⓦwww.fish-hotel.co.uk. The smaller *Fish Hotel* has history, romance and price on its side. Bar meals are available at lunch and dinner (the beer here is Theakston's), while packed lunches cost £7. No advance bookings for single-night stays. Parking. ❹

B&Bs and campsites

Dalegarth Buttermere, 1.5 miles southeast of the village ☎017687/70233. The grounds at Dalegarth extend to the lakeside. There are nine B&B rooms in the main house (not all en-suite), plus camping (with the use of a shower-and-toilet block). Closed Nov–March. Parking. ❷

Gatesgarth Farm Buttermere, 2 miles southeast of the village ☎017687/70256. Farmhouse B&B and campsite, set back from the end of the lake. Parking. No credit cards. ❷

Syke Farm Buttermere ☎017687/70222. The farm offers simple camping near the lake (toilet and shower block provided). Parking. No credit cards.

Wood House Crummock Water ☎017687/70208, ⓦwww.wdhse.co.uk. Quite the nicest choice is this attractive non-smoking house in a serene setting on Crummock Water, just a few hundred yards from the village. Three elegant bedrooms and the drawing room enjoy marvellous views, while the gardens and surrounding woodland harbour red squirrels and woodpeckers. There's a self-catering cottage in the grounds too (£280–420 a week). Packed lunches are £5, a good dinner £26. Parking. Closed Nov–Easter. No credit cards. ❺

Youth hostel

Buttermere YHA Buttermere, 0.25 miles southeast of the village ☎0870/770 5736, ⓔbuttermere@yha.org.uk. Overlooks the lake on the road to Honister Pass. There's one two-bedded room, otherwise accommodation in this quiet lakeland slate house is in four-or six-bedded rooms. Reception opens 5pm; evening meal served. Closed Mon–Thurs & Sun in Jan; also closed Sun & Mon in Feb, March, Nov & Dec. Dorm beds £16, includes breakfast.

Travel details

For Ravenglass & Eskdale Railway, see p.175.

From Keswick

Bus #77/77A circular route to: Honister Pass (40min), Buttermere (50min), Lorton (1hr 10min), Whinlatter Pass (1hr 20min); or to Whinlatter Pass (15min), Lorton (25min), Buttermere (45min), Honister Pass (1hr). Service operates April–Oct 4 daily.

From Buttermere

Bus #263 "Ennerdale Rambler" to: Loweswater Waterend (25min), Ennerdale Bridge (45min) and Bowness Knott (1hr); and to Lorton (15min) and Cockermouth (30min). Service operates July & Aug Sun & bank hol Mon 3 daily.

From Barrow-in-Furness

Furness coastal rail line to: Millom (25min), Silecroft (30min), Bootle (37min), Ravenglass (45min); and then via St Bees (1hr 5min), Whitehaven (1hr 15min) and Workington (1hr 30min) to Carlisle (2hr 25min). Barrow-in-Furness to Whitehaven service operates Mon–Sat 7 daily, though there is a limited Sunday Whitehaven to Carlisle service.

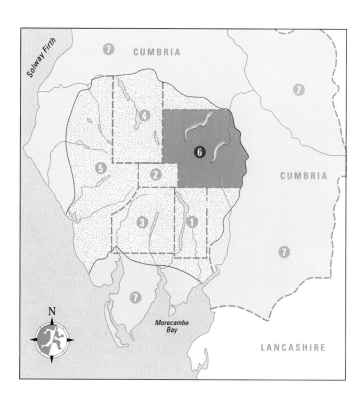

6

Ullswater

CHAPTER 6

Highlights

✻ **A steamer ride on Ullswater** Get off for some marvellous local walks or stay aboard for the round-the-lake cruise. See p.199

✻ **Striding Edge** There's no more exciting mountain walk than inching your way along Striding Edge, en route to the summit of Helvellyn. See p.200

✻ **Aira Force** Visit the romantic lakeland waterfall whose daffodil-strewn surroundings inspired Wordsworth to pen one of his most famous poems. See p.201

✻ **Queen's Head, Tirril** A cracking old inn with gastro-pub cuisine and its own brewery. See p.203

✻ **Dalemain** Successive generations of the same family have lived in this handsome stately home since 1679. See p.204

✻ **St Martin's, Martindale** This isolated stone chapel in a remote valley near Ullswater makes a fine target for a stroll. See p.205

△ Brothers Water

Ullswater

Wordsworth declared Ullswater "the happiest combination of beauty and grandeur, which any of the Lakes affords", a judgement that still holds good. At almost eight miles long, Ullswater is the second longest lake in Cumbria and much of its appeal derives from its serpentine shape, a result of the complex geology of this area. The glacier that formed the two-hundred-foot deep trench in which the lake now lies had to cut across a couple of geological boundaries, from granite in the south, through a band of Skiddaw slate, to softer sandstone and limestone in the north. The resulting fells are a dramatic sight, while the shores are stippled with woods of native oak, birch and hazel – one of the best surviving examples of pre-plantation lakeland scenery. The surrounding grandeur is matched by the means of transport on the lake: lake steamer services on Ullswater started in 1859 and the same two vessels, *Lady of the Lake* and *Raven*, have been in operation for almost as long – though both were converted to diesel in the 1930s. The newest addition to the fleet, the *Lady Dorothy*, though not as venerable, is the first steamer to run winter services on Ullswater.

On spring and summer days the A592 up the western side of the lake is packed with traffic, everyone looking for space in one of the few designated car parks. Twin lakeside settlements, **Patterdale** and **Glenridding**, less than a mile apart at the southern tip of Ullswater, soak up most of the visitors intent upon the local attractions: namely **cruises** from Glenridding, the falls of **Aira Force**, the Wordsworthian daffodils of **Gowbarrow Park** and the considerable heights of **Helvellyn**, the most popular of the four tallest mountains in Cumbria. From **Howtown** on the lake's eastern side, much less-tramped walking routes run up glorious hidden valleys such as Fusedale and Martindale and along the High Street range. **Pooley Bridge** at the head of Ullswater is the last lakeshore stop before Penrith, though outlying sights might delay you further, such as the historic house at **Dalemain** or the attractive village of **Askham**, gateway to the rolling Lowther parklands.

The northeastern lakes finish with a flourish in the crinkled valleys between the southern foot of Ullswater and the desolate Shap Fells at the eastern edge of the National Park. The A592, heading south from Ullswater for the Kirkstone Pass and Ambleside, passes **Brothers Water**. Otherwise the only roads are the minor lanes south from Askham and west of Shap, which meet at **Haweswater**, easternmost and very possibly the least visited of all the lakes (and, with Thirlmere, the Lake District's other main reservoir).

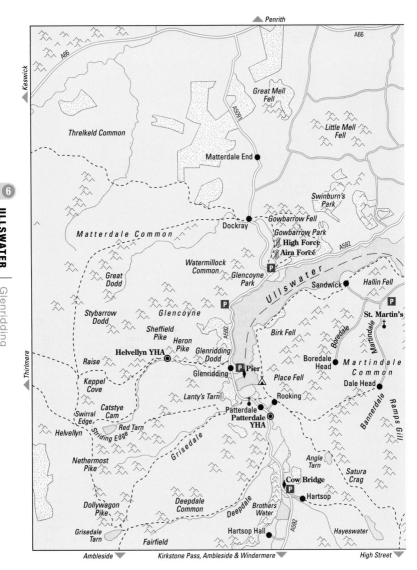

Penrith ▲

▲ Ambleside ▼   Kirkstone Pass, Ambleside & Windermere ▼   High Street ▼

Glenridding

A fast-flowing beck, flanked by stone buildings and cottages, tumbles through
the centre of **GLENRIDDING**, formerly a mining village and now the
busiest of Ullswater's lakeside settlements. Although the village itself hardly
consists of any more than a couple of rows of cottages set back from the lake,
there's also a huge car park, two or three tearooms, a general store, post office,
outdoors store and a fair amount of accommodation. There are rowboats to
rent and plenty of places to sit on the grass banks or wade into the water from

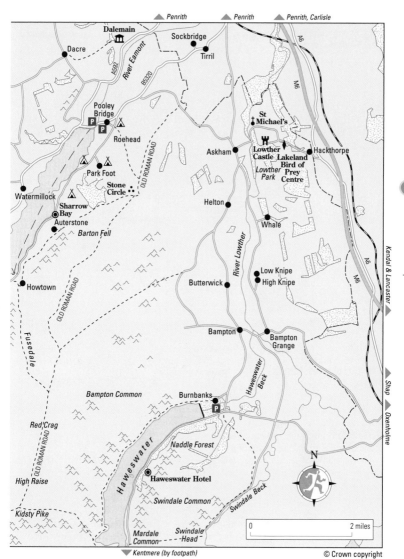

Dalemain
Dacre
Sockbridge
Tirril
River Eamont
A592
B5320
Pooley Bridge
Roehead
Park Foot
Watermillock
Stone Circle
Sharrow Bay
Auterstone
Barton Fell
Howtown
OLD ROMAN ROAD
Fusedale
St Michael's
Askham
Lowther Castle
Lowther Park
Lakeland Bird of Prey Centre
Hackthorpe
Helton
Whale
River Lowther
Low Knipe
High Knipe
Butterwick
Bampton
Bampton Grange
M6
A6
Bampton Common
Burnbanks
Haweswater Beck
Red Crag
OLD ROMAN ROAD
Naddle Forest
Haweswater
Haweswater Hotel
Swindale Common
Swindale Beck
High Raise
Kidsty Pike
Mardale Common
Swindale Head
N
0   2 miles

▼ Kentmere (by footpath)   © Crown copyright

the stony shore. If it sounds too popular for comfort it isn't particularly, since many visitors just park up for a day's walking and by early evening the placid lakeshore regains much of its peace and quiet.

If you're not here to climb Helvellyn, you can at least stretch your legs in the local valley and follow **Glenridding Beck** half a mile west as far as Rattlebeck Bridge. It's another mile up to the *Helvellyn* youth hostel, which sits amid old lead **mine workings**, which were first exploited in the seventeenth century and only ceased operation in the 1960s. The other way from the bridge, south and east, you can wind up to pretty little **Lanty's Tarn**, set in a grove of trees

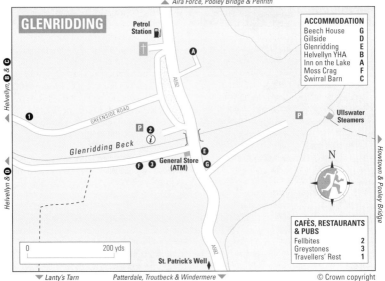

GLENRIDDING

Petrol Station

A592

GREENSIDE ROAD

Glenridding Beck

① ② ⓘ

Ⓟ

General Store (ATM)

Ⓕ ❸ Ⓖ

Ⓔ

◄ Helvellyn, Ⓑ & Ⓒ

◄ Helvellyn & Ⓓ

Ullswater Steamers Ⓟ

Howtown & Pooley Bridge ►

N

ACCOMMODATION	
Beech House	G
Gillside	D
Glenridding	E
Helvellyn YHA	B
Inn on the Lake	A
Moss Crag	F
Swirral Barn	C

CAFÈS, RESTAURANTS & PUBS	
Fellbites	2
Greystones	3
Travellers' Rest	1

0 ————— 200 yds

A592

St. Patrick's Well

▼ Lanty's Tarn   Patterdale, Troutbeck & Windermere ▼   © Crown copyright

and with nearby views from a knoll over Ullswater. The name is probably a corruption of "Lancelot", bestowed more in hope than accuracy on any romantically sited stretch of water that might conceal an Arthurian sword.

Practicalities

Buses #108 (from Penrith), #208 (from Keswick) and #517 (from Bowness/Windermere) stop on the main road (the A592) through the village. Pier House and the **steamer pier** are just five minutes' walk away on the lakeside. An Ullswater **Bus & Boat ticket** (£12) is available for a day's travel between Penrith and Glenridding/Patterdale, using the #108 bus and the steamer service – buy the ticket on board the bus.

There's an ATM inside the general store on the main road, and two or three other shops selling walking gear or supplies. The **National Park Information Centre** (Easter–Oct daily 9.30am–5.30pm; Nov–Easter Fri–Sun 9.30am–3.30pm; ☎017684/82414) is sited on the edge of the **car park** and posts a daily weather report for walkers. Glenridding is only a small place, with everything just a few minutes' walk from the car park. Two big traditional slate **hotels** dominate the village, the *Inn on the Lake* and the *Glenridding Hotel*, and there are several cheaper **B&Bs**. Hikers make a beeline for the out-of-village youth hostel, campsite, bunkhouse and camping barn, all lying en route to the area's major peak, Helvellyn.

Hotels and B&Bs

Beech House On the main road ☎017684/82037, ⓦwww.beechhouse.com. Bill and Lynn Reed offer a cheery welcome and a spick-and-span base for local walks and excursions. Eight rooms (half share a bathroom), though small, are prettily furnished, and a couple sport inlet and fell views. Breakfast is good, and there's no lounge "because

there's a pub [*Ratcher's*] next door". Packed lunches cost £2 or £4. Parking. ❸

Glenridding On the main road ☎017684/82228, ⓦwww.glenriddinghotel.co.uk. Standard and lakeview rooms available (supplement charged for the latter). There are also plenty of facilities, including an indoor pool and sauna and oak-panelled library with sun lounge. Walkers can borrow a map and a thermos flask. *Kilner's Coffee House* has Internet access, there's a good restaurant (*table d'hote* dinner £20, though D, B&B rates available, a price category higher), and a so-so tavern, *Ratcher's*, serving moderately priced pizza, pasta and grills. Parking. **❼**

Inn on the Lake Ullswater lakeside ℡017684/82444, ⊛www.innonthelakeullswater.com. Rooms and public areas have been upgraded and decked in flowers, there are some splendid views, and fifteen acres of gardens stretching down to Ullswater. The *Ramblers' Lodge* is the place for a beer, a bar meal and a game of pool, but there's also a more sophisticated lounge bar, lake-view restaurant (*table d'hote* menu £30, though D,B&B rates available), gym, sauna, jacuzzi, croquet lawn and tennis court. Parking. **❼**

Moss Crag On the south side of the beck near the shops ℡017684/82500, ⊛www.mosscrag.co.uk. One of a line of cottages, this genial non-smoking B&B has half-a-dozen cottage-style rooms (a couple of them en-suite, one with a four-poster) and an attached tearoom. Dinner available (£17). Closed Dec. Parking. **❸**

Campsite, hostel and camping barn

Gillside Caravan & Camping ℡017684/82346, ⊛www.gillsidecaravanandcampingsite.co.uk. A quarter of a mile up the valley behind the village – follow the path along the beck. There are also caravans for rent (from £40 a night, minimum two nights) and a good bunkhouse with a modern kitchen (£7 a bed), though you need your own sleeping and cooking equipment. Closed Nov–Feb.

Helvellyn YHA Greenside ℡0870/770 6110, ℮helvellyn@yha.org.uk. Walkers wanting an early start on Helvellyn stay at this dramatically sited hostel, 900ft and a mile-and-a-half up the valley road from Glenridding (the last half unmetalled, but suitable for vehicles if taken with care). The nearest pub, the *Travellers Rest*, is a mile away. Lots of beds (most two- or four-bedded). Reception opens 5pm; evening meal served. Open daily in July & Aug, though flexible opening during the rest of the year – call for availability. Dorm beds £11.

Swirral Barn ℡017687/72645. A hundred yards beyond the YHA, there's self-catering bunk-barn space in accommodation converted from former mine buildings. It's pretty basic (eg, unheated) and the toilet's in a separate building. Beds £5.

Cafés

Fellbites ℡017684/82664. The stylish café in the car park opens at 9am for walkers' breakfasts (served all day), after which it's light meals and drinks, and lunches and dinners using locally sourced lamb, beef and trout. Dinner is Fri & Sat only; also closed Tues & Wed from Nov–Easter. Moderate.

Greystones Coffee House and Gallery ℡017684/82392. Alongside the beck, and brightened by the local art and contemporary sculpture, *Greystones* dishes up teas and cappuccinos and tasty bites such as ciabatta sandwiches, or beans on toast. A few outdoor tables catch the sun in summer. Daytime only. Nov–Easter open weekends only. Inexpensive.

Pub

Travellers' Rest ℡017684/82298. It's worth the 500-yard tramp up the hill from the village centre to this unpretentious pub, with fell and partial lake views from its outdoor terrace. Filling bar meals and cask ales available.

Ullswater lake services

The Ullswater Navigation & Transit Company (℡017684/82229, ⊛www.ullswater-steamers.co.uk) has steamers operating from Glenridding to Howtown (£4.40 one-way, £7 return; 35min); and from Howtown to Pooley Bridge (£4.10 one-way, £6.70 return; 20min). Alternatively, you can buy a ticket between Glenridding and Pooley Bridge that effectively makes a two-hour round-the-lake cruise (£9.80).

Between June and September, there are up to ten daily departures from Glenridding to Howtown and five daily as far as Pooley Bridge. Services are reduced, though still daily, from mid-April to May and throughout October; from November to March, there are three services daily, between Glenridding and Howtown, and two daily to Pooley Bridge.

There's a bar on board the steamers, and parking, a café and picnic area at Glenridding's Pier House. At Pooley Bridge, a kiosk sells drinks and snacks.

The climb to the summit of **Helvellyn** (3114ft) is among the region's most challenging. You are unlikely to be alone on the yard-wide approaches – on summer weekends and bank holidays the car parks below and paths above are full by 9am – but the variety of routes up and down at least offers a chance of escaping the crowds.

Striding Edge

The most frequently chosen, and most direct, route to the summit is via the infamous **Striding Edge**. Purists negotiate the undulating ridge top of Striding Edge; slightly safer, but no less precipitous tracks follow the line of the ridge, just off the crest. However you get across (and some refuse to go any further when push comes to shove), there's a final, sheer, hands-and-feet scramble to the flat **summit** (2hr 30min from Glenridding). People do get into trouble on Striding Edge: if you're at all nervous of heights you'll find it a challenge to say the least.

Swirral Edge, Red Tarn and Catstye Cam

The classic return from the summit is via the less demanding **Swirral Edge**, where a route leads down to **Red Tarn** – the highest Lake District tarn – then follows the beck down to Glenridding past the disused slate quarry workings and the **Helvellyn youth hostel**. Another route climbs back up to **Catstye Cam** (2917ft) and drops down the northern ridge path into Keppel Cove, where you cross the dam and continue to the hostel. Either of these approaches and descents makes a seven-mile or five- to six-hour walk.

Grisedale

South from the Helvellyn summit, you can follow the flat ridge past **Nethermost Pike** (2920ft) and **Dollywagon Pike** (2810ft), after which there's a long scree scramble down to **Grisedale Tarn** and then the gentlest of descents down **Grisedale** valley, alongside the beck, emerging on the Patterdale–Glenridding road – a good six hours all told for the entire circuit.

See Basics, p.40, for general walking advice in the Lakes; recommended maps are detailed on p.27.

Patterdale

PATTERDALE, less than a mile south of Glenridding down the A592 (a path avoids the road for much of the way), lies at the foot of **Grisedale**, which provides access to a stunning valley hike up to Grisedale Tarn. St Patrick is supposed to have preached here (Patterdale is "Patrick's Dale") and the water in St Patrick's Well, on the road between Glenridding and Patterdale, was once thought to have miraculous powers. The saint's church, at the northern end of the village, is a nineteenth-century replacement of the medieval original, known for the locally made embroidered tapestries that hang inside.

The #108, #208 and #517 **bus** services stop in Patterdale. You're just off the lake in the village – though never very far away – but there's some reasonable **accommodation** strung along the road. Patterdale's only pub, the *White Lion* (☎017684/82214; ❸), has seven rooms available and *Castle Eden* beer on tap in the bar; sizzling steak platters are the house speciality, or try the trout with almonds. There's also a public bar at the large *Patterdale Hotel* up the road (☎0845/458 4333, ⓦ www.patterdalehotel.co.uk; ❺) – its front beer garden fills up quickly on a summer's day. South, past the pub, on the bend in the road, *Old Water View* (☎017684/82175, ⓦwww.oldwaterview.co.uk; ❸; closed mid-Dec to mid-Jan) is an attractive, non-smoking guest house with four rooms, private gardens and parking. They're used to walkers – even Alfred Wainwright stayed here on occasion. Just beyond lies Patterdale's popular ski-lodge-style **youth hostel**, *Patterdale YHA* (☎0870/770 5986; dorm beds £12.50, ⓔpatterdale@yha.org.uk; restricted opening Nov–March), on the banks of Goldrill Beck, with very comfortable beds, spacious public areas with open fire, Internet access and good food. A number of rooms here are available for couples and families, and reception is open all day. There's **camping** at *Side Farm* (☎017684/82338; closed Nov–Easter) – the track to the farm is across from the church, with the campsite on the eastern shore of the lake – and the only other service is a small **village shop-post office** opposite the pub.

Aira Force, Dockray and Gowbarrow

To avoid the crowds trailing up the needle-carpeted woodland paths to **Aira Force**, three miles north of Glenridding (where the A5091 meets the A592), get there first thing in the morning or last thing in the evening. This is one of the prettiest, most romantic of lakeland forces – a seventy-foot waterfall that's spectacular in spate and can be viewed from stone bridges spanning the top and bottom of the drop. It's only a thirty- to forty-minute round-trip from the car park, though you'll soon leave most of the visitors behind if you extend your walk further up the valley to High Force and on to **DOCKRAY** (where there's a pub with a beer garden, the *Royal*) and back – a three-mile, two-hour, circuit. Keep an eye out for red squirrels in the woods on the way. Back at the Aira Force car park there's an attractive **tearoom** (closed Nov–Easter) with an outdoor terrace; buses #108 and #208 stop nearby.

The falls flank the western side of **Gowbarrow Park**, whose hillside still blazes green and gold in spring, as it was doing when the Wordsworths visited in April 1802. Dorothy's sprightly recollections of the visit in her journal inspired William to write his "Daffodils" poem, though it was not until two years later that he first composed the famous lines (borrowing many of Dorothy's exact phrases). Despite its fame now, nothing much was thought of the poem at the time; it didn't even have a title on first publication in 1807 (in *Poems in Two Volumes*).

The walking is tougher going on adjacent **Gowbarrow Fell** (1579ft), which you can climb in an hour from Aira Force car park. The route runs via the viewpoint of Yew Crag and then up the boggy slopes to the cairn at the summit. From here you can descend to Dockray and the pub or, more directly, over the top to Green Hill and thence to Aira Force (2hr return). The National Park Authority is trying to cut the number of sheep grazing the fell in an attempt to lure back some of the wildlife, while every spring there's a battle of wits with visitors intent on picking the famous daffs.

Pooley Bridge

POOLEY BRIDGE, at the head of the lake, has a boulder-speckled shore with wonderful views south. The bridge itself is the sturdy example that crosses the River Eamont on the way into the village, evidence – along with the old village square, once used for markets – that this was a substantial settlement

△ Ullswater

in past times. Its market charter was granted by King John in the twelfth century – the modern equivalent is the thriving farmers' market (last Sun of month, April–Sept, 10.30am–2.30pm) held behind the *Sun Inn*. Pooley Bridge itself is a cute retreat, rendered less so once the car parks on either side of the bridge are full, but it's still not a bad lunch or overnight stop, with a couple of tearooms and three pubs. Apart from the **steamer** (whose jetty is a couple of hundred yards from the bridge), there's a daily, year-round **bus service** (the #108) from Penrith to Pooley Bridge (and on to Glenridding/Patterdale), as well as a limited post bus from Penrith (not Sun), which continues on to Howtown and Martindale.

The best **accommodation** is listed below; in addition, a few local B&Bs advertise vacancies and you can ask for help at the **tourist office** in The Square (Easter–Oct daily 10am–5pm; ☎017684/86530). Plenty of local **campsites** make the Pooley Bridge area popular with families. Those on the northeastern lake shore (listed below) are easiest to reach from the village. Another group of campsites lies two miles away on the northwest shore, behind Watermillock, but you'll need your own transport to reach these. The village pubs all provide **meals**, but the best food is found either at *Sharrow Bay* country house hotel, to the south of the village, or at the two country gastro-pubs just to the north, the *Queen's Head* at Tirril and the *Gate Inn* at Yanwath.

Hotels, B&Bs and inns

Elm House ☎017684/86334, @www.elmhouse .demon.co.uk. Non-smoking village B&B, 100 yards from the *Sun Inn*, opposite the church. Five rooms available (only one not en suite), plus a good breakfast, and walkers' flasks filled for free. Parking. ❸

Pooley Bridge Inn ☎017684/86215, @www .pooleybridgeinn.co.uk. Just across from the tourist office, this Alpine-style hotel seems to have been plucked out of a *Heidi* story. Breakfast in the wicker chairs on your own balcony is tempting, though standard rooms without a balcony are priced a category lower. Food is available in the rustic bar, including Ullswater trout and Cumberland sausage. Two-night minimum stay on summer weekends. Parking. ❺

Queen's Head Tirril, B5320, 2.5 miles north of Pooley Bridge ☎01768/863219, @www .queensheadinn.co.uk. The traditional inn certainly looks the part, with its oak beams and stone flags, while half a dozen charming rooms upstairs have solid furniture and decent bathrooms. As a gastro-pub it excels, serving things like locally smoked sausage salad, snapper on pesto noodles or fell-bred lamb (mains £9–13), bolstered by the house beers (brewed at nearby Brougham Hall), guest ales and forty malt whiskies. ❾

Sharrow Bay 2 miles south of Pooley Bridge, on the Howtown road ☎017684/86301, @www .sharrow-bay.com. England's first country-house hotel, in business since 1948, offering fine service and gourmet food (dinner is included in the room rate). There's a variety of lovely, antique-filled rooms available in the main Victorian house, a garden annexe, the Edwardian gatehouse or in a converted, elevated Elizabethan farmhouse a mile away. Lake and fell views abound, there are acres of gardens and woods to wander in, and books and games in the rooms to pass the time when it pours. The dining room is also open to non-residents; afternoon tea (£16) here is famous, while dinner (£50, booking essential) is a formal affair of highly refined cuisine. Parking. ❾

Sun Inn ☎017684/86205. The best of the village pubs (100 yards up the road from the tourist office) is the eighteenth-century *Sun*, with a terrific carved, panelled bar and a beer garden to catch the rays. There are nine good-value rooms and small discounts for multi-night stays. Bar meals served. Parking. ❹

Campsites

Cross Dormont On the Howtown road ☎017684/86537, @www.crossdormont.co.uk. Family-run site on a working farm (raising Herdwick sheep on the local fells). You can launch dinghies and kayaks from the lakeside fields.

Hill Croft ☎017684/86363. The nearest site to the village, a family-run affair just 100 yards from the Howtown crossroads. Closed mid-Nov to Feb.

Park Foot On the Howtown road ☎017684/86309. Has its own lakeside access and club-house facilities, including a bar. Closed Nov–Feb.

Waterside House On the Howtown road ☎017684/86332, @www.watersidefarm -campsite.co.uk. Right on the water, this is a tent- and motorhome-only site, and has canoes, rowboats and bikes for rent. Closed Nov–Feb.

Café

Granny Dowbekin's ☎017684/86453. Terraced riverside tea garden, by the bridge, serving soup and sandwiches, plus homemade cakes inspired by the recipes of the owner's great-great Lancastrian granny. Daytime only. Closed Jan. Inexpensive.

Pub

Gate Inn Yanwath, B5320, 3.5 miles north of Pooley Bridge ☎01768/862386. Trading as an inn for over 300 years, the *Gate* is making new friends under new owners and winning plaudits for its food. Tastes range from creamy seafood chowder to goat's cheese and smoked tomato salad, while classic dishes (ale-braised beef, Cumberland sausage, etc) are given a new lease of life. No food Mon. Moderate.

⑥ Dalemain

Two miles north of Pooley Bridge, up the A592, is the stately home of **Dalemain** (Easter–Oct Mon–Thurs & Sun 11am–4pm, gardens & tearoom same days 10.30am–5pm; Nov, Dec & Feb–Easter gardens & tearoom only Mon–Thurs 10am–4pm; £6; gardens only £4; ☎017684/86450, 🌐www.dalemain.com). Residence to the same family since 1679, it started life in the twelfth century as a fortified tower, but has subsequently been added to by every generation, culminating with a Georgian facade grafted on to a largely Elizabethan house. It's set in ample grounds – terraces, roses and Tudor gardens provide the main interest, best in late May and June – while the estate stretches west to encompass the fourteenth-century keep of Dacre Castle (no public access), which you can reach on a mile-long footpath from the house.

Inside Dalemain itself you're given the run of the public rooms, which the family still uses – hence the photographs and contemporary portraits alongside those of the ancestors. It's heavy with oak, hewn from the estate's plantations, though lightened by unusual touches such as the eighteenth-century handpainted wallpaper in the Chinese Room. The servants' corridors and pantries offer a glimpse of life "below stairs", commanded from the Housekeeper's Room – at the rear of which was discovered a priest's hole. Outside, the medieval courtyard and Elizabethan great barn doubled as the schoolroom and dormitory of Lowood School in a TV adaptation of Charlotte Brontë's *Jane Eyre*. There's an agricultural and countryside collection in the great barn, and plenty of other displays and exhibits throughout the house, from dolls' houses and old toys to Gillows and Chippendale furniture and the family glassware. The Medieval Hall provides drinks, lunches and afternoon teas – you don't need a ticket to visit this.

Askham and Lowther Park

Three miles east of Pooley Bridge, and five south of Penrith, the serene little village of **ASKHAM** lies across the River Lowther from the rolling lands of **Lowther Park**, seat of the eighteenth-century coal-mining and shipping magnates, the Lowthers, creators of the Georgian port of Whitehaven. The most notorious family member, Sir James, employed Wordsworth's father as his agent but, when John Wordsworth died, refused to pay his back-salary to the Wordsworth children. Not that there was any shortage of Lowther money in those days, as attested to by an extravagantly built Gothic Revival castle in the estate grounds, though eventually its ruinous upkeep was too much, even for the Lowthers. The **castle** is now roofless and partly in ruins – there's no public access, but it's visible from the road – but you can catch a glimpse of the Lowther heritage at the **church of St Michael**, just outside Askham, on a ridge above the river. Effectively the family chapel, this is filled with memorials to one Lowther or another – whose scions took the title Earl of Lonsdale – including a fine brass portraying a splendidly bewhiskered Henry Lowther. A later Lowther, the fifth Earl, Sir Hugh, was a keen sportsman, whose title at least is remembered in boxing's Lonsdale Belt, while the estate's **horse trials**, held here every August, are one of the region's major sporting events.

As well as the castle ruins, the Lowther estate includes two small villages, various farms and plantations and a deer park, past which you'll drive en route to the **Lakeland Bird of Prey Centre** (April–Oct daily 11am–5pm; £6; ☎01931/712746), outside Askham. Here eagles, hawks, falcons and owls are put through their paces twice a day (call for current times), though they are also all on show in the aviaries set in the walled garden. There's a tearoom here, too.

Public transport to Askham is limited to the "Haweswater Rambler" **bus** from Penrith, which runs year-round on Saturdays and also on Sundays during the school summer holidays; however, there's no bus out to the bird of prey centre. Askham itself has a couple of local B&Bs and two traditional **inns**, at either end of a sloping village green. At the top, the *Queen's Head* (☎01931/712225, ⓦwww.queenshead-askham.co.uk; ❸) has been sympathetically renovated – one of its rooms is a mini-suite with lounge and four -poster (priced a category higher). At the bottom, near the river, the *Punch Bowl* (☎01931/712443, ⓔpunchbowlaskham@aol.com; ❹) retains a bygone charm in its ancient public bar. Both have a choice of real ales and some sunny outdoor seats, while the bar food at either is a cut above the usual pub fare. The Lowther Estate (ⓦwww.lowther.co.uk) also maintains the *Lowther Holiday Park* (☎01768/863631; closed Nov–March), for **camping** and caravans, signposted within the estate and from main roads nearby, as well as two superior **holiday cottages** (☎01931/712577), one in Askham village and one just to the south in the hamlet of Whale.

Howtown and Martindale

HOWTOWN – best reached by regular steamer services in summer from Glenridding – is tucked behind a little indented harbour, four miles south of Pooley Bridge. It's a popular spot that lies at the start of several fine walks. Many people cross to Howtown by boat and then walk back (6 miles; 3hr), following the shore of Ullswater around Hallin Fell to **Sandwick** and then through the woods and on around the bottom of the lake to Patterdale.

There are only a few houses in Howtown, huddled around the *Howtown Hotel* (☎017684/86514; no credit cards; ❼), which has a cosy wood-panelled and stained-glass snug bar around the back where hikers can revive themselves with a beer or a cup of coffee. Dinner is included in the overnight room rate, though non-guests can also take advantage of the moderately priced cold-table lunch or *table d'hôte* dinner (£17, Sunday supper £11) available in the hotel dining room.

The minor road from Pooley Bridge runs south through Howtown and climbs up in switchbacks to a car park at the foot of **Martindale**. The road, in fact, continues another couple of miles up to Dale Head, but it's best to abandon the car and walk the ten minutes along to **St Martin's**, the most beautifully sited of all the Lake District's isolated churches. An Elizabethan stone chapel of

For some of the nicest but least-vaunted walking in the Lake District, cross Ullswater on the steamer from Glenridding. Various routes radiate from Howtown, including the two described below.

Fusedale

A strenuous route (8 miles; 4–5hr) cuts past the *Howtown Hotel* and heads up lovely **Fusedale**, at the head of which there's an unrelenting climb up to the **High Street**, a broad-backed ridge that was once a Roman road. The path is clearly visible for miles and following the ridge south you meet the highest point, **High Raise** (2632ft) – two hours from Howtown – where there's a cairn and glorious views. The route then runs south and west, via the stone outcrops of **Satura Crag**, past **Angle Tarn** and finally down to the A592, just shy of Patterdale's pub and post office.

To Pooley Bridge

Time the steamer services from Glenridding right and you can cross to Howtown, walk **to Pooley Bridge** and catch the boat back. The most direct route (5 miles; 3hr) leaves Howtown pier and runs northeast under Auterstone Crag before cutting up to the **Stone Circle** on the Roman road, south of Roehead, a couple of miles from Pooley Bridge. But for the best views and most exhilarating walk climb up to High Street from Fusedale (see above) and then charge straight along the ridge to the Stone Circle (7 miles; 3–4hr).

See Basics, p.40, for general walking advice in the Lakes; recommended maps are detailed on p.27.

great simplicity, all there is inside is a stone-flagged floor, a seventeenth-century altar table and lectern and rows of plain wooden benches. It's barely changed in centuries and, outside, the feeling of time immemorial is emphasized by the vast spreading yew tree, thought to be a thousand years old, whose gnarled branches shroud the tomb of Martindale's nineteenth-century curate George Woodley.

If these remote surroundings appeal, consider renting *The Bungalow* (℡017684/86450; sleeps up to 12; £450–900 per week), an isolated shooting lodge built in 1912 by the Earl of Lonsdale and maintained now by Dalemain Estates. The lodge is a mile or so from Dale Head (marked on the OS map), with rough access for cars and no electricity (though there is gas lighting and heating). Red deer are easily seen from the lodge.

Brothers Water, Hartsop and Hayeswater

The car park at **Cow Bridge**, two miles south of Patterdale, is the jumping-off point for the short stroll along a quiet stretch of Goldrill Beck to **Brothers Water**. The Water itself (possibly taking its name from a corruption of the Norse name "Brothir") is a mere liquid scoop, but the path along the western shore takes you under the canopy of some of the Lakes' oldest oak woodlands. This was the way Dorothy Wordsworth came on Good Friday in April 1802, after her daffodil-spotting excursion of the previous day, and it's easy to trace her exact route from her journal: "I left William sitting on the bridge, and went along the path on the right side of the lake through the wood. I was delighted with what I saw. The water under the boughs of the bare old trees, the simplicity of the mountains, and the exquisite beauty of the path." When she got back to Cow Bridge, William was busy writing a poem, which he later entitled (mistakenly) "Written in March".

The path alongside Brothers Water runs a mile or so up to the 500-year-old Hartsop Hall Farm – standing on land which experts reckon has been farmed since the Bronze Age. You can press further on if you're in the mood for a hike, or return to the car park and cross the main road for the tiny hamlet of **Hartsop** itself, from where it's a mile-and-a-bit walk east up the valley to **Hayeswater**, a limpid little lake sitting under the High Street range. It's hard to believe now, but Hartsop was once a thriving mining and quarrying centre, the biggest in the region, and the track up to Hayeswater sits beneath crags riddled with old workings.

Haweswater

With the example of Thirlmere already set, there was less opposition when **Haweswater** was dammed in the 1930s to provide more water for the industrial northwest. The Lake District's easternmost lake became almost twice as long as a result (now four miles in length), while the water level rose by 100 feet, completely drowning the village of Mardale. (It was visible in the hot summers of 1976, 1984 and 1995, when its deluged buildings emerged briefly from the depleted reservoir.) Such brutal dealings seem a long way off nowadays: the water company manages the valley and lake as a nature reserve, where woodpeckers and sparrowhawks inhabit Naddle Forest, and buzzards, peregrine falcons and the only pair of golden eagles in England swoop to the fells.

You can park at **Burnbanks**, at the northern end, near the dam wall, which is the best place to start the moderately strenuous **round-the-lake walk** (10 miles; 5hr), perhaps the best lakeside walk in the entire region – you'll usually be completely on your own on the way round. The path meanders above the water and through the woods on both sides of the lake, and if you walk anti-clockwise you can reward yourself near the end with a drink at the nicely old-fashioned *Haweswater Hotel* (☎01931/713235, ⓦwww.haweswater-hotel .com; ⓺), built in 1937 to replace the inn at Mardale, lost when the valley was drowned. The terrace, dining room and bar all have magnificent views, as do the rooms, while the three at the front have lake-facing balconies (though these aren't en suite). Homemade soup and sandwiches are available at lunch; for dinner there's a two- or three-course *table d'hôte* menu (£21/24.50).

The road ends at the southern foot of the lake where there's an official car park at **Mardale Head**: from here, walkers can climb south over the passes to Kentmere and Longsleddale or west up to High Street for Troutbeck, Patterdale or Howtown. The traditional circular day walk from Mardale Head (7 miles; 5hr) is up Riggindale to High Street (2719ft) and then south along the ridge to Mardale Ill Bell (2496ft) and Harter Fell (2539ft) before dropping down Gatescarth Pass back to the car park. On a clear day, the views for most of the way around are magnificent.

There are no other local facilities, save a pub and a post office-store-café in the small village of **BAMPTON**, which is a couple of miles beyond the head of the lake (and four miles south of Askham). A weekend (and public holiday) **bus** service, the #111 "Haweswater Rambler", runs from Penrith to Bampton and Burnbanks (all year, Sat only) and on to the foot-of-the-lake car park (mid-July to early Sept Sun & bank hols only).

Travel details

From Penrith

Bus #108, "Patterdale Rambler" (4–5 daily) to: Pooley Bridge (23min), Gowbarrow Park (35min), Glenridding (45min), Patterdale (50min).

Bus #110 postbus to: Pooley Bridge (quickest journey time 25min), Howtown (40min) and Martindale (45min). Service operates Mon–Sat 2 daily. Of the two, the much quicker afternoon service (shown here) is the only real option for most travellers.

Bus #111, "Haweswater Rambler" (3 daily) to: Askham (15min), Bampton (22min), Burnbanks (27min) and Mardale Head (1hr). Service operates Sat all year to Askham, Bampton and Burnbanks; and as far as Mardale Head on Sun & bank hols from mid-July to early Sept only.

From Glenridding/Patterdale

Bus #208 (5 daily) to: Aira Force (12min) and Keswick (38min). Service operates late-May to mid-July, Sat, Sun and bank hols; mid-July to Aug daily.

Bus #517, "Kirkstone Rambler" to: Brothers Water (10min), Kirkstone Pass Inn (25min), Troutbeck Queen's Head (35min), Windermere (50min) and Bowness (1hr). Service operates Easter to mid-July Sat, Sun & bank hols 3 daily; mid July to early Sept 3 daily.

From Bowness/Windermere

Bus #517, "Kirkstone Rambler" to: Brotherswater (45min), Patterdale (50min) and Glenridding (55min). Service operates Easter to mid-July Sat, Sun & bank hols 3 daily; mid-July to early Sept 3 daily.

Out of the
National Park

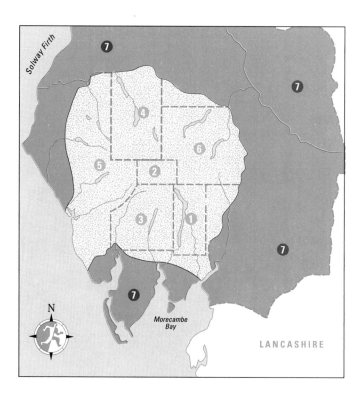

CHAPTER 7 # Highlights

✳ **L'Enclume, Cartmel** A cutting edge gastronomic retreat in one of the region's prettiest medieval villages. See p.221

✳ **Laurel and Hardy Museum, Ulverston** Picking over the life of Ulverston's finest son, Stan Laurel, provides a happy diversion from the lakes and fells. See p.222

✳ **Furness Abbey** The romantic sandstone pillars and arcades of Cumbria's finest religious ruin lie only a few miles off the beaten track. See p.225

✳ **Whitehaven** West Cumbria's most captivating town has a Georgian centre and revitalized harbour. See p.225

✳ **Wordsworth House, Cockermouth** Wordsworth's childhood home has been enterprisingly restored as a working Georgian household. See p.229

✳ **Rheged** A wet-weather attraction *par excellence*, Rheged visitor centre lures visitors with a giant-format cinema screen and Britain's national mountaineering museum. See p.237

△ Penrith Castle

7

Out of the National Park

When the Lake District National Park boundary was drawn around the lakes and fells, it excluded several peripheral Cumbrian towns, nearly all of the west Cumbrian coast and the southern Furness peninsulas. Most visitors to the Lakes will pass through at least one of these areas – indeed, the usual approaches to the Lake District make it hard to avoid Kendal or Penrith. And there's a case for aiming to see several other destinations not strictly within the National Park on any trip to the region. The distances help: it's not much more than thirty miles between Penrith and Cockermouth, and about the same around the west coast, making it easy to nip from lakeland valley to outlying town. This chapter highlights half a dozen of the most interesting destinations on the fringes of the National Park, all close enough to be considered part of the Lake District. You may well also pass through the largely industrial towns of the west coast – between Barrow-in-Furness and Maryport – and visit the county capital of Carlisle or the Morecambe Bay resort of Grange-over-Sands; but you won't find those places covered in this guide. For these, you'll need to get hold of a copy of the *Rough Guide to England*.

The towns outside the National Park are all larger than those within, not least **Kendal**, in the southeast, once the county town of Westmorland and still an enjoyable market town with a pair of fine museums, an arts centre and other attractions. **Penrith**, to the north, is also an ancient commercial centre and, like Kendal, retains the ruins of the castle that defended it during the turbulent medieval border wars. It's a minor stop on the Wordsworth trail, while many pass through before or after seeing nearby **Rheged**, the Cumbrian visitor centre and film experience, which also houses the National Mountaineering Exhibition. Religious foundations established in the south at **Cartmel** and **Furness Abbey** had a lasting regional significance; the enterprising Furness monks could be said to have made early Cumbria an economic powerhouse well before the Industrial Revolution. Of the Cumbrian ports and towns that boomed in the eighteenth and nineteenth centuries, **Ulverston** still thrives as a market town (and claims comedian Stan Laurel as its own), while **Whitehaven**, on the west Cumbrian coast, has been rejuvenated by investment in its fine harbour and quayside. Here, and at nearby **Cockermouth** – yet another handsome market town – the Georgian well-to-do (including the young Wordsworth family) lived out their comfortable lives.

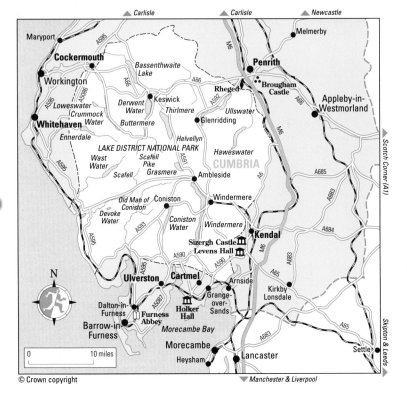

© Crown copyright

All the places covered in this chapter are accessible by **public transport** and details are given where necessary. Cumbria's **Traveline** ☎0870/608 2608, Ⓦwww.traveline.org.uk can provide specific routes and timetables.

Kendal

The self-billed "Gateway to the Lakes" (though nearly ten miles from Windermere), limestone-grey **KENDAL** is the largest of the southern Cumbrian towns, with a population of 25,000. Upwardly mobile Norman barons created a medieval market town on the banks of the fast-flowing River Kent and built the first castle here, whose skeletal remains still stand. They also bequeathed to the town its most characteristic feature by establishing uniform building plots along a single main street in an attempt to increase their rents. This resulted in the layout visible today on both sides of Highgate and Stricklandgate: houses and shops to the fore, stables and workshops to the rear in the numerous "yards" and "ginnels". The town became known for its archers – who fought at Crécy and Poitiers in the Hundred Years War with France – and for its cloth, particularly the "Kendal green" (plant-dyed wool), which earned the town a mention in Shakespeare's *Henry IV*. No wonder that the town motto became the no-nonsense "Cloth is my bread". By the eighteenth century Kendal was a major European cloth distribution centre, while its tanneries (which grievously polluted the River Kent) laid the foundation for today's most important industry, shoe-making. However, you could be forgiven for thinking that **Kendal Mintcake** is what keeps the contemporary coffers filled. This solid, energy-giving block of sugar and peppermint oil, invented by accident in the mid-nineteenth century, has been hoisted to the top of the world's highest mountains and is on sale throughout the Lakes.

The Town

The old **Market Place** has long since succumbed to development, with the market hall now converted to the Westmorland Shopping Centre (off Stricklandgate), but traditional stalls still do business outside every Wednesday and

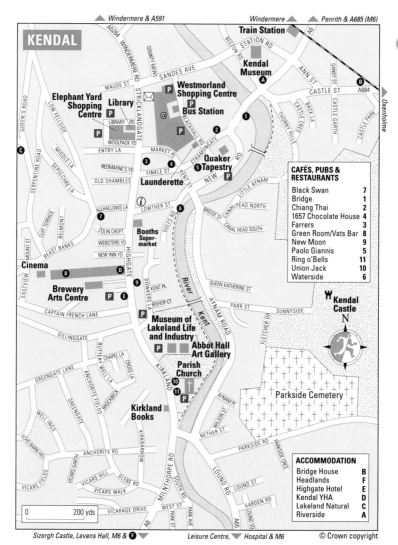

KENDAL

Windermere & A591   Windermere   Penrith & A685 (M6)

Train Station

Kendal Museum   **A**

Westmorland Shopping Centre

Elephant Yard Shopping Centre   Library

Bus Station

Kendal

CAFÉS, PUBS & RESTAURANTS

Black Swan	7
Bridge	1
Chiang Thai	2
1657 Chocolate House	4
Farrers	3
Green Room/Vats Bar	8
New Moon	9
Paolo Giannis	5
Ring o'Bells	11
Union Jack	10
Waterside	6

Quaker Tapestry

Launderette

Booths Supermarket

Cinema

Brewery Arts Centre

Museum of Lakeland Life and Industry

Abbot Hall Art Gallery

Parish Church

Kendal Castle

Parkside Cemetery

Kirkland Books

ACCOMMODATION

Bridge House	B
Headlands	F
Highgate Hotel	E
Kendal YHA	D
Lakeland Natural	C
Riverside	A

0   200 yds

Sizergh Castle, Levens Hall, M6 &   Leisure Centre,   Hospital & M6   © Crown copyright

213

Saturday and there's a well-established farmers' market on the last Friday of the month. The long main street – Stricklandgate and then Highgate – is backed by historic yards and alleys, many now renovated and containing shops and businesses. Strolling along here will eventually take you down to the riverside, past restored almshouses, mullioned shop fronts and old trade-signs, among them the pipe-smoking Turk outside the snuff factory on Lowther Street.

At Kirkland, by the river at the bottom of Highgate, the wide aisles of the Early English **Parish Church** house a number of family chapels, including that of the Parr family, who once owned the ruined **Kendal Castle** (free access) on a hillock to the east across the river. First erected in the early thirteenth century, it's claimed as the birthplace of Catherine Parr, Henry VIII's sixth wife, but the story is apocryphal – she was born in 1512, at which time the building was in

⑦ Alfred Wainwright

If ever a person has changed the way others look at the Lake District hills it's **Alfred Wainwright** (1907–91), whose handwritten walking guides – studied with the intensity normally reserved for religious texts – are among the most common sights on the fells. Wainwright was born in Blackburn in Lancashire, left school at 13 and worked his way up through the Borough Treasurer's office, qualifying as an accountant in 1933. After a first visit to the Lake District in 1930 he became a keen walker and returned to the Lakes at every possible opportunity. So taken was he with the fells that he engineered a move to Kendal in 1941; he was Borough Treasurer from 1948 until his retirement in 1967.

His love of walking was taken to obsessional lengths, setting off alone at the crack of dawn every weekend to tackle distant fells, peaks and valleys. In 1952, dissatisfied with the accuracy of existing maps of the paths and ancient tracks across the fells, he embarked on a series of seven walking guides, each painstakingly handwritten with mapped routes and delicately drawn views. These *Pictorial Guides* to the Lake District were a remarkable undertaking, especially since the original idea was only for his own amusement. The first book, *The Eastern Fells*, was published in 1955 and was an unexpected success; six others followed by 1966, thus completing the task he had set himself of recording in detail 214 separate lakeland fells. Many other titles followed: a *Pennine Way Companion* (1968), the *Coast-to-Coast* route he devised from St Bees to Robin Hood's Bay (1973), endless sketchbooks and guides to the Lake District, Scotland, Wales, the Yorkshire Dales and the Lancashire hills; fifty-odd books in all. His first wife, Ruth, left him in 1966 and in 1970 Wainwright married Betty McNally, with whom he'd corresponded (and secretly met on his walking trips) for years. He died in 1991, having given away most of his considerable earnings to animal rescue charities, and his ashes were scattered on Haystacks in Buttermere.

The effect his books have had is plain to see. People who don't normally consider themselves walkers are happy to follow his guidance through the Lake District – easy to do since little has changed up on the fells themselves in the fifty years since the *Pictorial Guides* were first written. But some decry their popularity, which has led to the ravaging of the land he so adored, especially on his most trekked route, the Coast-to-Coast – much of Wainwright's original route (subsequently amended) was not on designated rights of way and often crossed sensitive wildlife areas and archeological sites. It's also wrong to treat Wainwright as gospel, as many do in their attempts to "bag" the 214 fells he recorded. The number was an entirely arbitrary figure – most of the Wainwright fells are over 1400ft high, but there are plenty of other crags and fells lower than that but just as spectacular, not to mention the lakes, tarns and valleys which he covered only in passing.

an advanced state of decay. To reach the castle, follow the footpath from the end of Parr Street, across the footbridge just north of the church.

Kendal's other attractions – town museum, tapestry exhibition and the art gallery and museum at Abbott Hall – spread themselves along the River Kent, between the train station and the parish church.

Kendal Museum

The **Kendal Museum** on Station Road (Mon–Sat: Easter–Oct 10.30am–5pm; Nov, Dec & mid–Feb to Easter 10.30am–4pm; closed Jan to mid–Feb; £2.50; ℡01539/721374, ⊛www.kendalmuseum.org.uk) is the repository of the district's natural history and archeological finds. Founded as early as 1796, what was essentially a gentleman's private collection was later given to the town and moved into an old wool warehouse in 1913, where it's been stationed ever since. It's far from dull, since as well as the usual flints and stuffed birds there are plenty of well-presented displays relating to the town's history and various pieces of ephemera – from a penny-farthing bicycle to a stuffed grizzly bear, shot by the Earl of Lonsdale. There are also finds from local Roman and Viking sites, including part of a tenth-century cross with similar Christian symbols to that of the more famous Gosforth cross. Later exhibits include a medieval coin hoard and even a key from the town castle. Kendal's former borough treasurer, Alfred Wainwright (see box on p.214) was honorary clerk at the museum between 1945 and 1974: his office, various pen-and-ink drawings and a few of his personal effects are preserved, as well as many of the museum artefact labels written in his distinctive hand.

Quaker Tapestry

Just off the river, between New Road and Stramongate, one of Britain's largest Quaker Meeting Houses (built 1816) contains the 77 embroidered panels of the **Quaker Tapestry** (April–Oct Mon–Sat 10am–5pm; Nov to mid–Dec Mon–Fri 10am–5pm; £3.75; ℡01539/722975, ⊛www.quaker-tapestry.co.uk). This area of the southern Lakes was at the heart of early Quakerism, beginning with the travelling ministry of George Fox (1652), a seeker after truth, whose followers were dubbed Quakers "because we bid them tremble at the Word of the Lord". The tapestry – produced by almost four thousand people gathered in embroidery groups between 1981 and 1996 – forms a narrative history of Quaker experience through the ages, with the delicately worked panels portraying historical subjects such as Elizabeth Fry's work in Newgate prison and the anti-slavery "underground railroad" in the USA, as well as contemporary Quaker campaigns for peace, relief work and reconciliation. Embroidery workshops and demonstrations are held throughout the year, while there's a vegetarian café – in summer you can sit outside on the lawn. You can enter the Meeting House from either New Road or Stramongate.

Abbot Hall Art Gallery and Museum of Lakeland Life and Industry

The town's other two attractions – Art Gallery and Museum of Lakeland Life and Industry – are found at the Georgian **Abbot Hall** (Mon–Sat: April–Oct 10.30am–5pm; Nov to mid–Dec & mid–Jan to March 10.30am–4pm; closed mid–Dec to mid–Jan; gallery £3.50, museum £4.75, combined ticket £6.50; ℡01539/722464, ⊛www.abbothall.org.uk), by the river near the parish church. The main hall, painstakingly restored to its 1760s town-house origins, houses the **Art Gallery**, whose upper floors host temporary exhibitions of modern art. The lower-floor galleries are more locally focused, concentrating on the works of the eighteenth-century "Kendal School" of portrait painters, notably Daniel Gardner and, most famously, George Romney. Born in Dalton-in-Furness (and buried there), Romney set himself up as a portrait painter in Kendal in 1757, where he stayed for five years before moving to London to further his career. His society portraits are the pick of the gallery's collection, though you'll also find changing displays of works by those who came to the Lakes to paint, such as Constable, Ruskin, Turner and Edward Lear. Two large paintings of Windermere by Phillip James de Loutherbourg depict Belle Isle and its round house respectively beset by storms and becalmed. In addition, eighteenth-century chairs, writing desks and games tables designed and built by famed furniture-makers Gillows of Lancaster have all survived in Abbot Hall in excellent condition, and there's also a good café below the gallery.

A Barbara Hepworth sculpture, *Oval Form*, graces the grass between the hall and its former stables, which now house the **Museum of Lakeland Life and Industry**. Here, reconstructed house interiors from the seventeenth, eighteenth and nineteenth centuries stand alongside workshops that make a vivid presentation of rural trades and crafts, from mining, spinning and weaving to shoe-making and tanning. The museum also contains a room devoted to the life and work of the children's writer Arthur Ransome, whose widow donated his pipes, typewriter and other memorabilia to the collection after his death.

Sizergh Castle and Levens Hall

Three miles south of Kendal stands **Sizergh Castle**, tucked away off the A591 (Easter–Oct Mon–Thurs & Sun 1.30–5.30pm; gardens same days from 12.30pm; castle & gardens £5.80, gardens only £3.50; NT;

Walks from Kendal

Although Kendal isn't the most obvious hiking centre, you can in fact walk straight out of town and on to the nearby hills. There are no particularly dramatic heights to gain, but it's pretty countryside. The two moderate walks below offer a variety of scenery, while you're also only a short drive or train ride away from Staveley (p.82), the access point for Kentmere and its walks.

The River Kent to Staveley

Follow the path along the **River Kent** north out of Kendal (or jump the train one stop) to Burneside (the *Jolly Anglers* is a good pub), where you cut northeast up minor roads and farm tracks before climbing to **Gurnal Dubs** and **Potter Tarn**, two prettily sited tarns. The path skirts both before descending to Staveley (good café and pub), where you pick up the signposted Dales Way, which then meanders back down the River Kent through pastoral country to Burneside. From Burneside, this is a 7.5-mile (4hr) circular walk, though if you walk in and out of Kendal you can add another three miles (1hr) to this.

Scout Scar

The high limestone ridge known as **Scout Scar** is 5km southwest of Kendal and, on a clear day, provides some scintillating views. Again, you can walk out of Kendal if you want to make a day of it, though it's more usually climbed from either the Underbarrow road (north) or from Brigsteer (south) – there's parking at both places and a pub in Brigsteer.

See Basics, p.40, for general walking advice in the Lakes; recommended maps are detailed on p.27.

ⓣ015395/60070); take bus #555. Home of the Strickland family for eight centuries, the castle owes its epithet to the fourteenth-century pele tower at its core – one of the best examples of these towers, which were built as safe havens during the region's protracted medieval border raids. The Great Hall underwent significant changes in Elizabethan times, when most of its rooms were panelled in oak with their ceilings layered in elaborate plasterwork. At nearby **Low Sizergh Barn** (daily 9.30am–5pm; ⓣ015395/60426, Ⓦwww .lowsizerghbarn.co.uk), four miles south of Kendal on the A591, there's a really good farm shop and craft gallery, while the tearoom has a viewing window onto the organic dairy herd's milking parlour (cows milked daily around 3.45pm)

Two miles south of Sizergh, **Levens Hall** (April to mid-Oct Mon–Thurs & Sun noon–5pm; gardens same days from 10am; £8, gardens only £6; ⓣ015395/60321, Ⓦwww.levenshall.co.uk), also built around a pele tower, is more uniform in style than Sizergh, since the bulk of it was built or refurbished in classic Elizabethan style between 1570 and 1640. The dining room here is panelled not with oak but with goat's leather, printed with a deep-green floral design. Upstairs, the bedrooms offer glimpses of the beautifully trimmed topiary gardens (the world's oldest, according to *Guinness*), where yews in the shape of pyramids, peacocks and top hats stand between blooming bedding plants. The #555 bus stops outside the hall.

Practicalities

Kendal's **train station** is the first stop on the Windermere branch line, just three minutes from the Oxenholme main-line station. By catching bus #41 or #41A (to the Town Hall) from Oxenholme (Mon–Sat every 20min) you can avoid the wait for the connecting train. From Kendal station, head across the river and up Stramongate and Finkle Street to reach Highgate, a ten-minute walk. All buses (including National Express services) stop at the **bus station** on Blackhall Road (off Stramongate). Locally, the #599 (to Windermere, Bowness, Ambleside and Grasmere) and #555/556 (to Windermere, Ambleside, Grasmere and Keswick, or to Lancaster or Carlisle) are the main services. Driving in from the M6, take junction 38 (north) or 36 (south). There are signposted **car parks** all over town, including one at the Westmorland Shopping Centre (Blackhall Road) and a couple off Highgate, plus free unlimited parking on New Road by the river.

The **tourist office** (March–Dec Mon–Sat 9am–5pm, July & Aug until 6pm, Sun 10am–4pm, July & Aug until 5pm; Jan & Feb closed Sun; ⓣ01539/725758, Ⓦwww.kendaltown.org.uk) is in the Town Hall on Highgate (at the junction with Lowther Street). It has current details of the **guided walks** organized by the local Civic Society and held on various days throughout July and August.

Accommodation

Kendal makes a reasonable overnight stop on the way to or from the Lakes, and can be a useful base for the southern region – though walkers should note that the central fells and valleys are all a good drive or bus ride away. There's not a massive amount of town centre accommodation, save for the **youth hostel** and a handful of **pubs** offering rooms. Most of the local **B&Bs** lie along Windermere Road, north of the centre, and on Milnthorpe Road, to the south, while the most convenient campsite (and a few other good accommodation options) lies four miles northwest of town, near Staveley (see p.82).

B&Bs, guest houses and hotels

Bridge House 65 Castle St ☎01539/722041, ⓦwww.bridgehouse-kendal.co.uk. Georgian family house, not far from the station (it was once the station master's residence), with just a couple of pretty rooms available. No credit cards. ❸

Headlands 53 Milnthorpe Rd ☎01539/732464, ⓦwww.smoothhound.co.uk/hotels/headlands. The pick of the bunch on this popular road for guest houses is this traditional stone house, five minutes' walk south of the centre. Good prices for the rooms, which are small but smart – the one at the top of the house, a family room with a couple of bunks, is the most spacious. There's a licensed lounge-bar and a pick-up service offered from the train or bus stations. Parking. ❷

Highgate Hotel 128 Highgate ☎01539/724229, ⓦwww.highgatehotel.co.uk. Originally built for the town's first doctor, the rambling Georgian town house now conceals various spick-and-span rooms. There's a family room available (priced a couple of categories higher) and a small garden and patio, while you're just yards from the town's pubs and restaurants. Parking. ❸

Lakeland Natural Low Slack, Queen's Rd ☎01539/733011, ⓦwww.lakelandnatural.co.uk. Best B&B choice by far, an impressive, detached vegetarian guest house standing on high ground above the town, five minutes' walk west of the centre. There are expansive views from the lounge and five rooms in country pine, one of them (with two connecting rooms and a bathroom, priced a category higher) handy for families. Breakfasts incorporate homemade muffins and damson jam, organic yoghurt and fresh fruit salad; dinner (£17) is by arrangement. Parking. ❹

Riverside Stramongate Bridge ☎01539/734861, ⓦwww.riversidekendal.co.uk. Kendal's leather industry bequeathed the town several old riverside tanneries, of which this is a prime example. The rows of riverside windows let light into spacious, traditionally furnished rooms, fitted with baths and showers, while a restaurant makes the most of the riverside setting. Parking. ❺

Youth hostel

Kendal YHA 118 Highgate ☎0870/770 5892, ⓔkendal@yha.org.uk. Straightforward hostel accommodation in a building attached to The Brewery arts centre. The multi-bunked rooms are a bit barrack-like (though a few two-bedded rooms are available) and the hostel's tight on space, but the location's great and there's a lively arts centre bar next door. Reception opens 1pm; evening meals by prior arrangement. Weekends only Oct–Dec, plus flexible opening Jan & Feb – call for details. Dorm beds £16, includes breakfast.

Eating, drinking and entertainment

Kendal has the best selection of places to **eat and drink** in the south Lakes, so if you're moving on to the fells you'll want to get your cappuccinos and veggie specials while you can. Many of the town-centre **pubs** have had unsympathetic makeovers, but there are also still one or two traditional boozers left. However, the main focus of evening entertainment is the **Brewery Arts Centre**, 118 Highgate (☎01539/725133, ⓦwww.breweryarts.co.uk), with its foyer café-bar, restaurant, pub, cinema, theatre, galleries and concert hall. There's live music here throughout the year (including live outdoor concerts on summer Sundays), a special season of Christmas events, and a renowned annual **jazz and blues festival** every November. Other annual events in Kendal include the town's **Torchlight Procession** and **Westmorland County Show** (both Sept) and the **Mountain Film Festival** (Oct), which presents films and speakers from around the world on climbing and the mountains.

Cafés

1657 Chocolate House 54 Branthwaite Brow, Finkle St ☎01539/740702. Olde-worlde spot that sells hot chocolate in dozens of guises, plus two dozen cakes and filled croissants. Daytime only; closed Sun Jan–April. Inexpensive.

Farrers Tea & Coffee Merchants 13 Stricklandgate ☎01539/731707. Historic merchant's quarters on the main street, with tea and coffee sold by the weight in the shop and by the cup and cafetiere in the café at the back. Daytime only; closed Sun. Inexpensive.

Union Jack 15 Kirkland ☎01539/722458. If you want veggie food but also crave chips and beans, this is the spot – a family-run diner where full breakfasts and mixed grills take their place on the menu alongside homemade blackbean cakes with red lentil sauce, veggie country bake and bean burgers. Daytime only; closed Sun. Inexpensive.

Waterside Café Gulfs Rd, bottom of Lowther St ☎01539/729743. Veggie wholefood snacks and meals – eat either in one of the homely little rooms or outside, looking over the river. Soups, salads, bakes and cakes form the mainstay of the menu, but stuffed tortillas and other specials provide daily variation. Daytime only; closed Sun. Inexpensive.

Restaurants

Chiang Thai 54 Stramongate ☎01539/720387. Northern Thai dishes are the speciality in this intimate restaurant – such as *laab*, a spicy, minced-meat salad – but all the usual stir fries are available, alongside fragrant "mussaman" curries (with coconut, pineapple and peanuts) and delicate dishes like poached salmon and coconut soup. Tues–Sun dinner only. Moderate.

Green Room Brewery Arts Centre, Highgate ☎01539/725133. The funky arts centre café-restaurant serves pizzas, pastas, stir fries, sandwiches and salads at lunch – and you can eat on the terrace in summer. The dinner menu is similar, though with more choice, and adds steaks, grills and other specials (last orders are usually at around 9.30pm). Moderate.

New Moon 129 Highgate ☎01539/729254. Kendal's longest-serving foodie choice has had a sharp contemporary makeover, with a seasonally changing menu to match, presenting dishes that

mix locally sourced ingredients with Mediterranean and other flavours. There are always two vegetarian and two fish courses available. Expensive.

Paolo Giannis 21a Stramongate ☎01539/725858. Rustic Italian with tables placed cheek by jowl. No surprises on the menu – pizzas, pasta, grills – but it's a cheery place to dine, with a bargain happy-hour menu (noon–2pm & 5–6.30pm) when pizza or pasta is just £3.25. Moderate.

Pubs

Black Swan 8 Allhallows Lane ☎01539/724278. A locals' local, with a roaring fire in winter to thaw the chilliest souls and a range of decent beers.

Bridge Hotel Stramongate ☎01539/724170. A classic old pub with well-kept beer and a small riverside beer garden. It's right at the bottom of Stramongate, by the bridge.

Ring o' Bells 37 Kirkland ☎01539/720326. This pub, uniquely, stands on consecrated ground by the parish church, making it the bell-ringers' local. Does its holy location make the beer taste better? You decide.

Vats Bar Brewery Arts Centre, Highgate ☎01539/725133. More a pub than a bar, with a selection of real ales available – the huge "vats" provide circular booth seating. You can eat well here too, as the menu is the same as in the adjacent *Green Room* (see "Restaurants" above).

Listings

Banks and exchange ATMs at Barclays (9 Highgate); HSBC (64 Highgate); Lloyds-TSB (Finkle St); and NatWest (70 Stricklandgate). You can exchange travellers' cheques at the post office (see below).

Bookshop Kirkland Books, 68 Kirkland ☎01539/740841 (closed Sun). Offers an excellent selection of second-hand and antiquated books, and is especially strong on local interest, walking and topography.

Car rental Westmorland Vehicle Hire, Westmorland Business Park, Gilthwaiterigg Lane ☎01539/728532.

Emergencies Westmorland General Hospital, Burton Rd, Kendal ☎01539/732288.

Internet access Dot Café, 31–34 Westmorland Shopping Centre, Market Place (Mon–Sat 9am–5pm; ☎01539/740313); Kendal Library, Stricklandgate (Mon & Tues 9.30am–5.30pm, Wed & Fri 9.30am–7pm, Thurs 9.30am–1pm, Sat 9am–4pm; ☎01539/773520).

Laundry Kendal Laundrette, Greencoats Yard, Blackhall Rd (Mon–Fri 8am–6pm,

Sat 8am–5pm, Sun 9am–5pm; ☎01539 /733754).

Left luggage *Union Jack* café, 15 Kirkland, will look after your bags during the day for free; you should at least buy a cup of tea in return.

Pharmacies Boots, 10 Elephant Yard ☎01539/720180; Highgate Pharmacy, 41 Highgate ☎01539/720461; Lloyd's, Station Yd ☎01539/723988.

Police station Busher Walk ☎01539/722611.

Post office 75 Stricklandgate (Mon–Fri 9am–5.30pm, Sat 9am–12.30pm; ☎0845/722 3344).

Swimming pool Kendal Leisure Centre, Burton Rd ☎01539/729777, ⓦ www.kendal-leisure-centre .co.uk. Public admission usually lunchtime and evenings only during term-time, otherwise all day, but call for specific times; there's also a sauna, exercise room and squash court.

Taxis Blue Star Taxis ☎01539/723670; Crown Taxis ☎01539/732181; Cumbria Cars ☎01539/720620; K. & C. Taxis ☎01539/724117.

Cartmel

CARTMEL grew up around its twelfth-century Augustinian priory and is still dominated by the proud **Church of St Mary and St Michael** (daily: Easter–Oct 9am–5.30pm; Nov–Easter 9am–3.30pm; tours Easter–Oct Wed 11am & 2pm; free), the only substantial remnant of the priory to survive the Dissolution. A diagonally crowned tower is the most distinctive feature outside, while the light and spacious Norman-transitional interior climaxes at a splendid chancel, illuminated by the 45-foot-high East Window. The misericords are immaculate, carved with entwined branches, bunches of grapes, tools, leaves and crosses, while chief of the numerous sculpted tombs is the Harrington Tomb – the weathered figure is that of John Harrington, a fourteenth-century benefactor. Another patron of the church was one Rowland Briggs who paid for a shelf on a pier near the north door and for a supply of bread to be distributed from it every Sunday in perpetuity "to the most indigent housekeepers of this Parish". Before you leave, peruse the gravestones on the church floor, reminders of men and women swept away by the tide while crossing the sands – a short cut into the region from Grange-Over-Sands to the south.

Everything else in the village is modest in scale, centred on the attractive **market square**, with its Elizabethan cobbles, water pump and fish slabs. Refreshment is at hand at any of the village's three pubs, all on, or close to, the square, and you can then walk down to the **racecourse** whose delightful setting by the River Eea deserves a look even if the races (held on the last weekend in May and August; Ⓦwww.cartmel-steeplechases.co.uk) aren't in action. Given Cartmel's rather twee attraction, you'll not be surprised to find several **antique and craft shops**, as well as weekly antiques fairs (April–Oct) held in the village hall. On the square, Peter Bain Smith's **bookshop** has a huge selection of local books and guides, while the **Cartmel Village Shop** is known to aficionados for the quality of its sticky-toffee pudding.

A couple of miles west of the village, on the B5278, one of Cumbria's most interesting and well-presented country estates, **Holker Hall** (Easter–Oct Mon–Fri & Sun 10am–5.30pm; last admission 4pm; various combination tickets available; gardens £4.50, all-in ticket £9.25; Ⓣ015395/58328, Ⓦwww.holker-hall.co.uk), is still in use by the Cavendish family who've owned it since the late seventeenth century. Only the New Wing is open to the public and the real showpieces here are the cantilevered staircase and the library, which is stocked with more than three thousand leather-bound books, some of whose spines are fakes, constructed to hide electric light switches added later. The 25-acre gardens incorporate a variety of water features, while next to the house the **Lakeland Motor Museum** (Easter–Oct Mon–Fri & Sun 10.30am–4.45pm) displays more than a hundred vehicles, from 1880s tricycles and wartime ambulances to funky 1920s bubble cars and 1980s MGs. A special exhibition concentrates on the speed-freak Campbells – Sir Malcolm and son Donald.

Practicalities

Cartmel lies a few miles inland of Morecambe Bay and just five miles south of Lakeside, the southern tip of Windermere. **Trains** stop at Cark-in-Cartmel, two miles southwest of the village; the #532 **bus** (not Sun) from Grange-over-Sands train station or from Cark runs to the village. The turnoff from the M6 is junction 36; the **car park** is by the racecourse.

There's no **information** office in Cartmel, but you might look at the local website, Ⓦwww.cartmelvillage.com, for events and listings. Save for race meeting weekends, **accommodation** is easy to find, either in a local

B&B or in one of the old pubs, while Cartmel boasts one of Britain's finest restaurant-with-rooms operations. Otherwise, the village **pubs**, all on and around the square, form the basis of the evening's entertainment – the two listed below also offer accommodation, though the *King's Arms*, with tables outside on the square, is the best bet for real ales and good-value bar meals. For a stay in one of its delightful estate **cottages** (from £400–800 per week, cheaper outside school summer holidays), contact *Longlands at Cartmel*, at the base of Hampsfell just a mile north of the village (☎015395/36475, ⓦwww.cartmel.com), where guests get free use of a nearby pool, spa and sauna.

Bank Court Cottage Market Sq ☎015395/36593. Just through the arch by the bookshop, this family house B&B has one double and one twin room available. No credit cards. ❷

Cavendish Arms Cavendish St ☎015395/36240, ⓦwww.thecavendisharms.co.uk. The most celebrated of Cartmel's inns – on the road through the gatehouse – is an atmospheric place that retains many of its original sixteenth-century features and an open fire in the public bar. It sits on the site of a monastic guest house and offers ten rooms and popular, moderately priced meals in the restaurant or bar. ❸

Howbarrow Farm 2 miles west of Cartmel ☎015395/36330, ⓦwww.howbarroworganic .demon.co.uk. Farmhouse B&B with one pleasant double room and two singles in a quiet part of the region – this is a really nice place to kick back and relax. The farm's organic, which means your breakfast couldn't be much better for you, with most ingredients produced on the premises. No credit cards. ❸

L'Enclume Cavendish St ☎015395/36362, ⓦwww.lenclume.co.uk. Seriously classy restaurant-with-rooms on the site of Cartmel's medieval blacksmiths (*enclume* is French for anvil). The seven highly individual rooms have stylish fabrics, excellent bathrooms and flat-screen TVs – the pricier ones face the gardens or priory – or small groups can take over Bluebell House (four double rooms) in the village, a fifteenth-century house given the contemporary treatment. The food is simply extraordinary, with artfully constructed dishes presented in succession (think of it as designer tapas and you're not far off) – a single seared sea scallop on ginger-and-greentea foam is a typical example, while other dishes are accompanied by intensely flavoured jellied cubes or mousses, or adorned with wild herbs and exotic roots. It's Michelin-starred and very expensive (*a la carte* £40–50 plus drinks, tasting menus at £50, £75 and £95), though lunch is less stratospherically priced. Restaurant closed Mon; and whole place closed first two weeks Jan. ❽

Market Cross Cottage Market Sq ☎015395/36143, ⓔdburgess@marketcross .freeserve.co.uk. Seventeenth-century cottage with simple guest rooms upstairs (some without private facilities) and oak-beamed tearoom downstairs, where you can sample Morecambe Bay potted shrimps and other traditional delights. Tearoom closed Mon. Midweek and off-season rates shave a few pounds off the price. No credit cards. ❹

Royal Oak Market Sq ☎015395/36259, ⓦwww .royaloak-cartmel.co.uk. Old pub on the square with a riverside beer-garden and smart modern rooms upstairs, decked out in country pine. ❹

Ulverston

The railway line winds westwards from Cartmel to **ULVERSTON** – eleven miles by road – a close-knit market town on the Furness peninsula that formerly prospered on the cotton, tanning and iron-ore industries. The cutting of Britain's shortest, widest and deepest canal in 1796 allowed direct shipping access into town and boosted trade with the Americas and West Indies, while exports from the heart of the Lake District (from wooden bobbins and linen to copper and slate) passed out through Ulverston and made it wealthy. It's still an attractive place today, enhanced by its dappled grey limestone cottages and a jumble of cobbled alleys and traditional shops zigzagging off the central Market Place.

The Town

What looks like a lighthouse high on a hill to the north of town is the **Hoad Monument**, built in 1850 to honour locally born Sir John Barrow, a former Secretary of the Admiralty. It's open on summer Sundays and public holidays (if the flag's flying) and the walk to the top grants fine views of Morecambe Bay, the town and – to the north – the lakeland fells. To get there, follow Church Walk from the end of King Street, past the parish church.

In town, stalls set up in **Market Place** and in the surrounding streets every Thursday and Saturday for the outdoor market, held since the thirteenth century – the granting of the town charter, by Edward I, is still celebrated here every autumn during Ulverston's Charter Festival. In addition, a **food fair** and farmers' market occupies Market Street on the third Saturday of every month. On all other days the **Market Hall** on New Market Street (9am–5pm; closed Wed & Sun) is the centre of commercial life.

Ulverston's most famous son is Stan Laurel (born Arthur Stanley Jefferson), the whimpering, head-scratching half of Laurel and Hardy. The duo are celebrated in a mind-boggling collection of memorabilia at the **Laurel and Hardy Museum** up an alley at 4C Upper Brook St (daily 10am–4.30pm;

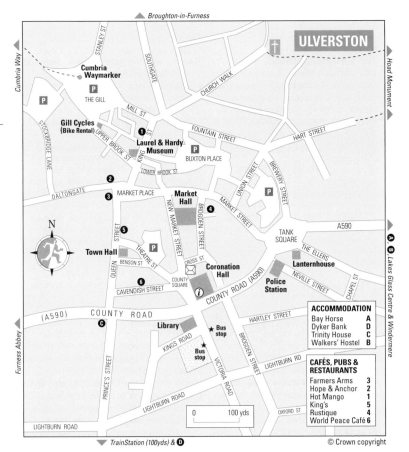

© Crown copyright

£2.50; closed Jan; ☎01229/582292, ⓦwww.laurel-and-hardy-museum.co.uk), thirty yards off Market Place down King Street. The copy of Stan's birth certificate (June 16, 1890, in Foundry Cottages, Ulverston) lists his father's occupation as "comedian" – young Arthur Stanley could hardly have become anything else. The eccentric showcase of hats, beer bottles, photos, models, puppets, press cuttings and props is complemented by a 1920s-style cinema, with almost constant screenings of Laurel and Hardy films.

It's also worth checking to see what's on at the **Lanternhouse**, on The Ellers (exhibitions, when on, Wed–Sat 11am–4pm; free; ☎01229/581127, ⓦwww .welfare-state.org), just off the A590, at the bottom of Market Street and across Tank Square (a traffic roundabout). A group of multimedia artists known as Welfare State International occupy this award-winning conversion of an old school, presenting imaginative exhibitions, concerts and events relating to the "celebratory arts".

The other main attraction is the **Lakes Glass Centre**, at Oubas Hill on the A590, behind Booths supermarket (☎01229/584400, ⓦwww .lakesglasscentre.co.uk), where you can watch the crystal-making process from blowing to painstaking carving, either at Heron Glass or Cumbria Crystal (factories open Mon–Fri 8.30/9am–4.30/5pm; free). Each also has a factory shop on site (Mon–Sat 9am–5pm, Sun 10am–4pm), and there's a café (daily 10am–4.30pm).

Practicalities

Ulverston **train station**, serving the Furness and Cumbrian coast railway, is only a few minutes' walk from the town centre – walk up Prince's Street and turn right at the main road for County Square. **Buses** arrive on nearby Victoria Road from Cartmel, Grange-over-Sands, Barrow, Bowness, Windermere and Kendal. The **Cumbria Way**, the long-distance footpath from Ulverston to Carlisle, starts from The Gill, at the top of Upper Brook Street – a waymarker spire signals the start. The turnoff from the M6 for Ulverston is junction 36; there are **car parks** off Market Street and at The Gill. The **tourist office** is in Coronation Hall on County Square (Mon–Sat 9am–5pm; ☎01229/587120, ⓦwww.ulverston.net).

Accommodation

Ulverston is certainly worth a night of anyone's time and is particularly well-provided for at either end of the budgetary scale – boasting one of the best "restaurants with rooms" in Cumbria as well one of the region's most accommodating backpackers' hostels. The nearest YHA hostels are on the Duddon Estuary in Millom or in Coniston.

Bay Horse Canal Foot, 1.5 miles east of town ☎01229/583972, ⓦwww.thebayhorsehotel .co.uk. Ulverston's best address for rooms and food, this old inn on the edge of the Leven estuary (30min walk) soothes you with water views and fine cooking. Most rooms open onto a terrace; dinner (included in the room rate) is served in the candlelit conservatory. Non-guests are also welcome for dinner (reservations essential), and for coffee and shortbread or lunch (daily except Mon) in the public bar or at the outdoor tables. From town, follow the A590 and turn off at the signpost for Canal Foot, running through an industrial estate to reach the inn, by the last lock on the Ulverston canal. Parking. ❾

Dyker Bank 2 Springfield Rd ☎01229/582423. A welcoming family home just up from the train station, this Georgian house has three spacious rooms available, including one with views to the hills and another (actually two connecting rooms) suitable for families. Parking. No credit cards. ❷

Trinity House Hotel Prince's St, junction with A590 ☎01229/588889 ⓦwww.traininghotel .co.uk. Half a dozen decently proportioned rooms in a handsome Georgian town house, once the rectory and still retaining its polished floors and impressive fireplaces. The staff here are all under training for the local hospitality industry, so the prices for rooms and food are fairly competitive. Two superior rooms offer a bit more space and a seating area, while a weekend room-only (no breakfast) rate is a real bargain. Parking. ⑤, weekend room-only ②

Walkers' Hostel Oubas Hill, Canal Head ☎01229/585588, ⓦ www.walkershostel.co.uk. Jean Povey's well-kept house is run on eco-friendly lines and sustains Cumbria Way walkers, backpackers, cyclists and outdoor types of all kinds. Beds are in small shared rooms (couples and families accommodated), with packed lunches (£4) and four-course vegetarian evening meals (£8) also available. Plenty of local information to hand, including details of Ulverston's annual walking festival. The house is near the canal basin, east on the A590, at the foot of the Hoad Monument, a 15min walk from the centre (look for the "big boots" painted on the house). Parking. Closed Nov & Dec. No credit cards. Beds £14, including breakfast.

Eating, drinking and entertainment

As befits a market town, there's plenty of choice when it comes to eating and drinking, and the best **cafés**, **pubs** and **restaurants** are listed below. Hartley's **beers**, a traditional Ulverston favourite, are available all over town (though the beer is no longer made here). For picnic food, you can't beat the markets, though there's also a good deli on King Street and a large Booths **supermarket** just out of the centre on the A590, at Canal Head, in front of the Lakes Glass Centre. Year-round entertainment – theatre, opera, music and other events –is provided at **Coronation Hall** in County Square (☎01229/587140, ⓦ www.corohall.co.uk). The tourist office can provide details of the town's many annual **festivals** – Ulverston is trumpeted as "Festival Town" and there's a celebration of one kind or another almost every month.

Cafés and restaurants

Hot Mango 27 King St ☎01229/584866. Come here for cappuccinos, breakfasts, hot baguette sandwiches, pastas and other dishes. Daytime only; closed Sun & Mon. Inexpensive.

King's 15–17 Queen St ☎01229/588947. Unpretentious wine bar with pasta, pizza and melts at lunch, and a full bistro menu in the evening. The early-bird dinner (£5.95) is popular. Moderate.

Rustique Off Brogden St ☎01229/587373. Very classy restaurant with a Modern European menu that changes every couple of weeks. Fish is a speciality, fashionably served with mash or risotto among other ways. Closed Sun dinner and all Mon. Expensive.

World Peace Café 5 Cavendish St ☎01229/587793. Veggie organic café with bagel or rice-cake sandwiches, and a short list of hot daily dishes for under a fiver. Daytime only; closed Sun & Mon. Inexpensive.

Pubs

Farmers Arms Market Place ☎01229/584469. Best pub in town for food, ranging from sandwich lunches and traditional bar meals to pricier blackboard specials, with fish always a good choice (a big bowl of mussels, clams and langoustines is a house special). There are half a dozen real ales, not a bad wine list and a cosy set of armchairs, plus outdoor tables with views down Market Street.

Hope & Anchor Daltongate ☎01229/583934. Cracking little local pub featuring Hartley's beers, open fire, low beams, garden patio and good-value bar meals (not Sun).

Listings

Banks and exchange ATMs at Barclays (County Sq); HSBC (New Market St); Lloyds-TSB (Union St); NatWest (Queen St). You can exchange travellers' cheques at the post office (see below).
Bike rental Gill Cycles, The Gill (Mon–Sat 9am–5pm; ☎01229/581116).
Car rental Alan Myerscough (Ford), The Ellers ☎01229/581058.

Emergencies Local doctors are based at the Health Centre, Victoria Rd ☎01229 /583093. Non-emergency matters are dealt with at Ulverston Hospital, Stanley St ☎01229/583635; otherwise, the nearest full hospital is in Barrow-in-Furness (Furness General Hospital, Dalton Lane; ☎01229/870870).

Internet access At Ulverston Library, King's Rd
(Mon, Tues, Thurs & Fri 9am–6pm, Wed 9am–1pm,
Sat 9am–4pm; ☎01229/894151).
Pharmacies Boots, Market St ☎01229/582049;
J. Hewitt, 10 Market Place ☎01229/582003.
Police station Neville St ☎01539/722611.
Post office County Sq (Mon–Fri 9am–5.30pm, Sat
9am–12.30pm ☎0845/722 3344).

Swimming pool At Ulverston Leisure Centre,
Priory Rd ☎01229/584110.
Taxis Bay Taxis ☎01229/869843; DJs
☎01229/587110; Joe's ☎01229/586700;
McKenna's ☎01229/582180; Mike's
☎01229/582427.

Furness Abbey

Cumbria's wealth used to be concentrated at **Furness Abbey** (April–Sept
daily 10am–6pm; Oct daily 10am–5pm; Nov–March Thurs–Mon 10am–4pm;
£3.30; EH; ☎01229/823420), which at the peak of its influence possessed
much of southern Cumbria as well as land in Ireland and the Isle of Man.
Founded in 1124, the Cistercian abbey had a remarkably diverse industry
– it ran sheep farms on the fells, controlled fishing rights, produced grain and
leather, smelted iron, dug peat for fuel and manufactured salt. By the fourteenth
century it had become such a prize that the Scots raided it twice, though it
survived until April 1536, when Henry VIII chose it to be the first of the large
abbeys to be dissolved. The abbot and 29 of his monks, who had hitherto
resisted (and, indeed, had encouraged the locals to resist Dissolution – a trea-
sonable offence), were pensioned off for the sum of two pounds each.

Now one of Cumbria's finest ruins, the abbey's roofless red sandstone arcades
and pillars lie hidden in a wooded vale north of Barrow-in-Furness. It's been
a popular tourist diversion since the early nineteenth century, when a train
station was built to bring in visitors, among them Wordsworth who was very
taken with the "mouldering pile". Borrow an audio-guide from the reception
desk to get the best out of the site, since there are no maps or explanatory signs.
The transepts stand virtually at their original height, while the massive slabs of
stone-ribbed vaulting, richly embellished arcades and intricately carved *sedilia*
in the presbytery are the equal of any in England. A small museum houses some
of the best carvings, including rare examples of effigies of armed knights with
closed helmets and – as medieval custom dictated – crossed legs. Only seven
others have ever been found intact. The *Abbey Tavern* at the entrance serves
drinks at tables scattered about some of the ruined outbuildings.

The abbey lies a mile-and-a-half out of the industrial town of Barrow-
in-Furness, on the Ulverston road (and about six miles from Ulverston).
Local **buses** (including the hourly #X35) between Kendal, Ulverston,
Dalton-in-Furness and Barrow pass by; details are available from Ulverston
tourist office.

Whitehaven

Some fine Georgian houses mark out the centre of **WHITEHAVEN**, one of
the few grid-planned towns in England and the most interesting destination on
Cumbria's west coast. The economic expansion here was as much due to the
booming slave trade as to the more widely recognized coal traffic. Whitehaven
spent a brief period during the eighteenth century as Britain's third busiest
port (after London and Bristol), making it a prime target for an abortive raid

△ Whitehaven harbour

led by Scottish-born American lieutenant John Paul Jones. Disgusted with the slave trade he witnessed while ship's mate in America, Jones returned to the port of his apprenticeship to rebel, but, let down by a drunk and potentially mutinous crew, he damaged only one of the two hundred boats in dock and his mini-crusade fell flat. All this and more is explained in **The Beacon** (Easter–Oct Tues–Sun 10am–5.30pm; Nov–Easter 10am–4.30pm; £4.25; ☎0845/095 2131, ⓦwww.thebeacon-whitehaven.co.uk), an enterprising heritage centre on the harbour. Resembling a squat lighthouse, and with an interactive Met Office weather gallery on the top floor, The Beacon entertainingly covers the town history, from slaving to smuggling, with a special emphasis on the local characters who have shaped the town. The **harbour** itself sits at the heart of a renaissance project that has spruced up the quayside and provided new promenades, sculptures and heritage trails. The **Crow's Nest**, a forty-metre-high tower, lit at night, is the dramatic centrepiece of the marina. The whole waterfront comes alive during the biannual **maritime festival** in June (next events 2005 and 2007).

For all the changes round the harbour, it's Whitehaven's Georgian streets and neatly painted houses that make it one of Cumbria's most distinguished towns. There's a **market** held here every Thursday and Saturday, which adds a bit of colour. Otherwise, stroll up Lowther Street to **The Rum Story** (daily: April–Sept 10am–5pm; Oct–March 10am–4pm; £4.95; ☎01946/592933, ⓦwww.rumstory.co.uk), housed in the eighteenth-century shop, courtyard and warehouses of the Jefferson rum family. This is another place you could easily spend an hour or so, discovering Whitehaven's links with the Caribbean and learning all about rum, the Navy, temperance and the hideousness of the slaves' Middle Passage, amongst other matters. Across Lowther Street is the seventeenth-century church of **St Nicholas**, though all that stands is its tower (containing a café). The rest succumbed to a fire in 1971, but there's a lovely garden now surrounding the former nave – a further American connection with the town is that George Washington's grandmother, Mildred Gale, wife of a Whitehaven merchant, lies buried here. Also on Lowther Street, don't miss **Michael Moon's bookshop** at no. 19 (☎01946/599010; closed Wed Jan–Easter, & closed Sun all year), a bookworm's secondhand treasure trove.

On the cliffs above Whitehaven, you can get to grips with the industry that set the town on its way at the **Haig Colliery Mining Museum**, Solway Road, Kells (daily 9.30am–4.30pm; free; ☎01946/599949, ⓦwww.haigpit.com), twenty minutes' walk from the harbour. This was Cumbria's last deep-coal mine (closed in 1986), and you can view the restored winding engines (operated every day) and learn about the dreadful living and working conditions that, in part at least, funded the elegant Georgian town below. A special walking tour (by arrangement, contact the museum) shows visitors the ruins of the early eighteenth-century Saltom Pit, the world's first undersea pit.

Five miles south of Whitehaven, the lighthouse on the sandstone cliffs of **St Bees Head** marks the start of Wainwright's 190-mile Coast-to-Coast walk. The beach below is one of the finest on the coast, wide and sandy, while half a mile inland lies the quiet village of **St Bees**, set around its twelfth-century priory.

Practicalities

Trains follow the coastal route south to St Bees, Ravenglass, Millom and Barrow, or north via Maryport to Carlisle. From the station you

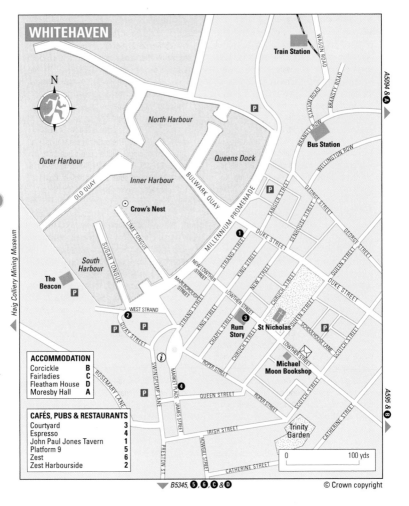

WHITEHAVEN

Train Station

North Harbour

Queens Dock

Bus Station

Outer Harbour

Inner Harbour

Old Quay

Crow's Nest

Millennium Promenade

South Harbour

Sugar Tongue

The Beacon

West Strand

Rum Story   St Nicholas

Michael Moon Bookshop

Quay Street

Rosemary Lane

Swingpump Lane

Market Place

James Street

Queen Street

Roper Street

Irish Street

Howgill Street

Preston St

Catherine Street

Trinity Garden

ACCOMMODATION	
Corcickle	B
Fairladies	C
Fleatham House	D
Moresby Hall	A

CAFÉS, PUBS & RESTAURANTS	
Courtyard	3
Espresso	4
John Paul Jones Tavern	1
Platform 9	5
Zest	6
Zest Harbourside	2

0   100 yds

B5345, ❺, ❻, ❻ & ❹

© Crown copyright

can walk around the harbour to The Beacon in less than ten minutes. The **bus station** is just across Tesco's car park from the train station, with regular services to Gosforth, Ravenglass and Muncaster (#6/X6), Cockermouth and Carlisle (#600, not Sun), and St Bees (#20). There's limited-time disc zone **parking** in town (pick up a disc from local shops); you're better off following signs to a central car park. The helpful **tourist office** is in the Market Hall on Market Place (Easter–Oct Mon–Sat 9.30am–5pm, plus July & Aug Sun 11am–3pm; Nov–Easter Mon–Sat 10am–4pm; ☎01946/852939, ⓦwww.copelandbc.gov.uk), just back from the harbour.

The Coast-to-Coast walk aside, Whitehaven itself is the start of the 140-mile **C2C cycle route** to Sunderland/Newcastle – a metal cut-out, protruding from the harbour slipway, marks the spot. Haven Cycles on Preston Street (☎01946/63263) is a park-and-hire outlet for bikes.

Hotels and B&Bs

Corcickle Guest House 1 Corcickle
℡01946/692073, Ⓔcorcickle@tinyworld.co.uk.
Whitehaven's best B&B is the very comfortable
Corcickle, five minutes' walk from the centre
– keep on up Lowther Street, past Safeway and
McDonald's to find the row of Georgian town
houses. It's impeccably maintained, with a cheery
welcome. No credit cards. ❷

Fairladies Barn Main St, St Bees
℡01946/822718, Ⓦwww.fairladiesbarn.co.uk.
Converted seventeenth-century sandstone barn
with gardens, right in the centre of the village,
offering a variety of smart rooms. Parking. No
credit cards. ❸

Fleatham House High House Rd, St Bees
℡01946/822341, Ⓦwww.fleathamhouse.com.
Just five minutes from the station (first left off
Main St), this lovely house is set in its own secluded grounds – Tony Blair and family stayed here on
a rare UK holiday. It's very informal: tea and cakes
are offered on arrival, there are six large rooms
(three of them singles) and a good breakfast,
while dinner is served in the Italian restaurant at
the house (Tues–Sat dinner only; moderate). And,
unlike most places, weekends have the cheapest
rates, when rooms are £10 less. Parking. ❺

Moresby Hall Moresby, 2 miles north of Whitehaven ℡01946/696317, Ⓦwww.moresbyhall
.co.uk. Medieval in origin, the hall provides quality B&B in an attractive Grade I listed building
with walled gardens, and sea and fell views.
Dinner is available (£22, advance booking
required). Parking. ❺

Cafés and restaurants

Courtyard Café In *The Rum Story*, Lowther St
℡01946/592093. Serves wraps, sandwiches,
baked potatoes and snacks under a glass roof.
Daytime only. Inexpensive.

Espresso 22 Market Place ℡01946/591548. A
classic espresso bar of the old school, dishing up
frothy coffees, fry-ups and grills for forty years.
Daytime only. Inexpensive.

Platform 9 Station House, Main St, St Bees
℡01946/822600. The bistro at the station is a
cosy, romantic spot with a good-value *table d'hote*
menu (£16.95, Fri & Sat £21.50), plus steaks, a
meat fondue and other similar dishes. Creative
tapas are also served Tues–Thurs. Dinner only.
Expensive.

Zest Harbourside West Strand ℡01946/66981.
Harbourside café-bar doing mix-and-match tapas-
style bowls and dishes, plus wraps and sandwiches, pasta, salads and more. Food served until
9.30pm, 10pm at weekends. Moderate.

Zest Low Rd, B5349, ℡01946/692848. The sister
restaurant is three-quarters of a mile out of the
centre on the Whitehaven–St Bees road. It's a stylish stop for Modern British cuisine, and bookings
are recommended as it's Whitehaven's classiest
night out. Wed–Sat dinner only. Expensive.

Pub

John Paul Jones Tavern Duke St
℡01946/690916. You can get a decent pint here,
in a modern pub that delivers a nod to the father
of the American Navy by modelling its interior on
that of a sailing ship.

Cockermouth

COCKERMOUTH, midway between the industrial coast and Keswick at
the confluence of the Cocker and Derwent rivers, dominates the flat vales that
leach out of the northwestern fells, an obvious strategic stronghold. Its Norman
castle was at the heart of the medieval border skirmishes, but the town later
thrived as a market centre – market day is Monday. Cockermouth tries hard
to please, with its impressive Georgian facades, tree-lined streets and riverside
setting, but after the dramatic fellside approaches from the south and east it can
fall a little flat. However, there's no shortage of local attractions, not least the
logical first stop on the Wordsworth trail – the house where the future poet
was born.

The Town

The single, long, Main Street crosses the River Cocker and runs parallel to
the Derwent through the town. At the western end is the **Wordsworth
House** (Easter to first week in Nov Mon–Sat 11am–4.30pm, last entry 4pm;
£4.50; NT; ℡01900/824805, Ⓦwww.wordsworthhouse.org.uk), a handsome,

terracotta-hued Georgian building that was the birthplace of all five Wordsworth children, including William (1770) and Dorothy (1771). It's a house suitable for the professional man that Wordsworth's father was, though he only rented it from his employer, Sir James Lowther, for whom he spent much of his time away on business. The children, too, though happy in the house, were often sent to their grandparents in Penrith and when Wordsworth's father died in 1783 – with the children already either away at school or living with relations – the family link with Cockermouth was broken. The building has been beautifully restored, but rather than a pure period piece it's presented as a functioning eighteenth-century home – with a costumed cook willing to share recipes in the kitchen and a clerk completing the ledger with quill and ink. Many of the fittings and furnishings are of the period (though actual Wordsworth relics are few), while others – kitchen equipment to carpets – have been specially commissioned. In around half the rooms you're encouraged to touch the items on display – children can dress up in one of the bedrooms – or lend the servants a hand, while the walled kitchen garden beside the river has been planted with fruit, vegetables and herbs that would have been familiar to the Wordworths. It's an education, in the best sense, and a really excellent visit.

Various rainy-day attractions occupy the historic buildings and yards ranged along the Main Street – including small museums of minerals and fossils, printing, toys and models, and motoring – while if you follow your nose you're likely to stumble upon **Jennings Brewery** on Brewery Lane by the river confluence. Jennings have been brewers in the town since 1874 and you

Herdwick sheep

The hardiest of indigenous British sheep breeds is the **Herdwick**, its name derived from the "herdwyck" (or sheep pasture) on which it was raised in medieval times. Other sheep breeds are more numerous but it's the grey-fleeced (black when young), white-faced Herdwick that's most characteristic of the Lake District – and which, in many ways, echoes the enduring struggle of lakeland hill farmers. The sheep, bred over the centuries to withstand the local terrain, live out on the inhospitable fells for almost the whole year – most are so good at foraging they never require additional feed. They are territorial, knowing their own "heafs" or particular grazing areas on the fells, and are historically concentrated in the central and western fells of Borrowdale, Buttermere, Langdale, Ennerdale, Wasdale, Eskdale and the Duddon Valley. The National Trust has been instrumental in maintaining the breed on its own farms by obliging tenants to keep Herdwicks. Beatrix Potter was also a keen sheep farmer and encouraged the breed on the farms she left to the Trust on her death.

Partly, the emphasis on maintaining the numbers of Herdwicks is to do with heritage: much of the existing lakeland landscape has been created for and around them, from the intensively grazed fields of the valley bottoms to the dry-stone walls further up the fells. But there's also an economic imperative not to let upland sheep farmers (guardians of much of the landscape) go to the wall without a fight. Even before the foot and mouth crisis of 2001, which saw many flocks destroyed, lakeland sheep farmers found it tough to make a living. While the medieval sheep were bred for their wool, the fleeces today are barely worth clipping as wool prices are so low and it's as high-quality meat that the farmers are attempting to position their flocks. To see the sheep at their best, visit one of the Lake District's summer agricultural shows (see p.39), when the Herdwick Sheep Breeders' Association hands out prizes to the healthiest and best-looking sheep. There's more information on the Herdwick Sheep Breeders' Association website ⓦ www.herdwick-sheep.com.

don't have to step far to sample their product, available in any local pub. For those sufficiently interested in the brewing process, take the hour-and-a-half-long **brewery tour** (July & Aug 2 daily; March–June, Sept & Oct Mon–Sat 2 daily; Nov–Feb Mon–Sat 1 daily; £4.50; ⓣ0845/129 7190, ⓦwww .jenningsbrewery.co.uk); it's advisable to book and note that there's a free tasting at the end. Also, it's always worth checking to see what's on at **Castlegate House** (March–Dec Mon–Wed & Fri–Sat 10.30am–5pm, Sun 2–5pm; free; ⓣ01900/822149, ⓦwww.castlegatehouse.co.uk), a Georgian mansion on Castlegate, opposite the entrance to Cockermouth Castle – itself a private residence and closed to the public. The house and sculpture garden supports a changing programme of contemporary art displays, specializing in the work of accomplished local artists.

Less rarefied lakeland affairs are dealt with in the out-of-town **Lakeland Sheep and Wool Centre** (daily 10am–6pm; closed for two weeks in Jan; ⓣ01900/822673, ⓦwww.sheep-woolcentre.co.uk), a mile south of town on the Egremont road (A66/A5086 roundabout), where various exhibits introduce visitors to the complexities of country life. Most come for the entertaining indoor sheepdog trials and sheep-shearing displays (March–Oct; 4 shows daily Mon–Thurs & Sun; £4), during which you'll learn how to be able to spot a Herdwick sheep, the most characteristic lakeland breed. On Fridays and Saturdays, when there are no shows, you'll be able to see the centre's video introduction to the region. Access to the visitor centre, video show, shop and café is free.

Practicalities

All **buses**, including National Express services, stop on Main Street, from where you follow the signs east to the **tourist office** in the Town Hall, off Market Place (April–June & Oct Mon–Sat 9.30am–4.30pm; July–Sept Mon

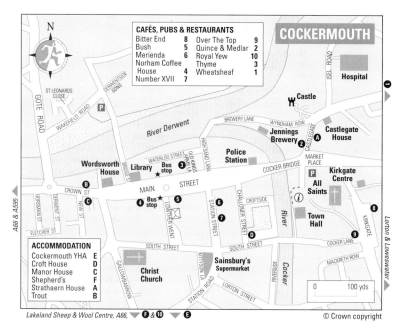

CAFÉS, PUBS & RESTAURANTS

Bitter End	8	Over The Top	9
Bush	5	Quince & Medlar	2
Merienda	6	Royal Yew	10
Norham Coffee House	4	Thyme	3
Number XVII	7	Wheatsheaf	1

COCKERMOUTH

ACCOMMODATION

Cockermouth YHA	E
Croft House	D
Manor House	C
Shepherd's	F
Strathaern House	A
Trout	B

Lorton & Lowesater

Lakeland Sheep & Wool Centre, A66, ▼ **F** & **10** ▼ **E**

–Sat 9.30am–5pm, Sun 10am–2pm; Nov–March Mon–Fri 9.30am–4pm, Sat 10am–2pm; ☎01900/822634); there's **online information** at ⓦwww.cockermouth.org.uk. Driving in, the A66 (from Keswick or Workington) bypasses the town to the south; turn in on either the B5292 (Whinlatter Pass road) or A5086 (from Loweswater and Ennerdale). The **car park** in front of the tourist office is the best place to park, since parking on Main Street is limited to an hour (and you need to display a disc in your car, available from local shops).

Accommodation

Cockermouth makes a handy base for the western Lakes – not far from Loweswater, Ennerdale Water and Buttermere – and there's a good range of accommodation. The best are picked out below, or the tourist office posts a list of other local options outside its office. The **youth hostel** is reasonably central, while the two local **campsites** are around a mile out of town, off the Lorton (B5292) road.

In Cockermouth

Croft House 6–8 Challoner St ☎01900/827533, ⓦwww.croft-guesthouse.com. A stylish revamp of a Georgian town house on a quiet residential street. It's decidedly chintz free – maplewood floors throughout, contemporary furnishings and bed linen – while the owners offer veggie and vegan alternatives for breakfast as well as Fair Trade coffee and tea. Six rooms available, one (with bunks) suitable for families. Parking. Closed Jan. ❸

Manor House Crown St ☎01900/828663. A favourite mid-range choice, the small family-run hotel spreads thirteen rooms across several floors of a tidy, Georgian-style detached house, complete with rotunda and spiral staircase. Space is at a bit of a premium inside the rooms, though most have a bath as well as a shower. Parking. ❺

Shepherd's At the Lakeland Sheep and Wool Centre, Egremont Rd, 1 mile south of Cockermouth ☎01900/822673, ⓦwww.shepherdshotel.co.uk. Thirteen, good-value modern motel-style rooms – and definitely the only hotel in Britain with its own "live sheep show". There's a café and restaurant. Parking. ❷

Strathaern House 6 Castlegate ☎01900/826749, ⓔwaters.boyle@virgin.net. The house is a grand (eighteenth-century and earlier) period piece, complete with impressive staircase and panelling, though the effect is lightened by half a dozen freshly painted, nicely furnished rooms and a jolly welcome. If they're full here, the owner's mother, over the road at The Rook (☎01900/828496), also offers B&B in a period town house. No credit cards. ❶, en-suite ❸

Trout Crown St ☎01900/823591, ⓦwww.trouthotel.co.uk. On the banks of the Derwent, this is the top choice in Cockermouth, well known among the fishing fraternity. It's a comfortable base, retaining something of its traditional aspect with its ornate staircase, panelled bar and silver-service restaurant, but the rooms are large and modern, with comfortable beds and good bathrooms, and there's a contemporary lounge-bar, *The Terrace*, with courtyard seating. Rates vary – river and garden views are pricier – but special two-night weekend deals (including dinner) and other special offers can be a real bargain. Parking. ❻

Youth hostel

Cockermouth YHA Double Mills ☎0870/770 5768. Housed in a seventeenth-century watermill down a track by a bend in the River Cocker: the double wheels (that lend the mill its name) and grindstones are still *in situ* and though the hostel needs modernizing, it's in a very peaceful spot – fifteen minutes' walk south from Main Street, along Station Rd and then Fern Bank. Reception opens 5pm; self-catering only. Closed Nov–March. Dorm beds £10.

Campsites

Graysonside Lorton Rd ☎01900/822351. Small site with space for just a few tents, but with good fell views. Closed Oct–March.

Violet Bank Simonscales Lane, off Lorton Rd ☎01900/822169. Holiday park for caravans and RVs, but there's plenty of tent space too. Closed Dec–Feb.

Eating, drinking and entertainment

You'll find most of the **cafés and restaurants** in town spread along Main Street and up Market Place. There are lots of **pubs**, too – this is the home ground of Jennings brewery, remember – and if you're in the mood, Cockermouth provides the hostelries for one of the more bizarre pub-crawls-of-the-rich-and-famous. Soccer manager Sir Matt Busby, cricketer Ian Botham and (strange but true) crooner and fisherman Bing Crosby have all had a drink in the bar of the *Trout Hotel*; while Robert Louis Stevenson plus local lad (and father of atomic theory) John Dalton frequented the front bar of the *Globe Hotel* on Main Street.

Cafés and restaurants

Merienda 7A Station St ☎01900/822790. Bright, contemporary café-bar – it's Spanish for "snack" – offering a range of breakfasts, sandwiches and light meals, with the emphasis on locally sourced and Fair Trade products. Also open Friday nights for tapas and music. Daytime only, though Fri until 10pm; closed Sun & Mon. Inexpensive.

Norham Coffee House 73 Main St ☎01900/824330. Trades on its history – it was formerly the home of John Christian, grandfather of *Mutiny on the Bounty*'s Fletcher Christian – and its courtyard seating. Daytime only; closed Sun. Inexpensive.

Number XVII 17 Station St ☎01900/822622. Amiable deli with café seating at the back, for brunch, lunch, salads, wraps and sandwiches. The eagle-eyed will notice it's a sister café to the one in Keswick – which, spookily, is also located at 17 Station St. Closed Sun. Inexpensive.

Over The Top 36 Kirkgate ☎01900/827016. One of Cockermouth's longest-serving places, an easygoing café-restaurant catering for veggies and meat-eaters alike with an eclectic menu of home-cooked dishes from around the world, available during the day (until 4pm) and in the evening (from 7.30pm). You can just drop in for a coffee, but it's also licensed and there's Internet access too. Closed Sun, Mon & Tues. Moderate.

Quince & Medlar 13 Castlegate ☎01900/823579. Gourmet vegetarian dishes served in a wood-panelled, candlelit Georgian house. Reservations advised. Dinner only; closed Sun & Mon. Expensive.

Thyme 7 Old Kings Arms Lane ☎01900/821223. A bit of metropolitan chic in this sleek-looking restaurant and bar serving a mix of classic and up-to-the-minute tastes, from rib-eye steak to Thai green curry. Menus change daily, but service and food are assured. Tues–Sat dinner only, also open Sun lunch; closed two weeks Jan. Expensive.

Pubs

Bitter End 15 Kirkgate ☎01900/828993. The nicest pub in town also contains Cumbria's smallest brewery, producing ales like "Farmers'", "Cockersnoot" and "Cuddy Lugs", or there's a long list of imported bottled beers. The bar food is really popular here.

Bush Main St ☎01900/822064. Probably the pick of the Jennings pubs in town and best place for a pint of the local beer.

Royal Yew Dean, 5 miles south of Cockermouth ☎01946/861342. The best destination for a drive out to a country pub, a traditional inn with a handsome yew tree outside and good food and beer within.

Wheatsheaf Embleton, 3 miles east of Cockermouth ☎017687/76408. The local folkie choice, with gigs on the first and third Thursdays of the month (details from Terry Haworth on ☎01900/604765), plus bar meals and real ales.

Arts centre

Kirkgate Centre Kirkgate ☎01900/826448, ⓦwww.thekirkgate.com. The converted Victorian school offers a wide-ranging programme of theatre, cinema, music and the arts.

Listings

Banks and exchange ATMs at Barclays (30 Main St); HSBC (1 Main St); Lloyds-TSB (50 Main St); NatWest (23 Station St).
Emergencies Cockermouth Cottage Hospital, Isel Rd ☎01900/822226.
Internet access Cockermouth Library, Main St (Mon–Wed & Fri 10am–7pm, Thurs & Sat 9am–noon; ☎01900/325990); *Over The Top* café, 36 Kirkgate (Wed–Sat 10am–4pm & 7.30–9pm; ☎01900/827016).
Laundry DIY Wash & Dry, Meadow Bank, Windmill Lane (daily 8.30am–6.30pm; ☎01900/827219).
Pharmacies Allison, 31 Main St ☎01900/822292; Boots, 56–58 Main St ☎01900/823160.

Police station Main St ☎ 01900/602422.
Post office Lowther Went, Main St (Mon–Fri 9am–
5.30pm, Sat 9am–12.30pm; ☎0845/722 3344).
Swimming pool Cockermouth Sports
Centre, Castlegate Drive ☎01900/823596

(public admission hours vary; call for exact
times).
Taxis Cockermouth Taxis ☎ 01900/826649;
G. & J. Taxis ☎ 01900/826307; Karl's Taxis
☎ 01900/827393.

Penrith

PENRITH – four miles from Ullswater and sixteen east of Keswick – has a long pedigree and an historic significance greater than anywhere else in the Lakes. Probably Celtic in origin, it was the capital of the independent kingdom of Cumbria until 1070, a thriving market town on the main north–south trading route from the thirteenth century onwards and harried by the Scots until the sixteenth century. Its castle, built as a bastion against raids from the north, was one of the northern headquarters of Richard III. It still prospers today as an important local market centre and has positioned itself as one of the main gateways to the Lake District; reasonable enough given that it's a stop on the London–Scotland train route and lies off the M6 motorway and A66 to Keswick. It does, however, suffer from undue comparisons with the improbably pretty settlements of the nearby Lakes and certainly its brisk streets, filled with no-nonsense shops and shoppers, have more in common with the towns of the North Pennines than the stone villages of south Cumbria.

The Town

Come on market day, Tuesday, if you want to get to grips with the local economy. The narrow streets, arcades and alleys off **Market Square**, the old **Corn Market** and the open space of **Great Dockray** provide traditional shopping for stalwart Cumbrian families, in the butchers' shops, fishmongers, outfitters, tobacconists and agricultural feed merchants. **St Andrew's Church** (possibly designed by Nicholas Hawkmoor) sits back from the square in a spacious churchyard surrounded by Georgian houses. The so-called "Giant's Grave" is actually a collection of pre-Norman crosses and "hogsback" tombstones. If you walk back round to the square and up Devonshire Street to the **George Hotel** – where Bonnie Prince Charlie spent the night in 1745 – you'll pass Arnison's, the drapers and milliners. The shop stands on the site of the town's old Moot Hall, owned in the eighteenth century by Wordsworth's grandparents. The young William and Dorothy often stayed here and their mother died in the house in 1778 (she's buried in St Andrew's churchyard, though the grave isn't marked).

Beyond the *George*, at the end of Middlegate, the tourist office shares its seventeenth-century schoolhouse premises with a small local **museum** (for hours, see below; free). After a quick review of the town's history, you'll want to climb up to the immaculately kept sandstone ruin of **Penrith Castle** (daily: Easter–Sept 7.30am–9pm; Oct–Easter 7.30am–4.30pm; free), opposite the train station, whose warm colour is at its best at sunset. Traditionally, warnings of attack or – in Napoleonic times – of possible invasion came from the north side of town, from the site of the sandstone beacon tower on **Beacon Hill**. To get there, head up Sandgate and Fell Lane to Beacon Edge (15min), turn left and follow the signposted right turn up through the woods. It takes about an hour, there and back, though the best views of Penrith and the fells beyond are on the way up rather than from the tree-shrouded summit.

The more impressive local fortification is actually that of **Brougham Castle** (April–Sept daily 10am–6pm; Oct–March Mon & Thurs–Sun 10am–4pm;

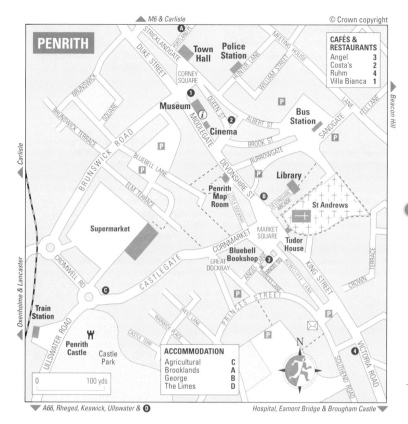

PENRITH

CAFÉS & RESTAURANTS	
Angel	3
Costa's	2
Ruhm	4
Villa Bianca	1

ACCOMMODATION	
Agricultural	C
Brooklands	A
George	B
The Limes	D

M6 & Carlisle

Town Hall · Police Station · Museum · Cinema · Bus Station · Library · Penrith Map Room · St Andrews · Supermarket · Tudor House · Bluebell Bookshop · Market Square · Train Station · Penrith Castle · Castle Park

Carlisle · Oxenholme & Lancaster

A66, Rheged, Keswick, Ullswater & D

Beacon Hill

Hospital, Eamont Bridge & Brougham Castle

0   100 yds

£2.60; EH), a mile and a half south of Penrith in a pretty spot by the River Eamont. You can climb the towering sandstone keep, in which you'll find remnants of Roman tombstones used as building material, plundered from an earlier Roman fort on this site. Coming back (follow the B6262), you can detour past **Brougham Hall**, an unusual fourteenth-century fortified country house now in service as a crafts centre and numbering a smokehouse, brewery, chocolate and truffle-maker and small café among its businesses. Devoted stone-chasers can also track down the minor standing stones in the vicinity, known as **King Arthur's Round Table** and **Mayburgh**, just south of Eamont Bridge.

Practicalities

Trains from Manchester, London, Glasgow and Edinburgh pull into Penrith station, five minutes' walk south of Market Square and Middlegate. The bus station is on Albert Street, behind Middlegate, and has regular services to Patterdale, Keswick, Cockermouth and Carlisle. Coming in off the M6, take junction 40; there's a **car park** off Brunswick Road and others signposted around town, though spaces are hard to come by on Tuesdays (market day). The **tourist office** is on Middlegate (Easter–Oct Mon–Sat 9.30am–5pm, Sun 1–4.45pm; Nov–Easter Mon–Fri 10am–4pm, Sat 10.30am–4pm; ☎01768/867466, ⊛www.visiteden.co.uk).

Accommodation

Penrith isn't overly blessed with **accommodation** and if you're aiming for the Lakes themselves it doesn't make much sense to stop, with Ullswater and Keswick both under half an hour away. But there's enough choice if you fancy a town stopover, though hostellers and campers will want to press on. The bulk of the standard B&Bs line noisy Victoria Road, the continuation of King Street, two minutes' walk south of Market Square. Portland Place has a rather more refined row of guest houses.

Agricultural Castlegate ☎01768/862622. Down-to-earth pub choice across from the castle, whose four letting rooms share a bathroom. The Victorian interior has been carefully restored and there are popular meals served in the bar. Parking. **②**

Brooklands 2 Portland Place St ☎01768/863395, Ⓦ www.brooklandsguesthouse.com. A very handsome house of the 1870s that's been well restored. Seven colour-coordinated rooms have pine furniture, one has a four-poster (priced a category higher); those at the rear overlooking the churchyard are the quietest. **③**

George Devonshire St ☎01768/862696, Ⓦ www .georgehotelpenrith.co.uk. The traditional choice in Penrith, this atmospheric old coaching inn right in the centre has pretty good prices. Rooms vary in size (some can be a bit of a squeeze), though the gloriously old-fashioned interior compensates – there are cosy wood-panelled lounges with roaring fires, rustic bric-a-brac and armchairs you could hibernate in. Also a decent bar and restaurant – the sort of place where Cumbrian ladies-who-lunch come to take tea and sip sherry. Parking. **⑤**

The Limes Redhills, 1 mile southwest of Penrith ☎01768/863343, Ⓔjdhanton@aol.com. A comfortable Victorian guest house with six rooms in a rural setting. Parking. **③**

Eating, drinking and entertainment

The best of the **cafés and restaurants** are highlighted below, while for picnic food and local produce the fantastically stocked J. & J. Graham's deli-grocery in Market Square (closed Sun) can't be beaten. Penrith **pubs** are a bit of a disappointment, save perhaps the *Agricultural Hotel*, which has a good selection of real ales. The local **cinema**, the *Alhambra*, is on Middlegate (☎01768/862400), next to the tourist office.

Penrith is the regional arts and music hub. **Penrith Playhouse** at the top of Castlegate (box office information from the tourist office) puts on theatrical productions throughout the year and also hosts regular **gigs** (Sept to May) in the theatre bar, including once-a-month concerts sponsored by Penrith Live Blues (Ⓦwww.penrithliveblues.co.uk). A three-day annual music festival, **Edenfest**, takes place each summer (usually Aug) in the Deer Park, off the A6 at Brougham, with separate days devoted to jazz/blues, indie and family/tribute bands. The sixty-year-old **Penrith Music Club**, meanwhile, hosts monthly classical concerts and recitals (Sept–April) in town. **Eden Arts** (☎01768/899444, Ⓦwww.edenarts.co.uk) has details of other events in town and throughout the region – one of the more unusual shows is **Potfest in the Pens** (Ⓦwww.potfest.co.uk), an annual exhibition (August) of ceramics in the sheep and cattle auctions mart, just outside town on the A66.

Angel 15 Angel Sq ☎01768/890170. Café-bar with decent coffee that's also open Friday and Saturday nights for cocktails and platters of "finger food" – crudités and dips to tapas and chicken wings. Mon–Thurs daytime only, Fri & Sat until 11pm; closed Sun. Inexpensive.

Costa's 9 Queen St ☎01768/895550. Tapas bar and Spanish restaurant where you can just snack and drink, or tuck into charcoal-grilled meat and fish specials. Closed Mon. Moderate.

Ruhm 15 Victoria Rd ☎01768/867453. Interesting gallery displaying art, ceramics and furniture; the café meanwhile dispenses toasted organic breads, croissants, wraps and rolls of all kinds, teas and cappuccino. Daytime only. Inexpensive.

Villa Bianca Corney Sq ☎01768/862221. Italian restaurant in characterful cottage surroundings.

Friendly service and decent prices for pizzas (the "Villa Bianca" comes with rocket and Parma ham) and traditional pastas make this a good choice for fill-me-up dining. Moderate.

Listings

Rheged

Rheged (daily 10am–5.30pm; ☏01768/868000, ⓦwww.rheged.com) – a Cumbrian "visitor experience", just outside Penrith – is billed as Europe's largest earth-covered building. Sited in a disused limestone quarry, it's designed to blend in with the surrounding fells, which it does admirably – from the main road you wouldn't know it was there. It's at Redhills, on the A66, half a mile west of the M6 (junction 40); buses #X4, #X5 and #X50 (between Penrith and Keswick) all call at the centre.

It takes its name from the ancient kingdom of Cumbria, which once stretched from Strathclyde in Scotland as far south as Cheshire. Entrance to the building itself is free – inside, an impressive atrium-lit underground visitor centre fills you in on the region's history by way of a giant format cinema screen showing a specially commissioned film (*Rheged: The Movie*; admission £5.95). Most visitors try to coincide with the movie, which shows at various times during the day, but there are plenty of other distractions, all aiming to showcase the best of Cumbria, so you'll also find shops and galleries displaying arts and crafts, seasonal exhibitions and demonstrations, and a café, restaurant and contemporary "food bar", *Taste*, specializing in local foods. It's a good place to bring children, especially in wet weather; allow at least a couple of hours for the whole experience.

Anyone even remotely interested in mountaineering shouldn't miss the separate **National Mountaineering Exhibition** (same times; £5.50) at Rheged, celebrating British mountaineering achievement from the very early days. Its centrepiece is an exhibition on the 1953 Everest climb, while other displays home in on historic artefacts (including the ice axe belonging to the first person to climb the Matterhorn) or the development of climbing equipment. Local characters are remembered too, none more important in advertising the early sport than the Abraham brothers of Keswick, whose 1897 camera and tripod are on display. If you think the equipment looks cumbersome to operate on the level, bear in mind they had to carry it up the fells to get their pictures.

Your entrance ticket gets you a sit down in the tent-like Summit Theatre to watch a film about the Hillary and Tensing expedition of 1953, complete with howling wind and dropping temperatures in the theatre just to get you in the mood.

For a different view of Everest, you can also buy a ticket to see the thrilling large-format film, *Everest*, a staple of IMAX theatres around the world and shown throughout the day on the Rheged big screen, along with a couple of other film presentations (each £5.95). Various combination tickets (£9.95 to £20.10) are also available if you want to see the Rheged, Everest and other movies plus the mountaineering exhibition.

Contexts

Contexts

History

The Lake District remained a land apart for centuries, its features – rugged and isolated – mirrored in the characteristics of its inhabitants. Daniel Defoe thought it "eminent only for being the wildest, most barren and frightful of any that I have passed over" – and, as he went on to point out, he'd been to Wales so he knew what he was talking about. Two factors spurred the first waves of tourism: the reappraisal of landscape brought about by such painters as Constable and the writings of Wordsworth and his contemporaries, and the outbreak of the French Revolution and its subsequent turmoil, which put paid to the idea of the continental Grand Tour. Later, as tourism to the Lakes was cemented by the arrival of the railway, Wordsworth – while bemoaning mass travel – wrote in his *Guide to the Lakes* that he desired "a sort of national property, in which every man has a right and interest who has an eye to perceive and a heart to enjoy". His wish finally came to fruition in 1951 when the government established the Lake District as England's largest national park. It's subsequently become one of the most visited parts of England.

Early times

Although human habitation is relatively recent, geologically speaking the Lake District is extremely old. The rocks which make up the Skiddaw and Blencathra massif consist of 500-million-year-old slate, while 100 million years later occurred the immense volcanic activity which shaped the high central mountains. The granite outcrops visible at Ennerdale and Eskdale were formed 350 million years ago. Later still, a tropical sea covered the region (320 million years ago) whose shell remains formed the ubiquitous limestone and sandstone.

At the heart of the region is Scafell, the remnant of a volcanic dome that had already been weathered into its present craggy shape before the last **Ice Age**, when glaciers flowed off its flanks to gouge their characteristic U-shaped valleys. As the ice withdrew, moraines of sediment dammed the meltwater, creating the main lakes, all of which radiate from Scafell's hub – Wordsworth, in a famous image, described them as immense spokes. The gentler terrain to the south was formed after this main burst of activity, with subsequent mini-ice ages (the last around 12,000 years ago) gouging out smaller tarns, flattening the valley bottoms and modifying the shape and scale of the mountains. Consequently, the Lake District as it appears today comprises a huge variety of terrains and geological material within a compact region.

The first humans

Human interaction has also played a significant part in the shaping of the Lake District. Before **Neolithic peoples** began to colonize the region around 5000 years ago, most of the now bare uplands were forested with pine and birch, while the valleys were blanketed with thickets of oak, alder, ash and elm. As these first settlers learned to shape flints into axes, they began to clear the upland forests for farmland – remnants of shaped stone axes have been found in so-called "factory" sites on Pike of Stickle (in Langdale) and on the slopes of Scafell. During the later **Stone and Bronze ages**, the subsistence existence of Lake District settlers is unlikely to have changed much. Their hunter-gathering lifestyle was augmented by early stock-rearing and planting, though evidence of their lives is sketchy. Bronze tools and weapons have been found (around Ambleside, Keswick and St John's in the Vale), though few burial or settlement sites have been pinpointed. The **stone circles** at Castlerigg (near Keswick), Melmerby (near Penrith) and at Swinside (near Duddon Bridge) are the region's most important sites and even the purpose of these is unclear. Some have suggested they had a time-keeping function or were used for religious purposes; others that the circles were a commercial focus or meeting-place. What's clear is the high degree of cooperation between people required to erect the stones in the first place.

By the third century BC, **Celtic peoples** from the south and east were pushing into the region. From their hillfort settlements (like that on Carrock Fell) they exploited the local metal deposits and employed advanced farming techniques. Sophisticated religious practices (including burial) and basic systems of law and communal defence (against raiders from the north) were established features of their lives by the time the Romans arrived in Britain in 55 BC.

The Romans and Celts

The **arrival of the Romans** in the north of England after 69 AD led to the first large-scale alteration of the region's landscape. **Hadrian's Wall**, from the Tyne to the Solway Firth – marking the northern limit of the Roman Empire – was completed by 130 AD. Associated with the wall were roads, forts and supply routes which cut through the heart of the Lakes. There are the remains of fortresses still to be seen at Hardknott Pass and at Waterhead, near Ambleside, while Roman roads can be traced between Kendal and Ravenglass and, most obviously, from Troutbeck to Brougham (near Penrith) along the ridge known as High Street.

The roads and forts were principally a means of subduing the local population. Throughout the Roman period the Lake District was essentially a **military zone**, policed by auxiliaries (recruited from all parts of the Roman Empire) rather than true legionnaires. However, around the bases grew **civilian settlements** as at Ambleside – which formed the basis of later towns and villages. Lead-mining was first practised during Roman times, while upland forests continued to be replaced by agricultural land as cereal crops were planted to supply the various permanent settlements. At Ravenglass, on the Cumbrian coast, are the extant remains of a bathhouse, part of a fort which survived in Ravenglass until the fourth century.

In the face of constant raids and harassment, England had become irrevocably detached from what remained of the Roman Empire by the start of the fifth century AD. The original **Celtic inhabitants** of the northwest had never fully abandoned their traditions and practices in the face of Roman might, and surviving Celtic place-names (Derwent, Blencathra) indicate strong local ties. Indeed, from the Celts comes the word they used to describe themselves – *Cymry* – from which derives the modern place-name Cumbria. **Christianity** secured an enduring toehold in the region too. St Kentigern (or Mungo), the Celtic missionary, founded several churches in the region, passing through Crosthwaite in Keswick in 553 AD.

The Saxon and Norse invasions

The **Saxon invasion** of England's south and east during the sixth century initially had little impact on the Lake District, which slowly fell under the control of the newly established **kingdom of Northumbria**. However, place-name evidence does suggest that Saxon farmers later settled on the lakeland fringes – names ending in "ham" and "ton" betray a Saxon influence, as does the suffix "-mere" attached to a lake.

A greater impact was made by **Norse (ie Norwegian) Vikings** during the ninth and tenth centuries. Although they eventually supplanted much of the native lakeland population, it would be wrong to see the Norse arrival as a violent invasion. Unlike the Danes, who had sacked Lindisfarne on the east coast in 793, the Norse invasion was less brutal, with Viking settlers (rather than warriors) gradually filtering into the Lake District from their established bases in Scotland, Ireland and the Isle of Man. They farmed the land extensively and left their indelible mark on the northern dialect – dale, fell, force, beck, tarn and the suffix "-thwaite" (a clearing) all have Norse origins. Physical remains are scarce, the finest example being the splendid Norse cross in the churchyard at Gosforth, which combines Pagan and Christian elements in a style reminiscent of similar crosses in Ireland and the Isle of Man. By the end of the eleventh century, wherever they originated, Lakelanders were living in small farming communities in recognized shires, or administrative districts, whose names survived for the next nine hundred years: Cumberland and Westmorland.

However, the region began to be disputed in a burgeoning number of turf wars between rival kingdoms. **Dunmail**, a Cumbrian warlord, was defeated in battle in 945 by the Saxon **King Edmund**, who granted control of the region to the kings of Scotland. This heralded six hundred years of political manoeuvring, between Scottish kings keen to push the border south and, after the Conquest, Norman rulers intent upon holding the line at Carlisle. The Lakes themselves, and their farming communities, were largely left alone as the opposing armies marched north and south, but the northern and western lowlands became a cross-border battleground. Castles at Cockermouth, Penrith and Kendal attest to the constant political threat, while raiding "**reivers**" or local clans made the borderlands ungovernable.

Medieval and Elizabethan times

By medieval times, most of the Lake District's **traditional industries** had been firmly established. The native breed of sheep, the Herdwick (black, with white faces), had proved itself a hardy species since at least Roman times, surviving harsh winters on the fells, while in summer cropping the hills of their wild flowers and preventing the regeneration of the woodland. **Religious houses** bordering the Lake District, such as Furness Abbey in the south, Carlisle in the north and St Bees in the west, came to hold large rural areas, establishing outlying farms – or "granges" – which further exploited the land. The **wool** produced found its way into markets throughout Europe and beyond, with **packhorse routes** meandering across the region to and from market towns such as Kendal, Keswick, Penrith and Cockermouth. The monks also maintained woods, or **coppices**, whose timber they used to produce charcoal (for iron-smelting) and bark (used in tanneries). The **dissolution of the monasteries** in 1536 had little effect on these industries. The new crown tenants and the emerging "**statesman**" **farmers**, who bought their own smallholdings, merely continued the age-old practices, denuding the uplands further with every passing year.

Mining was also altering the contours of the land. Plumbago, or graphite, had been discovered in Borrowdale and in 1564 Elizabeth I gave royal assent to an Anglo-German venture to exploit the ore – invaluable for pencil-making, glazing, black-leading iron weapons (to stop them rusting) and making casting moulds for cannon bore and shot. German miners settled in Keswick, while locals found employment in providing lodging, transport and charcoal. Later, copper mining took hold in the Keswick and Coniston areas, while slate quarrying in Borrowdale had always taken place on a local basis and was to boom in later centuries. For most people, though, **domestic life** probably altered very little for three hundred years – clothes were still produced locally, while primitive agricultural methods and poor land kept yields relatively low. The general diet was largely unchanged since Viking times, based around oatmeal cakes or porridge, bread and cheese – potatoes weren't widely cultivated until the eighteenth century. Increasingly, however, houses were being built of durable stone (rather than turf and timber) and many of the Lake District's farms and cottages – including notable examples such as Townend at Troutbeck – can trace their origins back as far as the seventeenth century.

The Picturesque and the Romantic

Until the eighteenth century, it was difficult to persuade the wider world – or at least fashionable England – that the Lake District had anything to offer. Indeed, the old county of Cumberland (containing the northern part of the Lake District) was viewed as a dangerous, unstable corner of the kingdom, too close to lawless Scotland for comfort. William, Duke of Cumberland, the "butcher" son of George II, put down the Jacobite rebellion of 1745, and the fortified towers and castles on the lakeland periphery tell their own story of border raids and skirmishes.

A sea change occurred with the advent of the so-called **Picturesque Movement** in the late eighteenth century, when received notions of beauty shifted from the classical to the natural. Vivid, irregular landscapes were the fashion amongst writers and artists, and it was with a palpable sense of excitement that the era's style arbiters discovered such landscapes on their doorstep. The poet **Thomas Gray** made the first of two visits in 1767 and recorded his favourable impressions in his journal (published in 1775), while in 1778 **Thomas West** produced the first guidebook dedicated solely to the region, waxing lyrical about the "Alpine views and pastoral scenes in a sublime style". These, and a dozen other books or treatises touching on the Lake District published during the 1770s, merely reinforced the contemporary Romantic view that contact with nature promoted artistic endeavour and human development. **Thomas Gainsborough**, **J.M.W. Turner** and, later, **John Constable** were all eager visitors to the Lakes, and all drew inspiration from what they saw. The first visitors were encouraged to view the mountains and lakes in a methodical manner – from particular "stations" (ie viewpoints) and through a "claude-glass" (or convex mirror) to frame the views.

The pre-eminent Romantic, **William Wordsworth**, was born in Cockermouth in 1770, moving to Dove Cottage outside Grasmere in 1799 and, in 1813, to nearby Rydal Mount. He became the centre of a famous, if fluctuating, literary circle – not only one of the so-called **Lake Poets** with **Samuel Taylor Coleridge** and **Robert Southey**, but also friend of the critic, essayist and Opium-Eater **Thomas De Quincey** and of the writer **John Wilson** ("Christopher North" of *Blackwood's Magazine*), and inspiration of future lakeland arrivals such as the Victorian social philosopher and critic **John Ruskin**. Wordsworth's own *Guide to the Lakes* – a mature distillation of all his thoughts on nature and beauty – was first published in 1810 and had gone through four further editions by 1835.

The eighteenth and nineteenth centuries

The **Industrial Revolution** didn't so much pass the Lake District by as touch its periphery. Carlisle was a cotton manufacturing town of some repute, while the coastal ports became important shipping centres and depots for nearby coal and iron industries. Georgian Whitehaven was Britain's third busiest port for a time in the late eighteenth century; Barrow-in-Furness is still an important shipbuilding town.

Within the Lakes themselves, sheep farming remained the mainstay of the economy. Textile production still tended to take the form of home-spun wool, as it had for centuries. However, the manufacture of wooden **bobbins** for the northwest's cotton mills later became an important local industry. There were also improvements in farming as turnips were introduced widely as a crop, which meant that cattle and sheep could be kept alive throughout the winter. Meanwhile, the French Revolution and the ensuing **Napoleonic wars** (1803–15) not only precluded European travel (in part explaining the growing popularity of the Lakes with the English gentry), but also pushed food prices higher. As a consequence, farmers began to reclaim the once-common land of the hillsides, a tendency sanctioned by the General Enclosure Act of 1801. Most of the region's characteristic dry-stone walls were built at this time.

Copper mining at Coniston became increasingly important, as did **slate quarrying** at Honister Pass and around Elterwater. The still-visible scars, shafts and debris on the Old Man of Coniston and at Honister Pass are evidence of these booming trades.

Transport and communications improved slowly. Roads and packhorse routes that had been barely altered since Roman times saw improvement following the passing of the Turnpike Acts in the 1750s. High passes opened up to the passage of stagecoaches; while England's burgeoning canal system reached Kendal in 1819. The **railway age** arrived late, with early railway lines associated with the mining and quarrying industries. The first passenger line, in 1847, connected Kendal with Windermere – and prompted a furious battle with the elderly Wordsworth who, having spent years inviting appreciation of the Lake District by outsiders, now raged against the folly of making the region easier to visit. Not only was it easier to visit, but after 1869 the Lake District even had its very own indigenous candy to sweeten the tooth of visitors – **Kendal Mintcake**, a peppermint candy that's been the mainstay of climbing expeditions ever since. It's still made in Kendal today.

With the passing of Southey (1843) and Wordsworth (1850), the mantle of local literary endeavour passed to writer **Harriet Martineau**, who lived at Ambleside between 1845 and 1876, and **Ruskin**, who settled at Brantwood near Coniston in 1872. Meanwhile, a seemingly endless succession of men and women of letters continued to visit or take a house, pronounce upon and then write about the region – **Sir Walter Scott**, **Percy Bysshe Shelley**, **Matthew Arnold**, **Alfred (Lord) Tennyson**, **Thomas Carlyle**, **George Eliot**, **Charlotte Brontë**, **Ralph Waldo Emerson** and **Nathaniel Hawthorne** all spent various periods in the Lake District. **Charles Dickens** and **Wilkie Collins** came together and climbed Carrock Fell, a trip recounted in Dickens' *Lazy Tour of Two Idle Apprentices* (1857).

The twentieth century: protecting the Lake District

C

Some of those who made a career of boosting the Lake District were also among the first to notice that two thousand years of farming and two hundred years of industrialization were taking their toll. Ruskin's unsuccessful campaign to prevent the damming of Thirlmere was just one example of an increased **environmental awareness** which manifested itself most obviously in the **creation of the National Trust** in 1895. Ruskin's disciple, Octavia Hill and a Keswick clergyman, Canon Rawnsley, were the Trust's co-founders (with Rawnsley its first secretary) – Brandlehow Woods on Derwent Water's western shore was the Trust's first purchase in the Lakes (1902). The Trust is now the largest landholder in the Lake District, gaining early impetus from the generous bequests of **Beatrix Potter**, who has probably done more than anyone – after Wordsworth – to popularize the region through her children's stories.

The **formation of the Forestry Commission** in 1919 presented another threat to the natural landscape as afforestation gathered pace, turning previously bare valleys and fellsides into thick conifer plantations. Successful environmental battles in the 1930s limited the scope of the plantations, but afforestation is still an emotive subject today.

Similarly, **water extraction** had long fuelled fears for the landscape. The Lake District has been used as a water source for northwestern England since Thirlmere was dammed in 1892. Construction at Haweswater in the 1930s raised the water level there by ninety feet – and drowned a village in the process. (Ennerdale Water still supplies the coastal towns and as late as 1980 there were serious proposals to raise levels there and at Wast Water in an attempt to drain more water for industrial use.)

Legal protection of the Lake District was, therefore, long overdue by the time of the establishment in 1951 of the **Lake District National Park**, spreading over 880 square miles. For the first time, there was to be direct control over planning, building and development within the Lake District, as well as systematic maintenance of the footpaths, bridleways, dry-stone walls, open land and historic monuments. The widely recognized National Park emblem – the outline of Great Gable – was adopted in 1953, and the Queen made the first royal visit to the park in 1956.

The National Park:
the first fifty years

The establishment of the National Park didn't, of course, end the threats to the social and natural environment of the Lake District, but it did provide the framework to defend the region from mass commercialism and development. Even so, many of the current problems facing the National Park were signalled in its earliest years.

As rationing ended and the privations of the postwar years were reduced, the number of leisure visitors increased dramatically. The first dedicated car park, at Tarn Hows, was established in 1954, while traffic in the National Park doubled in the five years until 1959. The number of caravan sites increased and there were early worries about litter on the fells and other obtrusive irritants. In the 1960s, speed restrictions were imposed on Derwent Water, Ullswater and Coniston for the first time and the first full-time park warden was employed as tourism to the Lakes became a year-round phenomenon. The house at **Brockhole**, near Windermere, was acquired in 1966 and opened in 1969 as the country's first National Park Visitor Centre. Meanwhile, in 1974, centuries of tradition were abandoned when local government reorganization resulted in the scrapping of the old counties of Cumberland, Westmorland and Lancashire: the Lake District became part of the new county of **Cumbria**.

During the 1970s and 1980s, **conservation** became the new watchword as visitor numbers steadily increased, fuelled in part by the extension of the M6 motorway to Penrith. Car park charges were introduced for the first time, to provide revenue and deter drivers; meanwhile, footpath erosion had become a major problem in many areas. Attempts were made to educate visitors about the impact of their presence on the lakes and landscape – information centres were opened at Keswick, Bowness Bay and Seatoller among others, while 10mph limits were imposed on craft using Derwent Water, Ullswater and Coniston. Cars were kept out of ancient villages such as Hawkshead, whose centre became pedestrianized, and the centre of Ambleside became the Lakes' first formal conservation area.

However, the underlying fragility of the park's ecosystem was exposed in 1986, after the accident at the nuclear power station at Chernobyl in the Soviet Union. Radioactive fallout contaminated Cumbrian soil , acting as a reminder – if one were needed – of the danger on the Lakes' own doorstep presented by the presence of the **Sellafield nuclear-reprocessing plant**, near Ravenglass, symbol of all that threatens the local environment.

Great strides were made during the 1990s to address some of the most fundamental problems facing the National Park. Coordinated traffic management and erosion control schemes were formulated, which began to have a significant effect on the environment. In 1993, Bassenthwaite became the first lake in Britain to be declared a National Nature Reserve and, in the same year, the Lake District Environmentally Sensitive Area (ESA) was established to protect traditional buildings and landscapes. Upland farmers – struggling with the downturn in their industry, and affected by the BSE crisis and other health scares – were given grants to maintain dry-stone walls and hedgerows, renovate traditional buildings and stock wildflower meadows.

The Lakes today

The National Park celebrated its half-centenary in 2001, with its successes balanced equally against its numerous challenges. There's no doubt that it's been a force for good – for example, defending the lakes from over-exploitive water extraction and preventing mass development in scenic areas. But, at times, it seems as if it's fighting a losing battle with the wider problems facing rural England as a whole.

Hill farming everywhere is in crisis, with farmers unable to turn a profit on their animals. In the Lake District, the unproductive nature of much of the land means that hill farming is basically undertaken at subsistence level, and would hardly be possible at all without European Union and central government subsidies. Prices for sheep and cattle halved in the late 1990s and just when it looked like things couldn't get any worse, Cumbria was hardest hit of all English counties by the **foot and mouth crisis** of 2001. As their animals were burned on pyres, farmers watched their incomes disappear – along with the tourists who were asked to keep away from infected areas as footpaths and farms were closed. Related businesses – rural accommodation, cafés, local attractions and activity centres – all suffered a drastic loss in trade. Although many Cumbrian farms subsequently restocked, replacing the many thousands of animals slaughtered in the government's programme to contain the disease, not all businesses survived. The truth is, there were probably too many farms trying to make a living in inauspicious economic circumstances (a deep-rooted problem for British farming as a whole) and no amount of diversification – from camping barns to pony rides – could save some businesses from going under.

In a region where **hunting** with hounds dates back to Norman times, local concern about the fate of agriculture manifests itself in solid support for the pro-hunting "Countryside Alliance" cause. The government's proposed hunting ban has already caused outrage and anger, not just in Cumbria. Others rail at the necessary **development restrictions** imposed by the National Park Authority, the National Trust (which owns a quarter of the land) and the district councils, which – to many locals – seem only to conspire against people from making a living on "their" land. At the same time, second-homers from the towns and cities ("off-comers" in the local parlance) push up **housing** prices, thus forcing the lakeland youth away from home and from the land – in line with other rural British holiday regions, it's estimated that a fifth of all Lake District houses are second or holiday homes. The situation was exacerbated by the council-house sales of the 1980s which further reduced the availability of affordable housing stock. But housing pressure has been a constant problem since the inception of the National Park, when early planning applicants first submitted plans to convert old barns into accommodation.

Indeed, the National Park faces its own pressures since, as a destination, it's simply too successful for its own good. At its first meeting in 1951, the authority dealt with fifteen planning applications. Today, it deals with over 1200 a year. A local population of just 42,000 is swamped by annual **visitor numbers** topping fourteen million, with all the traffic and environmental pressure that that entails. Expanded bus services, the promotion of cycling and an integrated **transport strategy** are starting to have some effect, but it's a long haul to persuade people to leave their cars at home. Around 350 **voluntary wardens** help manage the environment (patrolling lakeshores, maintaining footpaths, planting trees, restoring hedgerows and rebuilding stone walls), but they are faced with an exponential increase in leisure activities which impinge directly upon the Park's habitats – such as mountain biking, ghyll scrambling, four-wheel-drive safaris and water sports. The long-running and contentious saga of speed restrictions on Windermere presented the park authorities with the classic dilemma of balancing business needs with those of the environment. Water-sports companies and related businesses fought a long campaign against the restriction but from 2005 powered craft on England's largest lake will be restricted to 10mph.

On the land, a statutory "right to roam" across open countryside provides new rights for the public while safeguarding the landscape and wildlife. At least a quarter of the National Park area is open for public access: over two thousand miles of **paths and bridle ways** are virtually all clear of obstructions and some have been made suitable for wheelchair users. Erosion control is well in hand on all the most popular walking routes. **Employment** initiatives are working to provide more opportunities for local people, not just in tourism and hospitality, but also in the retail, small business and technology industries.

Projects designed to preserve some of the Lake District's most threatened species (such as the red squirrel) are under way and new native woodlands are being established. **The Lake District Environmentally Sensitive Area** (ESA), set up in 1993 and covering almost the entire National Park, provides the supportive framework for traditional farm buildings to be restored, hedges and orchards replanted, and moorland and riverbanks protected. One hundred **Sites of Special Scientific Interest** (SSSIs) cover another sixteen percent of the Park; and there are six **National Nature Reserves** (NNRs); and another eighty-odd **Regionally Important Geological Sites**. Conservation, at last, is being made fundamental to the National Park's well-being; the future challenge is to extend the same protection to lakeland traditions and the way of life.

Books

W e've highlighted a selection of books below which will give you a flavour of Lake District life, past and present, as well as the impressions of the visitors, writers and poets who have toured and settled in the region. As a glance in any bookshop will show you, there are hundreds of Lake District titles available. We've concentrated on titles of interest to the general reader (which discounts most of the academic literary criticism of the Lake Poets) and those most useful to the non-specialist visitor – for rare historical monographs, mountain-climbing guides, lavish limited-edition pop-up Beatrix Potter books and other arcana, consult a specialist bookshop or the comprehensive website of the Internet bookseller Amazon: ⓦwww.amazon.co.uk in the UK, ⓦwww.amazon.com in the US. A specific Lake District books website, ⓦwww.lakelandbooks.com, is particularly good for tracking down walking guides, outdoors books of all kinds, and historical and literary works associated with the Lakes. Books marked o/p are out of print, though many of those covered below are available in secondhand and antiquarian bookshops in the region.

Lakeland life, travel and topography

John Boardman *Classic Landforms of the Lake District.* A thin volume (one of a series) published by the Geographical Association and aimed at explaining the landscape to general observers, covering topics like lakeland geology and valley formation.

Melvyn Bragg *Land of the Lakes.* Scholarly yet highly readable large-format introduction to lakeland history, society and culture.

Hunter Davies *A Walk Around the Lakes; Strong Lad Wanted for Strong Lass.* The journalist and author Davies takes every opportunity to plug the Lakes in print. His account of a

walk around the region is an entertaining mix of anecdote, history and reportage, while *Strong Lad Wanted for Strong Lass* is his wry account of growing up in Carlisle in the 1950s.

A.H. Griffin *The Coniston Tigers; Inside the Real Lakeland; In Mountain Lakeland; Pageant of Lakeland; The Roof of England; Still the Real Lakeland; A Year in the Fells; Adventuring in Lakeland;* and others. The veteran lakelander climber, writer, journalist and *Guardian* newspaper country diarist, Harry Griffin (1911–2004) produced a dozen volumes that range around the fells with a keen eye for nature and tradition. The

---

Second-hand and antiquarian bookshops

The places listed below are all recommended, especially if you're searching for out-of-print or interesting lakeland titles.

Carlisle: Bookcase, 17 Castle St ☎01228/544560, ⓦwww.bookscumbria.com.
Cartmel: Peter Bain Smith, Bank Court, Market Square ☎015395/36369.
Gosforth: Archie Miles, Beck Place, Main St ☎019467/25792.
Kendal: Kirkland Books, 68 Kirkland ☎01539/780841.
Whitehaven: Michael Moon, 19 Lowther St ☎01946/599010.
Windermere: Fireside Bookshop, 21 Victoria St ☎015394/45855.

early books, written in the 1960s and 1970s, are mostly out of print. However, *The Coniston Tigers* (1999) is a climbing and walking memoir recalling seventy years of mountain adventure.

Norman Nicholson *The Lakers*; *Portrait of the Lakes* (o/p); *The Lake District: An Anthology* (o/p). Cumbria's best-known poet turned to prose with his informed, sympathetic studies of lakeland life, history, geology and people. The comprehensive *Anthology* is a joy, with extracts from writings of every period since the first visitors, and incorporating dialect verse, legends, letters and journals.

Nikolaus Pevsner *Cumberland and Westmorland*. The regional edition of Pevsner's classic architectural guide to the old counties of England. First published in 1967 (when there was still a Cumberland and Westmorland, rather than Cumbria) and detailing every church, hall, house and cross worth looking at.

Jim Watson *Lakeland Towns*; *Lakeland Villages*; *Lakeland Panoramas*. The first two titles are coffee-table format books covering all the lakeland towns and villages in chatty, anecdotal fashion, with the text accompanied by black-and-white pen-and-ink drawings and detailed hand-drawn maps. Not guidebooks as such (though walks and viewpoints are included), more background information and observations by the Penrith-born artist and cartoonist. His *Lakeland Panoramas* are Wainwright-style drawings presenting the widescreen view from the top of 49 easy-to-get-to viewpoints.

William Wordsworth *Guide to the Lakes*. The old curmudgeon's guide to the Lakes went through five editions between 1810 and 1835. This facsimile of the last, and definitive, edition is full of his prejudices (on the "colouring" of buildings, the shape of chimneys, forestation, the railway, the great unwashed) and timeless scenic observations.

Walking guides

Bill Birkett *Complete Lakeland Fells*; *Lakeland Fells Almanac*; *Exploring the Lakes and Low Fells*. The *Complete* edition is the definitive, modern fell-walking reference guide from a leading Cumbrian mountain writer and photographer; classic walks to the top of 541 separate fells for all levels of walker. The *Almanac* distils the *Complete* fells into 129 circular walks taking in the tops, with maps, times and route details. Less adventurous walkers can tour the lake perimeters, tarns, valley bottoms, viewpoints and low fells in his company, too, using eighty easy-to-follow, half-day circular routes laid out clearly over two small-format hardback volumes of *Exploring the Lakes and Low Fells*.

Anthony Burton *The Cumbria Way*. This is the best guide to pack for the 72-mile Cumbria Way (Ulverston to Carlisle), which cuts right through the heart of the Lakes. Durable format, clear walking instructions, Ordnance Survey map extracts, plus history and anecdotes.

Eileen and Brian Evans *North Lakeland*; *South Lakeland*; *West Lakeland*. A three-volume series of informative, nicely produced, pocket-sized walking guides which cover fifty half-day (four- to eight-mile) walks in each lakeland region, concentrating on the lower fells, valleys and woodlands. Some classic routes are included, but the emphasis is more on out-of-the-way tracks and secluded areas.

Pathfinder Guide *Lake District Walks; More Lake District Walks.* The best walking guides for the day-pack: slim volumes of walks, graded from short-and-easy to challenging, with accompanying text and Ordnance Survey map extracts.

W.A. Poucher *The Lakeland Peaks.* First published in 1960 and updated intermittently, Walter Poucher's classic guide for fell-walkers and peak-baggers has almost as many fans as the Wainwright volumes. The pocket-sized guide details 142 routes up fourteen separate mountain groups, accompanied by Poucher's impressive black-and-white landscape photographs (on which are superimposed the various summit routes).

Graham Thompson *The Backpacker's Guide to the Lake District.* Covers forty two-day fell walks in the Lake District, an ideal companion for weekend hikers who want to experience the high fells. The walks are either circular or point-to-point, backed up by useful planning information and some fine photography.

A. Wainwright *A Pictorial Guide to the Lakeland Fells (7 vols); In the Valleys of Lakeland; On the Lakeland Mountain Passes; Favourite Lakeland Mountains; Fellwalking with Wainwright.* Wainwright's *Pictorial Guide* is his masterpiece: seven beautifully produced small-format volumes of handwritten notes and sketches (written between 1952 and 1966) guiding generations of walkers up the mountains of the Lake District. Later spin-off publications (most with superb photography by Derry Brabbs) include Wainwright in elegiac mood, holding forth on the majesty of lakeland mountains, passes and valleys.

Jim Watson *The Cumbria Way and the Allerdale Ramble.* Single-volume walking guide to the two long-distance trans-Lakes footpaths; in particular it's the best guide to the less-walked fifty-mile Allerdale Ramble (from Seathwaite in Borrowdale to the Solway Firth). It's a useful map-pocket-sized book and Watson's hand-drawn maps keep you company every step of the way.

Cycling guides

Nick Cotton *Cycle Tours: Cumbria and the Lakes.* The trusted choice for cyclists – 24 one-day bike routes in Cumbria and the Lakes; ring-bound, with clear maps and detailed directions.

Tim Woodcock *Mountain Bike Route Guide: Lake District.* Twenty off-road routes, from eight to 38 miles, to suit all abilities, accompanied by colour route maps.

Lakeland books, novels and journals

Melvyn Bragg *Without A City Wall; The Silken Net; The Second Inheritance; For Want of a Nail; The Maid of Buttermere; The Cumbrian Trilogy; The Soldier's Return; A Son At War; Crossing the Lines.* The writer, broadcaster, professional Cumbrian (born in Wigton) and butt of Dame Edna Everage – "don't write any more, Melvyn dear, or we'll never catch up" – Bragg is at his historical best in *The Maid of Buttermere*, a fictionalized romantic tragedy involving one of the Lakes' most enduring heroines. *The Soldier's Return* and its sequels, *A Son At War* and *Crossing the Lines*, all very moving portraits of small-town life in the years after World War II, draw heavily on the experiences of his own family in Wigton. Other novels also lovingly explore the Cumbrian past and present, notably *The Cumbrian Trilogy* (comprising *The Hired Man*, *A Place in England* and *Kingdom Come*), which traces the lives of four generations of a Cumbrian family through the twentieth century.

Sarah Hall *Haweswater*. In the 1930s, as the remote village of Mardale is destined to be flooded to create Haweswater resevoir, all kinds of passions are released. Hall's lyrical first novel delves graphically into the lives and loves of a simple farming community attempting to come to terms with progress.

Magnus Mills *All Quiet on the Orient Express*. Strange goings-on in an un-named lakeland community as the outsider-narrator is slowly sucked into the confused relationships of the hard-to-fathom locals. Great, and increasingly sinister, fun.

Beatrix Potter *The Tale of Peter Rabbit; The Tale of Jemima Puddle-duck; The Tale of Squirrel Nutkin;* and many more. Rabbits, pigs, hedgehogs, mice and ducks in lakeland stories of valour, betrayal, adventure and romance. The original twenty-odd titles have metamorphosed into literally hundreds of different formats at varying prices – colouring books, pop-up books, foam-filled fabric books . . .

Arthur Ransome *Swallows and Amazons; Swallowdale; Winter Holiday; Pigeon Post; The Picts and the Martyrs*. Ransome's innocent childhood stories of pirates and treasure, secret harbours and outdoor camps, summer holidays and winter freezes still possess the power to entrance. The series starts with *Swallows and Amazons* (first published 1930), and there's no better evocation of the drawn-out halcyon days of childhood.

Hugh Walpole *Rogue Herries; Judith Paris; The Fortress; Vanessa.*

Guidebooks

The first guidebook to the Lake District was written in the late-eighteenth century and dozens more followed as the region opened up to people of leisure. Most of the earliest guides are long out of print but a trawl through the stock in any local second-hand/antiquarian bookshop throws up old copies of other classic publications. They make interesting souvenirs, while you'll often find that the landscapes described have hardly changed in more than a century.

The earliest lakeland writings were contained in the journal of the poet **Thomas Gray**, first published as part of **Thomas West's** *Guide to the Lakes in Cumberland, Westmorland and Lancashire* (1778). In 1810, **William Wordsworth** wrote down his own observations, appearing in the most complete form as his *Guide to the Lakes* (1835), which, alone of all the historic guides, is still in print. His friend in later life, the writer and political observer **Harriet Martineau** of Ambleside, produced her own *Complete Guide to the English Lakes* (1855). Fifty years later, **W.G. Collingwood's** *The Lake Counties* (1902) set new standards of erudition, while **Canon H.D. Rawnsley** (founder of the National Trust) also found time to produce a multitude of lakeland volumes: *Round the Lake Country* (1909) is typical. In the days before cheaply available colour photography, landscape watercolourist **Alfred Heaton Cooper** illustrated guidebooks for A. & C. Black; the Lake District titles are fairly easy to come by, as are the four lakeland books illustrated by his son **William Heaton Cooper**, starting with *The Hills of Lakeland* (1938). The *Lake Counties* (1937) volume in **Arthur Mee's** classic "King's England" series is widely available too.

Largely forgotten now, Walpole was a successful writer by the time he moved to the Lake District in 1923. He immersed himself in the local history to produce these four volumes covering two hundred years of the rip-roaring lives and loves of the Herries clan – too flowery for today's tastes but full of lakeland lore and life.

Dorothy Wordsworth *The Grasmere Journals; Home at Grasmere.* Was she a poet in her own right? Judge for yourself from the sharply observed descriptions of nature and day-to-day Grasmere life contained in the *Journals. Home at Grasmere* lets you see the debt Wordsworth owed his sister by placing journal entries and completed poetry side by side.

People

Juliet Barker *Wordsworth: A Life.* The latest big Wordsworth biography is a very readable book by an author who gets right to the emotional heart of her subject's life and loves. Barker manages to make the irascible man of letters seem more human, even more likeable, as a consequence, and the evenly paced account of his quiet death, which came in 1850, is a moving read.

John Batchelor *John Ruskin: No Wealth But Life.* This book provides the best background material yet on Ruskin's life for the non-academic reader. The subtitle is Ruskin's own evaluation of "wealth" and Batchelor conveys well Ruskin's journey from precocious child to visionary and moralist.

Hugh Brogan *Signalling From Mars: The Letters of Arthur Ransome.* Ransome's biographer adds flesh and bones to a fascinating man – Ransome was a journalist and Russian political expert before he was a childrens' writer – and gets to the bottom of the books' influences. The edited letters chart Ransome's life, marriages, sailing and writing career – a useful counterweight to Brogan's *The Life of Arthur Ransome* (o/p) and Ransome's own *Autobiography* (o/p).

⭐ **A.S. Byatt**, *Unruly Times.* Authoritative, insightful study of Wordsworth and Coleridge "in their times", which charts their

relationship, ideas, work and family situation against a lively backdrop of contemporary politics, society and culture.

Hunter Davies *Wainwright: The Biography; William Wordsworth.* Davies turns his informal, chatty style upon two of the Lake District's biggest enigmas. Hard biographical detail aside, there's not much to learn about the character of either man that a close reading of their respective works won't tell you already – but then that's not Davies's fault.

Stephen Gill *William Wordsworth: A Life.* The standard academic biography (published 1989) relies on close readings of the manuscripts and contemporary records to build up a cradle-to-grave account of a poet's single-minded dedication to his work at the expense of friends, relationships and politics.

⭐ **Richard Holmes** *Coleridge: Early Visions; Coleridge: Darker Reflections.* The supreme account of the troubled genius of Coleridge, who emerges from Holmes's acclaimed two-volume biography as an animated intellectual and creative poet in his own right as well as the catalyst for Wordsworth's poetic development.

⭐ **Kenneth R. Johnston** *The Hidden Wordsworth.* For "hidden" read "young", as Johnston's controversial book focuses on the creation of the poet by examining his early life and work in exhaustively researched detail. The book ends in 1807 with more than half of Wordsworth's life yet to run, but the argument is that "his young life was his most important life". And along the way are sprinkled the controversies, with Wordsworth variously touted as lover, rebel and – most contentiously – spy.

Kathleen Jones *A Passionate Sisterhood*. Welcome feminist take on the lives of the sisters, wives and daughters of the Lake Poets, whose letters and journals reveal not quite the rustic idyll we've been led to expect by the poetry.

Margaret Lane *The Tale of Beatrix Potter*. The standard biography (written in 1946, shortly after her death, and revised in 1985) of the tale-writing, sheep-farming Mrs Heelis. No reason to disagree with the author's assessment that this is a "modest and unsensational" account of Potter's life and work.

★ **Thomas De Quincey** *Confessions of an English Opium-Eater, Recollections of the Lakes and the Lake Poets*. Tripping out with the best-known literary drug-taker after Coleridge – "Fear and Loathing in Grasmere" it isn't, but neither is the *Confessions* a simple cautionary tale. The famous *Recollections* collected together magazine features De Quincey wrote in the 1830s, providing a highly readable, often catty, account of life in the Lakes with the Wordsworths, the Coleridges and Southey.

Mark Storey *Robert Southey: A Life*. Generally eclipsed by the shining lights of Coleridge and Wordsworth, Southey's reputation is somewhat rehabilitated by this biography. Although he's little known now, in his day Southey was a major man of letters, author of 45 books, and expert on Brazil, Portugal and Spain (not to mention surrogate father and husband to the Coleridge brood). In his own time, he was thought of primarily as a poet, his reputation established by *Joan of Arc* and subsequent epics and by his appointment as Poet Laureate. Despite his poetry, however, what has endured most is his clear, plain prose style – thought "perfect" by Byron – and his biographical history of Nelson. As Southey himself recognized, "I have done enough to be remembered among poets, though my proper place will be among the historians."

Andrew Wilson *An American President's Love Affair with the English Lake District*. The president in question is Woodrow Wilson (1865–1924), whose mother was born in Carlisle. He visited the Lake District five times between 1896 and 1908, cycling along Ullswater, staying in local inns and hotels, paying his respects at the literary shrines and discovering his Cumbrian roots. This definitive account traces Wilson's Cumbrian heritage and records his local tours and friendships, and is a handy companion if you want to retrace the presidential steps.

Poetry

Samuel Taylor Coleridge *Selected Poems*; *The Complete Poems*; *Critical Edition of the Major Works*. Final texts of all the poems in varying editions: the Penguin *Selected* (edited by his biographer Richard Holmes) also includes extracts from Coleridge's verse plays and prefaces; the Penguin *Complete* edition includes unfinished verses.

Norman Nicholson *Collected Poems*. The bard of Cumbria – who lived all his life in Millom, on the coast – produced five books of verse by the time of his death in 1987, collected here. He writes beautifully and movingly of his country, its trades, its past and its people.

 William Wordsworth *The Prelude*; *Lyrical Ballads*; *Poetical Works*; *Selected Poems*. There are dozens of editions of the works of Wordsworth on the market, but these are the current pick. The major poems, sonnets and odes are all collected in *Selected Poems* (Penguin), which has the advantage of being a cheap, pocket-sized edition. For the full text of major works, you'll need *Lyrical Ballads* and *The Prelude* (both Penguin) – the latter presenting the four separate texts of 1798, 1799, 1805 and 1850. (Wordsworth revised his original, 1798, text three times, the last published after his death.) *Poetical Works* (OUP) contains every piece of verse ever published by Wordsworth.

Habitats of the Lake District

The Lake District National Park covers 880 square miles, or half a million acres – approximately one percent of Britain's land area. For such a relatively small region it has a highly varied landscape, geology and climate, and possesses a unique combination of spectacular mountains, rugged fells, pastoral and wooded valleys, and tarns, lakes and rivers. These physical aspects – climate, soil type, topography and altitude – influence the habitats for a rich selection of plants and animals, though other determining factors are at work too, including human and economic influences. This section gives a general introduction to the various habitats of the Lake District, including a rundown of the threats posed by modern agricultural methods and human encroachment. Each habitat description includes brief details of the flora and fauna found there, while some of the more prominent nature reserves in the National Park are also covered. For more information about local habitats and wildlife, don't miss the interesting exhibits at the Lake District Visitor Centre at Brockhole (see p.67).

Whichever habitat you encounter, it's crucial to realize that the landscape you see today bears little resemblance to that which has endured for the majority of time since the last ice age. Five thousand years ago, for example, nearly all of Britain was covered in woodland. Over time, people began to clear selected fell areas for settlement and **agriculture**, which created new habitats as the previously almost unbroken tracts of forest were opened up. The process gained speed during the Norse settlement of the Lake District – place-names ending in "thwaite" (signifying a clearing in the forest) are a clue to the changing landscape – and again during monastic times, with the rapid development of sheep farming. Since then, a "semi-natural" pattern of habitats has evolved, reflecting the area's strong history of farming. Indeed, in the absence of grazing and other management regimes, much of the land in the Lake District would revert to oak woodland – the so-called "climax vegetation".

Today's landscape and habitats within the Lake District National Park are heavily protected and maintained for future generations. There are currently eight **National Nature Reserves** (NNR), over a hundred **Sites of Special Scientific Interest** (SSSI), three **RAMSAR** sites (an internationally important wetland designation), two **European Special Protection Areas** (SPA) and 23 candidate Special Areas of Conservation (cSAC). In addition, in an attempt to combat the threat of agricultural intensification the Lake District National Park was designated an **Environmentally Sensitive Area** (ESA) in 1993. By providing them with financial incentives, farmers are encouraged to reduce chemical inputs such as fertilizers and pesticides; to safeguard and restore hedges, dry-stone walls, traditional farm buildings and archeological remains; and to take care of wildlife habitats such as flower-rich hay meadows, heather moor, wetlands and native woodland. At the same time, the National Park Authority works closely with organizations such as the Cumbria Wildlife Trust, the National Trust and the Royal Society for the Protection of Birds to monitor important habitats and ensure they are protected and maintained for future generations.

Woodland and forest

There is more **native woodland** in the Lake District than in any other upland National Park in Britain. The most widespread type, sessile-oak woodland, occurs on the acid rocks that make up most of the Lake District, with birch, rowan, hazel and holly also present alongside the dominant oaks. On limestone it's ash woodland that dominates, though elm, hazel, silver birch, yew and rowan might also be present. The woodlands provide food, shelter and breeding sites for many different birds such as buzzard, pied flycatcher, warbler and tawny owl, and animals including deer, badger, fox, bat, wood mouse, weasel, shrew and stoat. As for ground flora, plants common on limestone – but found in other types of woodland too – include bluebell, primrose, wood anemone, cowslip and wild daffodil. Shrubs such as blackthorn and buckthorn are typical. In more acidic soil, bilberry, wavy hair and other grasses, ferns and bracken are common, shrubs less so. Woodlands in **Borrowdale** are particularly important for their lichens and their rich moss and liverwort communities, which depend upon high rainfall and humidity.

There's little, if any, true natural forest, or "wildwood", remaining in the Lakes – most had already been cleared by Roman times. However, there are sites that have been continually wooded for at least the past 400 years, which are known as **ancient semi-natural woodland**. The continuity of woodland cover over such a long period of time has allowed a rich flora and fauna to develop. **Roudsea Wood NNR**, on the southern fringes of the National Park (a mile southwest of Haverthwaite village), is a good example of this kind of habitat, featuring a large variety of trees, ferns and woodland birds. East of Windermere, near Staveley, **Dorothy Farrer's Spring Wood** shows the continuing benefit of coppicing (cutting trees, often hazel, back to a stump) in ancient semi-natural woodland. The tree canopy is periodically opened up, allowing more light to reach the woodland floor and encouraging the growth of plants and fungi. The National Park also contains the highest-altitude woodland in England and Wales, including the **Eskdale and Birkrigg woods** in the Newlands Valley, which are both thought to be descended from original wildwood.

Conifer plantations occupy large areas of the Lake District. They often contain fast-growing, non-indigenous, tree species such as spruce and pine, which are favoured by commercial timber growers but support only a limited range of wildlife. They are, however, used by several birds of prey, including the sparrowhawk, goshawk and merlin, and provide refuge, feeding and nesting areas for the native red squirrel. Recent moves towards more varied planting and felling patterns are producing a mosaic of smaller stands of different aged trees, seen for example in plantations at **Thirlmere** and in **Grizedale Forest**. These are more botanically diverse and of much greater value to wildlife. For example, young plantations often harbour small mammals such as voles and mice which, in turn, are a food source for kestrels and owls. Other coniferous plantations worth visiting include **Dodd Wood**, four miles north of Keswick (harbouring red squirrel and various birds of prey), **Ennerdale Forest** (roe deer, red squirrel and badger) and **Thornethwaite Forest** (buzzard and sparrowhawk).

Overgrazing by stock and deer is perhaps the greatest cause of decline in the natural regeneration of broadleaved woodlands. A diverse age structure within a woodland is vital to ensure the long-term survival of the habitat and its associated species. In some areas where regeneration is not occurring naturally, woodland management (providing stock-proof fencing or undertaking coppicing and so on) is being practised. Other threats are posed by the **ornamental species** introduced by the Victorians, such as rhododendron and laurel, which have escaped from the private gardens for which they were intended and spread into surrounding woodland. Their dense canopy prevents light from reaching the woodland floor, while the roots produce toxic chemicals that prevent other plants from growing. This makes the surrounding soil very acidic and reduces the species diversity of woodlands.

Grassland

The National Park has many different kinds of grassland, reflecting the diversity of rocks, climate and topography. Before people began to clear the forests for agriculture and settlement, open grassland was a rare feature below the tree line. Most grasslands have been created by humans and grazing animals. Some areas have been drained, ploughed and re-seeded with "improved" grass mixtures for agriculture and so have limited wildlife value. Others remain as unimproved pasture, which supports a greater diversity of plants and animals.

Acid grassland is common on upland sheep pasture where high rainfall, coupled with a long history of burning and grazing, has favoured this relatively species-poor habitat. However, the invertebrate species associated with grasslands provide a vital food source for birds such as skylark and meadow pipit, along with small mammals such as mouse and vole. Acid grasslands often contain small areas of richer habitat in the form of wet flushes, springs and mires where many interesting plants, such as the insectivorous sundew and butterwort, can be found.

Calcareous grassland occurs on the limestone outcrops in the Lake District, which were formed during the last ice age when huge glaciers scoured the bedrock. In limestone areas this created a smooth, flattened surface, which is characteristic of **limestone pavements**. Weathering and run-off from rainwater widened and deepened any cracks in the rock, giving rise to a complex pattern of solid blocks called **clints**, separated by fissures (sometimes several feet deep) known as **grikes**. These habitats form distinctive niches for a range of plants and animals. For instance, rare ferns thrive in the deep grikes, while above you may catch a glimpse of the Duke of Burgundy or other rare butterflies.

The flattened area of limestone known as limestone pavement is a nationally rare habitat of international importance and, outside Britain, it's found in only a few other areas of Europe. Limestone, of course, has been extracted for decades, to build walls, gateposts and decorative rockeries. Commercial exploitation of limestone pavement has led to large-scale destruction of this fragile habitat and, today, most pavement in England is protected. Cumbria holds 36 percent of Britain's limestone pavement and examples at **Whitbarrow NNR** are some of the finest in Britain. Here, just to the southeast of Cartmell Fell and Bowland Bridge in the Winster Valley, the limestone ridge of Whitbarrow Scar is dominated by the rare blue moor grass, but also contains the hart's tongue fern, dog's mercury, yellow rockrose and limestone bedstraw, as well as the rarer dropwort, dark-red helleborine and rigid buckler fern. Uncommon orchids and distinctive plants, such as crested hair-grass, can also be seen, along with four species of fritillary butterfly, plus the grayling, northern brown argus and common blue butterfly.

Further south, near Witherslack village, a very different mix of grassland flora occupies the small reserve of **Latterbarrow**. Grazing has cleared much of the ancient woodland here, allowing over 150 flowering plant species to be recorded, including numerous orchids.

Hay meadows support a rich variety of wild flowers and tall-growing grasses, and provide nectar for invertebrates. Their richness is maintained by the fact that plants can flower and set seed before mowing, enabling them to be dispersed during summer hay-making. Unfortunately, many hay meadows have been lost over recent years due, in part, to the intensification of agriculture. The move away from hay-making towards silage production (which requires an earlier cut and often relies on the input of artificial fertilizer) has led to a considerable loss of species diversity on many grasslands or pastures. However, under the Environmentally Sensitive Area scheme, farmers are now being encouraged to take care of traditional hay meadows, which can sometimes support over a hundred different species of flowering plants.

Upland heath

Heathland is an open habitat dominated by dwarf shrubs such as heather. It is thought that such areas were originally cleared for agriculture, but their poor acidic soils made them unsuitable for farming. This enabled the acid-tolerant heather to colonize the land. These open habitats are particularly important for insects and over 170 species of butterfly and moth have been identified at **Rusland Moss NNR** in the south of the National Park (three miles north of Haverthwaite village), along with numerous spiders, flies, beetles, birds and reptiles.

Large areas of upland heath have traditionally been managed as shooting estates. A diverse age structure of vegetation is maintained through systematically burning strips of heather to promote seed germination and encourage the growth of new shoots. This practice ensures a constant food supply for birds, such as the red grouse (found only in Britain), and provides an important breeding ground for the short-eared owl as well as Britain's smallest bird of prey, the merlin.

Heathland needs careful management to prevent it reverting to woodland. This is commonly achieved through stock grazing. However, if stocking densities are too high, the regeneration of heather cannot keep pace with the consumption of young shoots by the sheep, and the heather dies back. This continues to be a problem in the Lake District, although financial incentives aimed at tackling overgrazing have been introduced as part of the Environmentally Sensitive Areas scheme.

Mires

The cool, wet climate of the Lake District provides ideal conditions for the development of peat, and the area is considered to be of national importance for both the extent and quality of its **mires**. Peat is characteristic of waterlogged conditions and consists of partially decomposed plant material. In areas where soil micro-organisms cannot complete their natural breakdown processes due to highly acidic conditions and a lack of oxygen, organic remains accumulate as peat. Many mires are nutrient-poor ecosystems, unsuitable for farming. The vegetation depends almost entirely on dilute nutrient supplies present in rainwater and atmospheric dust. Mosses and liverworts flourish, along with many species of lichen and dwarfed forms of heathers and sedges.

Blanket mire (ie where there's a blanket covering of peat) is a scarce habitat, particularly important for breeding moorland birds such as red grouse, golden plover and merlin. Many sites have become impoverished through burning, grazing and drainage, but extensive areas remain on some of the flatter fell tops within the National Park. Here you'll find cross-leaved heath, purple moor grass, cotton grass, bog asphodel, sundew and sphagnum mosses. Small fragments of **raised mire** (flattish, boggy areas of deep peat) also occur within the National Park, such as **Meathop Moss SSSI** – one of the best remaining examples in southern Cumbria – which supports a wide range of plants, over two hundred species of moth and butterfly (including the large heath butterfly), and several species of dragonfly and damselfly. At **Roudsea Mosses NNR** (a mile southwest of Haverthwaite village in the southern Lakes), a raised mire provides a breeding site for over fifty species of bird including woodcock, curlew, greater spotted woodpecker and reed bunting. **Dubbs Moss**, a small reserve just to the southwest of Cockermouth, is a mostly wet mixture of mire, fen, meadow and woodland, with plenty of mosses and ferns in evidence.

Like many wildlife habitats, mires were once more numerous and extensive, but vast tracts have disappeared over the last century, mainly as a result of reclamation for agriculture and horticulture. Artificial drainage of sites, coupled with the increased demand for peat by gardeners, has led to a widespread decline of this wetland habitat. To try to reverse this situation, attempts are being made to raise gardeners' awareness of alternatives for soil conditioning (such as home-made compost), and steps are being taken to protect and manage existing mires more sympathetically. A few have been rewetted and are managed by controlling water levels. In areas where rare plants such as the bog orchid have been found, grazing has been controlled.

Lakes, tarns and rivers

Lakes and tarns make a vital contribution to the identity and beauty of the National Park and support an exceptional variety of aquatic plants and animals. They were formed in the last ice age by huge glaciers gouging out depressions, which were later filled by meltwater and rain. They vary considerably in their size, depth and nutrient status. Some lakes in particular have a long tradition of recreational use, while others are valued for their tranquil and relatively undisturbed atmosphere.

The deep, cold, clear lakes of **Buttermere**, **Ennerdale** and **Wastwater** provide habitats for a restricted range of plants and animals, but these include some rare crustaceans specifically adapted to nutrient-poor environments. In contrast, lakes such as **Windermere** and **Bassenthwaite** support a more diverse range of species. Their more wooded shorelines, with shallow bays and areas of reedbed, provide valuable nesting haunts for swans, grebes, ducks, geese and other birds. **Esthwaite Water** is the most nutrient-rich of the lakes, supporting white and yellow water lilies and rare pondweeds as well as nesting grebes, plus wild rainbow and brown trout. Windermere is of national importance for wintering wildfowl, while Bassenthwaite Lake is very rich in aquatic plants (including the scarce floating water plantain) and is one of only two lakes in Britain known to support the rare fish, vendace – the other, **Derwent Water**, also attracts various wintering wildfowl, including the pochard and tufted duck. In 2001, the first pair of ospreys to nest in northern England for 150 years bred near the shores of Bassenthwaite Lake, and ospreys continue to return here. However, recreational use of some lakes can sometimes conflict with nature conservation interests. The lakeshore habitat is a fragile "soft shore" environment that is highly susceptible to erosion. The trampling action of feet, coupled with grazing by livestock and waves created from passing boats, can lead to soil and organic material being washed away. Over time the reedy shoreline may begin to resemble a pebble beach, which contains only a fraction of the invertebrate species and little or no aquatic vegetation.

Many of the **rivers** within the National Park are of considerable ecological importance. The significant populations of fish, together with other species such as native crayfish, freshwater pearl mussel, water vole and otter, reflect the generally high standards of water quality. The fast-flowing upland streams provide ideal conditions for birds such as dippers and yellow and grey wagtail.

Rock and scree

Glacial activity has produced a wide variety of crags, knolls, ledges and other rock features. In some places, steep-sided **gills** cut deeply into the fellsides. These ravines provide a damp, sheltered environment and are largely inaccessible to grazing animals, which enables them to support many unusual plants. Steep rocky cliffs, known locally as **crags**, support a mixture of lowland plant species and the more distinctive arctic-alpine flora (including yellow, purple and mossy saxifrage and alpine lady's mantle). Sheltered **rock ledges** and **screes** provide a habitat for tall herbs and ferns (including the parsley fern, common in the Lake District, but fairly rare elsewhere) along with many mosses, liverworts and flowering plants.

Crags and ledges also provide a habitat for a varied range of bird species, including stonechat, wheatear and ring ouzel, and nest sites for the buzzard, raven, peregrine falcon and golden eagle. The population of peregrine falcons, in particular, suffered a huge decline during the 1950s and 1960s due to widespread use of pesticides and illegal persecution. Their numbers dropped to just six pairs in Cumbria, though over the last twenty years they have made a considerable recovery and the Lake District today supports the highest density of peregrines anywhere in Europe. Golden eagles are far less numerous; in fact, the only pair in England have been seen on the outcrops and open fells above **Haweswater**, along with buzzards and peregrine falcons. The very high fells (particularly in Langdale) are also the only place you'll spot the mountain ringlet butterfly, Britain's only true alpine butterfly.

Cliff, rock and scree habitats are, of course, highly vulnerable to the activities of climbers, walkers and scramblers. Many agencies are working in partnership to promote responsible use of the countryside and seasonal access restrictions to crags with nesting birds are negotiated annually. Walkers should always keep to marked paths and trails, since going "off trail" – even just stepping off a marked path – can spoil a fragile habitat.

Coastal environments

Coastal environments include areas of shingle, dune, grazing marshes, coastal heath, mudflats and the banks of tidal rivers. Five sites of international importance for nature conservation are located on the coast of the National Park, while on its southern boundary the National Park encompasses small parts of the **Duddon Estuary** and **Morecambe Bay**. These extensive areas support huge numbers of breeding and wintering birds for which they are awarded special European protection – RAMSAR status. Depending on the time of year, you're likely to see flocks of knot, dunlin and oystercatcher, plus grey and ringed plover, curlew, greenshank, spotted redshank, mallard, shelduck and wigeon.

In the west, the National Park's coast stretches from **Drigg Local Nature Reserve** (SSSI) for twelve miles south to **Silecroft**. Large numbers of the natterjack toad are found here along with the palmate, great crested and smooth newt, and the common lizard, while other important species include the adder and the slow worm. Over two hundred plant species are found in the coastal habitats, from sea campion, sea beet and sea kale established on the shingle beaches to typical saltmarsh plants such as glasswort and sea arrowgrass. On the dunes, marram grass and lyme grass help stabilize the sand, while in the hollows, or "slacks", of the dune systems (sometimes filled with fresh or sea water) rarer species such as creeping willow, marsh pennywort and various other marsh orchids can often be found. Shingle and dune habitats also provide breeding areas for five species of tern and large colonies of gulls. The **Hodbarrow** nature reserve, near Millom – a habitat fashioned from a former iron-ore mining site – sees a huge variety of coastal bird species, including great crested grebe, tufted duck, shelduck, oystercatcher and ringed plover, as well as birds of prey such as the kestrel, sparrowhawk and barn owl.

This feature is based on literature kindly provided by the Lake District National Park Authority.

C

CONTEXTS | Habitats of the Lake District

Climbing in the Lake District

Two centuries ago, no one climbed rocks for fun. That's not to say that people didn't go up mountains, but they would never have thought of themselves as climbers or what they were doing as a sport. Shepherds, soldiers and traders ventured onto high ground, but only with good reason. Mountains were the stuff of myth and legend – useless to farmers, dangerous to travellers, largely unknown and often feared. Daniel Defoe, writing of the Lake District in the 1720s, thought the region's mountains "had a kind of inhospitable terror in them"; and Dr Johnson, some fifty years later, was "astonished and repelled by this wide extent of hopeless sterility". But revolution was afoot in the late-eighteenth century, as much in man's perception of the natural world as in politics, and two new influences were making themselves felt upon the landscapes of Europe: Romanticism and the urge for scientific discovery.

Early steps

In August 1786, Mont Blanc in the French Alps (the highest summit in Western Europe) was climbed for the first time by a young Chamonix doctor, **Michel-Gabriel Paccard** and his porter **Jacques Balmat**. The pair made notes and collected botanical and geological specimens as they went – and picked up a substantial prize in addition, offered by the Swiss scientist and explorer Horace-Benedict de Saussure for the first successful ascent. Given that only eighty years previously a serious attempt had been made to seek out and classify "alpine dragons", Paccard's climb was both a mountaineering tour de force and a triumph of scientific rationalism over superstition.

In England it was the artistic, rather than the scientific, community which began to influence the general attitude towards the Lake District's own, lesser, mountain range. **The Picturesque Movement**, precursor of Romanticism, had made the depiction of landscape fashionable and, by the 1760s, various English artists were making good money out of the developing public taste for mountainous scenery. Idealized prints of Derwent Water by Thomas Smith and William Bellers proved both popular and profitable; while in 1783, the renowned artist Thomas Gainsborough visited the Lakes and produced three well-received works (including one of the Langdale Pikes).

Capturing the prevailing Romantic spirit, other visitors published successful accounts of their lakeland expeditions, and in the writings of **William Gilpin**, **Thomas West** and novelist **Mrs Ann Radcliffe** are found the first descriptions of mountains as objects to be climbed (primarily for the "picturesque" views from the top). But the relatively easy ascent of Skiddaw aside (which could be conquered on horseback), most Lake District mountain tops were still well off-limits. It took the energy and vision of an opium-riddled, rheumatic poet to transform the way people regarded lakeland crags and cliffs.

Coleridge and the birth of rock climbing

If Wordsworth was the great walker in the Lake District, then **Samuel Taylor Coleridge** was the pioneer of rock climbing. In August 1802, setting off from his home in Keswick, he made a nine-day solo tour – which he dubbed his "circumcursion" – taking in the peaks and valleys of the central and western Lakes in a hundred-mile circuit. Coleridge was escaping a troubled marriage and an ebbing literary career and, recording his travels in his journal and in a series of letters to his beloved "Asra" (Wordsworth's sister-in-law, Sara Hutchinson), he became the sport's first great writer.

Coleridge had no time for most contemporary visitors to the Lakes, who tended to follow the same routes set down by early guidebook writers, viewing picturesque beauty spots from predetermined stations and idling in boats. Coleridge's was a wilder spirit and it was with a real sense of exhilaration that he found himself on the top of **Scafell** on the fifth day of his tour. In a famous passage from his journal he records his hair-raising descent, dropping down the successive ledges of **Broad Stand** by hanging over them from his fingertips. In this manner, he soon found himself in a position where: ". . . every Drop increased the Palsy of my Limbs . . . and now I had only two more to drop down, to return was impossible – but of these two the first was tremendous, it was twice my own height, and the Ledge at the bottom was so exceedingly narrow, that if I dropt down upon it I must of necessity have fallen backwards and of course killed myself". A moment's reflection brought respite: "I know not how to proceed, how to return, but I am calm and fearless and confident."

This ability to overcome the body's response to fear is a quality all climbers must possess and Coleridge's breathless account marks him out as a true mountaineer. His descent of Broad Stand may have been accidental but his reasons for being on the fells, and his response to them, would be understood by any modern climber. He revelled in the activity for its own sake and in his "stretched and anxious state of mind" he discovered calm and an escape from the cares of home.

Others followed Coleridge onto the fells. The description of Ennerdale's **Pillar Rock** as "unclimbable" by a guidebook writer, John Otley, in 1825, led to a competition among local dalesmen to ascend the only sizeable summit in the area that could not be gained by walking alone. It was duly scaled in 1826 by a shepherd, **John Atkinson**. By 1875, some fifty annual ascents were being recorded, amongst them that of the first woman, a Miss Barker of Gosforth, and a 14-year-old boy, Lawrence Pilkington, later a pioneering Alpine climber (and the founder of the famous glass company).

Wasdale and the Victorian climbers

For the most part, the Lake District crags were largely ignored by daring English gentlemen climbers and their professional guides. Mountaineering meant Alpine glaciers and snow ridges, and most Alpinists regarded lakeland rock climbers as mere "chimney sweeps" and "rock gymnasts". But change was in the air. A handful of more broad-minded climbers began to gather for winter practice at **Wasdale Head**, from where Coleridge had set off for Scafell in 1802. On the whole they were professional men from the industrial cities or academics, with the time and energy to indulge their passion for the mountains. From their ranks came the Cambridge classicist and unlikely sporting revolutionary **Walter Parry Haskett Smith**. Having been introduced to the high fells at Wasdale in 1881, Haskett Smith returned the following year and set out to discover challenging routes up the gullies and chimneys that cleave their way through the rocks. Climbing for the sheer thrill of it, Haskett Smith began to record his routes, guiding those who might choose to follow his footsteps and hand-holds. The visitor's book at the **Wastwater Hotel** (now the *Wasdale Head Inn*) became the lakeland climber's bible, and the hotel doubled as the rock climbers' clubhouse.

An almost chivalrous code developed amongst the climbers: comradeship tempered the excesses of competition and bar-room bragging was not tolerated. These men found in climbing an escape from the demands of their professions, families and society, and a few days spent at Wasdale each year was an excuse for the sort of behaviour not usually associated with the staid lives of Victorian gentlemen. After a hard day on the crag, there were often evening gymnastic revelries: the "billiard room traverse" – circling and leaving the room without touching the floor – or the "passage of the billiard table leg", completed by climbing beneath the table and around a table leg. Boyish games, certainly, but by the end of the century these supple lakeland climbers were pioneering routes unmatched anywhere else in the country.

In 1886, Haskett Smith made the first ascent of **Napes Needle**, that slender pillar of rock that rises on the southern flank of Great Gable. This was no simple gully scramble, nor could it be rationalized as merely an alternative route to a fell top. This was climbing pure and simple, and climbing for its own sake at that. If one climb set the standard for a new sport, this was it. The route is short, but exposed, and is still many a novice's first lakeland climb. Haskett Smith did it alone, unroped and in nailed boots, at the end of a full day in the hills. (He later repeated this pioneering climb on its fiftieth anniversary, when he was a sprightly 76-year-old.)

Haskett Smith's exploits didn't go unnoticed. **Owen Glynne Jones**, the son of a Welsh carpenter, was teaching at the City of London School when, in 1891, he saw a photograph of Napes Needle in a shop on the Strand and within a fortnight had climbed it during his Easter holidays. He was a bold, brash man ("The Only Genuine Jones", as he called himself), who climbed ferociously well and pioneered several physically demanding routes, eagerly taking up the right of first ascenders to name new climbs (a tradition that remains to this day) – "Jones's Route Direct" on Scafell owes its name to him.

Jones came to dominate lakeland climbing in the 1890s, doing much to publicize the new sport in the process. In 1897, his book, *Rock Climbing in the English Lake District* was published, including thirty magnificent full-page photographs by Keswick brothers and photographers **George** and **Ashley Abraham** – examples of these pictures still hang in Keswick shops and pubs, and in the *Wasdale Head Inn*. Jones's accompanying descriptions of the routes included **grades** allocated according to the difficulty of the climb – from Easy to Severe. This was the first attempt to put some order into what had been, until now, a sport without classification and Jones's basic grading framework still stands, although there are now some twenty intermediate and additional grades (to accommodate the huge rise in standards over the last century).

Danger and progress on the fells

Jones was killed in a fall in the Alps in 1899 and his death highlighted the dangers facing the early climbers. Their **specialist equipment** was basically limited to nails arranged in varying patterns on the sole or around the edge of the boot to help grip the rock. Heavy hemp ropes (as used when crossing crevasse-strewn Alpine glaciers) were of dubious benefit on lakeland crags. Two or more climbers might rope themselves together but, as the rope itself was not attached to the rock (as it is today), the chances of surviving a fall were slim. Put bluntly, it was "one off, all off" and the tragic results can be seen in St Olaf's graveyard at Wasdale Head, where three headstones mark the graves of a roped party who fell together from the Pinnacle Face of Scafell in 1906.

Some measure of organization came to lakeland rock climbing with the establishment in 1907 of the **Fell and Rock Climbing Club (FRCC)** of the English Lake District. Ashley Abraham became its president, with honorary memberships granted to Haskett Smith, Cecil Slingsby (a great lakeland climber on Scafell and Gable, and probably the first Englishman to learn the art of skiing) and Norman Collie (an experienced climber in Skye, the Alps, the Rockies and the Himalayas, who also found time to discover the gas neon and develop the first practical application of the X-ray). The Fell and Rock, as the club came to be known, not only promoted safer climbing techniques but helped usher the sport out of the Victorian age with its revolutionary acceptance of women members (something the more established Alpine Club didn't do until after World War II).

Meanwhile, lakeland climbers continued to push at the boundaries of possibility. **Siegfried Herford** (Welsh-born but with a German mother) began climbing in 1907 and his eventual ascent of **Central Buttress** on Scafell in the spring of 1914 was a landmark climb, requiring a new grade to be added to the grading framework – it was so tough, no one else repeated the climb for seven years.

A democratic sport

By the **mid-1930s**, climbing had become a popular, rather than a specialist, pastime. Partly, this was because it was now a safer sport than it had been: rubber-soled gym shoes were worn in dry weather rather than nailed boots and rope techniques had improved markedly. But, more importantly, what had once been the preserve of daring gentlemen was now open to all – better road access, more holiday time and the establishment of youth hostels and rambling clubs all brought new faces (known as "crag rats") onto the crags.

Jim Birkett, a quarryman from Langdale, and **Bill Peascod**, a Workington coal-miner, were typical of the new breed of climber. Birkett was a reserved man and a traditionalist, who kept climbing in nailed boots long after his contemporaries had abandoned them. On May 1, 1938, he pioneered his first classic route on **Scafell East Buttress**, calling it "May Day". This was followed by "Gremlin's Groove" on the same face and two other classics on **Esk Buttress** ("Afterthought" and "Frustration"), before Birkett turned his attention to **Castle Rock** in Thirlmere, climbing what was then known as the Lakeland Everest in April 1939 by a route he called "Overhanging Bastion". Meanwhile, the more extrovert Peascod was making similar advances in **Buttermere**, with routes such as "Eagle Front", climbed in June 1940, followed by nine other new routes of a similarly severe standard in 1941.

Popularity and professionalism

By **the 1960s,** thanks to the conquest of Everest, climbing rode high in the public conscience. Men like **Joe Brown** and **Chris Bonington** became household names – although they were better known for their achievements in the Alps and Himalayas than for any of the notable lakeland routes they had also created. Other British climbers were also branching out from the Lakes, not only to Scotland and Wales but to the warmer rocks of France, Spain and Morocco. However, fashions come and go and the Lake District has always attracted climbers back, drawn by the huge variety of rock faces crammed into such a tightly packed mountain range.

By **the 1970s,** an increasing number of professional climbers were taking a new approach to their sport, training as hard as any top athlete in order to push the boundaries still further. Typical of this single-minded athleticism were the exploits of the Yorkshireman **Pete Livesey**, whose great lakeland season came in 1974. In **Borrowdale** alone he put up four routes of such a magnitude that many at first thought them impossible without using "aid" (pitons, ropes or other artificial help on the rock). But Livesey maintained the tradition of so-called "free climbing" (whereby equipment is used only to provide safety in the event of a fall), thus proving it was simply another psychological barrier that had to be broken. Soon others were climbing even more "impossible" routes than Livesey. **Bill Birkett** – son of the Langdale climber, Jim – undertook some audacious climbing in the Patterdale area, most notably on **Dove Crag**, in the 1970s and 1980s. And today, **Dave Birkett**, Bill's cousin, is creating a new standard right back in the heart of Langdale: on Pavey Ark, his "Impact Day" (graded Extreme 9) is about as tough as it gets in the Lakes.

Modern equipment and challenges

Climbing equipment has developed alongside the athletic professionalism. Nailed boots and gym shoes have given way to specialized climbing shoes, first developed in the 1950s by the French climber Pierre Allain (and known by his initials as PAs). Where Haskett Smith would have climbed in tweeds, modern climbers don multi-coloured Lycra leggings: chalk bags hang from belts, ready to dry sweat-dampened fingers, along with a battery of safety chocks and slings, placed in the rock to give the nylon rope a secure anchor point in the event of a fall. Despite the severity of today's climbing, accidents are few and far between, since a securely placed sling or "runner" (through which the rope is clipped) holds anyone whose ambition out-runs their ability. There was a move towards "**aid climbing**" in the Lakes in the 1960s, when pitons and screws were used to assist an ascent, but it was largely frowned upon and today nearly all lakeland climbers climb "**free**"; that is by their own efforts alone. It's a technique championed by Cumbria's latest young gun, **Leo Houlding**, a climber with rock-star looks and boundless confidence – one of a bunch of young British climbers (including Ian Parnell, Andy Kirkpatrick and Airlie Anderson) scaling crags and peaks from Yosemite to Patagonia.

The number of climbers on the Lake District's crags has increased to such an extent that queues now form on popular routes in the summer. But there are still **challenging routes** to be discovered alongside the classics on Gable and Scafell. Hikers, meanwhile, have the history of climbing all around them. Take a walk up from the *Wasdale Head Inn* and the very names of the features around the Great Napes on Great Gable – Sphinx Ridge, Needle Gulley and Napes Needle itself – are all attributable to the pioneer climbers. You may not know it, and it will not be listed by the Ordnance Survey, but on Scafell Crag you could pass by "Botterill's Slab" (1903, F.W. Botterill), "Pegasus" (1952, A. Dolphin & P. Greenwood) or "The White Wizard" (1976, C.J.S. Bonington & N. Estcourt), and find climbers on each. All are finding something different in the challenge of hand and foot on rock, and all are, in their own way, conquering the impossible. In that, nothing has changed.

William Wordsworth: A Life

Wordsworth was of a good height, just five feet ten, and not a slender man . . .
Meantime his face . . . was certainly the noblest for intellectual effects that, in
actual life, I have seen.

Thomas De Quincey, *Recollections of the Lake and Lake Poets*

William Wordsworth and the Lake District are inextricably linked,
and in the streets of Grasmere, Hawkshead and Cockermouth, and
the fells surrounding Ullswater, Borrowdale and the Duddon Valley
you're never very far away from a house or a sight associated with
the poet and his circle. His birthplace, houses, favourite spots and final resting-
place are all covered in the Guide, together with anecdotes about, and analysis
of, his day-to-day life, his poetry and personal relationships. Below, a general
biographical account of Wordsworth's life is provided to place the various sites
and accounts in context.

Childhood, school and university

William Wordsworth was **born in Cockermouth** (April 7, 1770), the second
eldest of four brothers and a sister, Dorothy. His father, John, was agent and
lawyer for a local landowner, Sir James Lowther, and the family was comfortably off, as the surviving Wordsworth home in Cockermouth attests. The
children spent much time with their grandparents in Penrith – William even
attended a school there – and when their mother Ann died (she was only 30)
in 1778, the family was split up: Dorothy was sent to live with relations in
Halifax in Yorkshire, while William and his older brother Richard began life at
the respected **grammar school in Hawkshead**, lodging with **Ann Tyson**
and going back to Penrith or Cockermouth in the holidays. On his father's
death in 1783, William and the other children were left in relative poverty as
the Lowthers refused to pay John Wordsworth's long-owed salary (indeed, it
was almost twenty years before the debt was honoured).

At school in Hawkshead, Wordsworth (now supported by his uncles) flourished, storing up childhood experiences of ice-skating, climbing, fishing
and dancing that would later emerge in his most celebrated poetry. In 1787,
finished with school and clutching new clothes made for him by Ann Tyson
and the already devoted Dorothy, Wordsworth went up to **St John's College**,
Cambridge, where his uncles intended that he should study to become a
clergyman. His academic promise soon fizzled out. Despite a bright start – to
his evident amusement, De Quincey later recalled that Wordsworth briefly
became a "dandy", sporting silk stockings and powdered hair – he abandoned
his formal studies and left in 1790 without distinction and with no prospect
of being ordained. His uncles were furious, but Wordsworth had other plans
for his future.

In France

A walking tour through **France and the Alps** in the summer of 1790 excited the young, idealistic Wordsworth who had grand thoughts of being a poet. His interest was fired by the contemporary revolutionary movements of Europe. The Bastille had fallen the previous year and Wordsworth's early republicanism flowered. ("Bliss was it in that dawn to be alive, but to be young was very Heaven!") He returned to France in 1791 where he met one **Annette Vallon**, with whom he fell in love – she became pregnant, giving birth to their child, Caroline, in December 1792. But by this time, Wordsworth had returned to England, to oversee the publication, in 1793, of his first works, *Descriptive Sketches* (inspired by his revolutionary travels) and the lakeland reverie *An Evening Walk*. When war broke out between England and France in 1793 Wordsworth was unable to return to France or to Annette; they didn't meet again until 1802.

Depressed by the events of the Terror in France, which rather dented his revolutionary enthusiasm, Wordsworth alternated between fretting and idling in London and making walking tours around England. He thought he might become a teacher and shared Dorothy's oft-expressed dream of setting up home together and devoting his life to poetry – something that at last seemed possible when a small, but unexpected, bequest from the dying **Raisley Calvert**, the brother of an old schoolfriend, gave him just enough to live on.

Becoming a poet: the Lyrical Ballads and Germany

William and Dorothy moved to **Dorset** in 1795 (where they'd been offered a house), and William became acquainted with a fiery, widely read, passionate young critic and writer. **Samuel Taylor Coleridge** had read and admired Wordsworth's two published works and, on meeting Wordsworth himself, was almost overcome with enthusiasm for his ideas and passions. There's no doubt that they inspired each other and the Wordsworths moved to **Somerset** to be near Coleridge – "three people, but one soul", as Coleridge later had it. Here they collaborated on what became the **Lyrical Ballads** (1798), a work which could be said to mark the onset of English Romantic poetry and which contained some of Wordsworth's finest early writing (quite apart from Coleridge's "The Rime of the Ancient Mariner"): not just the famous "Lines Written above Tintern Abbey", but also snatches later incorporated into *The Prelude* (Wordsworth's great autobiographical work, unpublished during his lifetime – Wordsworth only ever knew it as the "Poem on my own Life"). It's hard to see today quite how unusual the *Lyrical Ballads* were for their time: conceived as "experiments", the mixture of simple poems with a rustic, natural content and longer narrative works flew right in the face of contemporary classicism. Sales and reviews were universally poor.

Wordsworth, Dorothy and Coleridge went to **Germany** in 1798, during which time their joint idea for a long autobiographical, philosophical work began to gel in Wordsworth's mind. He produced a first version of *The Prelude* in Germany, along with the affecting "Lucy" poems (including "Strange fits of passion have I known"), which some say pointed to an unnatural passion for his sister. It was certainly an unusual relationship: Dorothy devoted herself entirely to William (her favourite brother since childhood) and his work; she kept house for him, walked with him, listened to his poems, transcribed and made copies of them, and he wrote passionate poems about nameless women who could be no one else but Dorothy. But there's no evidence – to be blunt – that she slept with him, despite the claims of some critics.

Grasmere

In 1799 William and Dorothy moved to **Grasmere** (and Coleridge followed), in the search both for conducive natural surroundings in which Wordsworth's work could flourish and for somewhere they could survive on a restricted budget. William was to spend the last two-thirds of his life in and around the village.

Brother and sister first moved into **Dove Cottage** where they remained until 1808, a period in which Wordsworth established himself as a major poet. A new edition of the *Lyrical Ballads* (1801) appeared, including some of the poems he'd written in Germany together with his first major Grasmere poems, such as "The Brothers" and "Michael", based on local stories and characters. This edition also included its famous **preface** expounding his theories of poetry (against "inane phraseology"; for simple, natural, emotive language), which many critics found arrogant. Wordsworth was at his most productive in the years to 1805, resulting in the publication of *Poems in Two Volumes* (1807), containing the celebrated odes to "Duty" and "Immortality", the Westminster Bridge sonnet, the "Daffodils" poem (untitled when first published) and a hundred other new poems and sonnets. A third edition of *Lyrical Ballads* appeared, and he had also found time to expand and complete a second version of *The Prelude*. All this early work set new standards in poetry: questioning the nature of perception, challenging contemporary prejudices and orchestrating a highly original vision of the human soul within nature.

Dorothy, meanwhile, kept a **journal** recording life at Dove Cottage which has become a classic in its own right. Her skilled observations of the local people and landscape prompted some of William's best-known work, most famously the "Daffodils" stanzas – Wordsworth relied heavily on her journal for the famous images of the flowers dancing and reeling in the breeze.

Marriage and money

Wordsworth's dire financial position slowly improved. His sales and reviews weren't getting any better (Byron trashed most of *Poems in Two Volumes*) but the Lowthers finally stumped up the debt owed to William's long-dead father. This allowed him to marry an old childhood friend from Penrith, **Mary Hutchinson**, in 1802, having first travelled with Dorothy to France to make amends with his first love Annette; Wordsworth later provided an annuity for Annette and their young daughter. Outwardly, the **marriage to Mary** seemed precipitous and passionless and scholars have speculated about Wordsworth's motives, though letters between William and his wife (discovered in the 1970s) tend to scotch the myth that he was marrying out of duty. **Children** followed – John, Dorothy (always known as Dora), Thomas, Catherine and William – though Catherine and then Thomas, both infants, succumbed to mortal illnesses in the same tragic year of 1812.

Dove Cottage became too small for comfort as the family grew. His wife's sister, Sara Hutchinson, was a permanent fixture, as was Coleridge (by now separated from his wife) and his visiting children. The Wordsworths moved to other houses in Grasmere (Allan Bank and the Old Rectory), and then in 1813 finally settled on **Rydal Mount**, a gracious house two miles south of the village. Here William lived out the rest of his life, supported for some years by his salaried position as **Distributor of Stamps for Westmorland** (good fortune, caused as De Quincey noted, by the current incumbent distributing "himself and his office into two different places"). It was hardly a sinecure – he had to travel through the county, collecting dues and granting licences, work which he undertook assiduously – but it brought him in £200 a year.

The Rydal years

Wordsworth may have already written his finest poetry, but after the move to Rydal he was at the peak of his fame. Over the years, the literary world made its way to his door, a procession recorded in detail by the critic and essayist **Thomas De Quincey** who first made the pilgrimage to Grasmere to meet his hero in 1807. After a long friendship interrupted by disagreements, De Quincey's frank series of articles on Wordsworth and his family in 1839 (later published as *Recollections of the Lakes and the Lake Poets*) caused an irreparable rift. **Coleridge**, too, was persona non grata after a falling-out in 1810, though the two old friends did come to some kind of an accommodation in later life, and *The Prelude* remained dedicated to him.

There were family setbacks. The death of William's brother, John, in 1805 had affected him deeply (and led later to a burgeoning religious faith); after 1828, his beloved sister Dorothy suffered a series of depressive illnesses, which incapacitated her mind for most of the rest of her long life; and his wife's sister, Sara Hutchinson – who had so besotted Coleridge and who had lived with them for thirty years – died of the flu in 1835.

Wordsworth continued to be productive, at least in the early Rydal years. The *Excursion* (1814), long enough in itself, was conceived as part of an even longer philosophical work to be called "The Recluse", which he never completed. His first *Collected Poems* appeared the following year, together with *The White Doe of Rylstone*; but it wasn't until *Peter Bell* (1819) and *The River Duddon sonnets* (1820) that sales and reviews finally flourished. His *Vaudracour and Julia* (1819) also had deep significance: a tale of seduction, it was a fictionalized account of his affair with Annette.

As Wordsworth grew older he lost the radicalism of his youth, becoming a loud opponent of democracy, liberalism and progress. Political developments in France and the threat of the mob and the Reform Bill at home appalled him. His views on nature and the picturesque had led him to produce his own descriptive **Guide to the Lakes** ("for the minds of persons of taste"), at first published anonymously (1810) to accompany a book of drawings; its later popularity (a final, fifth edition, appeared in 1835) did much to advertise the very charms of the region he was keen to preserve. In the end, fulminating against the whitewashed houses and fir plantations he thought were disfiguring the Lakes, Wordsworth retreated to his beloved garden at Rydal Mount.

Apart from the rare crafted sonnet or couplet, Wordsworth's later work was largely undistinguished. The third major revision of *The Prelude* had been completed in 1838; the poem didn't see the light of day until after his death, when Mary gave it a name and handed it over for publication. But in 1843, on the death of Robert Southey and at the age of 73, Wordsworth's position as Grand Old Man of the literary establishment was confirmed by his appointment as **Poet Laureate**.

After his **death in 1850**, William's body was interred in St Oswald's churchyard in Grasmere, to be later joined by Dorothy (1885) and by his wife Mary (1889).

small print and

Index

A Rough Guide to Rough Guides

In the summer of 1981, Mark Ellingham, a recent graduate from Bristol University, was travelling round Greece and couldn't find a guidebook that really met his needs. On the one hand there were the student guides, insistent on saving every last cent, and on the other the heavyweight cultural tomes whose authors seemed to have spent more time in a research library than lounging away the afternoon at a taverna or on the beach.

In a bid to avoid getting a job, Mark and a small group of writers set about creating their own guidebook. It was a guide to Greece that aimed to combine a journalistic approach to description with a thoroughly practical approach to travellers' needs – a guide that would incorporate culture, history and contemporary insights with a critical edge, together with up-to-date, value-for-money listings. Back in London, Mark and the team finished their Rough Guide, as they called it, and talked Routledge into publishing the book.

That first *Rough Guide to Greece*, published in 1982, was a student scheme that became a publishing phenomenon. The immediate success of the book – with numerous reprints and a Thomas Cook prize shortlisting – spawned a series that rapidly covered dozens of destinations. Rough Guides had a ready market among low-budget backpackers, but soon also acquired a much broader and older readership that relished Rough Guides' wit and inquisitiveness as much as their enthusiastic, critical approach. Everyone wants value for money, but not at any price.

Rough Guides soon began supplementing the "rougher" information about hostels and low-budget listings with the kind of detail on restaurants and quality hotels that independent-minded visitors on any budget might expect, whether on business in New York or trekking in Thailand.

These days the guides – distributed worldwide by the Penguin group – offer recommendations from shoestring to luxury and cover more than 200 destinations around the globe, including almost every country in the Americas and Europe, more than half of Africa and most of Asia and Australasia. Our ever-growing team of authors and photographers is spread all over the world, particularly in Europe, the USA and Australia.

In 1994, we published the *Rough Guide to World Music* and *Rough Guide to Classical Music*; and a year later the *Rough Guide to the Internet*. All three books have become benchmark titles in their fields – which encouraged us to expand into other areas of publishing, mainly around popular culture. Rough Guides now publish:

- Travel guides to more than 200 worldwide destinations
- Dictionary phrasebooks to 22 major languages
- History guides ranging from Ireland to Islam
- Maps printed on rip-proof and waterproof Polyart™ paper
- Music guides running the gamut from Opera to Elvis
- Restaurant guides to London, New York and San Francisco
- Reference books on topics as diverse as the Weather and Shakespeare
- Sports guides from Formula 1 to Man Utd
- Pop culture books from *Lord of the Rings* to Cult TV
- World Music CDs in association with World Music Network

Visit www.roughguides.com to see our latest publications.

Rough Guide credits

Text editor: Ann-Marie Shaw
Layout: Amit Verma
Cartography: Jai Prakash Mishra
Picture research: Mark Thomas
Proofreader: Tamara Colloff-Bennett
Editorial: London Martin Dunford, Kate
Berens, Claire Saunders, Geoff Howard, Ruth
Blackmore, Gavin Thomas, Polly Thomas,
Richard Lim, Clifton Wilkinson, Alison Murchie,
Sally Schafer, Karoline Densley, Andy Turner,
Ella O'Donnell, Keith Drew, Edward Aves,
Andrew Lockett, Joe Staines, Duncan Clark,
Peter Buckley, Matthew Milton, Daniel Crewe,
Nikki Birrell **New York** Andrew Rosenberg,
Richard Koss, Chris Barsanti, Steven Horak,
AnneLise Sorensen, Amy Hegarty
Design & Pictures: London Simon Bracken,
Dan May, Diana Jarvis, Mark Thomas, Jj
Luck, Harriet Mills, Chloë Roberts; **Delhi**
Madhulita Mohapatra, Umesh Aggarwal, Ajay
Verma, Jessica Subramanian, Amit Verma
Production: Julia Bovis, Sophie Hewat,
Katherine Owers

Cartography: **London** Maxine Repath,
Ed Wright, Katie Lloyd-Jones
Delhi Manish Chandra, Rajesh Chhibber,
Jai Prakash Mishra, Ashutosh Bharti, Rajesh
Mishra, Animesh Pathak, Jasbir Sandhu,
Karobi Gogoi
Online: New York Jennifer Gold, Cree
Lawson, Suzanne Welles, Benjamin Ross;
Delhi Manik Chauhan, Narender Kumar,
Shekhar Jha, Rakesh Kumar, Lalit Sharma
Marketing & Publicity: London Richard
Trillo, Niki Hanmer, David Wearn, Demelza
Dallow, Kristina Pentland; **New York** Geoff
Colquitt, Megan Kennedy, Milena Perez;
Delhi: Reem Khokhar
Custom publishing and foreign rights:
Philippa Hopkins
Finance: Gary Singh
Manager India: Punita Singh
Series editor: Mark Ellingham
PA to Managing Director: Megan McIntyre
Managing Director: Kevin Fitzgerald

Publishing information

This third edition published April 2005 by
Rough Guides Ltd,
80 Strand, London WC2R 0RL.
345 Hudson St, 4th Floor,
New York, NY 10014, USA.
Distributed by the Penguin Group
Penguin Books Ltd,
80 Strand, London WC2R 0RL
Penguin Putnam, Inc.
375 Hudson Street, NY 10014, USA
Penguin Group (Australia)
250 Camberwell Road, Camberwell
Victoria 3124, Australia
Penguin Books Canada Ltd,
10 Alcorn Avenue, Toronto, Ontario,
Canada M4V 1E4
Penguin Group (New Zealand)
Cnr Rosedale and Airborne Roads
Albany, Auckland, New Zealand
Typeset in Bembo and Helvetica to an original
design by Henry Iles.

Printed in Italy by LegoPrint S.p.A

288pp includes index
A catalogue record for this book is available from
the British Library

ISBN 1-84353-418-5

1   3   5   7   9   8   6   4   2

Help us update

We've gone to a lot of effort to ensure that
the third edition of **The Rough Guide to
The Lake District** is accurate and up-to-
date. However, things change – places get
"discovered", opening hours are notoriously
fickle, restaurants and rooms raise prices or
lower standards. If you feel we've got it wrong
or left something out, we'd like to know, and if
you can remember the address, the price, the
time, the phone number, so much the better.

We'll credit all contributions, and send a
copy of the next edition (or any other Rough

Guide if you prefer) for the best letters.
Everyone who writes to us and isn't already a
subscriber will receive a copy of our full-colour
thrice-yearly newsletter. Please mark letters:
"**Rough Guide The Lake District Update**"
and send to: Rough Guides, 80 Strand,
London WC2R 0RL, or Rough Guides, 4th
Floor, 345 Hudson St, New York, NY 10014. Or
send an email to **mail@roughguides.com**
Have your questions answered and tell
others about your trip at
www.roughguides.atinfopop.com

SMALL PRINT

Acknowledgements

The author would like to thank the following for invaluable information, advice and assistance: Melanie Clarkson and the Cumbria Tourist Board; Annie Duckworth and the Lake District National Park Authority; Helen Roebuck; Bill Kenmir of the RSPB; Liz Evans and Jon Gould at the Youth Hostels Association; Liz Houseman at the National Trust; Barbara Spearman at English Heritage; Barney Hill; Janet and Graham Edwards; Matt Edwards and Marta Bakinowska; Barry Surtees at Muncaster; Honister Slate Mine; Suzanne Dimmock at Blackwell; and Allan King at the Wordsworth Trust.

Thanks also to: Annie, for editing with aplomb; to mum and dad for all their help; to Greg who went up a mountain; and to Katie, Fox and Rips for keeping things going at home. Sadly, Capt. I. Little never returned from his bold attempt to conquer every Wainwright peak by Space Hopper and will be sorely missed.

The editor would like to thank Helena Smith for sterling support, and Jules for making it all so enjoyable.

Readers' letters

Thanks to all the readers who took the trouble to write in with their comments and suggestions (and apologies to anyone whose name we've misspelt or omitted):

Dawn Barnes, John Boardman, Alison Columbine, Keith, Sarah, Harriet and Imogen Davey, Joanne Dixey, Roger Green, Christel Lemmens, Michael Moon, Kevin Paszalek, Brian and Dorothy Pearson, Alex Polkinghorne, Rob Romano, Dave Willis.

Photo credits

Index

Map entries are in colour.

INDEX

0

INDEX

F

G

H

I

INDEX

T

W

U

V

INDEX

Y

Map symbols

– – –	Chapter division boundary
– – –	National park boundary
▬▬▬	Motorway
═══	Major road
───	Minor road
- - - - -	Path
▬▬▬	Railway
— —	Ferry route
────	Waterway
▪▪▪▪	Wall
⊃⊂	Bridge
♜	Castle
🏛	Stately home
🏛	Abbey
⚲	Church (regional maps)
♦	General point of interest
⊥	Gardens
⋎	Viewpoint
⌒	Cave

⚠	Campsite
▲	Mountain peak
⌃⌃	Hills/mountains
⩵	Pass
⚘	Waterfall
⌁	Rocks
∴	Ruin
★	Bus stop
🅿	Parking
⛽	Petrol station
◉	Accommodation
ⓘ	Tourist office
⊠	Post office
@	Internet access
▮	Building
⊞	Church (town maps)
⊤	Cemetery
▢	Park
▢	Marsh